Collins

EDEXC

science

FOR EDEXCEL GCSE ADDITIONAL SCIENCE

AVALANCHE RESEARCH

Brian Arnold SERIES EDITOR
Gareth Price
Phil Routledge
Rob King
Mike Tingle
Jane Cartwright
Gurinder Chadha

William Collins' dream of knowledge for all began with the publication of his first book in 1819. A self-educated mill worker, he not only enriched millions of lives, but also founded a flourishing publishing house. Today, staying true to this spirit, Collins books are packed with inspiration, innovation and practical expertise. They place you at the centre of a world of possibility and give you exactly what you need to explore it.

Collins. Do more.

Published by Collins
An imprint of HarperCollins*Publishers*
77–85 Fulham Palace Road
Hammersmith
London
W6 8JB

Browse the complete Collins catalogue at
www.collinseducation.com

10 9 8 7 6 5 4 3 2 1

ISBN 13: 978 0 00 721640 6
ISBN 10: 0 00 721640 8

British Library Cataloguing in Publication Data. A Catalogue record for this publication is available from the British Library.

Commissioned by Cassandra Birmingham

Publishing manager: Michael Cotter

Project editor: Kate Wigley

Project management: Jo Kemp

Editor: Ros Woodward

Cover design by John Fordham

Cover artwork by Bob Lea

Prepared by Starfish Design, Editorial and Project Management Ltd.

Internal design by JPD

Illustrations by Rory Walker and Peters and Zabransky Ltd.

Exam questions by Dr Martin Barker, Lesley Owen and Karen Nicola Thomas

Glossary by Gareth Price

Production by Natasha Buckland

Printed and bound by Printing Express, Hong Kong

Acknowledgements

The authors and publisher are grateful to the following for permission to reproduce copyright material: Met Office, Hadley Centre and the Climate Reseach Unit at the University of Anglia, © Crown Copyright (p. 76, Figure 2); image courtesy of the Marian Koshland Science Museum of the US National Academy of Sciences (p. 76, Figure 3); *New Scientist* (p. 145); the Department for Transport (pp. 213 and 215); the British Parachute Association (p. 215) . Whilst every effort has been made to trace the copyright holders, in cases where this has been unsuccessful or if any have been inadvertently overlooked, the publisher will be pleased to make the necessary arrangements at the first opportunity.

Contents

Hormonal bananas

PAGE 144

How hot to melt a rock?

PAGE 156

Bionic bones

PAGE 222

What kind of energy?

PAGE 258

Magic or physics?

Welcome to Collins GCSE Science!

This book aims to give you a fascinating insight into contemporary science that is relevant and useful to you, right now today. We have written it to convey the excitement of Biology, Chemistry and Physics, and hope it will help you to carry a knowledge and understanding of science and scientific thinking with you throughout life.

USING THIS BOOK

What you should know

It is amazing how much knowledge you gain each year in your studies. Hopefully you can then build on this in the following years. In science there are many key ideas that are continually revisited and developed. To remind you of these, there are summaries for each of the main sections: biology, chemistry and physics.

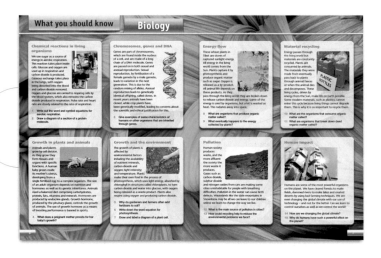

Unit opener

Altogether there are six units: two biology, two chemistry and two physics. At the start of each unit there is an introductory spread, consisting of a large image showing just some of the exciting science you will learn about. Also listed on this page are the spreads you will work through in the unit.

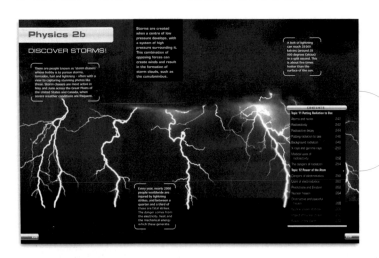

Main content

Each of the six units contains two topics and each topic has approximately 10 double page spreads. An introductory paragraph at the start of each spread puts the material in an everyday context. Separate sections then look at progressively more demanding ideas and applications. Titles marked with an (H) mean the following paragraphs are Higher Tier.

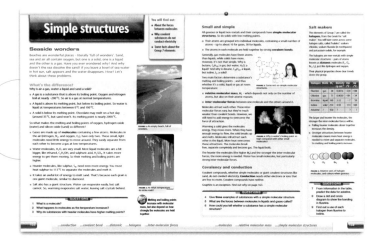

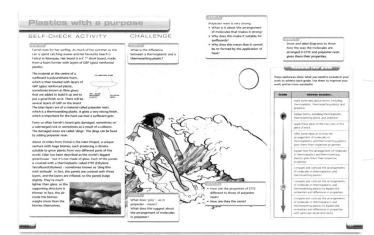

Mid-unit assessment

The mid-unit assessment questions enable you to recap on several weeks' work and assess your own level of understanding. Achieving good marks in these will confirm your progress and highlight any areas of weakness that need to be addressed.

Unit summary

Unit summaries offer the opportunity to visualise links between key ideas through the use of spider diagrams. Constructing your own versions of these would be a useful way to begin your revision. The unit finishes with a number of questions designed to sharpen up your skills in these areas.

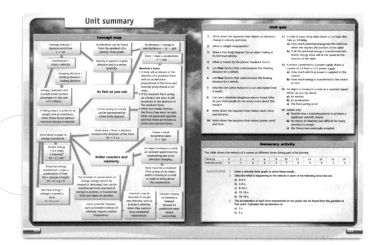

Exam practice

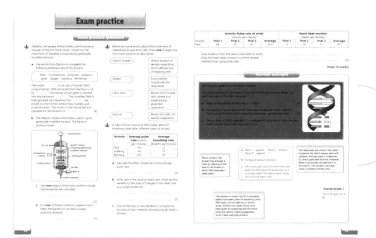

Developing a good exam technique will ensure that you take full advantage of the skills and knowledge you have gained. You need to give clear answers with working out and reasoning shown, in order to earn top marks. To help you achieve this we have included some practice questions. Try your best with these and don't rush them. Tackle one or two, see where you went wrong and then try some more, ensuring that you don't make the same mistakes. Remember: practice makes perfect – so use the questions well.

Your guide to GCSE Additional Science

While you are studying GCSE Science, your teacher will assess your practical skills, and give you assessment activities to complete. These pages should give you some helpful guidance and practice.

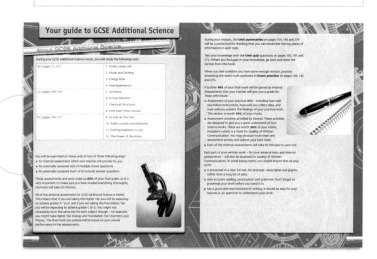

Chemical reactions in living organisms

We use sugar as a source of energy in aerobic respiration. This reaction takes place inside cells. Glucose and oxygen are used up in respiration and carbon dioxide is produced. Gaseous exchange takes place in the lungs, with oxygen being absorbed into the blood and carbon dioxide removed. Oxygen and glucose are carried to respiring cells by the blood system, which also removes the carbon dioxide produced in respiration. Pulse rate and heart rate are closely related to the rate of respiration.

1   Write out the word and symbol equations for aerobic respiration.

2   Draw a diagram of a section of a protein molecule.

Chromosomes, genes and DNA

Genes are part of chromosomes, which are found inside the nucleus of a cell, and are made of a long chain of a DNA molecule. Genes are passed on in both sexual and asexual reproduction. Sexual reproduction, by fertilisation of a female gamete by a male gamete, leads to variation in the next generation. This is due to the random mixing of alleles. Asexual reproduction leads to genetically identical offspring, called clones. In recent years animals have been cloned, while crop plants have been genetically modified, leading to concerns about the scientific and ethical justification for this.

3   Give examples of some characteristics of humans or other organisms that are inherited through genes.

Growth in plants and animals

Animals and plants grow by cell division. As they grow they form tissues and organs with specific functions. A human baby grows inside its mother's uterus, developing from a single fertilised egg to a complex organism. The size of an adult organism depends on nutrition and hormones as well as its genetic inheritance. Animals need a balanced diet comprising carbohydrates, protein, fats, vitamins and minerals. Hormones are produced by endocrine glands. Growth hormone, produced by the pituitary gland, controls the growth of animals. The use of growth hormone as a means of boosting performance is banned in sports.

4   What does a pregnant mother provide for her baby's growth?

Growth and the environment

The growth of plants is affected by environmental factors including the availability of nutrient minerals, carbon dioxide and oxygen; light intensity; and temperature. Plants make their own food in the process of photosynthesis, which uses light energy, absorbed by chlorophyll in structures called chloroplasts, to turn carbon dioxide and water into glucose, with oxygen being released as a waste product. Plants also respire using oxygen and producing carbon dioxide.

5   Why do gardeners and farmers often add fertilisers to soil?

6   Write down the word equation for photosynthesis.

7   Draw and label a diagram of a plant cell.

Energy flow

These wheat plants in Tibet are stores of captured sunlight energy. All energy in the living world comes from the Sun. Plants capture it by photosynthesis and produce organic matter such as sugar. Oxygen is released as a by-product. All animal life depends on these products. As they

pass through the living world they are broken down to release carbon dioxide and energy. Some of the energy is used by organisms, but a lot is wasted as heat. This radiates away into space.

8   What are organisms that produce organic matter called?

9   What eventually happens to the energy collected by plants?

Material recycling

Energy passes through the living world but materials are constantly recycled. Plants are consumed by animals. The materials they were made from eventually pass back to plants through animal faeces or when the animal dies and decomposes. These living cycles, driven by

energy from the Sun, make life on Earth possible. Some modern materials, such as plastics, cannot enter this cycle because living things cannot degrade them. This is why it is so important to recycle them.

10   What are the organisms that consume organic matter called?

11   What are organisms that break down dead organic matter called?

Pollution

Human society produces waste, and the more affluent the society the more waste it produces. Gases such as carbon dioxide, sulphur dioxide

and nitrogen oxides from cars are making some cities uninhabitable for people with breathing difficulties. Pollution in the water can cause birth defects. Wastelands like the slate mountains in Snowdonia may be all we can leave to our children unless we learn to change the way we live.

12   What is the main source of pollution in cities?

13   How could recycling help to reduce the environmental problems we face?

Human impact

Humans are some of the most powerful organisms on the planet. We have cleared forests to make fields, dammed rivers to make lakes and created deserts by using bad farming techniques. We are even changing the global climate with our use of technology – and not for the better. Can we learn to control ourselves as well as we control the world?

14   How are we changing the global climate?

15   Why do humans have such a powerful effect on the planet?

Carbon compounds

Water and crude oil are the only natural liquids on Earth. Water is essential for life. Oil isn't, but our lives would be very different without it. We rely on oil for fuels, plastics, medicines and many other items.

Before we can use crude oil, we must refine it. Refineries distil oil to separate it into fractions, such as petroleum gases, gasoline, kerosene, diesel, fuel oil and bitumen. We also make fuels like ethanol and biodiesel using carbon compounds from plants.

1   Why is petroleum so important in our everyday lives?

2   Name the refinery process that separates crude oil into fractions.

Using chemical reactions

Chemists take raw materials and perform chemical reactions to turn them into a vast range of different substances. There are different types of reaction, including combustion, reduction/oxidation, neutralisation and decomposition. Redox reactions, for example, involve substances exchanging oxygen; neutralisations involve acids and bases forming salts.

Chemists describe reactions using equations with symbols and formulae to show what reactants are used, what they produce, their composition, and relative amounts.

3   What do we mean by 'raw materials'?

4   Why do reduction and oxidation always take place together (as a redox reaction)?

Elements

Elements are only made up of one type of atom. They cannot be broken down to form other substances. Atoms have a central nucleus. This is a lot smaller than the atom, and contains particles called protons and neutrons. Electrons orbit the nucleus. Protons and neutrons are much heavier than electrons. The proton has a positive charge, the neutron has no charge and the electron has a negative charge.

Only 90 chemical elements occur naturally (e.g. carbon, oxygen, nitrogen, sulphur and sodium). Each element has a shorthand symbol – symbols for the five elements above are C, O, N, S and Na. In most chemistry classrooms, you will see a chart of the chemical elements called the periodic table.

5   What is a chemical element?

6   What is the symbol for sodium?

Compounds

Compounds are made of more than one element chemically combined. They have chemical formulae showing which elements are present. Numbers show how many atoms of each element there are. For example, the formula H_2SO_4 means that in one sulphuric acid molecule, 2 hydrogen, 1 sulphur and 4 oxygen atoms are bonded together.

Other important compounds include:

Water	H_2O	Calcium carbonate	$CaCO_3$
Carbon dioxide	CO_2	Hydrochloric acid	HCl
Methane	CH_4	Sodium carbonate	Na_2CO_3

7   What is meant by the term 'chemical compound'?

6   How many atoms in total are present in one molecule of carbon dioxide?

Understanding molecules

Molecules have come in different 3-dimensional shapes. The shapes are difficult to draw but can be modelled on a computer.

A molecule's shape depends on the arrangement and size of the atoms that make it. Some molecules are mirror images of each other.

The structures of some molecules have been discovered by mistake, such as 'buckyballs', which are in the shape of a football!

9   Apart from using a computer, how else could you model the shape of a molecule?

10   What is the proper name for 'buckyballs'?

Chemical bonds

Atoms make up everything in our Universe. Atoms are able to combine or interact with other atoms to form molecules and chemical compounds.

When atoms join together they are chemically bonded. If the chemical bond needs to be broken, heat energy must be supplied in order to break the bond.

11   When atoms join together, they make groups of atoms called ....

12   Atoms are joined together by chemical ....

Hot and cold reactions

Chemical reactions that give out heat are called exothermic reactions. Examples of exothermic reactions include all combustion (burning) reactions and neutralisations.

Some displacement reactions like zinc metal reacting with copper(II) sulphate solution are also exothermic.

Reactions that feel cold to the touch are called endothermic reactions. These absorb heat energy.

We can show that a reaction is exothermic or endothermic by the temperature change. If the temperature increases, the reaction is exothermic, and if it decreases, the reaction is endothermic.

13   Give one example of an exothermic reaction?

14   What is meant by a displacement reaction?

Rates of reaction

Chemical reactions happen at different rates. Some are very slow, such as the rusting of iron in damp air. Others are very fast, as when sodium metal reacts with water.

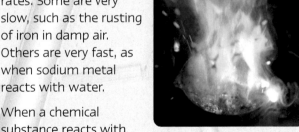

When a chemical substance reacts with another substance, the particles in each substance collide and react to produce a new chemical substance. There are many ways of increasing the rate of a reaction.

15   In order for chemical substances to react, particles must be able to ....

16   Give three ways of making a reaction go faster.

Up to speed

The speed of an object measures its rate of change of distance:

$$speed = \frac{distance}{time}$$

Speed can be measured in metres per second (m/s).

An object whose speed is increasing is said to be accelerating.

An object whose speed is decreasing is said to be decelerating.

1. Which of these objects (A, B or C) will have the lowest speed?
   A moves 100 m in 12 s
   B moves 50 m in 12 s
   C moves 50 m in 8 s
2. What is the speed in metres per second of an object that moves 30 m in 6 s?.

Force facts

Force is measured in newtons (N). The gravitational attraction between an object and the Earth causes a force an object called 'weight'.

Balanced forces cause no change to the motion of an object, but unbalanced forces will cause on object to change its speed or direction of travel.

Frictional forces act against motion.

3. Give three examples (other than weight) of types of force.
4. If an object is moving at a constant speed in a straight line, what must be true about the forces acting on it?

Full of energy

There are different types of energy including potential, kinetic and electrical energy.

Energy is measured in joules (J). It is never created or destroyed but can be changed into different types.

Energy can be stored in forms such as potential and chemical energy.

5. What type of energy does a moving object have?
6. Give an example of potential energy.

In a spin

Many objects move in curved paths, such as planets orbiting the Sun. Moving in a circle requires a force such as gravity.

Albert Einstein made an important contribution to the history of science.

7. Give two examples of objects that move in circular paths (other than the planets).
8. What is always changing for an object moving in a circle, even if its speed is constant?

Atoms

Everything we can feel and touch is made up of tiny particles called atoms. The atom is quite small. There can be as many as 10 million atoms on a single pinhead. Atoms consist of electrons, protons and neutrons. Electrons have a negative charge, protons have a positive charge and the neutrons have no charge. The atoms of a particular element have the same number of protons. The atoms of one element are very different from the atoms of another element.

9   Name all the particles within an atom.

10 What is the charge of a proton?

Electromagnetic waves

Radio waves, visible light, X-rays and gamma rays are all examples of electromagnetic waves. These waves have different wavelengths and frequencies. Electromagnetic waves can travel through a vacuum at an incredible speed of 300 000 kilometres per second. X-rays and gamma rays are dangerous to humans because of their high frequencies.

11 Name another electromagnetic wave not mentioned in the text above.

12 How long would it take for radio waves to travel from the Earth's North Pole to the South Pole – a distance of 20 000 km?

Insulators

Electrical insulators are opposite to electrical conductors. Electrical conductors, like copper, can conduct electrical current easily round circuits. Electrical conductors have low electrical resistance because they have lots of 'free' electrons. Insulators, like rubber, have high electrical resistance because they have fewer 'free' electrons. Copper cables connected to domestic appliances are encased in plastic to prevent us from getting an electrical shock!

13 Name an insulator.

14 Use the Internet to find a metal that is a better conductor than copper.

Energy

Energy is measured in joules (J). A moving object has kinetic energy. An object moving faster has greater kinetic energy than when it is moving slowly. The atoms of a gas move faster when it is warmed and its temperature rises. Increasing the temperature of a solid makes the atoms vibrate more. Heat is a form of energy.

15 Give an example of a form of energy.

16 What happens to the atoms of a gas when its temperature is increased?

Biology 2a

DISCOVER PROTEIN SYNTHESIS!

What is this? A creature from the ocean depths? A space monster attacking its prey? No – this photo shows a protein molecule being formed inside a cell.

Proteins are made of long, complex molecules and are constructed by ribosomes, following the code 'written' in the DNA.

This is a section of a RNA molecule, copied from DNA in the cell nucleus.

Here is the protein molecule that is being manufactured. It is made of smaller amino acids, joined in a chain.

CONTENTS

The DNA code

Happy families

Why do we look like our parents and our brothers and sisters? You already know that we inherit characteristics from our parents in chromosomes, which are found in the cell nuclei. Chromosomes are made up of genes, which control cells and carry information from our parents. We get our genes in an egg and a sperm, which is why we inherit characteristics from both parents.

FIGURE 1: The members of this family look alike because they share many genes.

Blueprint for you

DNA stands for **deoxyribonucleic** acid and it is a really huge molecule. Each cell contains over 2 metres of DNA, coiled up inside the nucleus! Engineers designing things such as cars, ships and aeroplanes used to draw their plans on blue paper called 'blueprints'. These contained all of the information needed to build the car, ship or aeroplane. Your DNA contains all of the information needed to make you, so it is like a blueprint for you. Your DNA is different from any other person's DNA (unless you have an identical twin).

Genes make up sections of chromosomes, so genes are made of pieces of DNA. DNA is a **double helix** shaped molecule. It is a bit like a ladder that has been twisted into the same shape as a spiral staircase. The 'steps' of the ladder hold together two long **strands**. It is these steps that carry all of the information stored in the DNA molecule, as a special code.

FIGURE 2: A short section of a DNA molecule showing the double helix shape.

WOW FACTOR!

Human chromosomes contain about 25 000 genes.

◼ QUESTIONS ◼

1   What does DNA stand for?
2   What substance are chromosomes made from?
3   Name the people who won a Nobel Prize for discovering the structure of DNA.
4   What shape is a molecule of DNA?

WANT TO KNOW MORE?

Read *The Double Helix* by James Watson or *Rosalind Franklin and DNA* by Anne Sayre.

...adenine   ...base   ...cytosine   ...DNA   ...double helix   ...guanine

DNA structure

DNA molecules are made of thousands of smaller units, called **nucleotides**. Each nucleotide consists of three parts:

- a phosphate
- a sugar
- a **base**.

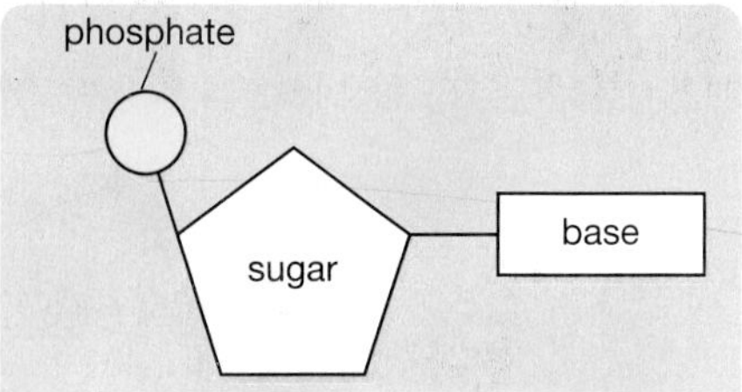

The sugar and the phosphate groups join together and make the 'backbone' of each strand of the DNA. The bases are bonded to the sugar group. They are also joined to a base on the other strand of the DNA, using a weak bond called a **hydrogen bond**. Although these bonds are weak, there are thousands of them holding the two strands of the DNA together. If you think about DNA as a twisted ladder, then the sugar and the phosphate form the uprights and the bases form the steps.

There are four different bases in DNA:

- **thymine** (T)
- **adenine** (A)
- **cytosine** (C)
- **guanine** (G)

These bases always pair up in the same way:

- Adenine to thymine
- Cytosine to guanine

The DNA code

The sequence of bases forms the coded genetic information. Each base is like one letter in a four-letter alphabet. These letters make up three letter groups called codon **triplets**. Each triplet is one piece of information.

WOW FACTOR!

The Human Genome Project took 13 years to determine the sequence of the 3 billion base pairs in human DNA.

FIGURE 3: A single nucleotide unit made up of a phosphate, a sugar and a base.

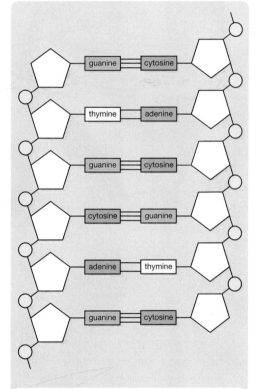

FIGURE 4: A short section of a DNA molecule showing how the different parts fit together.

Making new DNA

Each time a cell divides, in the process called mitosis, to make two new cells it needs to make an exact copy of all of the chromosomes. This means making an exact copy of the entire DNA in the cell. A tall order for such a complex molecule? The structure of DNA makes it all fairly simple. This is how it works:

1 The hydrogen bonds holding the base pairs together break.
2 The double helix 'unzips' to make two separate strands. Each strand acts as a template.
3 Free nucleotides are each attracted to their 'partner' nucleotide on each strand.
4 Bonds form between the nucleotides forming two new strands.
5 Two new molecules of DNA are made, each being an identical copy of the parent DNA.

This process is called replication.

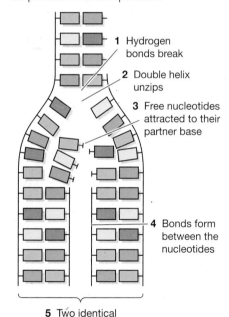

FIGURE 5: Replication makes two exact copies of the 'parent' DNA.

QUESTIONS

5 How many possible triplets can you make from the letters A, C, G and T?
6 What sequence of bases would pair up with this sequence: AAGTCTTCCGTC?
7 What is a nucleotide?
8 How do weak hydrogen bonds manage to hold together the DNA molecule?

QUESTIONS

9 Draw a flow chart to show the stages in DNA replication.
10 What would happen if there was an error in copying DNA?

...hydrogen bond ...nucleotides ...strands ...thymine ...triplets

Making protein

You will find out:

- That genes are the template for making proteins within cells
- That the order of the bases in DNA determines the order of the amino acids in a protein

Written in our genes

Genes control the development of all inherited characteristics. They do this because they contain the instructions for making proteins. Proteins are an important part of the structure of all living things. Enzymes, which control all of the chemical reactions in living things, are made of protein. Genes control exactly which proteins are made in cells and so they control the development, structure and functions of organisms.

FIGURE 1: Identical twins have exactly the same genes so they make exactly the same proteins.

What are proteins?

Proteins are large molecules. Egg white, antibodies, insulin, fingernails and hair are all made of protein. They are made of lots of smaller molecules called **amino acids**, which are joined together in long chains. These long chains are called **polypeptides**. In the drawing each coloured shape represents one amino acid, in a short polypeptide chain.

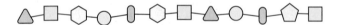

FIGURE 2: A short polypeptide chain.

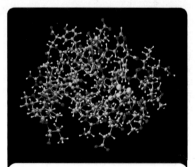

FIGURE 3: A model of an insulin molecule. Insulin has one of the simplest structures of all proteins!

One or more polypeptide chains link together to form a protein. Proteins have a complicated shape that helps them to carry out their jobs. If a protein molecule was the wrong shape, it might not be able to do its job properly. The shape of a protein molecule depends on the exact order of the amino acids in the polypeptide chains. DNA carries the code for putting amino acids in the correct order when making the polypeptide chains.

QUESTIONS

1. What is an enzyme?
2. What type of smaller molecule makes up larger protein molecules?
3. What is a polypeptide?
4. What could happen if an antibody molecule had an amino acid in the wrong place?

...amino acids   ...coding   ...messenger ribose nucleic acid   ...organelles

Making proteins (H)

To make a protein, hundreds or even thousands of amino acids need to be linked together in the correct order. The instructions for making each protein are stored on DNA in the cell nucleus. Each codon triplet identifies one amino acid in the protein. DNA is so big that it cannot leave the nucleus, yet proteins are made (**synthesised**) in **ribosomes**, tiny structures which are found in the cell cytoplasm. Ribosomes are one of the many types of **organelles** found in cells.

How does information for making proteins get from DNA in the nucleus to ribosomes in the cytoplasm? Cells make another type of nucleic acid, called **messenger ribonucleic acid** (mRNA), which is similar in structure to one strand of a DNA molecule (except that it has the base uracil instead of thymine.

A section of DNA for a particular protein unzips. A copy is made of one strand. This is mRNA, which passes out of the nucleus through a pore and moves to a ribosome. At the ribosome, other molecules, called **transfer RNA** (tRNA), carry amino acids to be linked together. Different tRNA molecules carry different amino acids. Each tRNA has a codon triplet that matches the triplets on the mRNA.

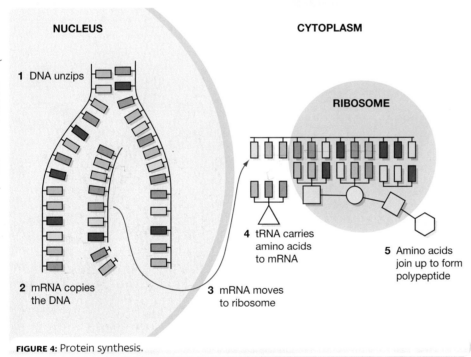

FIGURE 4: Protein synthesis.

Codons (H)

There are 20 naturally occurring amino acids, and proteins are made up of combinations of them. You will remember that the four bases, adenine, cytosine, guanine and thymine, can be arranged in 64 combinations of codon triplets, far more than are needed for the 20 amino acids. Each amino acid actually has more than one triplet **coding** for it. In addition, there are some codons that identify where to start and to stop copying the DNA.

Ribosomes

Ribosomes are tiny structures found in cells. They consist of protein and RNA. The picture below shows that ribosomes are made of two sub-units, with a groove between them. The mRNA (purple) is between the two sub-units, with the protein (yellow) forming on the mRNA.

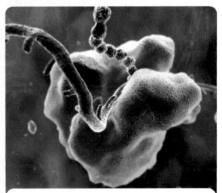

FIGURE 5: Protein being made by a ribosome.

QUESTIONS

5 Give **three** differences between DNA and mRNA.

6 How many codon triplets are there on a molecule of tRNA?

7 Draw a flow diagram to summarise the stages of protein synthesis from the DNA to a new protein molecule.

QUESTIONS

8 Why is it important that there are codon triplets that mean 'start' and 'stop'?

9 Where do we get the amino acids that we use to make new proteins?

Beer and wine

You will find out:

- That microorganisms can use substances as an energy source and make new materials
- That this process is called fermentation and requires suitable conditions

Alcoholic porridge!

Imagine an ancient Egyptian who makes a bowl of 'porridge' by boiling some wheat in water. It doesn't all get eaten and is left in a warm place for a few days. Then he tries some more. It tastes a bit odd but he keeps on eating it. After a while he starts to feel quite cheerful and decides that this stuff is so good that he invites some friends around to try it. He has made alcohol!

Making alcohol

Humans have been using grain and rotting fruit to make alcohol for thousands of years. Ancient people did not know how it worked but they knew how to make it. We now know that alcohol is made by the effect of yeast on sugar.

Fermentation

1 Set up the experiment in the diagram.

2 Leave it in a warm place.

3 Observe what happens to the limewater.

4 Put your results in a table.

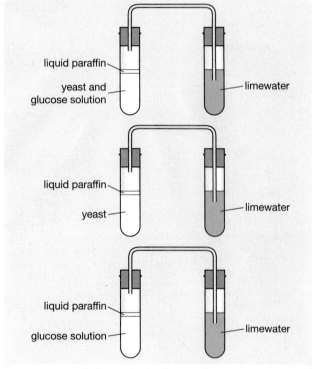

FIGURE 2: What is happening in this experiment?

FIGURE 1: I wonder what they are carrying in those pots!

Yeast uses sugar as a source of energy. Yeast can survive and reproduce without oxygen. The layer of liquid paraffin was used in the experiment to stop oxygen getting to the yeast. If there is no oxygen for the yeast it produces carbon dioxide and ethanol (alcohol). This is called **fermentation**. The chemical equation for fermentation is:

glucose → ethanol + carbon dioxide

QUESTIONS

1 How could you tell which tube(s) in the experiment fermented?

2 Why was there a layer of liquid paraffin in each tube?

3 Why were the other tubes used?

4 Explain the results of the experiment.

EXAM HINTS AND TIPS

It's easy to identify a sugar from its name as they all end in '-ose'.

...aerobic respiration   ...anaerobic respiration

Anaerobic respiration

Respiration is a chemical reaction that takes place in all living things. It uses a food source such as sugar to produce energy. Oxygen is usually used in respiration:

- Respiration with oxygen is called **aerobic respiration**.
- Respiration without oxygen is called **anaerobic respiration**.

Anaerobic respiration of sugar by yeast is an example of fermentation and is used to make alcoholic drinks. The ethanol which is produced makes the drinks alcoholic. The carbon dioxide gives some drinks, such as beer and champagne, their fizz.

Anaerobic respiration by yeast is also used to make bread. The carbon dioxide forms bubbles in the dough, making it rise.

What factors affect the rate of fermentation?

1 Mix 25 g of flour and 2 g of glucose in a beaker.

2 Mix 1 g of dried yeast into 20 cm³ of water.

3 Add the yeast mixture to the flour and glucose and stir it.

4 Pour the mixture into a 250 cm³ measuring cylinder.

5 Measure the volume of the dough every 2 minutes for 30 minutes.

6 Plot a line graph of your results.

Design an investigation to find out what factors affect the rate of fermentation. Factors that you investigate could include:

- temperature
- concentration of glucose
- amount of yeast.

Make sure you make your investigation a fair test.

FIGURE 3: Food from fermentation.

Wine and beer making (H)

Both wine and beer making involve using yeast to convert sugar into alcohol. The main difference between the two processes is the source of sugar. Wine making is easy. Grapes contain a lot of sugar so it's just a matter of crushing the grapes to release the sugar then adding some yeast. Beer, however, is made from barley, which contains a lot of starch but no sugar. This starch is a store of energy. When the barley starts to germinate, the starch is converted to a sugar, called maltose. The first stage in brewing beer is to add water to the barley and put it in a warm place. These are the best conditions to start germination.

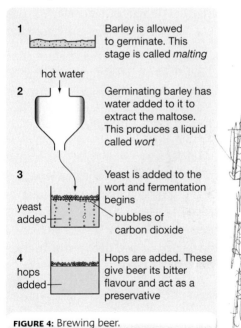

1 Barley is allowed to germinate. This stage is called *malting*

hot water

2 Germinating barley has water added to it to extract the maltose. This produces a liquid called *wort*

3 Yeast is added to the wort and fermentation begins
yeast added — bubbles of carbon dioxide

4 Hops are added. These give beer its bitter flavour and act as a preservative
hops added

FIGURE 4: Brewing beer.

QUESTIONS

5 Bread is made in anaerobic respiration. Why doesn't bread contain alcohol?

6 Why did the dough rise in the experiment?

7 Write a report on your investigation. Explain the effect on the rate of fermentation of the factor you investigated. Explain how you made your investigation a fair test.

QUESTIONS

8 Why does brewing beer involve the stage called 'malting'?

9 Fermentation is an anaerobic process. How is oxygen kept away from the yeast in fermentation?

...*fermentation* ...*glucose*

Genetic engineering

You will find out:

- That sections of DNA for specific proteins have been identified can be inserted into microorganisms

- That these micro-organisms can be cultivated in fermenters

Insulin

In the topic 'Electrical and chemical signals' you learnt that some people cannot make enough of the hormone **insulin**, which controls the concentration of blood sugar. People who do not have enough insulin suffer from **diabetes**. Many people with diabetes need to inject insulin every day. Up to the 1980s, the insulin they used was extracted from pigs and cattle, but insulin from other animals does not work as well as human insulin.

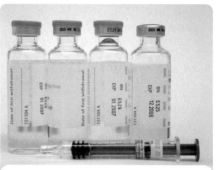

FIGURE 1: Many people with diabetes need daily injections of insulin.

Genetic engineering

Today, people with diabetes use human insulin instead of animal insulin. Scientists have found a way of making human insulin. There are three main reasons for using human insulin:

- Human insulin works better than animal insulin because the molecules are exactly the right shape for the body to use. Animal insulin has a slightly different structure from human insulin.
- Some people have an allergic reaction to animal insulin.
- Some people object to using any products extracted from animals.

Insulin is a protein. Your DNA contains a gene which has the instructions for making insulin. A gene is a length of DNA with the correct genetic code for all of the amino acids in a particular protein. To make human insulin, the exact piece of DNA in a human cell has to be identified. It is then cut out of the human DNA and inserted into the DNA of a **microorganism**. Then all you have to do is get the microorganism to grow in large quantities and it will make all of the insulin you need.

This method of making insulin uses **genetic engineering**. Genetic engineering means moving genes from one species to another.

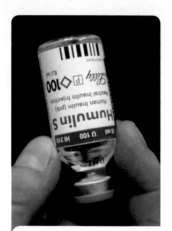

FIGURE 2: Humulin S is human insulin produced by genetic engineering.

ⅠⅠ QUESTIONS ⅠⅠ

1 What is a hormone?
2 Which part of the body makes insulin?
3 Why do you think that some people object to using insulin that is extracted from animals?
4 Why do you think that some people have an allergic reaction to animal insulin?

EXAM HINTS AND TIPS

A genetically modified organism is one whose genetic material has been altered.

...clones   ...diabetes   ...factor VIII   ...genetic engineering

Making human insulin

Although DNA is huge compared with other molecules, it is still far too small to see, so scientists have had to develop new 'tools' to be able to cut it and join sections of it together.

Bacteria do not have a nucleus like other cells. Instead, they have a long strand of DNA as well as some short sections of circular DNA called **plasmids**. The strand of DNA coding for insulin is inserted into one of these plasmids:

1 The section of DNA coding for insulin is identified.
2 Enzymes are used like scissors to cut out the insulin gene.
3 A plasmid is removed from a bacterial cell.
4 The plasmid is cut open using an enzyme.
5 Another enzyme is used to insert the insulin gene into the plasmid.
6 The plasmid is replaced into the bacterial cell.
7 The bacterial cells are allowed to multiply to make millions of **clones** (cells containing identical DNA).
8 The genetically modified bacteria are grown in a fermenter where they make insulin.

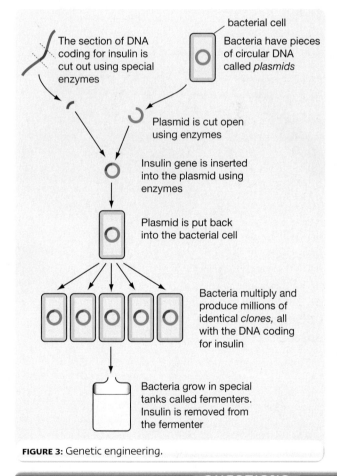

FIGURE 3: Genetic engineering.

More genetic engineering

The ability of blood to clot is very important. Clotting stops bleeding and prevents microbes from entering the body. **Haemophilia** is a condition where people lack a substance, called **factor VIII**, which is needed to form clots. If someone with haemophilia is injured then it is vital that they are injected with this missing substance. Previously this factor was extracted from blood given in transfusions. Many people with haemophilia were given factor VIII that was contaminated with HIV and went on to develop AIDS. Today, factor VIII is made using genetic engineering.

Other examples of genetic engineering include:
■ Producing *interferon*, a human protein which stops viruses multiplying inside cells.
■ Producing *human growth hormone* to treat abnormal growth.
■ Producing *crops* which are resistant to pests.
■ Producing *enzymes* for biological washing powder.

FIGURE 4: Genetic engineering even helps get your clothes clean!

QUESTIONS

5 What are the 'tools' that are used to cut and join together pieces of DNA?
6 What is a plasmid?
7 What is a 'clone'?
8 What is a fermenter?

QUESTIONS

9 Find out about why human growth hormone produced by genetic engineering is much safer than that extracted from the pituitary of people who have died.

…haemophilia …insulin …microorganism …plasmids

Fungi for food

You will find out:
- That fungi can be cultivated to provide food
- How microbes can be used to make food for humans

Fungi for food

People have been eating fungi for thousands of years. At first they collected fungi that they found growing naturally. Some people still collect mushrooms but most of us buy them from a greengrocer or supermarket. Growing mushrooms is a complicated business. The mushrooms need to be grown in the dark on a special compost of horse or chicken manure mixed with straw. The compost has to be heated to kill microbes. Fungi need the right temperature to grow properly.

FIGURE 1: Do you like mushrooms?

Growing mushrooms

Mushroom growing is a good example of how we can use waste material, such as horse manure, chicken manure and straw, to produce food. Mushrooms are only a small part of the fungus that produces them. Most of the fungus grows underground. Long threads called **hyphae** absorb nutrients from the soil. They get their energy from these nutrients. As the hyphae grow they produce the mushrooms (which are actually the reproductive organs of the fungus).

Mycoprotein 'meat'

Mycoprotein was first produced in the 1960s. Mycoprotein is protein that is produced from fungi. It has been on sale since the 1980s. You may have seen **Quorn**^{TM} products in the shops.

FIGURE 2: These tasty 'meat' products are actually made from a fungus!

Quorn^{TM} is made from a fungus called **Fusarium**. It was developed as a way of solving a world shortage of food because it can be made quickly and cheaply. The fungus is grown in huge fermenters. Vegetarians can eat Quorn because it contains no meat. Slimmers eat it because it is low in fat.

Mycoprotein is useful for making meat substitute because:

- it does not have much taste, so 'meat' flavours can be added
- it has a high protein content
- it forms fibres, which give it a texture like meat.

QUESTIONS

1. What are hyphae?
2. What is mycoprotein?
3. Who might want to eat Quorn and why?
4. Why is Quorn good for making meat substitutes?

WOW FACTOR!

Mycoprotein is a good source of protein and fibre while being low in fat and cholesterol.

Industrial fermentation

To get the maximum possible yield of mycoprotein, it is essential that the *Fusarium* is **cultivated** in the best possible conditions for growth. A fermenter provides these conditions. Industrial fermentation needs:

- **Aseptic** *conditions.* This means there should be no other microorganisms present as these would use some of the nutrients and could produce toxins that would prevent the *Fusarium* from growing.
- *Suitable nutrients.* These provide a source of energy and the raw materials for making mycoprotein.
- *Optimum temperature.* This means making sure that the microorganism is at the best temperature for growth. For *Fusarium* this is 32 °C.
- *Optimum pH.* This means that the acid/alkali balance is correct.
- *Oxygenation. Fusarium* needs plenty of oxygen to be able to respire.
- *Mixing.* The fermenter needs to be constantly mixed to ensure that the microorganism can use all the nutrients.

Industrial fermenters hold millions of litres of culture broth. They use a system called **continuous culture** to maximise yield. This means that nutrients are constantly added and the product is constantly harvested. Once the fungus starts to reproduce at its maximum rate, the amount of fungus in the fermenter doubles every five hours.

Although the example above refers to the production of mycoprotein from *Fusarium*, similar processes are used to cultivate other microorganisms to make products including penicillin, insulin and enzymes for washing powders.

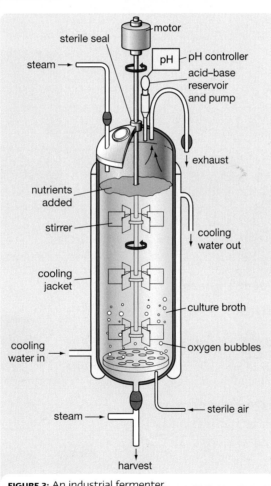

FIGURE 3: An industrial fermenter.

QUESTIONS

5 Make a labelled diagram of a fermenter. For each labelled part, explain its importance in getting the maximum yield of product.

6 If 10 kg of fungus is used to start the fermenter, how much will there be after 30 hours?

Food for the future?

Most of the protein in our diet comes from meat, fish, eggs, cheese and beans. Cultivating microorganisms, however, is a very economical way of producing protein:

- Growth of the microorganism is very fast. Animals do not double their mass every five hours!
- The protein can be made into a wide range of different 'meat' products.
- The process is not dependent on the weather as conditions inside the fermenter can be controlled to give maximum yield.
- Industrial fermentation often uses waste materials from other processes as the raw materials. For example, the raw material used for Quorn™ production is waste starch from crisp manufacturers.
- Industrial fermentation is a very efficient way of converting raw materials into protein:

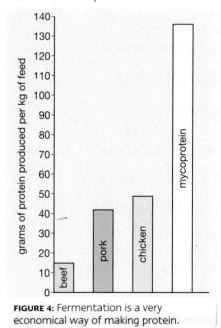

FIGURE 4: Fermentation is a very economical way of making protein.

QUESTIONS

7 Explain why more 'feed' is converted to protein by microorganisms than animals.

8 List some other advantages of producing mycoprotein rather than animal protein.

9 Why don't we all eat mycoprotein all of the time?

…hyphae …mycoprotein …Quorn™

Respiration

You will find out:

- That respiration provides energy
- That aerobic respiration uses O_2 and releases CO_2
- How inhaled air and exhaled air differ

Releasing energy

A car or motorcycle engine needs energy to make the car move. It uses a fuel such as petrol or diesel as a source of **chemical energy**. The fuel burns inside the engine. Oxygen is needed to make the fuel burn. Carbon dioxide is released in the reaction.

A similar thing happens in living organisms. Glucose is the fuel and oxygen is needed to release the energy.

FIGURE 1: The motorcycle engine uses petrol as a fuel while the rider uses glucose!

Using energy

You need energy so you can do lots of different things:

- controlling your temperature
- moving your muscles

- sending nerve impulses
- transporting substances around the body
- making new cells
- absorbing food.

FIGURE 2: Playing a sport uses lots of energy!

Respiration

You get energy from glucose in **respiration**. Fortunately respiration is controlled by your body so you do not burst into flames! Here is the chemical equation for respiration:

glucose + oxygen → carbon dioxide + water + energy

$$C_6H_{12}O_6 \quad 6O_2 \quad\quad 6CO_2 \quad\quad 6H_2O$$

This is called **aerobic respiration** because oxygen is needed for it to happen. Aerobic respiration is going on non-stop in all of the cells of your body.

We breathe in the oxygen we need for respiration and breathe out the carbon dioxide that is produced. This means that **inhaled** (breathed in) air is different from **exhaled** (breathed out) air.

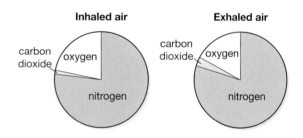

FIGURE 3: How do inhaled air and exhaled air differ?

QUESTIONS

1. Why do you think the word 'energy' is shown in red in the chemical equation for aerobic respiration?
2. Look at the list of reasons why we need energy. Which of them are taking place in the tennis player?
3. Explain the differences between inhaled and exhaled air.
4. In artificial resuscitation you breathe into the lungs of a person who has stopped breathing. How is this possible if we use the oxygen we breathe?

EXAM HINTS AND TIPS

Make sure you can remember the chemical equation for aerobic respiration. It is sure to be in your exam.

...aerobic respiration   ...chemical energy   ...exhaled

What happens in respiration?

Comparing carbon dioxide in inhaled and exhaled air

1 Set up the apparatus shown in the diagram.

2 Gently breathe in and out through the mouthpiece.

3 Observe what happens to the limewater.

■ Does inhaled air come in through tube 1 or 2?

■ Does exhaled air go out through tube 1 or 2?

■ In which tube did the limewater go cloudy first?

■ What does this tell us?

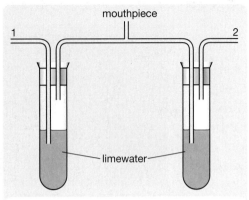

FIGURE 4: Comparing carbon dioxide in inhaled and exhaled air.

Comparing oxygen in inhaled and exhaled air

1 Put a lighted candle in a jar of air.

2 Time how long it takes for the candle to go out.

3 Repeat the experiment with a jar of exhaled air. (The diagram shows you how to collect a jar of exhaled air.)

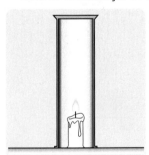

FIGURE 5: How long will a candle burn in inhaled and exhaled air?

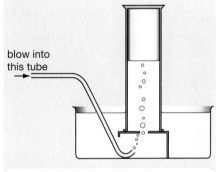

blow into this tube

FIGURE 6: Collecting exhaled air.

■ Make a table of your results.

■ Explain any differences you found in the length of time your candle burned in each jar.

EXAM HINTS AND TIPS

Remember that exhaled air contains oxygen. There's just less than in inhaled air. Likewise inhaled air contains less carbon dioxide than exhaled air.

QUESTIONS

5 We use energy even when we are asleep. List some of the activities that use energy while we are sleeping.

6 What is meant by aerobic respiration?

7 Write an account of each of the experiments in this section and explain how it confirms what we know about aerobic respiration.

Mitochondria (H)

Aerobic respiration takes place in cell organelles called **mitochondria** (singular *mitochondrion*). These are tiny structures found in all cells, although the more energy a cell uses, the more mitochondria there will be.

Mitochondria have a folded inner membrane. This provides a large surface area for the enzymes that control respiration.

ATP and ADP

Aerobic respiration is a complex chemical reaction which proceeds in many stages. Respiration releases energy from glucose but this energy is not used directly. Instead the mitochondria use the energy to make molecules of adenosine triphosphate (ATP). This acts as a store of energy that can be released instantly, rather than going through the long process of breaking down glucose molecules each time some energy is needed.

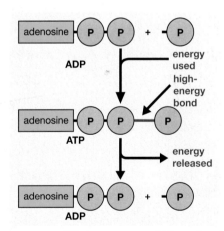

FIGURE 7: ATP stores energy which can be released very quickly.

QUESTIONS

8 Name some cells which you would expect to have a lot of mitochondria.

9 What do you think ADP stands for?

10 Explain why cells make ATP.

Breathing

You will find out:
- About the structure of the breathing system
- How we breathe in and out

Breath of life

How long can you hold your breath? A minute is a long time for the average person. After that you cannot help taking another breath. You know that you need to take in oxygen for your cells to release energy in aerobic respiration. You also produce carbon dioxide which you need to get rid of. Your lungs do this for you when you breathe. So where are your lungs and how do they work?

FIGURE 1: Divers usually take their own supply of air with them.

The breathing system

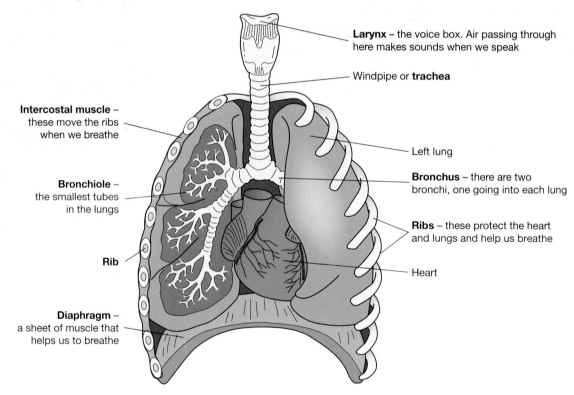

Larynx – the voice box. Air passing through here makes sounds when we speak

Windpipe or **trachea**

Intercostal muscle – these move the ribs when we breathe

Left lung

Bronchiole – the smallest tubes in the lungs

Bronchus – there are two bronchi, one going into each lung

Ribs – these protect the heart and lungs and help us breathe

Rib

Heart

Diaphragm – a sheet of muscle that helps us to breathe

FIGURE 2: The chest or **thorax**. The right side has been cut open to show inside.

▌▐ QUESTIONS ▐▌

1. What is the name of the gas in the air that is needed for respiration?
2. What is the name of the gas that is made in respiration and is breathed out?
3. Name two muscles that are used in breathing.
4. What are the jobs of the ribs?

WOW FACTOR!

Tom Sietas holds the world record for holding his breath – 9 minutes and 58 seconds – underwater!

...bronchiole ...bronchus ...diaphragm ...intercostal muscles

How we breathe

Look at the picture of a set of bellows. You can use them to get extra air into a fire to get it going.

- Squeezing the handles *decreases* the *volume* of the bellows.
- The pressure inside is *more than* atmospheric pressure and air is *forced out*.
- Pulling the handles apart increases the volume of the bellows.
- The pressure inside is *less than* atmospheric pressure and air is *forced in*.

Your breathing system works like a set of bellows.

FIGURE 3: Are you like these bellows?

Breathing in

1 **Intercostal muscles** contract.

2 **Ribs** move upwards and outwards.

3 **Diaphragm** contracts and flattens.

4 Volume of the **thorax** increases.

5 Pressure inside the thorax decreases.

6 Higher external pressure pushes air into the lungs.

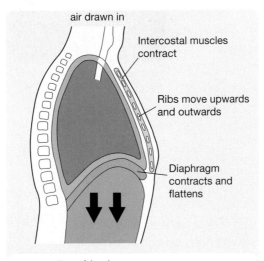

air drawn in

Intercostal muscles contract

Ribs move upwards and outwards

Diaphragm contracts and flattens

FIGURE 4: Breathing in.

Breathing out

1 Intercostal muscles relax.

2 Ribs move downwards and inwards.

3 Diaphragm relaxes and curves upwards.

4 Volume of the thorax decreases.

5 Pressure inside the thorax increases.

6 Higher internal pressure pushes air out of the lungs.

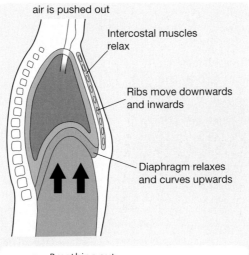

air is pushed out

Intercostal muscles relax

Ribs move downwards and inwards

Diaphragm relaxes and curves upwards

FIGURE 5: Breathing out.

Watch Out When you look at a diagram of the breathing system the left lung is on the right. That's because you are facing the diagram.

Deeper breathing

When you relax, the intercostal muscles do not move the ribs much. Movement of the diaphragm makes enough change in thoracic volume to breathe in the amount of air needed. It is only when you do exercise and need more air that the intercostal muscles start moving the ribs up and down.

There are actually two sets of intercostal muscles. The external intercostal muscles contact when we breathe in. The internal intercostal muscles are usually relaxed. When you need to cough or blow hard they contract and force the lungs down and inwards.

FIGURE 6: You need powerful internal intercostal muscles to play the bagpipes.

Iron lung

Until a vaccine was found, many people suffered from the disease polio. This disease affects the muscles and can leave people paralysed, often unable to breathe. Their lives were saved by a device called an iron lung.

QUESTIONS

5 In what ways do bellows work in a similar way to lungs?

6 In what ways do bellows work differently from lungs?

7 Between the lungs and the ribs there are fluid-filled pleural membranes. Why do you think these are important?

QUESTIONS

8 Why are the internal intercostal muscles especially important for people who play wind instruments?

9 Find out how an iron lung works. Draw a diagram to explain it.

...larynx ...ribs ...thorax ...trachea

Exchanging gases

You will find out:

- How O_2 gets from the lungs to respiring cells
- How glucose gets to respiring cells
- How CO_2 is removed from respiring cells

Inside your lungs

If you asked someone to describe their lungs they might well say that they are two bags inside their chest. They would be wrong! The inside of your lungs is more like a sponge, full of tiny air spaces. These air spaces are surrounded by millions of tiny blood vessels, called **capillaries**. These capillaries collect oxygen from the air you breathe in. They carry carbon dioxide to your lungs so you can breathe it out.

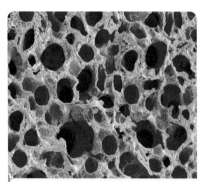

FIGURE 1: Not a photograph of a bath sponge but a small section of lung tissue!

Inside your lungs

The air you breathe in goes through the nasal cavities behind your nose. These are covered with a layer of water which moistens the air you breathe in. The nasal cavities are surrounded with blood vessels. They warm up the air you breathe in. The warm, moist air goes down the windpipe or trachea. The trachea splits into two tubes called **bronchi** (singular *bronchus*). Each bronchus divides into smaller and smaller tubes called **bronchioles**. At the end of the bronchioles are tiny air sacs called **alveoli** (singular *alveolus*).

Inhaled and exhaled air

The air we breathe in is different from the air we breathe out:

Gas	Inhaled air	Exhaled air
Nitrogen	79%	79%
Oxygen	21%	16%
Carbon dioxide	0.04%	5%
Water vapour	variable	variable

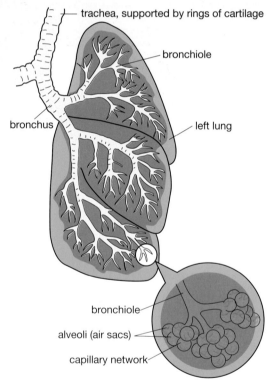

FIGURE 2: Inside the lungs. The part showing the alveoli is greatly magnified.

QUESTIONS

1. What are the smallest blood vessels of the body called?
2. Why are some capillaries in the diagram coloured red and some coloured blue?
3. Draw a bar chart to show the differences between inhaled and exhaled air.
4. What does the table tell you about the use of nitrogen by the body?

WOW FACTOR!

If all of the air sacs in the lung were spread out, they would cover about the same area as a tennis court.

...alveoli ...arteries ...arterioles ...bronchi ...bronchioles ...capillaries

Exchanging gases

Oxygen moves from the alveoli, where there is a high concentration, to the red blood cells, where there is a lower concentration. Carbon dioxide moves from the blood plasma, where there is a high concentration, to the alveoli, where there is a lower concentration. Movement of substances from areas of higher concentration to areas of lower concentration is called **diffusion**. The alveoli are very well adapted to carry out their job of exchanging gases:

■ The alveoli have very thin walls. They are only one cell thick. This makes it easier for oxygen and carbon dioxide to pass through them.

■ Each alveolus is surrounded by lots of **capillaries**. This means that there is plenty of blood to carry oxygen from the alveolus.

■ The inside of the alveolus is moist with a layer of water. This is because oxygen needs to dissolve in water before it can pass into the blood.

■ There are millions of alveoli in the lungs. They give the inside of the lungs a huge surface area. Plenty of oxygen can pass from the air in the lungs to the blood. Plenty of carbon dioxide can pass from the blood to the air in the lungs.

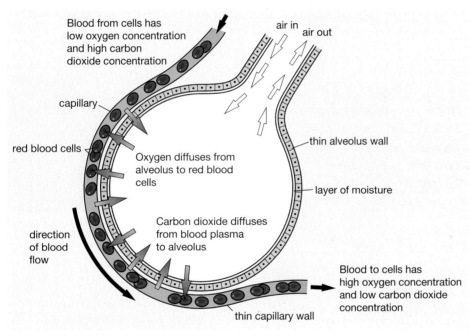

FIGURE 3: Gas exchange in an alveolus.

Fuel for respiration

Think about the chemical equation for aerobic respiration. Your cells need glucose to get energy. Glucose comes from food or from breaking down stores of glycogen. Your blood carries glucose to respiring cells from the small intestine, where it is absorbed from food, and from stores of glycogen, which are mostly in the liver.

QUESTIONS

5 What does 'diffusion' mean?

6 Why are the insides of the alveoli covered with a layer of water?

7 Why do the alveoli have very thin walls?

8 Describe **two** other features of alveoli that help them to carry out their function.

Into the cells

Once blood reaches the cells of the body, the reverse of the process in the alveoli takes place. Blood containing a high concentration of oxygen is carried from the heart in **arteries**. These divide into smaller vessels called **arterioles**. Arterioles divide further still to form capillaries. Each cell in the body has a capillary very close to it. In the cells of the body the concentration of oxygen is lower than in the red blood cells, while the concentration of carbon dioxide is higher than in the blood plasma. So oxygen, carbon dioxide and glucose diffuse from the area of higher concentration to the area of lower concentration. A difference in concentration like this is called a **concentration gradient**. Capillaries join together to form small vessels called **venules**. Venules join together to form veins which return blood to the heart.

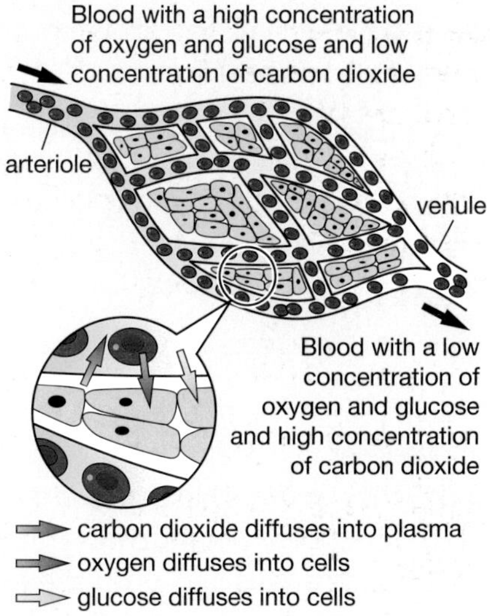

FIGURE 4: A capillary bed: oxygen and glucose diffuse from the blood to body cells and carbon dioxide diffuses from the cells to the blood.

QUESTIONS

9 Explain what is meant by a concentration gradient.

10 Draw a flowchart to show how glucose gets to a respiring cell.

11 Draw and label a diagram showing the diffusion of substances between blood and the body's cells

Exercise

You will find out:

● Why heart rate and breathing rate increase when we exercise

● That when we exercise vigorously, muscle cells may not get enough oxygen so they respire anaerobically

Hard at work

It takes a lot of energy to do a marathon. Remember that we get our energy from the respiration of glucose:

glucose + oxygen → carbon dioxide + water

The athlete needs to get glucose and oxygen to his muscles. He also needs to get rid of all of the extra carbon dioxide he is making. So how does he do it?

FIGURE 1: It's hard work doing a marathon!

Getting extra energy

What do you think the athlete's body will be doing as he races around the course? He will notice that:

■ *he is breathing faster and taking bigger breaths*– this gets more oxygen into his body and gets rid of as much carbon dioxide as possible
■ *his heart beats faster* – this gets blood pumping round his body faster
■ *he feels hotter* – respiration produces heat energy so his body temperature increases
■ *he sweats a lot* – this helps to cool him down.

The athlete in the photograph is being tested in a sports laboratory. Modern laboratories can make many measurements including heart rate, breathing rate and temperature. These measurements are made using electronic instruments which are much more accurate than old-fashioned methods. Measurements are being made as she pedals on the exercise bike. One measurement is of the amount of air breathed in. The results are shown in the graph.

Another measurement is of her heart rate. These results are shown in the table:

FIGURE 2: Sports laboratories can give athletes helpful information.

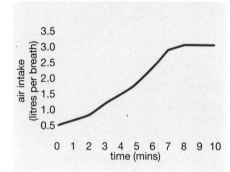

FIGURE 3: How would your air intake change with exercise?

Time (mins)	0	1	2	3	4	5	6	7	8	9	10
Pulse rate (beats per min)	80	90	110	130	140	150	160	165	170	170	170

⊞ QUESTIONS ⊞

1 What was the size of the athlete's normal breath?
2 Describe the pattern shown in the graph of air intake.
3 Plot a graph to show how the pulse rate changed when the athlete was on the exercise bike.
4 Why are modern electronic methods better than older methods of recording things such as heart rate?

...anaerobic respiration   ...concentration gradient

Exercise

Why do you breathe faster and deeper and why does your heart rate increase when you exercise? When you exercise your muscles need more energy. To get more energy you need to respire faster. To respire faster your muscle cells need more oxygen and glucose and they have more carbon dioxide to remove.

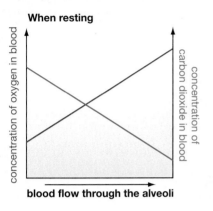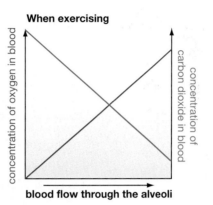

FIGURE 4: Concentration gradients of gases increase when we exercise.

The rate of diffusion of oxygen and carbon dioxide in the lungs and muscle cells increases when we exercise. This is because the difference in concentration is greater. The **concentration gradient** has increased.

Anaerobic respiration

Yeast can respire without oxygen.

Anaerobic respiration in yeast: **glucose → ethanol + carbon dioxide + energy**

If you do very vigorous exercise then eventually you cannot breathe any faster and your heart cannot pump blood any faster. You cannot get any more oxygen to your muscle cells. When this happens, your body gets energy from glucose by **anaerobic respiration** (although this is not the same reaction as in yeast).

Anaerobic respiration in animals: **glucose → lactic acid + energy**

Lactic acid is a poison. As it builds up in muscles it causes **cramp**, a pain in the muscles. Your body needs to get rid of lactic acid. It does this by reacting lactic acid with oxygen:

lactic acid + oxygen → carbon dioxide + water

Another problem with anaerobic respiration is that it does not produce very much energy compared with aerobic respiration:

- aerobic respiration   16.1 kJ/g glucose
- anaerobic respiration   0.8 kJ/g glucose

▭▭▭ QUESTIONS ▭▭▭

5   Why can sprinters run at top speed for only a few seconds?

6   Describe **three** differences between aerobic and anaerobic respiration.

7   Write word equations for all **three** types of respiration (without looking in the book!)

8   Explain the graphs of heart rate and breathing rate from the previous column.

Repaying the debt   (H)

You may have noticed that after you have finished exercising, you carry on breathing deeply and quickly for a while. It also takes a while for your heart rate to return to normal. This is because the muscle cells have to take in extra oxygen to break down lactic acid. The extra oxygen needed is called the **oxygen debt.**

FIGURE 5: After this sprint finish, cyclist Lance Armstrong will need to 'get his breath back'. He will be repaying his oxygen debt.

Your body cannot cope with much of a build-up of lactic acid. That is why long distance athletes run at a slower speed than sprinters. Long distance athletes might build up lactic acid at the end of a race in a short sprint finish as they will be able to repay their oxygen debt after the race.

▭▭▭ QUESTIONS ▭▭▭

9   Explain what is meant by oxygen debt.

10 Draw graphs to show the concentration gradients of carbon dioxide and oxygen between muscle cells and capillaries, while at rest and when exercising.

On a diet?

You will find out:
- About official advice on diets and exercise
- About the science behind some popular diets

Obesity

Obesity means being very overweight. A recent government survey estimated that 17% of 15 year olds in the UK are **obese**. 30 000 deaths per year in the UK are caused by obesity. People become overweight or obese because they get more energy in their food than they use up. There are over 20 000 different books about dieting and over 8000 about exercise so, with plenty of advice available, why do people become obese?

I'll get all of the exercise i need carrying these around!

Body mass index

You can work out if you are overweight or obese by calculating your **body mass index** (BMI):

mass (in kilograms) ÷ height^2 (in metres) = body mass index

When you have calculated your BMI you can check it against the table.

Body mass index	Description
Less than 18.5	underweight
20–25	normal
25–30	overweight
More than 30	obese

One Calorie is equal to 4.2 kJ.

Why do you gain weight?

Your body needs a certain amount of energy every day. You get your energy from the food you eat. If you eat more energy than you use, your body converts the excess into fat, which is stored under your skin. If you eat less energy than you use, your body uses up stores of fat.

Calories and joules

You will often hear people talking about the **calories** in food. A calorie is a measurement of the amount of energy. On food packets you will see it written as Calories (with a capital 'C') which is 1000 calories or a kilocalorie. Scientists now use **kilojoules** (kJ). One Calorie is equal to 4.2 kJ.

⊪ QUESTIONS ⊪

1. Calculate your own BMI. You can do this at home.
2. How could you decide if someone is obese?
3. A packet of crisps contains 154 Calories. How much is this in kJ?
4. What factors could affect the amount of energy you use each day?

...Atkins' diet ...body mass index ...calories ...glycaemic index

Food fads?

Many scientists describe modern diets as 'fads' – fashionable advice but not based on sound scientific evidence.

- *Government advice* in the UK is to eat a diet that is high in carbohydrates and fibre and low in protein and fat. It also suggests that you should get plenty of exercise. Carbohydrates give you the energy you need while fibre makes you feel full. Fat has much more energy than carbohydrate so it gives you more energy than you need.
- The *cabbage soup diet* has been around for a few years although nobody seems to know who invented it! People on this diet have to make cabbage soup, which is very low in energy. They can eat as much cabbage soup as they want to keep them full, then, each day, they are allowed additional foods in their diet. The cabbage soup diet is only recommended for a week.
- The *traffic light diet* sorts foods into three groups. Red foods are high in energy and have few useful nutrients. Amber foods are high in energy but are a good source of nutrients. Green foods are low in energy and high in nutrients.

- The GI (**glycaemic index**) *diet* is based on controlling the amount of sugar in the blood. All foods are given a glycaemic index (GI) which is a measurement of how quickly they release sugar into the blood. Foods with a high GI give you lots of energy all at once but this energy is quickly used up and you soon feel hungry again. Foods with a low GI release sugar into your blood more gradually giving you a steady flow of energy.

QUESTIONS

5. Summarise the advantages and disadvantages of the diets above.
6. Why is taking plenty of exercise an important part of losing weight?
7. Use diet books, magazines or the internet to research some other diets and explain how they are supposed to work.

Atkins' diet

The **Atkins' diet** has been in the news, with many famous celebrities claiming to have lost large amounts of weight. Eat lots of protein and fat and less than 20 g of carbohydrate per day. The theory behind this is that the more carbohydrate we eat, the more insulin we produce. Insulin encourages the body to convert carbohydrates to fats and to store them. If you do not eat carbohydrate then your body uses up reserves of fat instead. Many doctors, however, think that the Atkins' diet is unsafe.

FIGURE 1: This grocery store specialises in foods for the Atkins' diet.

When you break down fat your body produces chemicals called **ketones**. Your body has to remove these ketones which can cause damage to the liver and kidneys.

QUESTIONS

8. Use your knowledge of insulin to explain how the Atkins' diet works.
9. Why do many scientists believe that the Atkins' diet increases your chance of having a heart attack?

...ketones   ...kilojoule   ...obese

The right type of respiration

CHALLENGE

CONTEXT

Will is in Year 10 and is doing pretty well in cross-country running. It's sometimes not much fun when it's chucking it down with rain and he often ends up plastered in mud, but he's doing pretty well in the races and it's a good way of keeping fit. That's important to Will because he does a lot of surfing as well and stamina is important in that.

As he's got older, and moved up in the classes he enters in cross-country races, the distances get longer. Some of his races are up to 5700 m now and that can be a strain. Starts are important; it's no good holding back at the beginning of a race and then trying to catch up – you'd never do it. Will gets stuck in and is often well up with the leaders into the first bend.

It's later on in the race that he sometimes finds it difficult. He's not as tall as some of the runners and he sometimes finds himself dropping back a bit. Not much usually, but occasionally cramp sets in and that's a problem.

When Will is running his muscles need a supply of energy and that comes from respiration. Glucose is broken down to release energy, oxygen is used and the products are water and carbon dioxide. Although it leaves him panting and feeling tired at the end of a race, it's often no worse than that.

Sometimes he has to work harder ('dig deeper' as the team coach says) and the respiration process in his body runs short of oxygen. Glucose is still being broken down and energy is being released, but so is lactic acid, which builds up in the muscles. This is cramp and it hurts.

STEP 1

What are the scientific names given to:

1 respiration with sufficient oxygen?
2 respiration without sufficient oxygen?

STEP 2

Respiration releases carbon dioxide and water. How does Will dispose of the:

1 carbon dioxide?
2 water? (You should be able to supply more than one answer here!)

Will has quite a rigorous training regime. In fact, as the season wears on he finds that the cramp becomes a bit less of a problem. Suggest why this should be.

When Will is running his body responds in quite a different way from when he is standing or walking. The increased rate of respiration affects him in a number of ways. Look at the word equation for respiration on page 24 and think about how it feels to run fast. Write a short paragraph explaining which organs are behaving differently during a cross-country run and why that should be.

Maximise your grade

These sentences show what you need to include in your work to achieve each grade. Use them to improve your work and be more successful.

Grade	Answer includes...
F	Recall some ideas about the respiration equation and types of respiration.
	Recall ideas such as the respiration equation and types of respiration.
	Know that respiration applies to the human body.
	Start to apply the concept of respiration to the human body.
C	Apply the concept of respiration to the human body.
	Understand how the body adapts to changes.
A	Apply the concept of adaptation to the process of respiration to the human body.
	Apply the concept of adaptation to the process of respiration to the human body with clarity and detail.

Dizviding cells

You will find out:

- That cells divide by mitosis to produce two identical cells for growth and replacement

Starting off

You should remember that you started off from one cell that contained chromosomes from your parents. You have 46 chromosomes in total, 23 from your mother and 23 from your father. Your chromosomes are made of DNA, which is identical in all the cells in your body. The single cell that was the start of you had to divide millions of times to make the cells in your body, all with identical DNA.

FIGURE 1: An egg just at the point of fertilisation. You can see the sperm nucleus about to join with the ovum nucleus.

Mitosis

The cell that you started from was called a **zygote**, which was made when an egg (or **ovum**) was fertilised by a **sperm**. **Mitosis** is a type of **cell division** which makes **daughter cells** with identical DNA. Genetically identical cells are called clones. All the cells of the body, apart from eggs and sperms, are made by mitosis. Mitosis occurs when:

- an organism grows
- damage, such as a cut, is being repaired
- old or worn-out cells are replaced.

Normally the **chromosomes** are a long tangle of threads in the **nucleus**. Before mitosis, the threads contract and thicken. This makes them easier to see. The next stage in mitosis is to make an exact copy of all the

FIGURE 2: A cell dividing by mitosis. You can see the chromosomes moving to the opposite ends of the cell.

chromosomes. For a short time the cell nucleus has double the normal number of chromosomes. The cell then divides in two. One set of chromosomes moves into each new cell.

Human cells have 46 chromosomes. This is called the **diploid** number. Other animals have a different number of chromosomes. The diploid number in chimps is 48, in mice it is 40, and in dogs it is 78.

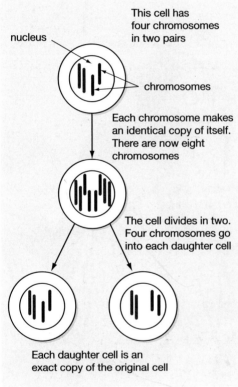

This cell has four chromosomes in two pairs

nucleus

chromosomes

Each chromosome makes an identical copy of itself. There are now eight chromosomes

The cell divides in two. Four chromosomes go into each daughter cell

Each daughter cell is an exact copy of the original cell

FIGURE 3: Mitosis – this cell has a diploid number of four.

QUESTIONS

1 What is meant by the diploid number?
2 Why do cells need to divide by mitosis?
3 What is the diploid number in a human?
4 Draw a flowchart to show what happens in mitosis.

...cell division   ...chromosomes   ...daughter cells   ...diploid   ...gametes   ...genes

Meiosis (H)

Human sperm cells and egg cells (ova) are called sex cells or **gametes**. They have only 23 chromosomes each. This is called the **haploid** number. The haploid number for any *species* is half the diploid number. Eggs and sperms are formed in a special type of cell division called **meiosis**.

Diploid to haploid to diploid

Meiosis produces gametes, which are haploid. Fertilisation produces diploid cells again. These then divide by mitosis to form a new organism. The diagram summarises this in humans.

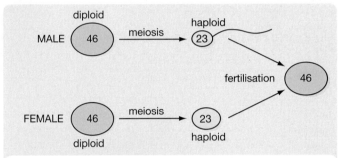

FIGURE 4: Fertilisation restores the diploid number.

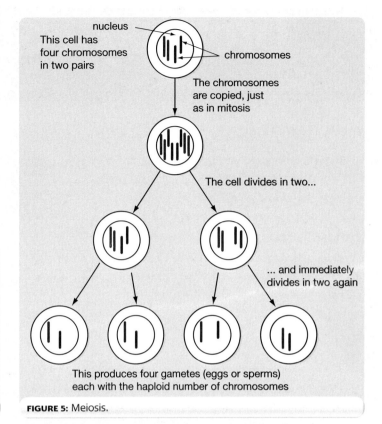

FIGURE 5: Meiosis.

Gene mixing

Unlike mitosis, meiosis does not produce exact copies of the parent cell – they cannot be identical because they only have half the number of chromosomes. In addition, however, all the gametes produced are different. This happens in two ways.

Meiosis is random. The two chromosomes in each pair will randomly mix when gametes form. In this cell, with just two pairs of chromosomes, there are four possible ways in which they can combine.

> **WOW FACTOR!**
>
> All the red blood cells in your body are replaced about every 100 days – but not all at once!

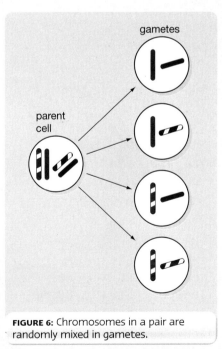

FIGURE 6: Chromosomes in a pair are randomly mixed in gametes.

Gene crossovers

Another way in which meiosis mixes up **genes** is by gene crossovers. During meiosis each pair of chromosomes lies side by side and genes can cross from one to another.

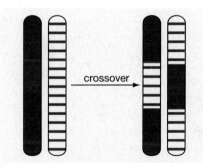

FIGURE 7: Genes have crossed over from one chromosome of a pair to the other.

QUESTIONS

9 In a cell with 23 pairs of chromosomes, in how many possible ways could the chromosomes mix?

10 Draw a table to summarise the differences between mitosis and meiosis.

QUESTIONS

5 What would happen if human ova and sperm had 46 chromosomes?

6 What is meant by the haploid number?

7 Where does meiosis take place in animals?

8 Draw a diagram to summarise how fertilisation restores the diploid number.

...haploid   ...meiosis   ...mitosis   ...nucleus   ...ovum   ...sperm   ...zygote

Growing a baby

You will find out:

- About how a zygote grows and develops to form a baby by cell division, growth and differentiation
- About the scientific evidence in the debate on abortion

Fertilisation to birth

The baby in the photograph is four days old. It's tiny. It has a lot of growing to do. But this baby has already grown at a faster rate than it will ever grow again. From fertilisation to birth it has grown from a single cell, about the size of a full stop, to a mass of about 3 kg. Its mass increases about 1 000 000 000 times in nine months!

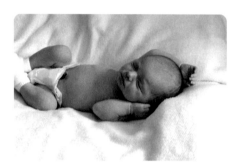

FIGURE 1: Only four days old but hasn't he grown!

In the uterus

Once a zygote has been formed, it starts to divide by mitosis:

- 3 days after fertilisation it is a ball of 16 cells.
- After 5 days it is a hollow ball of cells called a **blastocyst**. It starts to attach itself to the wall of the uterus. Cells on the outside form the **placenta**. Cells in the middle start to form the **embryo**.
- After 14 days it is a blob of cells and is now called an embryo. The cells are all pretty much the same.
- After 21 days it is 2 mm long and looks like a small worm. It has a tiny heart which has started to beat.
- After 28 days it is about 5 mm long and looks like a tadpole with a tail.
- After about 30 days it has a face and is losing its tail.
- By 60 days its brain has started to appear but it is still very primitive.
- By about 10 weeks it is starting to look human. It has arms, hands, legs and feet, and is beginning to develop the organs of the body. It is now called a **foetus**.
- By about 4 months the mother may be able to feel its movements and its heartbeat can be heard with a stethoscope.
- By 5½ months its lungs are becoming quite well developed. Neurones in the brain begin to link up with each other. It responds to sounds outside its mother's body and it is possible that it can feel pain.

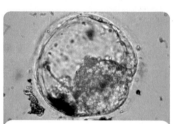

FIGURE 2: A blastocyst – the clump of cells near the bottom will become the embryo.

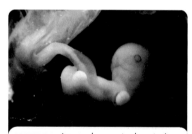

FIGURE 3: An embryo at about six weeks – it is about 15 mm long.

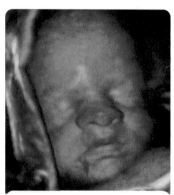

FIGURE 4: A foetus at about five months. The picture was taken from an ultrasound scan.

QUESTIONS

1. If your mass increased 1 000 000 000 times, how heavy would you be?
2. What is a zygote?
3. What is the difference between an embryo and a foetus?
4. Draw a timeline to show the development of a baby from a zygote.

...blastocyst ...differentiation ...embryo ...foetus

Termination

In the UK a woman is legally allowed to have her pregnancy ended at any time up to 24 weeks if two doctors agree that there is a risk to her physical or mental health by having a baby or if there is a risk to the health of any children she already has. There is no time limit if two doctors agree that a woman's health or life is seriously threatened by continuing with the pregnancy or that the foetus is likely to be born with severe physical or mental abnormalities. Ending a pregnancy in this way is called a **termination** or **induced abortion**. 90% of terminations in the UK take place before 12 weeks.

Many people think that it is totally wrong to terminate a pregnancy, as it is ending a life and is therefore murder. Other people think that a woman has the right to choose whether or not she carries on with her pregnancy. There are many views in between, based on moral, ethical and religious beliefs.

When induced abortion was first made legal in the UK, in 1967, the time limit was 28 weeks in cases where there was a risk to the woman's health. This limit was set because babies born earlier were not likely to survive. This was later reduced as medical and technological advances made it possible for premature babies to survive as early as 24 weeks of pregnancy. Babies have survived being born as early as 22 weeks but almost all have been seriously disabled.

FIGURE 5: People have strongly held views both for and against legally induced abortion.

Making a human

As the embryo grows, its cells divide, get bigger, then divide again. As well as getting bigger, the embryo needs to start making the tissues of a human body, which are all made from different types of cell. Making different tissue, with their specialised cells, is called **differentiation**.

Every cell in your body has exactly the same genes that were in the original zygote. A cell in your leg muscle has the information needed to make liver cells, while a cell in your liver has the information needed to make muscle cells, but they are unable to do this. Liver cells can make only new liver cells and muscle cells can make only new muscle cells. Only the cells that are present very early in pregnancy can differentiate into different tissues. We call these **stem cells**.

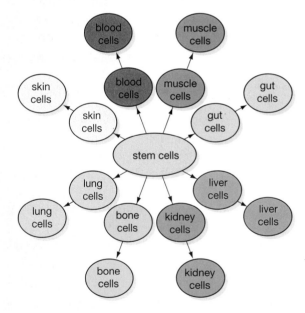

FIGURE 6: Stem cells can differentiate into all types of cells but specialised cells can only make more of the same type.

QUESTIONS

5   Find out more about the termination of pregnancies. Summarise the views of people who are for or against legal induced abortion. Use evidence, including scientific evidence, to decide whether the law should be changed or not and give reasons for your decision.

QUESTIONS

6   Do cells in the foetus divide by meiosis or mitosis?

7   What does differentiation mean?

8   What is special about stem cells?

9   Where are stem cells found?

Stem cells

You will find out:
- About some of the possible uses of stem cells
- That stem cells can differentiate into other cells but that cells from older animals cannot

What are stem cells?

Stem cells can **differentiate** into different cell types in the body. When a stem cell divides, each new cell is able to remain a stem cell or become another type of specialised cell, such as a muscle cell, a blood cell or a brain cell. Stem cells can divide forever to replace other cells while the person is still alive. Some scientists think that stem cells could be used to repair damaged parts of the body.

FIGURE 1: A round clump of stem cells. The picture was taken using an electron microscope.

Regeneration

Can you recognise the strange animal in the photograph? It's a starfish but why is one leg much bigger than the body and the other legs? This starfish was probably attacked by another sea creature. Its leg was removed from its body. The leg survived and a new body has grown from the remains of the leg. If the body survived then a new leg would have grown from it!

This ability to grow new body parts is called **regeneration**. A number of animals are able to do this, including reptiles, amphibians, worms and spiders. Many scientists hope that, by using stem cells, it may be possible to replace damaged tissues in humans.

Using stem cells

The cells in an embryo are stem cells called **embryonic stem cells**. They can grow into any of the 200 different types of cell in the body. Women who are infertile may have a baby by **in vitro** fertilisation (IVF) treatment, often called 'test-tube babies'. When this is carried out, several eggs are fertilised and allowed to grow for a few days to form a blastocyst. One or more of these is then implanted in the woman's body.

Women may allow doctors to use blastocysts to get stem cells for research. Some people think that this should not be allowed as they believe the blastocyst is already a human life.

FIGURE 2: This damaged starfish was able to grow a new body from a surviving leg!

WANT TO KNOW MORE?

Look at website http://www.luc.edu/depts/biology/dev/regen2.htm to see a newt regenerating a leg!

QUESTIONS

1 What is regeneration? Name some animals that can regenerate limbs.
2 Why do doctors think that stem cells may be very useful?
3 What is a blastocyst?
4 Should doctors be allowed to use stem cells from embryos in research?

...cancer cells   ...DA neurone   ...differentiate   ...dopamine   ...embryonic stem cells

Stem cell therapy

About 1 person in 50 over the age of 65 is affected by **Parkinson's disease**. It is caused by the breakdown of a type of neurone in the brain, called a **DA neurone**. These produce a chemical called **dopamine**, which helps to control the passing of nerve impulse across synapses. Without enough dopamine the patient suffers a lack of coordination in their movement that often appears as shaking, stiffness of muscles and joints, and difficulty in moving. Patients are treated with drugs that help the neurones to replace dopamine, but these only slow down the disease – they cannot cure it.

Scientists hope that stem cells may provide a cure for Parkinson's disease. They have identified the exact cells that need to be replaced and have developed ways to make embryonic stem cells differentiate into cells with many of the functions of DA neurones.

FIGURE 3: Actor Michael J. Fox suffers from Parkinson's disease. Here he is seen campaigning in favour of stem cell research.

Scientists are trying to find ways of producing DA neurones from human stem cells in the laboratory for transplantation into humans with Parkinson's disease.

One of the biggest hurdles in stem cell research is to find ways of 'switching on' particular genes. For example, all the cells in the body carry the gene for making insulin, but this gene works only in the cells in the pancreas. Scientists are trying to use stem cells to replace pancreas cells that do not produce insulin. The problem is to find a way of switching on the gene for producing insulin.

WOW FACTOR!

Cells taken from a cancer patient in 1951 are still dividing and are used in medical research, despite the fact that the patient died over 50 years ago.

Drug testing

Many drugs are tested on animals. In addition to ethical objections to using animals for research, animals do not always respond to drugs in the same way as humans. Medicines could be tested on differentiated cells from human **stem** cells, allowing drug testing in various cell types. To do this, scientists need to learn to control the differentiation of stem cells into the specific cell type on which drugs will be tested.

It is not possible to grow enough of a cell type for drug testing purposes from specialised cells from humans because there is a limit, called the **Hayflick limit**, to the number of times they can divide. Stem cells and **cancer cells** do not have a limit to the number of times they can divide. Cancer cells, for example, are used to test potential anti-cancer drugs.

FIGURE 4: Using stem cells for research could reduce the number of experiments carried out on animals.

QUESTIONS

5 Describe the causes and symptoms of Parkinson's disease.

6 Why do scientists need to be able to produce large numbers of stem cells?

7 What is meant by 'switching on' a gene?

QUESTIONS

8 What would be the advantages of using stem cells for medical research rather than animals?

9 What is the Hayflick limit?

Growth in animals

You will find out:

- That growth patterns are affected by genes, hormones and nutrition

- That size is a continuous variable

Growth

All living things, both animals and plants, grow. **Growth** is one of the characteristics of living things. You can grow a crystal in a beaker of a solution. As water evaporates from the solution, layers build up on the outside of the crystal, making it bigger. Growth in living things is much more complicated than this, however. Living things grow from within themselves. Cells divide and differentiate, forming new tissues and increasing in size.

FIGURE 1: You can grow a crystal like this in a science laboratory.

How do we grow?

As you know, you began as a single cell called a zygote, an egg fertilised by a sperm. This cell divided into two cells, which divided into 4 cells, then 8, then 16, and continued until you were made of billions of cells. In between dividing, the cells grew. Cells differentiate, forming the specialised cells that make up the tissues and organs of your body. Normally once cells have differentiated to form specialised cells, they do not divide any more.

The fastest period of growth in a human is in the time between fertilisation and birth. You continue to grow after being born but the rate of growth slows down and most people have stopped growing by the time they are about 18–20 years old. We stop growing because most of our cells stop dividing as we get older.

Some cells need to be replaced throughout our life and so some cells carry on dividing including:

- red blood cells
- skin cells
- cells lining your intestine.

FIGURE 2: By the time you are 20 you will almost certainly have stopped growing.

These new cells are made by a special type of **adult stem cells**. Unlike embryonic stem cells, which can make any type of cell, adult stem cells can make only a few different types of cell, depending on the part of the body they are in.

⠿ QUESTIONS ⠿

1 In what way is the growth of a crystal different from the growth of a human?

2 When do humans grow fastest?

3 By what age do humans stop growing?

4 What is the difference between adult and embryonic stem cells?

WOW FACTOR!

Most of the dust that gathers in a house is made of skin cells!

...adult stem cells ...continuous variable ...diet ...discontinuous variable

Measuring growth

There are various ways we can use to measure growth in humans. The table shows the height of an average male and female:

Age (years)	Male height (cm)	Female height (cm)
0	53	53
1	61	61
2	71	71
3	91	87
4	99	92
5	104	101
6	109	111
7	114	119
8	122	124
9	124	128
10	125	130
11	127	132
12	130	134
13	132	137
14	137	142
15	142	147
16	147	153
17	155	157
18	163	160
19	170	161
20	173	162
21	175	162
22	175	162

We could also measure the mass of the person. This is less reliable because a person's mass will vary from day to day depending on the amount they have had to eat, whether they have been to the toilet or whether they have sweated a lot.

What factors affect growth in humans?

Three main factors affect growth:

- **Inheritance** – we have genes that affect our *potential* size.
- **Diet** – we need protein and energy to grow. People who do not have a balanced diet with enough protein may not reach their potential size.
- **Hormones** – our size is affected by the amount of growth hormone that we produce. People who do not produce enough growth hormone may not reach their potential size. The ability to make growth hormone may be largely inherited in the genes, however.

Height survey

1 Carry out a survey of the heights of people in your class.

2 You might find it useful to put heights in **ranges**, e.g. 135–139 cm, 140–144 cm.

3 Make a tally chart of your classmates' height, then plot the data on a bar chart.

4 You may find it useful to use a spreadsheet.

- Work out the most common range.
- What was the average height?
- Was their a noticeable difference between boys and girls?
- Would it be more useful to plot separate bar charts for boys and girls?
- What was the overall size range from the shortest to the tallest?

Variation

There is a lot of **variation** in height among the members of your class. There are many other examples of variation within the members of a species. Within your class you could have looked at eye colour. Eyes can be blue, brown or green. This is an example of a **discontinuous variable**. Height, however, is an example of a **continuous variable**, as people can be any height within a range.

Drugs and sport

In 1988 Ben Johnson finished first in the 100 metres final at the Olympic Games. A few days later he was stripped of his title and sent home in disgrace. A urine test showed that he had used an artificial hormone to help him build muscle. The use of drugs is banned in sports. One reason is to make sure it is a fair contest but another reason is that drugs have harmful side effects, including kidney and liver damage.

FIGURE 3: Ben Johnson thought he was the Olympic champion but he was later stripped of his medal.

QUESTIONS

9 Explain the difference between continuous and discontinuous variation.

10 Carry out a class survey of some examples of discontinuous variation. Draw charts to display the results.

11 Why shouldn't athletes be allowed to use drugs if they want?

QUESTIONS

5 Plot a graph to show the growth of a human male and female.

6 Describe the pattern shown by the graphs.

7 What factors affect human growth?

8 How could you improve your height survey to make the data more reliable?

...*growth*   ...*hormones*   ...*inheritance*   ...*ranges*   ...*variation*

Growth in plants

You will find out:
- About factors that affect the growth of plants including light, temperature, carbon dioxide, nutrients, water, oxygen and pH

Perfect plants

These poinsettia plants look good – and they need to be. Their bright colour makes them a very popular houseplant in winter. Growers need to produce plenty of healthy looking plants for Christmas. That means getting exactly the right conditions for maximum growth. What are the best conditions for growing plants?

FIGURE 1: Perfect growth conditions mean perfect plants!

Feeding in plants

Plants make their own food through the process called **photosynthesis**. Plants use **light** energy to convert **carbon dioxide** and **water** to glucose. They use the glucose as a source of energy and as a raw material for producing all of the substances that make up the plant. Oxygen is produced as a waste product of photosynthesis. Plant leaves contain **chlorophyll**, a green substance that absorbs light.

carbon dioxide + water $\xrightarrow{\text{light and chlorophyll}}$ **glucose + oxygen**

The chemical equation for photosynthesis tells us about some of the things that plants need for growth. Without light, water and carbon dioxide they would not be able to make glucose. Without glucose they would not be able to make new plant cells.

Other factors also affect the growth of plants:

- **Temperature** – plants grow best at a particular temperature called the **optimum** temperature.
- **Nutrients** – plants need certain elements, which they usually absorb as minerals from the soil. These include nitrogen (absorbed as nitrate), phosphorus (absorbed as phosphate), potassium (absorbed as potassium ions) and magnesium, used to make chlorophyll.
- **Oxygen** – although plants make oxygen in photosynthesis, they also use it in aerobic respiration.
- **Hormones** – plants make a number of different hormones that affect the way they grow and develop.
- **pH** – the pH of soil affects how easy it is to absorb minerals.

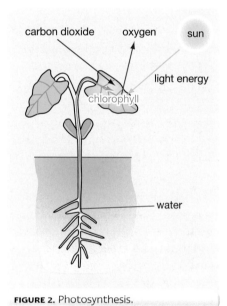

FIGURE 2. Photosynthesis.

QUESTIONS

1. List the factors that affect the growth of plants.
2. What is meant by an optimum temperature?
3. Cover up the top part of this page. Write out the chemical equation for photosynthesis.
4. Where do plants get minerals from?

...dry mass   ...eutrophication   ...fresh mass   ...hormones   ...leaching

Light

Plants need light for photosynthesis. What happens if you grow plants without light? Jack carried out an experiment to find out.

He got two plant pots and filled each one with identical soil. Each pot was given the same amount of water. He planted ten peas in each pot and left them on a warm windowsill. One pot was covered to keep out the light.

Jack *predicted* that the peas would grow bigger in the pot with light.

After two weeks he examined both pots. Here is a drawing of the plants:

light   dark

FIGURE 3: Jack's experiment.

Jack found that the plants from the dark were taller. He still thought that these plants had not grown as well as the others. He pulled out the plants, removed all of the soil and weighed them. The plants from the light weighed more than those from the dark. Jack decided that weight was a better measurement of plant growth.

(The plants in the dark were using food stored in the pea seed. Plants in the dark will grow very tall in an attempt to reach light so that they can then begin to photosynthesise.)

Weight is a useful measure of growth. Weight of a whole organism can be misleading, however, as it includes water. Plants that have been watered recently weigh more than plants that have been in dry soil. It is better to dry out the plant and find its **dry mass**. This measures new material made by the plant and is more reliable than measuring the **wet** or **fresh mass**.

Nutrients

You can buy bottles of liquid fertiliser, containing the minerals that plants need. These can be added to the soil. The label will have instructions about how much needs to be added.

> **WOW FACTOR!**
>
> The Venus flytrap lives in places where the soil lacks nitrate. They get nitrogen by trapping and digesting insects.

QUESTIONS

5   How did Jack make sure his investigation was a fair test?

6   Why did the peas in the dark grow taller?

7   Explain why dry mass is a more reliable indicator of growth than fresh mass.

8   Plan and carry out an investigation to find the optimum amount of fertiliser for growing plants.

Eutrophication

Fertilisers can lead to a problem called **eutrophication**. This occurs when too much fertiliser is added to soil or when it rains heavily after the fertiliser has been spread:

- Fertiliser is washed from the soil into streams and rivers – this is called **leaching**.
- Weeds and algae in the water grow very rapidly.
- Eventually they die and rot.
- Bacteria use the dead plants as food and multiply very quickly.
- The bacteria use up lots of oxygen from the water.
- Fish and other water creatures die.

To avoid this, it is important for farmers to know how much and what type of fertiliser is needed for a particular crop and to add just the right amount.

Lack of oxygen can kill water plants as well as animals. At night, when not photosynthesising, plants need oxygen from the water for respiration.

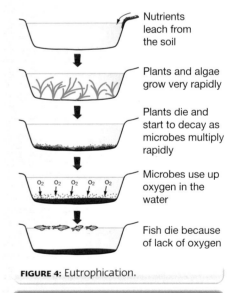

Nutrients leach from the soil

Plants and algae grow very rapidly

Plants die and start to decay as microbes multiply rapidly

Microbes use up oxygen in the water

Fish die because of lack of oxygen

FIGURE 4: Eutrophication.

QUESTIONS

9   Draw a flow chart to show the stages that lead to eutrophication.

10   Why should farmers check the weather forecast before spreading fertilisers?

11   Why is eutrophication more likely to occur in summer?

...nutrients   ...optimum   ...pH   ...photosynthesis   ...temperature   ...wet mass

Plant populations

You will find out:

● About factors that affect the distribution of plants including light, temperature, carbon dioxide, nutrients, water and oxygen

Weeds

Isn't it annoying that weeds always grow exactly where you don't want them? What is a weed anyway? People choose to grow poppies in their gardens. Yet poppies in a field of wheat are a weed to the farmer. So is a weed just something growing where it is not wanted?

Plants grow wherever the conditions are right. A garden or a farm provides the right conditions.

FIGURE 1: Those weeds grow everywhere!

Plant distribution

Plant growth is affected by:

- light
- temperature
- carbon dioxide concentration
- nutrients in the soil
- water
- oxygen concentration
- pH.

These factors also affect *where* plants grow. We call this the **distribution** of plants. Plants reproduce in two ways:

- From **seeds**, which are spread or dispersed in a number of ways including being blown by the wind and carried by animals. If it lands in a place with the right conditions then the seed **germinates** and a plant grows.
- By **vegetative reproduction**, where shoots or roots gradually spread out from a parent plant.

Both methods have advantages. Seeds spread widely from the parent plant. Many will find new suitable places to colonise but many will never germinate. Seeds increase variation within the species. Vegetative reproduction means there is a good chance of the new plants surviving but all of the plants have the same genes, so there is a lack of variation.

FIGURE 2: This plant found the right conditions for growth in a crack in the pavement.

WOW FACTOR!

Coconuts are actually part of a huge seed. They are dispersed by falling into the sea and floating away. When they land in the right conditions they germinate.

▥ QUESTIONS ▥

1 Which method of plant reproduction spreads plants more widely?

2 What do we know about the genes of plants that reproduce by vegetative reproduction?

3 Why is this a 'bad thing'?

4 Draw a table to summarise the advantages and disadvantages of the two methods of reproduction.

...*distribution*   ...*environmental factors*   ...*germinate*   ...*kite diagram*   ...*quadrat*

Environmental factors and plant distribution

You will survey an area to find out how **environmental factors** affect the distribution of plants. You will need to measure some environmental factors and estimate the distribution of plants in an area.

- *Soil pH*: If you are lucky you will be able to use a soil pH meter. Push the probe into the soil and read off the pH. If you are not so lucky you will need to take a sample of soil and test it in the laboratory.
  Add a spatula of soil to a test tube of distilled water. Shake the mixture then filter it to remove soil particles. Add a few drops of universal indicator solution and check the pH.
- *Soil moisture*: You may be able to use a soil moisture meter. If one is not available then collect a sample of soil and take it back to the lab.
  Weigh out 10 g of soil into an evaporating dish. Leave it overnight in an oven at 95 °C. Weigh it again. Work out the percentage moisture from the weight lost.
- *Light*: Use a light meter to measure the light intensity at ground level.
- *Temperature*: Use a thermometer to measure the temperature at ground level.
- *Sampling plants*: It would take a very long time to count every single plant in an area (unless it was very small). Instead we **sample** an area using a **quadrat**, a square of 0.25 m^2. Instead of counting all of the plants you estimate the **percentage coverage** within the quadrat.

Use your quadrat to make a **transect**:

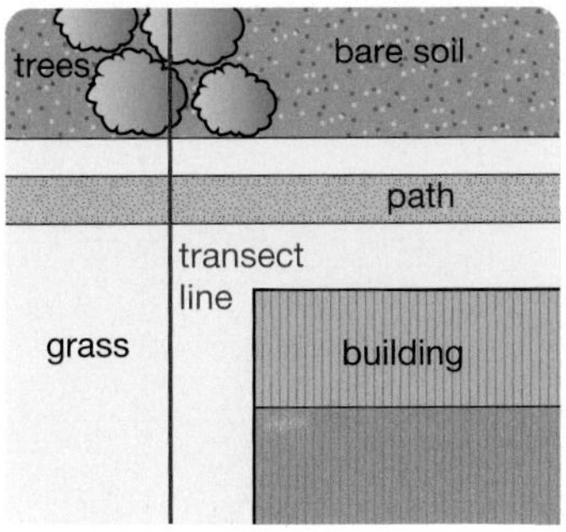

FIGURE 3: Make a map of your chosen area. Mark the transect on it.

	% cover						
Distance (m)	Grass	Daisy	Clover	Bare soil	pH	Moisture (%)	Temp (°C)
0	0	10	10	80	6.0	20	15
2.5	10	10	10	70	6.0	23	15
5.0	0	0	0	100	6.0	24	16
7.5	50	10	10	30	7.0	14	21
10.0	70	10	10	10	7.5	10	22

FIGURE 4: Follow your transect, estimating the percentage coverage of different plants. Make measurements of environmental factors. Make a table of your results.

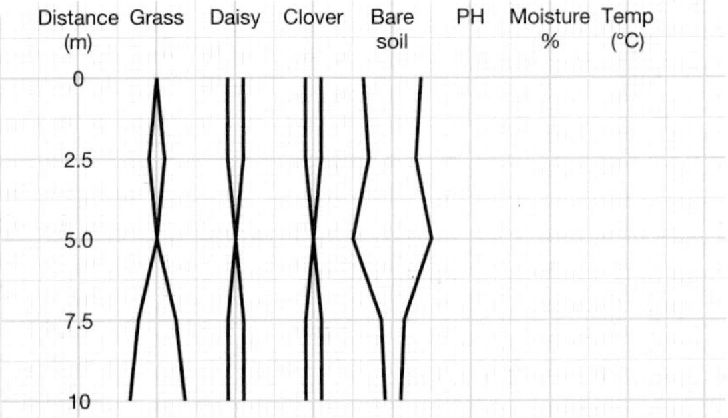

FIGURE 5: Use your results to draw a kite diagram.

QUESTIONS

5 Produce a report on your plant survey. Can you draw any conclusions about how the factors you measured affect the distribution of plants? How well did your investigation work? Were there any problems with the data you obtained or the method you used? Can you think of ways of improving it?

WOW FACTOR!

Fruits contain seeds that pass through an animal's intestines and end up with a nice pile of manure to grow in!

A knotty problem

In its native country, Japanese Knotweed is one of the first plants to appear on areas of volcanic ash after an eruption. It was introduced into the UK in the 19th century, where it was planted in gardens. By the end of the 19th century it was first seen outside gardens and it is now a major problem. In many parts of the UK it has totally displaced native plants. This is a problem for animals that feed on those plants. It spreads by underground roots called rhizomes. Even tiny pieces of rhizome dug up from the soil can grow new plants. This means that people trying to remove Japanese knotweed must burn all parts of the plant rather than dump them elsewhere. The leaves and stems die off in winter but take about three years to decompose.

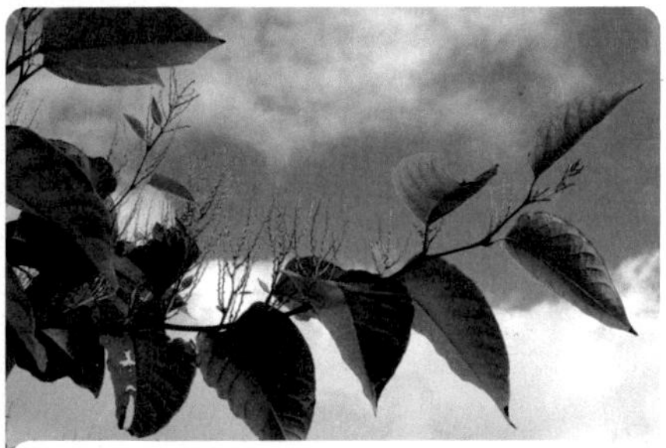

FIGURE 6: Japanese knotweed. It looks like a nice plant but its roots can damage buildings.

QUESTIONS

6 Japanese knotweed grows well on bare ground. Why do you think this is?

7 It grows well in many areas of the UK. What does this tell you about the conditions it needs for growth?

Plant hormones

Ripe bananas

Most of the bananas we eat in the UK come from the Caribbean. They are carried in ships that take a few weeks to cross the Atlantic. So how come the bananas are perfectly ripe when they reach us? The bananas are picked, transported and stored when they are unripe. Then just before they are ready to go on sale, they are treated with **ethene**, a **plant hormone** that makes fruit ripen.

FIGURE 1: Bananas are unripe when they are picked.

Plant hormones

If you cut off the tip of a plant shoot, it stops growing. Put the tip back on the shoot and it starts growing again. The shoot tip makes a plant hormone called **auxin**, which stimulates the shoot to grow. Shoots grow in the bit just below the tip. Cell division takes place near the tip. The new cells then **elongate**. This means they get longer. This is what makes the shoot grow. Auxin causes the cells to elongate.

Plant growth is affected by factors such as light, water and gravity. Some parts of the plants grow towards light, for example, and others grow away from it:

- Shoots grow towards light and away from gravity.
- Roots grow towards gravity and water.

We call these **tropisms**. Plant hormones control tropisms.

If you put a plant on a windowsill the plant will grow towards the light. This is called **phototropism**. This is how it works:

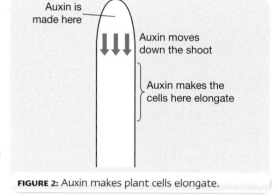

FIGURE 2: Auxin makes plant cells elongate.

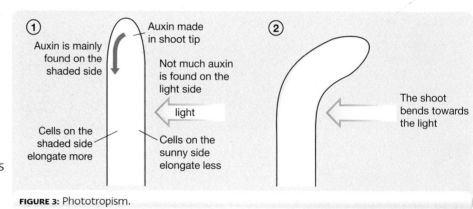

FIGURE 3: Phototropism.

QUESTIONS

1 Draw a flow chart to explain how bananas always arrive in the shops perfectly ripe.
2 Why is it important for plant cells to grow towards light?
3 What is a tropism?
4 Draw a flow chart to explain how phototropism happens.

...auxin   ...fruit initiation   ...elongate   ...ethene

Geotropism

Even if you plant a seed upside-down the root will always grow downwards. This is because it grows towards gravity, a response called **geotropism**.

Note that auxin encourages cell elongation in shoots but inhibits it in roots.

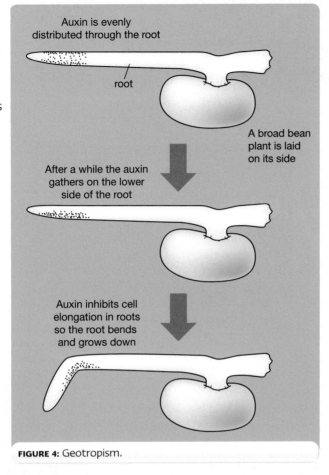

Auxin is evenly distributed through the root

root

A broad bean plant is laid on its side

After a while the auxin gathers on the lower side of the root

Auxin inhibits cell elongation in roots so the root bends and grows down

FIGURE 4: Geotropism.

Using plant hormones

Plant hormones are used artificially in a number of ways:

- *Rooting powder*: People often take cuttings to grow new plants. Dipping the cut end of the plant in a powder containing auxin encourages it to form roots.
- *Weedkillers*: Hormones are used as weedkillers in lawns and in fields of cereal crops. The hormone is sprayed on the plants. Broad-leafed weeds absorb a lot of the hormone. This makes them grow too quickly and they die. Narrow leafed grasses and cereals absorb less of the hormone and are not affected.
- *Cut flowers*: When flowers are cut they make a hormone that causes the flowers to die faster. Flowers are sometimes sold with a sachet of a chemical which, when added to the water in a vase, prevents this hormone being produced. Aspirin has the same effect!

FIGURE 5: Plant hormones encourage the growth of roots on cuttings.

Seedless fruits   (H)

Ovules are the plant's equivalent of an animal's egg. When an ovule is fertilised by pollen, an embryo plant forms, which produces auxin. This stimulates the ovary to develop, forming a fruit. This is called **fruit initiation**.

Fruit growers spray auxin on unpollinated flowers. The auxin encourages a fruit to form even though there is no embryo. This technique produces fruits, such as oranges and grapes, which are seedless.

FIGURE 6: Plant hormones are used to produce seedless grapes.

Other hormones are sprayed onto fruit trees to stop the fruits falling off. This gives the fruit more time on the tree so bigger fruits are produced.

QUESTIONS

5 Plan and carry out an investigation to check that roots grow downwards because they are growing towards gravity rather than away from light.

6 Use your knowledge of plant hormones to explain why plants kept in total darkness grow very tall.

7 Why don't lawn weedkillers kill the grass?

8 Explain what we mean by geotropism.

QUESTIONS

9 Draw a table to summarise the artificial uses of plant hormones.

10 Explain how and why hormones are used to stimulate fruit initiation.

...geotropism ...phototropism ...plant hormone ...tropism

Selective breeding

You will find out:

● That artificial selection (or selective breeding) can be used to improve the usefulness of plants and animals including the quality of milk, the number of lambs born to sheep and the yield from wheat

A wolf at the door

You would probably get a shock if you saw these wolves walking down the street. You would probably get out of the way – fast! Yet our domestic pet dogs were originally bred from wolves. Over thousands of years many different breeds of dogs have emerged, all descended from wolves. By **selective breeding** we have produced nearly 200 recognised breeds of dog.

FIGURE 1: Wolves – ancestors of our pet dogs.

Breeding for a purpose

Most dogs were originally bred to help humans. Different breeds were produced to help us do different jobs. Early people may have wanted a fast dog to help them to hunt. So they made sure that they chose the fastest dogs to breed from. These dogs were more likely to have genes for characteristics such as long legs and strong muscles. They were more likely to pass these genes on to their puppies. When the puppies grew up, the fastest ones would again be selected for breeding purposes. Gradually the perfect hunting dog was produced. Other people might have wanted to breed a dog that could help herd sheep. They chose intelligent dogs that could be trained and that would not try to attack and kill the sheep they were supposed to be herding. Always choosing the best dogs for a particular purpose to breed from is called selective breeding or **artificial selection**.

The way a dog looks or behaves can sometimes give us a clue about the job for which it was bred.

FIGURE 3: The long, low body of a dachshund was perfect for chasing foxes and badgers from their holes.

FIGURE 2: The Labrador was bred to swim into lakes and bring back birds that hunters had shot. It is a good swimmer and has a very soft mouth.

FIGURE 4: The strength of the St Bernard, along with its thick coat and good sense of smell, make it an ideal mountain rescue dog.

⊞ QUESTIONS ⊞

1   Your hobby is keeping pet mice. You decide to breed a new tailless mouse. Explain what you would do.

2   What is meant by selective breeding?

3   What characteristics would you look for to breed a dog to keep as a pet in a small house?

4   Find out about breed of dog. Write about the job it was bred for and how it is suitable for that job.

WOW FACTOR!

Despite the pictures you might have seen, St. Bernard dogs out on mountain rescues never carried a barrel of brandy on their collar!

...artificial selection   ...gene banks   ...genetic diversity

Cattle breeding

Cattle were originally kept for both meat and milk but have been selectively bred for meat or milk. Cows bred for meat have small udders and produce about 2 litres of milk per day, enough to feed one calf. Modern dairy cattle have huge udders and can produce up to 20 litres per day. Extra milk production means more money. But is it so good for the cow? It is claimed that the extra weight of milk makes dairy cows go lame.

Jersey cows are a breed that makes extra creamy milk. They were selectively bred to produce this milk. For health reasons, however, more people today use low-fat milk. This is made by skimming off the cream. Could cattle breeders produce cows that make low-fat milk?

FIGURE 5: Jersey cows make extra creamy milk. Could we selectively breed cow that make low-fat milk?

Sheep

Sheep have been selectively bred for centuries and there are now about 200 breeds of sheep. Breeds have been selectively bred for the quality of their wool, meat or milk. Wild sheep normally only give birth to one lamb at a time but through selective breeding the chances of having twins or even triplets has increased. Selective breeding has produced sheep with a strong 'flocking' instinct, which makes it easier to look after a herd. There is also a possibility of breeding sheep that are resistant to disease.

Wheat

It is not just animals that have been selectively bred. Few of the plants that we use for food are found growing wild. Cabbage, cauliflower, broccoli, turnip and Brussels sprouts have all been selectively bred from the same ancestor.

Wheat was selectively bred from a **species** of wild grass. Recently dwarf varieties have been developed. Less of the energy from photosynthesis goes into making stalks and more into making grain, thus increasing the yield.

Genetic diversity

Selectively breeding from the same group of animals decreases **genetic diversity**. This means that genes for particular characteristics disappear from the population because only individuals with the desired characteristics are selected for breeding. This may not be a problem at present but a change in climate, for example, could mean that we want to breed different characteristics. This might not be possible if the gene no longer exists. **Gene banks** store seeds of plant varieties so that if a particular gene is needed in the future it will still be available.

If there is a harmful gene in the population, then there is an increased chance of the offspring inheriting two recessive genes when breeding takes place between animals that are closely related (called **inbreeding**). That is one reason why human societies have strict laws to prevent a person marrying someone who is too closely related.

QUESTIONS

5 Make a list of some desirable qualities that have been bred into cattle and sheep.

6 What qualities have been bred into pigs that make them different from their ancestors, the wild boar?

7 Can you think of any characteristics that we might want to select in future?

QUESTIONS

8 What is meant by genetic diversity?

9 What is a gene bank?

10 Describe some of the problems of selective breeding.

11 What is meant by inbreeding?

...inbreeding ...selective breeding ...species

Cloning

You will find out:

- What we mean by a clone
- How plants can be cloned
- The risks and ethical dilemma involved in cloning mammals

Attack of the clones

That sounds scary! Clones are some sort of bad guys in science fiction movies, aren't they? Some identical aliens who descend from a spacecraft and cause havoc with ray guns? Well, no. Humans have been making clones for thousands of years and plants make clones naturally. The chips you ate yesterday came from a potato clone! You wouldn't worry about being attacked by a potato army – unless they had ray guns!

What is a clone?

Clones are organisms that have exactly the same genes. They are **genetically identical**. Vegetative reproduction in plants produces clones. Many plants do this naturally. You have probably seen the houseplant called a spider plant. It reproduces by growing runners. Each runner has a little 'plantlet' at the end. When these touch the ground, they grow roots. Eventually the runner withers away and a new plant is formed, genetically identical to the parent.

FIGURE 1: Each baby spider plant is a clone of its parent.

To grow potatoes you plant a tuber. All the tubers from a particular variety of potato are clones. Planting clones is a very useful way of growing plants. If people like the colour or taste of a particular plant, they will want the same thing to eat again. By growing clones you can be sure of getting identical offspring. Seeds are produced in sexual reproduction, which mixes up genes, so that you get variation. You can also grow new plants by taking **cuttings**:

- Find a suitable shoot on the parent plant.
- Cut off the shoot with a sharp knife.
- Dip it in rooting powder.
- Push it into a pot of compost.
- Cover it with a polythene bag to keep it moist.

Each cutting is a clone of the original plant so it will have the same colour flower, leaves, etc.

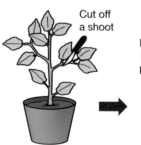

Cut off a shoot

Dip it in rooting powder

Plant it in compost and cover it with a polythene bag

FIGURE 2: Taking a cutting.

QUESTIONS

1 What is a clone?
2 How do you take a cutting?
3 What is in rooting powder and why do you use it?
4 Why do we plant potato tubers rather than seeds to grow potatoes?

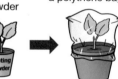

WOW FACTOR!

All of the Japanese knotweed plants in the UK are clones from a plant introduced from Japan.

...clones   ...cuttings   ...explants

Tissue culture

The problem with taking cuttings is that you can get only a few cuttings from one plant. **Tissue culture** can be used to get more plants:

- Pieces of plant about 1 mm^3 are cut from the parent plant.
- These are sterilised to kill microbes.
- The pieces of plant are then put in a tube of sterile agar jelly. The agar jelly contains nutrients and hormones.
- The plant cells divide and produce shoots, roots and leaves; they are called **explants**.

Tissue culture is used to produce expensive plants such as orchids.

Cloning mammals

Dolly the sheep is famous for being the first cloned mammal. Dolly was cloned in 1996 by scientists at Edinburgh University.

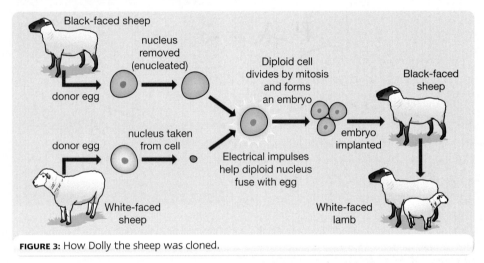

FIGURE 3: How Dolly the sheep was cloned.

In 2003 Dolly was put down after she was found to be suffering arthritis and lung disease. There has been a lot of debate about Dolly suffering from premature ageing, the conditions she suffered from being usual in older sheep.

Many other animals have since been cloned, including goats, cows, mice, pigs, cats, rabbits and a gaur, an endangered species of wild cow. Many of these animals have shown signs of premature ageing and damaged DNA. Yet many scientists are still trying to clone animals:

- It has been suggested that clones could be produced of much-loved pets when they die.
- There are claims of scientists trying to clone humans, although this is illegal in most countries.
- One wealthy Russian has offered a huge cash prize to anyone who clones a mammoth from remains found frozen in permafrost.

Problems with cloning

The success rate in cloning is low. Depending on the species being cloned, the success rate varies from 0.1% to 3%. That is between 1 and 30 births per 1000 attempts:

- The egg and the nucleus may not be compatible.
- An egg with a newly transferred nucleus may not begin to divide properly.
- Implantation of the embryo into the surrogate mother might fail.
- The pregnancy itself might fail due to miscarriage.
- Clones are often bigger than normal at birth. This can cause birth difficulties. It can also cause breathing and circulation problems.
- Some clones have malformed brains and kidneys.
- Some clones' immune systems do not work properly.
- Clones of some species show changes in their chromosomes normally only seen in older animals.

▥▥▥ QUESTIONS ▥▥▥

9   What is a surrogate mother?

10 Why do you think larger than average offspring have breathing and circulation problems?

11 Why might you expect a clone's chromosomes to show signs of ageing?

12 Should scientists carry on cloning animals?

▥▥▥ QUESTIONS ▥▥▥

5   What are the advantages of growing orchids by tissue culture?

6   Make a list of reasons why cloning animals could be useful.

7   Should scientists be allowed to clone humans?

8   If a mammoth was cloned, what animal would you use to carry the embryo?

Gene therapy

You will find out:

- About the benefits and problems of gene therapy
- About whether gene therapy would prevent genetic disorders being passed on to the next generation

Cystic fibrosis

The girl in the photograph has **cystic fibrosis**. She produces thick, sticky mucus in her lungs and digestive system. She has difficulty in breathing and absorbing food. The mucus in her lungs encourages the growth of microbes so she gets lots of chest infections. She inherited the disease in the genes passed on from her parents. There is no cure for cystic fibrosis, although daily physiotherapy helps to clear the mucus from the lungs.

Gene therapy

Cystic fibrosis is caused by a recessive gene. Scientists have been able to identify the 'healthy' allele of the gene and are trying to use this healthy gene to replace the unhealthy gene. This has been done in a culture of cells in a laboratory, but it is difficult to get the healthy gene into a cystic fibrosis patient.

FIGURE 1: Cystic fibrosis patients need daily physiotherapy to remove mucus from their lungs.

FIGURE 2: A scientist studies cells from patients with genetic disorders.

The healthy gene has been inserted into a 'cold' virus, but this triggered an immune response and the patient fought off the virus. Further attempts have been made to insert the healthy gene into the patient's DNA. So far none of these methods has been successful but scientists continue to try new ideas. Altering genes is called **genetic modification**.

Other diseases where it is thought that gene therapy may provide a cure include haemophilia, some forms of cancer and the disease phenylketonuria (PKU). PKU affects about 1 in 12 000 white children. Early detection means the child can be treated with a special low-protein diet. If it is not detected and treated early, it can result in severe mental retardation.

QUESTIONS

1. The boy's parents do not have cystic fibrosis, so how did he get it?
2. Why have scientists concentrated on inserting 'healthy' cystic fibrosis genes in lung cells rather than intestine cells?
3. Name some diseases that could be treated by gene therapy.
4. Would the gene therapy suggested prevent patients passing on the unhealthy gene to their children?

WANT TO KNOW MORE?

You can find out more about gene therapy and cystic fibrosis at http://news.bbc.co.uk/1/h/health/2340539.stm

...cancer cells ...cystic fibrosis ...genetic modification

What are the problems with gene therapy?

■ Some genetic disorders affect many parts of the body. There are problems with delivering the healthy gene where it is needed.

■ Some genetic disorders are caused by a combination of genes. This adds to the problems of identifying and replacing the defective gene.

■ It is difficult to find a safe way of delivering the healthy gene. In one experimental treatment a patient died because of a severe allergic reaction to the virus used to deliver the gene.

■ Could inserting a new gene cause **mutations** to occur or cause other medical problems?

■ One defective gene, for sickle cell anaemia, is helpful in some people by protecting against malaria. In Africa this gene has probably prevented more people from dying of malaria than it has killed due to sickle cell anaemia. Could other 'defective' genes have so-far undiscovered benefits?

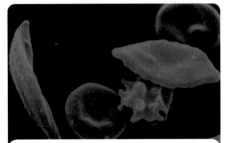

FIGURE 3: Sickle cell anaemia is caused by a defective gene, but this condition protects against malaria.

■ Some people believe that gene therapy could lead to attempts to create a race of 'superhumans'. Others think that altering a person's genes goes against the will of God.

■ Some people who have genetic disorders believe that trying to cure them indicates that society thinks they are of less value than other people, and that they manage perfectly well as they are.

Gene therapy and the next generation

One day there may be gene therapy treatments for diseases such as cystic fibrosis. All gene therapy research is concentrated on repairing genes in **somatic cells**, the cells of the body other than eggs and sperms. People who have defective genes replaced in the somatic cells would still produce gametes with defective genes. Preventing genetic disorders being passed would involve replacing defective genes in the eggs and sperms. Technical difficulties mean it is unlikely that germ line therapy could be tried on humans in the near future.

Gene therapy and cancer (H)

Some forms of cancer are caused by defective genes. Scientists have devised a gene therapy technique that has prevented cancer in mice and could be used in some human cancers. It does not cure cancer, but it could prevent the disease from developing in vulnerable people, such as smokers.

The researchers studied the *FHIT* gene. In many patients with breast or colon cancer, this gene is damaged. The *FHIT* gene causes damaged cells to break down before they can start the growth of cancer.

If the gene is defective, the cells keep dividing in an uncontrolled manner. One feature of **cancer cells** is that they keep on dividing and do not stay within the **Hayflick limit** like other cells. The gene can be damaged by toxins, such as those in cigarette smoke. The mice were given healthy copies of the *FHIT* gene via a virus similar to 'cold' virus.

FIGURE 4: Lab rats help us to find out about diseases such as cancer.

QUESTIONS

7 Is gene therapy a 'super cure' for cancer?

8 Make a list of the advantages and disadvantages of gene therapy. Should scientists continue with research into gene therapy?

QUESTIONS

5 Make a list of some of the problems that have so far prevented successful gene therapy.

6 What are the problems in preventing genetic disorders being passed on to the children of those people who have such disorders?

...Hayflick limit   ...mutation   ...somatic cells

Unit summary

Microbes can be grown in fermenters to produce food products.

Inside living cells

The cell nucleus contains chromosomes made of DNA, which forms a code for joining together amino acids in a specific order to make protein molecules.

This process is carried out in a fermenter which supplies microbes with nutrients and oxygen and provides the optimum conditions for growth.

Sections of human DNA can be inserted into microorganisms to make useful substances such as insulin.

When we exercise we need more energy. Heart rate and breathing rate increase to carry the materials needed for respiration to the muscles.

Energy

Aerobic respiration uses glucose and oxygen to produce energy, releasing carbon dioxide and water in the process.

In vigorous exercise cells may not receive enough oxygen so cells resort to anaerobic respiration, producing lactic acid.

Oxygen is absorbed into capillaries in alveoli in the lungs. Glucose is absorbed into capillaries in the intestine. Oxygen and glucose are carried to the site of respiration in the blood.

Cells divide by meiosis to produce gametes.

Divide and develop

Cells divide by mitosis to produce genetically identical cells for growth and repair. In the process of growth cells differentiate to produce different types of tissues.

Plants grow by cell division, elongation and differentiation. Plant growth is affected by nutrients, light, temperature, carbon dioxide, oxygen and plant hormones.

Plant hormones can be used artificially for many purposes including fruit initiation.

Stem cells are able to differentiate to form different types of cell. Cells in adults are unable to do this in most species.

Replacing faulty genes could, in the future, be used to treat diseases.

Gene manipulation

Certain beneficial genes can be selected in animal breeding programmes.

Genetically identical animals can be produced in the process of cloning.

Unit quiz

1. What are the differences between DNA and mRNA?

2. What shape is a DNA molecule?

3. One strand of a DNA molecule has the base sequence AAGCTTCAG. What sequence would be found on the other strand?

4. What smaller molecules join together to form a protein molecule?

5. What is meant by anaerobic respiration?

6. Write out the equation for anaerobic respiration in yeast.

7. What is insulin used for?

8. What is mycoprotein and how is it made?

9. Write out the equation for aerobic respiration in humans.

10. How are the lungs adapted for gaseous exchange?

11. Which muscles are used when breathing in?

12. What is a BMI and why might you want to work it out?

13. What are the differences between mitosis and meiosis?

14. Explain the difference between an embryo and a foetus.

15. What is a stem cell?

16. What is meant by limb regeneration?

17. What happens when cells differentiate?

18. Give three ways in which plant hormones can be used artificially.

19. What is meant by a clone?

20. What is meant by gene therapy?

Numeracy activity

Exercise

Two boys measured their pulse while at rest then again every minute for ten minutes after exercising. Here are their results:

Pulse rate (beats per min)	Before exercise	1 mins	2 mins	3 mins	4 mins	5 mins	6 mins	7 mins	8 mins	9 mins	10 mins
James	72	156	141	126	113	100	90	80	72	72	72
Joel	84	168	158	148	138	128	118	109	100	92	84

QUESTIONS
1. Draw a graph to compare the results of James and Joel.
2. What should they have done to make sure their investigation was fair?
3. Explain the pattern shown by James's results.
4. Who is fitter? Explain your results. How reliable are these results?

Exam practice

Exam practice questions

1 Diabetics are people whose bodies cannot produce enough of the hormone insulin. Insulin for the treatment of diabetes is produced by genetically modified bacteria.

a Use words from the box to complete the following sentences about this process.

> DNA   chromosome   enzymes   diabetics
> gene   oxygen   bacteria   fermenter

The insulin .... is cut out of human DNA, using enzymes. DNA extracted from bacteria is cut by .... The human insulin gene is inserted into the bacteria's .... This modified DNA is then put back into bacteria. The .... are placed in a fermenter, where they multiply and produce insulin. The insulin is then extracted and prepared for distribution to .... [4]

b The diagram shows a fermenter, used to grow genetically modified bacteria. The bacteria produce insulin.

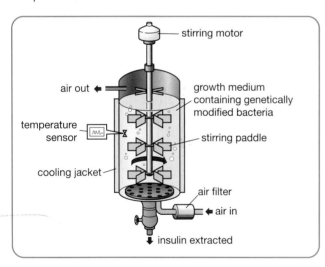

- stirring motor
- air out
- growth medium containing genetically modified bacteria
- temperature sensor
- stirring paddle
- cooling jacket
- air filter
- air in
- insulin extracted

i Give **two** ways in which the conditions inside the fermenter are controlled.

....

.... [2]

ii For **one** of these conditions, explain how it helps the bacteria to produce a large quantity of insulin.

.... [1]

2 Below are some words about the movement of substances to and from cells. Draw **one** straight line from each word to its description.

Carbon dioxide		Waste product of aerobic respiration, which diffuses out of respiring cells
Oxygen		Food used by muscle cells for respiration
Lactic acid		Moves from muscle cells, where it is made during anaerobic respiration
Glucose		Moves into cells, for aerobic respiration

3 A class of boys measured their pulse rates and breathing rates after different types of activity.

Activity	Average pulse rate (counts per minute)	Average breathing rate (breaths per minute)
Rest	64	12
Walking	86	14
Running	120	20

a Describe the effect of exercise on the average pulse rate.

.... [1]

b Pulse rate is the same as heart rate. What are the benefits to the body of changes to the heart rate as a result of exercise?

....

.... [2]

c One of the boys in class decided to compare the accuracy of two methods of measuring his heart's activity.

Activity	Activity Pulse rate at wrist (counts per minute)				Heart beat monitor (beats per minute)			
	Trial 1	Trial 2	Trial 3	Average	Trial 1	Trial 2	Trial 3	Average
Rest	68	75	67	70.0	71	70	71	70.7

Give evidence from the data in the table to show that the heart beat monitor is a more reliable method than using pulse rate.

....

....   [2]

(Total 15 marks)

Worked example

The diagram shows part of a DNA molecule.

The bases cytosine (C), thymine (T) and adenine (A) are exposed. Bases 1, 2 and 3 are part of the DNA molecule.

a What is the identity of the bases 1, 2 and 3?   [2]

b The pairing of bases allows DNA molecules to replicate (make copies of themselves). When do DNA molecules replicate in normal body cells?   [1]

c The purpose of DNA molecules is to make particular proteins within the cell. Briefly explain how DNA molecules do this.

a Base 1 ...guanine... Base 2 ...adenine... Base 3 ...adenine... 1

b During cell division (mitosis)

c RNA molecules 'read' the DNA molecules when the DNA and RNA bases pair up in a certain order. This makes amino acids line up in the right order.

This is correct. The student has ensured a mark by referring to the *type* of cell division in which DNA replication takes place.

Two responses are correct. Yes, base 1 is guanine (G), which always pairs with cytosine. And yes, base 2 is adenine (T), which pairs with thymine. However, Base 3 cannot also be adenine; it is thymine (T). The student may have made a careless mistake here.

The answer is correct, but it's incomplete. Marks have been given for explaining what RNA does, and for referring to amino acids. Another two marks would have been given for explaining that the amino acids are used to make polypeptides, which make particular proteins.

Overall Grade: C

How to get an A

This is a very popular topic with examiners. They will be looking for clear explanations of the different processes that are taking place. Equally importantly, they will be looking for you to use correct scientific terminology. Get to grips with the proper words and phrases.

Biology 2b

DISCOVER GLOBAL WARMING!

A beautiful sunset in the Arctic, and the resident polar bears are making the most of the scenery. But should they be worried about getting their toes wet?

It is estimated that, due to global warming, nearly 90% of the ice in the Arctic could disappear in the next 100 years.

The knock-on effect of the ice melting could mean changes to ocean currents and a quickening of global warming: bad news for polar bears, and for us!

The 'Big Thaw' could release as much as 400 billion tonnes of methane trapped in the frozen soil, accelerating global warming.

Most of the permafrost across North America, Alaska, Siberia and Scandinavia could melt to a depth of about 3 metres, leaving a trail of destruction in its path.

CONTENTS

Green world

You will find out:
- Why plants are so important to people
- Why coffee is so valuable

Plants are boring?

They're not cuddly like a kitten. They don't welcome you home like a puppy. And they don't bring Father Christmas every year like reindeer! So plants are boring? Wrong! Plants provide all of our food, keep our air fit to breathe and provide medicines, homes, clothes and fuel all over the world. Plants are superstars!

FIGURE 1: It's just a collection of plants but millions of visitors have made the Eden Project one of Cornwall's biggest tourist attractions.

Fancy a cuppa?

The coffee plant evolved in the mountains of Ethiopia. Monks used to roast the beans and make a thick black liquid. They found it kept them awake at night while they were working. The first coffee shops in London were just for the very rich. They were more like expensive clubs. Nowadays coffee comes from Africa, South America and the Caribbean. Wherever Europeans went, they took coffee plants with them to see if they would grow.

Tea was discovered about 5000 years ago in China. It was brought to England in about 1650 where it was served in the 'coffee houses'! In 1773, a group of Americans protested against unfair rules about tea importing imposed by the British government. They tipped crates of tea into Boston harbour in what became known as the Boston Tea Party. The British responded with strict new laws that made matters worse – and sparked the American War of Independence. Tea is the only drink that has started a revolution! Tea is now grown in Africa, India and China and in 2003 the UK imported tea worth £153 million!

The man in Figure 2 is an expert in tea. His shop in Guilin, China, only sells tea – but about 50 different varieties of it! And you always get a chance to try a few different types with him before you buy.

FIGURE 2: A modern tea expert at work.

my uncle

⊞ QUESTIONS ⊞

1 List at least **three** drinks made from plants.
2 Where did tea come from originally?
3 Where is tea grown nowadays?

WOW FACTOR!

At one time coffee beans cost more than gold!

Medicines from plants

Many of our common medicines come from plants. The active ingredients for some of them are now made artificially but they were discovered originally in plants. For the vast majority of people in the world, medicines made from plants and herbs are an effective way to cure many illnesses.

The agricultural revolution

Before humans started farming, they moved around the country following the animals they hunted. They did not set up permanent camps and they lived in small family groups. They were called **hunter-gatherers** because of how they got their food.

Then **agriculture** began. Suddenly people could:

- rely on food supplies – they could plant seeds and keep animals

- build towns and villages – there would always be enough food without having to move around all the time.

Fixed villages meant that new crafts developed as the farmers produced food for themselves and other people in the village. Even money was invented – to pay for food. And, suddenly, land became important because it could be used to grow crops. That meant we needed soldiers to guard the land and laws to decide who owned it. Writing was invented to keep records of who owned what and how much food was produced by each farmer. The invention of agriculture was a revolution that changed forever the way we live.

In Europe, agriculture was based on wheat, barley and oats. These grass-like plants still give us a lot of our food. In the Far East they had rice instead of wheat and in America they had maize. There were a handful of different vegetables as well but even today wheat, barley, rice and potatoes supply over half of the world's food!

Medicine	Original source	Use
aspirin	the bark of willow trees	painkiller
opium	seed heads of opium poppies	powerful painkiller – but only used under strict medical supervision because it is so strong and addictive
digitalin	foxgloves	stimulates the heart muscles
taxol	yew trees	a powerful anti-cancer drug
senna	the senna plant	treats constipation
vincristine	Madagascan periwinkle flower	a powerful anti-cancer drug used to treat some types of breast cancer and childhood leukaemia

FIGURE 3: Rice – an excellent source of carbohydrate and protein.

Species	Use
wheat	flour for bread and pasta
rice	eaten as grains
barley	some eaten as flour but a lot used to make alcoholic drinks such as whisky and beer
potatoes	the swollen roots, called tubers, are eaten all over the world

▦ QUESTIONS ▦

4   List **four** uses of plants.

5   Make a list of the plant products you have used today. Think about your food, your clothes, your home – even the pencils you use to draw diagrams!

6   What is the main group of plants that we use for food?

7   List **three** changes in human society brought about by the invention of agriculture.

Cells

You will find out:
- About the structures all cells contain
- About the differences between plant and animal cells
- How cells are organised

Built from cells

A human adult contains roughly 100 000 billion cells. A fully grown oak tree will contain many more. All of these cells are based around a common pattern. In some ways they are like different styles of wristwatches – they can look very different but they have to do the same job! How do cells manage to do this?

FIGURE 1: It may look strange but it's just a watch! It has to tell you the time and contains parts that are similar to many other watches.

All cells have...

Cells are the building blocks of plants and animals. All cells have some features in common:

- All contain **cytoplasm** – a thin jelly-like mixture that holds all of the parts of the cell in place. Many of the important chemical reactions that happen in the cell go on in the cytoplasm.

- Most contain a **nucleus**. The nucleus contains the genetic material that helps to control the cell.

- All contain a thin layer around the outside called the **plasma membrane**. This acts like a skin and controls what passes into and out of the cell.

- Many contain granules of starch or bubbles of oil which act as stores of food.

But cells are also different in some ways. They split into two major groups: **plant cells** and **animal cells**. Plant cells have everything that is present in animal cells but also have special structures:

- A **cell wall** that is made of **cellulose** and holds the cell in shape.

- Some cells have green organs called **chloroplasts** that make sugar by photosynthesis from carbon dioxide and water, using light as the energy source.

- Many cells also have a **vacuole**, which is a bit like a large bubble of watery liquid inside the cell.

QUESTIONS

1. What is a cell?
2. List **four** structures you would find in an animal cell.
3. List **four** structures you would find in a plant cell.
4. List the jobs each of the following does in cells: the nucleus, the plasma membrane, the cell wall.

...animal cells   ...cellulose   ...cell wall   ...chloroplast ...cytoplasm   ...membrane

More about cells

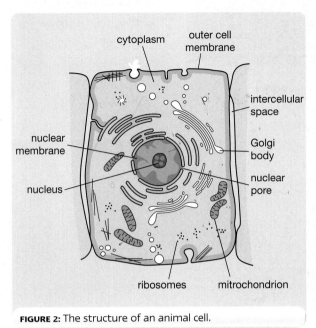

FIGURE 2: The structure of an animal cell.

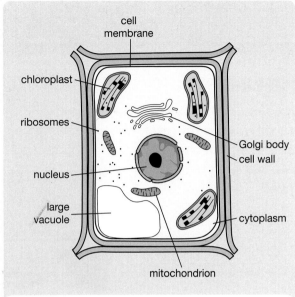

FIGURE 3: The structure of a plant cell.

Cells do not exist in isolation. They link to the cells around them and depend on the rest of the plant or animal body to keep them alive.

- A group of cells of the same type organised together is called a **tissue**.

- Different tissues are linked together in an **organ**.

- Different organs are linked into a **system** and different systems are linked together to make a complete organism.

Level of organisation	Plants	Animals
cells	epithelial cells	glandular cells
tissues	leaf epithelium	stomach lining
organs	leaves	stomach
system	photosynthetic system	digestive system
organism	daffodil	human being

Plants are green because their cells contain structures named chloroplasts. These are called organelles and are wrapped in their own **membrane**, almost like a cell within a cell. Chloroplasts have a complicated structure and contain the chemical chlorophyll. Chlorophyll is able to absorb light energy and use it to drive certain chemical reactions.

QUESTIONS

5   What is a tissue?

6   What do chloroplasts do?

7   List **three** differences between plant and animal cells.

...*nucleus*   ...*organ*   ...*plant cells*   ...*plasma membrane*   ...*system*   ...*tissue*   ...*vacuole*

Photosynthesis

You will find out:

- What is needed for photosynthesis
- Why photosynthesis is vital to life on Earth
- How light and carbon dioxide levels affect photosynthesis

Eat your greens!

You may think that salad is the stuff that falls on the floor when you take a bite out of your beefburger, but without green plants you would be dead! All life on Earth depends on green plants for food (even your beefburger!) to eat and oxygen to breathe. It's all about photosynthesis...

Photosynthesis

Photosynthesis is the manufacture of sugar and oxygen from carbon dioxide and water in green plants. Energy is needed for the reaction to work. Plants get this energy from sunlight. How do they do this?

Chlorophyll is the molecule that makes this all possible. It absorbs most colours of light but reflects green light. This is why plants look green. Chloroplasts contain chlorophyll and a mixture of other chemicals which can also absorb light. These chemicals are called **pigments**.

Laver bread is a Welsh delicacy made from ground-up seaweed! It tastes ... interesting. It is so dark in colour because it contains pigments that can absorb the widest possible range of light. This helps seaweed to grow underwater where the light often seems greenish-blue.

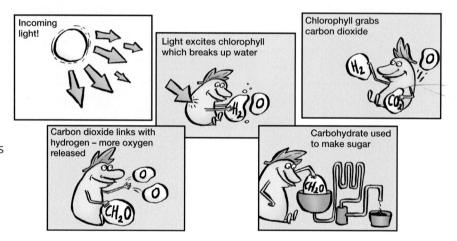

FIGURE 1: Laver bread – the black colour comes from chlorophyll and a mixture of other pigments including some that are red.

◾ QUESTIONS ◾

1. What chemicals are used up in photosynthesis?
2. What chemicals are made by photosynthesis?
3. What would happen to a plant if you kept it in green light for a couple of weeks?
4. Why does laver bread look black, and not green?

...chlorophyll   ...limiting factor

Speeding up photosynthesis

Since photosynthesis is so important can we speed it up to produce more food and oxygen? Photosynthesis needs:

- light
- carbon dioxide
- water.

A **limiting factor** is something that slows down a reaction. A group of walkers will have to go as slowly as the slowest walker – he becomes the limiting factor. In the same way, photosynthesis is a series of complex reactions. If one of these reactions is slow then the others just have to wait.

At low light levels, adding extra carbon dioxide will have no effect because light is the limiting factor. You can see that the graph levels off – no increase in photosynthesis at all. However, if you increase the light level, more carbon dioxide is needed. It has become the limiting factor and so adding more increases the rate of photosynthesis.

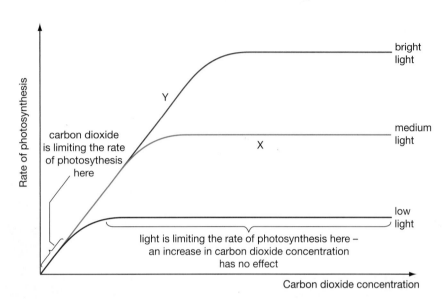

FIGURE 2: This graph shows how light and carbon dioxide levels affect the rate of photosynthesis.

Is water ever the limiting factor? Probably not. A plant that is lacking water has many more important problems than its rate of photosynthesis. Plants shut down their photosynthetic equipment in times of water stress. They do this to protect the concentration of important solutions in their cells. The effect of water stress is important and can reduce the yield of the plant even if more water is added later.

A gardener investigated the effects of water stress on the yield of tomato plants. A group of plants were divided into four sets and given different amounts of water. This enabled the gardener to see just how water supply affected the fruit supplied by the plants.

Watering regime	Eventual yield of fruit / kg
never allowed to wilt	20.4
allowed to wilt once before fruit formed	18.3
allowed to wilt once after fruit formed	17.5
allowed to wilt often	14.8

FIGURE 3: The greenhouses in Tibet are helping to raise the efficiency of the plants inside – and provide fresh vegetables for the local people.

QUESTIONS

5   What does the term 'limiting factor' mean?

6   What is the limiting factor for photosynthesis at point X on the graph above?

7   What is the limiting factor for photosynthesis at point Y on the graph above?

8   Draw a suitable graph to display the data in the table.

9   What advice would you give to a gardener about watering tomato plants?

Fuel or fertiliser?

You will find out:

- About nitrogen and plant growth
- How nitrogen passes through the world
- That decisions about use of resources can be complicated

Yak pancakes

What's brown and smelly, comes out of a yak and is good for cooking? That's right – yak faeces! Tibetans shape it into cakes and stick it on the walls of their houses to dry in the sun. Later they cook with it. They burn it to cook the food! What did you think I meant?

Too good to burn?

But yak faeces are a good fertiliser in exactly the same way as manure is in the UK. Why do Tibetans use them for fuel?

- Tibet has very few forests now because of logging by the Chinese. Wood to burn is very scarce and coal is expensive.

- The climate is cold, so not many plants grow. Fertiliser is most useful in areas that also have enough water and warmth for the plants to grow.

Fertilisers

Plants need water and light for photosynthesis but need other substances to grow well. These are called mineral nutrients and come from the soil. Faeces contain large supplies of one of the most valuable – nitrogen.

Plants use nitrogen to make proteins, nucleic acids and chlorophyll. If the soil does not contain enough nitrogen, the plants do not grow well. Their leaves are often yellowish in colour.

Fertilisers such as manure also contain a range of other chemicals that help to improve the soil. Because manure comes from a living source it is called an organic fertiliser. Modern fertilisers are made in chemical factories and are applied as a powder. These are called inorganic fertilisers.

FIGURE 1: Yak faeces mixed with straw and drying on a Tibetan wall. Think of them as the equivalent of a roaring log fire...

ORGANIC FERTILISERS

Organic fertilisers help to build a healthy soil structure and allow more air into the soil – essential for growth of healthy roots.

▥ QUESTIONS ▥

1 Give **two** possible uses of yak faeces.
2 What factors decide what you use yak faeces for?
3 How else could you fertilise ground to grow plants?
4 What does a plant need nitrogen for?

...algae ...decomposer ...denitrifying bacteria ...fertilisers ...microorganisms ...nitrates

The nitrogen cycle

The nitrogen in the air is no use to a plant. It must take in nitrogen as **nitrates** from the soil. A series of complex reactions in plant cells converts these nitrates into a range of chemicals, including protein, that are essential for healthy plant growth. The **nitrogen cycle** shows how nitrogen passes around the natural world. It takes many different forms during the cycle.

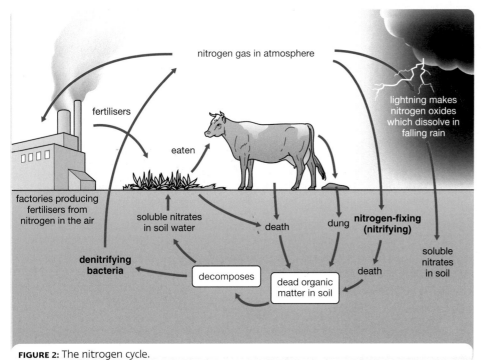

FIGURE 2: The nitrogen cycle.

Fuel or fertiliser?

What happens to the nitrogen that is added to the fields? Why doesn't it build up in the soil? The plants that grow there take it up and use it to make proteins. When the crop is harvested, the proteins (carrying their nitrogen) are taken away. This means that there is a constant export of nitrogen from the soil and explains why farmers need to add more every year.

QUESTIONS

5   List the factors that increase the level of available nitrogen in the soil.
6   List the factors that decrease the level of available nitrogen in the soil.
7   Adding manure to the soil increases the amount of nitrogen available to plants. How?
8   A field that is used to grow wheat loses fertility after a few years if fertilisers are not added regularly. Why?

Rice and algae

Rice and algae is not a recipe from an expensive restaurant! **Algae** (which are **microorganisms**) growing in the wet rice fields of Asia are able to fix nitrogen directly from the air. They build it into their bodies. When these die and decay, the nitrogen is released into the water and helps the rice plants to grow. Rice fields with a healthy supply of these algae produce much higher yields.

Sometimes farmers add inorganic nitrogen to the rice fields as powdered fertiliser. This does the same job as the algae but does it more quickly. However, fertiliser is not free and some research shows that it seems to reduce the growth of the algae and so less nitrogen is fixed 'for free'. Genetic engineers are now looking for a way to move the gene for nitrogen fixation from the algae into the rice. If they could do this, they could produce rice plants that make their own fertiliser.

FIGURE 3: The floating mats of algae help to fertilise this rice field ready for next season's crop.

QUESTIONS

9   Give **one** advantage of the algae compared with inorganic fertilisers.
10 Suggest **one** reason why a farmer might still use inorganic fertiliser even if the field contained algae.
11 How could you find out how much fertiliser you could add to the field before the algae were inhibited?

Mineral salts

You will find out:

- How plants take up minerals
- How minerals improve plant growth
- About the dangers of over-fertilising farmland

Cat fertiliser

In the 19th century thousands of mummified cats were imported from Egypt. They were ground up into powder and spread on the fields as a good fertiliser! The mixture of **mineral salts** in the powdered dead bodies increased the yield of the fields and helped to feed the growing city populations.

FIGURE 1: To you it's a dead cat. To the ancient Egyptians it was almost a god. To farmers – it's fertiliser.

Minerals and growth

The table shows the main mineral nutrients needed for healthy growth. These are needed in large amounts and so are called **macronutrients**. Many other minerals are needed in smaller amounts and are called **micronutrients**.

Mineral nutrients are absorbed into the plant through the **roots** as simple salts such as potassium phosphate or ammonium sulphate. Fertiliser packets often show how much of the key elements are present in the mixture. This allows a gardener or farmer to work out how much to add to the soil. It is important to get the dose right:

- Too little fertiliser and the plants will not grow well.
- Too much fertiliser can harm plant growth and high levels of nitrogen in the soil can damage nearby rivers and lakes. Fertiliser is also expensive – you don't want to waste it!

Mineral nutrient	Use in plant	Effects of deficiency
nitrogen	proteins, nucleic acids, chlorophyll	reduced growth and yellowish leaves
potassium	essential for some enzyme reactions	poor growth, older leaves become mottled
phosphorus	nucleic acids and a range of other substances including ATP	poor root growth
magnesium	to make chlorophyll	yellowish leaves, poor growth

QUESTIONS

1. Why does the plant need potassium?
2. What effect does lack of phosphorus have on plants?
3. 'Some fertiliser good, more fertiliser better'. Why is this not always true?
4. List **two** inorganic fertilisers.

...*active transport*   ...*eutrophication*   ...*macronutrients*   ...*micronutrients*

Enough already!

If plants need minerals, how can too much fertiliser be dangerous? The main problem occurs with nitrogenous fertilisers. If a farmer adds too much fertiliser to the ground the plants cannot take it all up. Some remains dissolved in the water in the soil. When it rains, water passes through the soil and drains into local streams and rivers – carrying the nitrogenous fertiliser with it. This is called run-off.

In the rivers and lakes the fertiliser encourages growth of water plants – particularly some sorts of algae. These cover the surface of the water and block light from the lower levels. This kills plants lower down in the water and they start to sink to the bottom and decay. This decay uses up the oxygen in the water. The plants need oxygen and some of them die. They decay and make the situation even worse. Soon the lake is a smelly mess of decaying organic matter. This process is called **eutrophication**.

Rivers also suffer from eutrophication but because they are constantly fed with fresh water the excess nitrogen is washed away more quickly.

And dead lakes and rivers are only part of the problem. In the UK we take drinking water out of rivers. If it contains high levels of nitrates the water can be dangerous. Nitrates cause particular problems for pregnant women and babies.

FIGURE 2: An over-fertilised lake.

QUESTIONS

5 What does the word 'eutrophication' mean?

6 What causes the fall in oxygen concentration in lakes polluted with fertilisers?

7 Why is run-off from fields into a large river less of a problem than run-off into a lake?

Getting mineral salts into plants (H)

Mineral salts enter plants in solution through the **root hairs**. The root hairs stick into the spaces between the soil particles where water collects. They absorb water and mineral salts and these pass into the root from cell to cell. In the middle of the roots are special water-conducting tubes called **xylem vessels**. They go all the way up to the leaves.

Mineral salts do not pass easily across a cell membrane. The plant uses an **active transport** mechanism. Special proteins in the cell membrane can react with mineral ions on the outside. The protein twists to bring the mineral ion to the inner surface and releases it into the cell. This needs energy as ATP.

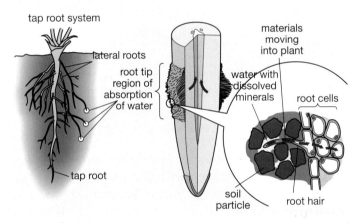

FIGURE 3: Root structure.

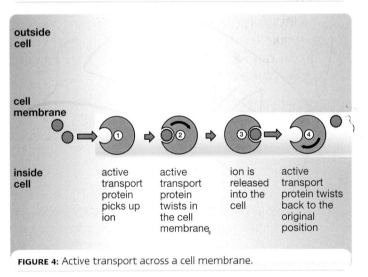

FIGURE 4: Active transport across a cell membrane.

QUESTIONS

8 Which part of the root absorbs mineral salts?

9 How do mineral salts pass from the roots to the leaves?

10 When a potted plant becomes waterlogged, the level of oxygen in the soil drops dramatically. Why does this reduce the rate of mineral salt uptake?

Maximising food production

You will find out:
- How to increase food production in greenhouses
- How fish farms increase food production

Dig for victory!

In World War II, food was in very short supply. People had to survive on rations – or what they could grow themselves. Suddenly everyone was interested in how to get more food out of the same sized patch of land! Producing more food is now more important than ever if we are to feed everyone in the world.

Optimum all the time

The best conditions for something to happen are called the **optimum conditions**. So, a plant will have an optimum water level and optimum temperature for growth. Unfortunately the weather in the UK means that optimum conditions cannot be guaranteed.

Sometimes optimum levels for different factors seem to fight against each other. Tomatoes grow best in hot, sunny conditions. Unfortunately that sort of weather is also dry and tomatoes need a lot of water! The only way to make sure you can keep all conditions at their optimum levels is to control them all. For tomatoes, this means growing them in a greenhouse.

For an excellent tomato crop make sure:

- the temperature never drops below 10 °C
- the sun shines for at least 14 hours a day
- the plants never dry out – or even wilt!
- the roots are supplied with plenty of fertiliser.

Maximising food production

The Eden Project in Cornwall has some of the largest greenhouses in the world – but it's not to provide food! The engineers and plant scientists who built the domes can control all the environmental factors inside to copy almost any area of the world. This means the Eden Project has a wide range of plants that would normally die in Cornwall.

PLANT A VICTORY GARDEN

OUR FOOD IS FIGHTING

A GARDEN WILL MAKE YOUR RATIONS GO FURTHER

FIGURE 1: Digging for victory!

FIGURE 2: Mediterranean plants growing in cold and wet cornwall!

QUESTIONS

1. What does the word optimum mean?
2. Where does the energy come from for the growing tomato plant?
3. Why do tomato plants need lots of fertiliser?
4. Suggest **one** other thing a good tomato grower would control to get a high yield.

...*fish farms*

Fish heaven!

Fish is an excellent low-fat, high-protein food and is becoming more popular every year. To supply this growing market, farmers are building **fish farms** where they can make sure the fish are kept in optimum conditions for growth. An open fish farm is little more than a large pond or lake where fish are kept. Carefully controlled amounts of animal manure are added to encourage growth of pondweeds. The fish feed on these weeds and can be netted when they are big enough to eat.

Salmon farming in Scotland uses a different system. The fish are kept in giant tanks in lochs. Food is added and the fish are harvested when they have reached a suitable size. To stock the farm, eggs and sperm are removed from adult fish by stroking their sides. They are then mixed in the laboratory. The eggs are hatched in tanks of gently flowing water and when the young fish, called fry, are a suitable size, they are added to the tanks in the lochs. Since the fish's breeding is controlled, it is possible to select for the best salmon rather like farmers choose the best cow to breed from.

FIGURE 3: Fish farms mean more fish for us to eat!

The cages are well stocked with salmon. This makes infection in the fish more likely. The farmer often adds pesticides to the fish food to protect the stock from pests such as the salmon louse. These pesticides can leak out into the environment beyond the cages.

Fish are very efficient converters of energy into meat. They do not keep their bodies above environmental temperature (as mammals do), so they do not waste food energy doing this.

Fish farmers maximise production by:

- stocking fish at high densities
- supplying food
- choosing the best fish to breed from
- protecting against pests with chemical pesticides.

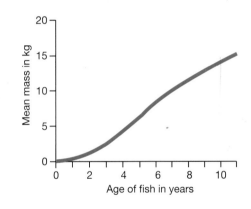

FIGURE 4: Growth rate of fish.

Fish per tank	Growth rate (gram per fish per day)
250	0.032
500	0.026
750	0.020
1000	0.014
1500	0.008

QUESTIONS

5 Why are fish so efficient at converting food into protein?

6 Assuming all the weight gain is protein, what is the total protein gain for a tank of 500 fish over a week?

7 Describe the relationship between stocking density of fish and growth rates shown by the data.

8 Why are salmon in fish farms more likely to be infected with pests than wild salmon?

9 At what age are fish growing at their fastest rate?

...optimum conditions

The carbon cycle

You will find out:

- Why carbon is so important
- How to draw a carbon cycle
- How changes in the carbon cycle threaten our survival

Fuel's paradise?

Every year, road traffic pumps millions of tonnes of carbon dioxide into the atmosphere. Almost all serious climate scientists believe that this carbon dioxide is causing global warming. But carbon dioxide is a natural chemical, so surely the Earth can clean up our mess?

Carbon everywhere

Carbon is an element that appears in every living thing. Look at the equation for **respiration**. Carbon enters as **glucose** on one side and leaves as carbon dioxide on the other. This process releases **energy** for living things to use. **Combustion** is the same basic reaction – but the energy comes out as heat and light.

$$\text{glucose} + \text{oxygen} \rightarrow \text{carbon dioxide} + \text{water} + \text{energy}$$

Photosynthesis drives carbon the other way. Carbon enters as carbon dioxide and leaves as sugar. This time energy is put into the reaction to drive it forward. This energy is supplied as sunlight.

Photosynthesis and respiration are the major controllers of gas concentration in the atmosphere but other factors also have an effect:

- Burning fossil fuels such as coal, oil and gas releases carbon dioxide.
- Burning fuels such as wood and straw releases carbon dioxide.
- Rising water temperature in the oceans reduces the solubility of carbon dioxide and it comes out into the atmosphere.

FIGURE 1: Every year the number of cars on our planet goes up. Every year more carbon dioxide is pumped into the air. Every year global warming gets a little worse.

Watch Out Photosynthesis and respiration are exact opposites of each other. If you learn one equation, the other is the same – just back to front.

FIGURE 2: This maize may end up in your cornflakes. It has trapped carbon dioxide by photosynthesis to make sugars and starch.

QUESTIONS

1 Which gas does respiration produce?
2 Which gas does photosynthesis take in?
3 How does carbon dioxide leave the atmosphere?
4 List **two** ways carbon dioxide can enter the atmosphere.

WOW FACTOR!

The average citizen in the USA uses enough fossil fuel to make 5.5 tonnes of carbon dioxide every year. An Indian farmer produces just under 0.5 tonnes in the same time.

...biomass fuels   ...calcium carbonate   ...carbon cycle   ...carbon dioxide   ...combustion

The carbon cycle

Millions of years ago, before plants evolved, there was no oxygen in the atmosphere. Today, the balance between photosynthesis and respiration is probably the most important controller of oxygen and carbon dioxide levels in the atmosphere.

Respiration breaks down carbon-containing chemicals to make carbon dioxide. These chemicals may be present in living organisms or be the decaying remains of dead organisms. All living organisms are eventually broken down into carbon dioxide, water and other non-living chemicals.

The only way to get carbon dioxide out of the air is by photosynthesis. Across the planet millions of plants are doing this and giving out oxygen. The oceans are full of microscopic plants called **phytoplankton** that take tonnes of carbon dioxide from the atmosphere every year.

Sometimes carbon is built into skeletons as **calcium carbonate**. This fixes the carbon because living things cannot respire calcium carbonate. You can see tonnes of this locked up carbon in the cliffs of chalk near Dover.

FIGURE 3: The white cliffs of Dover – almost pure calcium carbonate.

Sometimes plants and animals do not decay completely when they die. They may be covered with soil or water which keeps oxygen away from the dead remains. This prevents decay. Over millions of years this forms coal, oil or gas – **fossil fuels**. These are different from **biomass fuels** which are burnt as soon as they are grown. Wood is a good example of a biomass fuel.

Variations in carbon dioxide concentration

Carbon dioxide concentration remains remarkably constant, and low, in the atmosphere at only 0.03%. However, there is some variation, and over recent years the level has risen significantly owing to human activity.

Carbon dioxide levels also vary during the day as the graph shows. These measurements were taken in a field of grass over one day in May 1961.

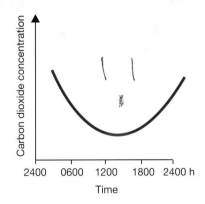

FIGURE 4: The carbon dioxide levels between the leaves of long grass.

▦ QUESTIONS ▦

5 How do phytoplankton affect the concentration of carbon dioxide in the air?

6 A rise in carbon dioxide concentration increases the rate of photosynthesis. How will this affect the concentration of carbon dioxide in the air?

7 Give an example of some carbon dioxide that has been fixed into other chemicals and is no longer available to the living world.

8 Biomass fuels are grown to provide fuel to burn. How does the production and use of biomass fuels affect the level of carbon dioxide in the air?

▦ QUESTIONS ▦

9 Explain what causes the variation in carbon dioxide concentrations over the day.

10 The data were collected in May. How would the graph be different if it had been collected in December? Give reasons for your answer.

...energy   ...fossil fuels   ...glucose   ...phytoplankton   ...photosynthesis   ...respiration

Global warming

You will find out:

- About the evidence for global warming
- How the greenhouse effect explains global warming
- About the choices for our planet

English champagne?

Some French champagne manufacturers are starting to buy farms in Kent. They have decided that if global warming happens, as some scientists are predicting, Kent will be the perfect place to grow vines for champagne grapes. Will we see Canterbury champagne in years to come?

FIGURE 1: Vineyards in Kent.

Is the globe getting warmer?

Our planet is changing. It is getting warmer every year – not by much, but enough to cause major problems. And there is no sign that the change is slowing down.

- The 1990s were the hottest decade in the UK since records began.

- Some migratory birds have stopped flying south for the winter because the temperature in the UK stays warmer.

- Average thickness of ice in Arctic:
  - 1958–1976: 3 metres (about 10 feet)
  - 11993–1997: 2 metres (about 6 feet).

Some scientists and politicians deny that **global warming** is happening at all – or that it is anything to worry about. They say that the Earth gets warmer and colder in a natural cycle and that we are currently in a warming time.

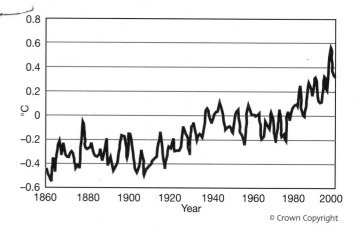

© Crown Copyright

FIGURE 2: The Earth appears to be getting warmer. Has this been caused by our activities?

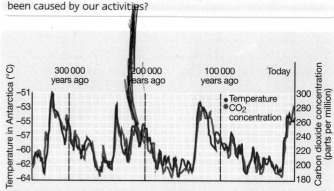

FIGURE 3: How temperature and carbon dioxide levels have changed in Antarctica.

QUESTIONS

1. What does the term 'global warming' mean?
2. Give **two** pieces of evidence that suggest global warming is occurring.
3. What are the dangers of not reacting to possible global warming?
4. What are the dangers of over-reacting to possible global warming?

...global warming   ...greenhouse gases

The greenhouse effect

The vast majority of serious scientists now accept that global warming is occurring. But what is causing it? This produces a little more disagreement. However, the majority view is that the levels of certain gases in the air, called **greenhouse gases**, are causing the warming.

It is possible to use data from bubbles of gas buried in the deep ice of the Antarctic to estimate the concentration of carbon dioxide in the atmosphere for the last few thousand years. It is also possible to estimate temperatures over the same period. What do the two lines on the graph seem to suggest?

A possible mechanism?

Sunlight reaches the Earth and passes through the atmosphere. It warms the ground and oceans and is responsible for all life on the planet. The Earth radiates heat rather like an infrared electric heater. It is the balance between incoming sunlight and outgoing heat that keeps our planet temperature constant.

Carbon dioxide and other greenhouse gases such as water vapour and methane seem to interfere with this balance. They let sunlight through, but reflect the infrared rays. So, they act like the glass in a greenhouse, keeping the energy in and raising the temperature. This explains why carbon dioxide levels seem to match the changes in global temperatures.

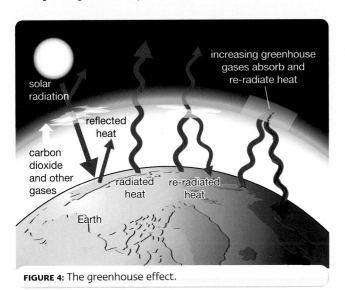

FIGURE 4: The greenhouse effect.

Monitoring the greenhouse

A global phenomenon such as the greenhouse effect needs global monitoring. Scientists from many countries are working on it and need to share data and thoughts. Looks like the internet arrived at just the right time!

Scientists post data on websites that can be accessed by anyone doing research in this area. The United Nations also collects data on temperature, carbon dioxide levels and so on from across the planet. Satellites orbiting the planet collect data about sea temperatures, concentrations of chlorophyll and amount of forest clearance.

Government bodies, scientists and even school pupils can now carry out global research using computers and secondary data. **Secondary data** are data collected by someone else.

QUESTIONS

9   Why is global monitoring so useful when looking at the greenhouse effect?

10 Give **three** sources of information available to scientists studying the greenhouse effect.

11 If the same data are available to everyone, why do scientists disagree about the causes of global warming?

12 If most scientists interpret data in one way, does that mean the minority of scientists who disagree must be wrong?

QUESTIONS

5   What is the 'greenhouse effect' and how is it different from 'global warming'?

6   State **one** piece of evidence that suggests a link between carbon dioxide concentration in the atmosphere and global temperature. Explain the reasons for your choice.

7   How can we collect data about atmospheres from 3000 years ago?

8   How does carbon dioxide in the atmosphere cause a rise in temperature at sea level?

...secondary data

Population bomb

You will find out:
- How fast the world's population is increasing
- About the dangers of non-sustainable growth

1, The Avenue, Mars

The human population is growing, but the Earth stays the same size. Will we get to the stage where there is just not enough room, or food, to go round? Perhaps the solution is to colonise other planets? Will your children, or their children, have an address on Mars?

Biospheres

A **biosphere** is a completely sealed environment. Materials such as oxygen and carbon dioxide are cycled inside it just like they are on planet Earth. Light gets into the biosphere through a clear roof to drive photosynthesis. Will these be built on Mars to house Earth's growing population? Well … maybe.

- Biospheres are not easy to make. They have to be very large to contain enough plants to produce oxygen and food for even a small number of people.

- Biospheres are very expensive to build, even on Earth. The cost of taking the materials to Mars to build them would be huge. We have only managed to land small spacecraft on Mars so far – the total weight is less than a very small car! How could we get the tonnes of steel we need for a biosphere to Mars?

- Managing biospheres is not easy! The problems with global warming look like we can't even manage our home planet properly.

But doctors used to think human beings could not move faster than 30 km/hour without dying. And flying in something heavier than air was considered impossible for many centuries. Who knows what technology we will have in a hundred years' time?

FIGURE 1: Islands in space?

QUESTIONS

1. What supplies the energy to support life in biospheres?
2. List **three** problems with building biospheres on Mars.
3. We have enough problems on Earth. Scientists should spend time and money solving those before we try to get to Mars. Do you agree?
4. Would you like to live on a biosphere in Mars?

…biosphere …deforestation

How big a problem? (H)

Our **population** is increasing, but this increase is not evenly spread. In the rich countries of the developed world populations have stabilised, while in the poorer developing countries they continue to rise.

Year	Predicted population (billions)
2005	6.5
2010	6.8
2020	7.6
2030	8.2
2040	8.7
2050	9.1

Can we do anything about population growth?

- A large population is not a bad thing. More people means more artists, more workers, more people to look after the ill. People are our greatest resource.

- Educated women have fewer children than women who did not go to secondary school. The population increase is the result of lack of education and opportunities – particularly for women. If we gave more people a better start in life, the world population would stabilise within a generation.

- There is no such thing as over-population ... only over-consumption by some people! But over the next few years our diets will change. More and more people will be eating meat – which means land will produce less food per hectare.

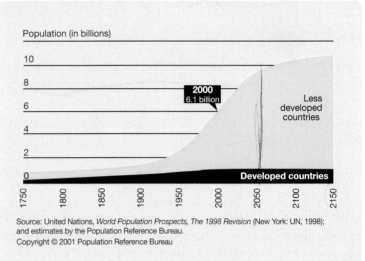

Source: United Nations, *World Population Prospects, The 1998 Revision* (New York: UN, 1998); and estimates by the Population Reference Bureau.
Copyright © 2001 Population Reference Bureau

FIGURE 2: How the world's population has grown from 1750, and how it is predicted to grow to 2150.

Deforestation

An African proverb says, 'Forests go before man, deserts follow'. Sadly, this seems to be true. Increasing global populations and expectations mean that we lose millions of acres of forests every year as trees are felled for timber or simply to clear the ground for food production.

Loss of forests around the world hurts us all. Perhaps an anti-cancer drug has already been lost as a rare rainforest plant was pushed into extinction. Forests help to take carbon dioxide out of the air by photosynthesis. **Deforestation** has a direct effect on global warming.

FIGURE 3: Deforestation from logging in Brazil. This forest is home to thousands of species of animals and plants – will we lose them all?

QUESTIONS

5 Describe the differences between population changes in the developed and developing countries over the next 100 years.

6 The rise in population in developed countries is placing a great strain on the Earth's resources. Why does a similar increase in a poorer country have less effect?

7 Why is it difficult to set a figure for the maximum number of people the Earth can support?

8 Is poverty created by a large population or is a large population created by poverty? What do you think?

A natural disaster?

You will find out:

- How famines can be created by food distribution rules
- About the distribution of food supplies in the world

Green River?

On Saint Patrick's Day in 2005 they dyed the river in Chicago green! Great fun, but why are there so many Irish people in the USA to celebrate Saint Patrick's day? Strangely, it is because of a famine in 1840 – a famine created partly by laws passed in London...

Potatoes with everything

Potatoes were the main food for Irish peasants in the 1800s. They were easy to grow in the damp, cool climate of Ireland and produced a good yield of food that was nutritionally almost as good as wheat. An English writer travelling in Ireland at the time was amazed to see that a typical Irish man might eat 5 kg of potatoes a day!

But there was another reason why so many potatoes were grown. Irish peasants rented their land from landlords, many of whom were English. This rent could be paid either as work in the landlord's fields or in crops such as wheat that could be sold to raise cash. If the rent was not paid, the peasants would be forced from their farms. This usually meant they lost their house as well. Potatoes were so easy to grow, the peasants could raise enough to eat and have time left over to work for the landlord.

The table shows the quality of diet in pre-famine Ireland.

FIGURE 1: The St. Lawrence river in Chicago – dyed green to celebrate St Patrick's Day!

Food component	Ireland 1839	Recommended Daily Allowance for active males in Britain
Protein/g	134.6	72
Fat/g	3.6	not specified
Carbohydrate/g	1099.1	not specified
Energy value/J	4720	2900
Calcium/mg	2398	500
Iron/mg	24.5	10

▥ QUESTIONS ▥

1 What weight of potatoes would a typical Irish male eat in the 1830s?
2 Was the potato diet healthy? Use figures from the table to support your answer.
3 Give **two** reasons why potatoes were so popular in Ireland in the 1800s.

...disease ...fairly-traded goods

Potato blight (H)

Potato blight is a **disease** of potatoes. It is caused by a **fungus** called *Phytophthora infestans*. In 1845 the first signs of blight were noticed. The harvest was poor, but little was done about it. This was a 'natural disaster' and hopefully next year's harvest would be better. In fact, things got worse and worse over the next few years.

The graph shows the main stages of what became known as 'The Great Famine'. It led directly to massive numbers of Irish people leaving Ireland for America – and the green river of Chicago!

Irish famine deaths

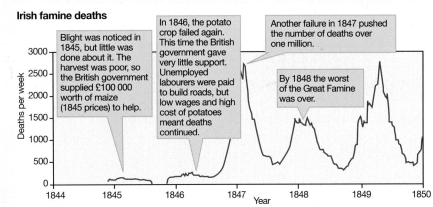

Blight was noticed in 1845, but little was done about it. The harvest was poor, so the British government supplied £100 000 worth of maize (1845 prices) to help.

In 1846, the potato crop failed again. This time the British government gave very little support. Unemployed labourers were paid to build roads, but low wages and high cost of potatoes meant deaths continued.

Another failure in 1847 pushed the number of deaths over one million.

By 1848 the worst of the Great Famine was over.

FIGURE 2: Graph of Irish famine deaths.

A natural disaster?

In fact, the Great Famine was not a natural disaster. The potato blight fungus caused the immediate problem, but it was the poverty of the peasants that killed them. They were too dependent on one crop. Even during the famine, Ireland was exporting grain to feed people in the cities in England. There was never a shortage of food – only an unequal distribution of it.

The table shows how Irish grain exports and imports changed from 1844 to 1848.

Year	Exports (millions of kg)	Imports (millions of kg)
1844	431	31
1845	521	29
1846	289	200
1847	148	903
1848	319	446

Learning from history?

So have we learnt from the Great Famine and is food now distributed fairly? Unfortunately not. Land in some of the poorest countries in the world is not used to grow food for local people but to raise flowers for British supermarkets. Coffee and tea plantations in Africa often occupy the best land, leaving the worst land for local **food production**.

The USA and EU subsidise their farmers so that crops they produce are artificially cheap. These crops are dumped on the world market and push the price down. This encourages farmers to grow less food, and more crops such as coffee, tea and bananas that cannot be grown in the developed countries. This is looking very similar to the Irish peasants being dependent on potatoes ...

How can we prevent another 'Great Famine'?

- Reduce subsidies to rich country farmers.
- Encourage farmers in poorer countries to grow more food for local consumption.
- Where possible buy **fairly-traded goods** which pay a proper price for crops like coffee, tea and chocolate.

QUESTIONS

4   Which groups of people in Ireland were most likely to
    a survive the famine?   **b** die of starvation?

5   Why did the starving peasants not buy some of the grain being exported to England during the famine?

6   How does reliance on a single crop make a 'natural disaster' more likely in a country?

7   Why does supplying cheap food to a country help to drive farmers out of business and make the food supply situation worse for some people?

Keeping the globe warm?

SELF-CHECK ACTIVITY

CONTEXT

Catherine is living in London with her family. She wasn't born there but her father works for a national organisation and they needed him to be working in their London offices for a couple of years. The area is very nice; they are near to the Thames and a bus or train ride to the West End with the theatres, shops and museums. She's settled in quickly and soon made friends at school. Several of the other children become good friends and soon she is being invited round to their homes at evenings and weekends.

One friend is called Ruth and Catherine goes round there quite a bit. After several months she notices something rather odd. Whenever she goes into Ruth's flat it is always at exactly the same temperature, no matter what the time of year. Like many of the houses in the area they have air conditioning to keep the house cool in the heat of the summer in the city.

'Well,' says Ruth, 'What we do is to set the air conditioning so that it comes on if the temperature rises above 20 °C. And if it drops below 20 °C the heating comes on. That way it's always the same temperature. Pretty neat, huh?'

Catherine nods and smiles but doesn't say anything. She looks out of the window and watches the Thames flowing past. In a couple of her science lessons recently she's been finding out about global warming and it has made her think. Ruth's flat is heated by gas-fired central heating and the air conditioning runs from electricity.

CHALLENGE

STEP 1

How does burning gas to run a central heating system contribute towards global warming?

STEP 2

Does the use of electricity (for the air conditioning) contribute towards global warming? Explain your answer.

STEP 3

Explain what the impact of global warming might be upon the level of the sea.

STEP 4

What do you think Catherine might be thinking, in the flat with its constant temperature and views over the river?

STEP 5

What changes might people have to make in their lives to avoid disasters from global warming?

Maximise your grade

These sentences show what you need to include in your work to achieve each grade. Use them to improve your work and be more successful.

Grade	Answer includes...
F	Have some idea about how burning fossil fuels can add to global warming.
	Know how burning fossil fuels can add to global warming.
	Apply knowledge about the causes of global warming to this context.
	Have some idea about the effects of global warming.
C	Explain how global warming may affect people's lives.
	Combine understanding of causes and effects of global warming.
A	Explain, in the context of causes and effects of global warming, how human behaviour may need to change.
	Explain clearly and comprehensively, in the context of causes and effects of global warming, how human behaviour may need to change.

On the edge

You will find out:

- About organisms that can survive boiling in poison
- How penguins are adapted to life in the Antarctic

Under pressure

Some microorganisms survive temperatures higher than those in hospital sterilising equipment! Some algae grow in solid ice in the Antarctic and make the ice look pink. And penguins – almost the symbol of Antarctica – seem perfectly happy in sub-zero conditions. How do these organisms manage?

Smokers!

Deep in the Pacific are cracks that lead down into hot rocks below the Earth's crust. Gases and superheated steam constantly stream out of these cracks to raise the temperature of the ocean near them to well over 90 °C. This is enough to kill almost all of the organisms you can see around you. These are some of the harshest **aquatic** environments on the planet. So are these areas dead?

Not exactly. Highly specialised bacteria grow in this environment. They can use the heat and the chemicals from the vents, called **smokers**, to get energy to survive. They actually need these harsh conditions – at sea level they would die!

Scientists study these microbes to find out how they can survive these conditions. Some of the chemicals common around these vents are poisons. They contain lots of sulphur. If we learn how these organisms handle these chemicals we might be able to extract enzymes which could clean wastes from industry. Imagine a chimney lined with an enzyme extract from these bacteria. The chimney might be able to clean the waste gases – also rich in sulphur – before they were released into the environment.

FIGURE 1: Superheated water escaping from a smoker deep in the Pacific Ocean.

QUESTIONS

1 What is a deep sea smoker?
2 Where does the heat to raise the water temperature near a smoker come from?
3 Why might the organisms that grow near smokers provide useful enzymes for industry?

...adaptation   ...aquatic   ...blubber   ...extreme environment

Pick up a penguin?

Penguins live in the Antarctic. This is a **terrestrial** environment, which means it is on dry land. For much of the year the temperature is below freezing point. The birds spend 75 per cent of their lives underwater where it is actually warmer! Penguins have a range of **adaptations** to help them survive:

- A layer of fat or **blubber** under the skin insulates the body from the severe cold.

- The characteristic black and white feathers also act as insulation.

- Heavy bones in the legs help the penguin to sink in the water.

- Wings have been modified to be more like flippers – penguins cannot fly but swim very well.

- Penguin feathers are very densely packed and oily to stop them absorbing water.

- The body has a **streamlined** shape and the feet are webbed like flippers.

- The black and white colours of the feathers are very good camouflage – penguins are almost invisible from above and below.

FIGURE 2: The brown fluffy birds are juveniles. As they grow they will develop the standard black and white plumage.

WOW FACTOR!

Penguins contain so much fat that Antarctic explorers used them as candles. Just light the head of a dead penguin and it burns down like a fat black and white candle!

Dark and dangerous

Very little light gets to the seabed and little food falls down from above. If a fish finds some food it needs to grab it and eat it quickly – who knows when the next meal will come along? The ugly angler fish lives deep in the sea and gives out light which attracts other fish. Unfortunately for the other fish the light is produced by an organ that hangs just in front of the angler fish's huge mouth. When the prey gets close to the light the angler fish pounces and swallows it in one gulp!

FIGURE 3: It would have to be dark! You wouldn't approach this fish if you could see what you were doing!

The eyes of deep sea fish are adapted to cope with this very dark **extreme environment**. They are often quite large and very sensitive. Some of the chemicals in the eyes of deep sea fish are much more sensitive to light than the chemicals in human eyes. By having a light-producing organ that hangs in front of the mouth the fish can produce enough light to see – and to attract **prey**. The skin of angler fish is also black so that it absorbs the faint blue light given out by the light organ. Why is this an advantage?

The ugly angler fish lives deep in the sea

QUESTIONS

4 List **three** adaptations of penguins to do with protecting them against low temperatures.

5 List **three** adaptations of penguins to do with improving their ability to swim in Antarctic waters.

6 List **two** adaptations of the deep sea angler fish.

7 Explain how each of the adaptations you listed helps the fish to survive.

Forestry

You will find out:

- How temperate forests can be sustainably managed

- What the term 'carbon neutral' means

Ent moot?

The ents are giant tree-like creatures from Tolkien's Lord of the Rings. They manage trees rather like shepherds manage sheep. Of course, they don't exist but there are 'human ents' who manage forests to make sure there are some left for future generations.

Forests

- Forests are not just a collection of trees. A mature forest is a complex ecosystem of large and small plants, animals and soil microorganisms. After years of development it becomes stable and new organisms only grow to replace those that die. Compare this with a wheat field where ground is cleared every year for new crops to grow. A mature forest has quite a low productivity.

- To solve this problem, foresters cut the trees back to the ground every few years. This is called **coppicing** and encourages vigorous growth. Coppiced forests are much more productive than unmanaged forests.

- In the UK willow is coppiced to produce wood for burning in power stations. This biofuel is very environmentally friendly because the carbon dioxide released when the willow burns only replaces the carbon dioxide taken out of the air while the willow was growing. This means the fuel is 'carbon neutral'.

- Alternatives to coppicing are **reforestation** and **replacement planting**. In reforestation a complete forest is removed and then replanted in one go. Replacement planting takes out individual trees and replants them one at a time.

FIGURE 1: Willow growing for biofuel.

█ QUESTIONS █

1. Give **two** ways forests are different from wheat fields.
2. Why not cut down the trees every year?
3. What does the term 'carbon neutral' mean?
4. Why do foresters coppice trees?

...coppicing

Advantages of coppicing

Coppicing increases the yield of forests by encouraging new growth. It also has a number of other benefits:

Biodiversity

Because different areas of the forest are coppiced at different times there is always a range of trees of different ages. In some areas of the forest more light gets through and there is increased growth on the forest floor.

Materials

Coppiced wood has a wide range of uses from making fences to firewood and even charcoal. This is different from only cutting mature trees which are only useful for timber.

Biofuels

Coppiced willow can grow up to 4 metres in a single season! This produces huge amounts of wood for burning in power stations. Charcoal made from coppiced wood burns at a temperature of 1100 °C – hot enough to melt iron!

Longevity

Trees that are regularly coppiced survive longer than trees that are not. This may be because dead wood above ground is removed regularly. This also takes away any damaged or diseased wood.

FIGURE 2: These rows of conifers on a Welsh hillside damage the soil and are far too densely packed to allow growth of anything else between them. From an environmentalist's point of view they are a disaster!

Reforestation

A healthy coppiced woodland can be productive for hundreds or even thousands of years – but what happens if the forest has already died? Reforestation is the process of planting a new forest. The mixture of trees must be carefully chosen to make sure a natural forest develops. This is very different from the huge plantations of conifers on hills in Wales and Scotland!

Replacement planting

Replacement planting aims to prevent a forest from being destroyed. Every time a tree is removed, another is planted in its place. Again careful management is needed because it will take many years for a young tree to replace a fully grown specimen. Felling a tree can also damage the forest – particularly if large machines are used to move the tree or logs away.

▦▦▦ QUESTIONS ▦▦▦

5 List **four** advantages of coppicing.

6 Why do coppiced forests tend to have a wider range of living things than plantations of conifers?

7 What is the difference between replacement planting and coppicing?

8 Wet wood does not burn as well as dry timber. Plan an investigation to find the heat energy of wood samples from a coppiced forest.

9 An area in Derbyshire can be used to grow coppiced broadleafed forest or coniferous plantations. Which type of forest should the local people go for? Give reasons for your answer.

...reforestation ...replacement planting

Save the rainforest

You will find out:
- How different organisms depend on each other
- About ecological services

Where the nuts come from

Many acres of Brazilian rainforest have been cleared for farms to grow grass to feed cattle. These farms last only a short time. Within a few seasons they become infertile, degraded land. Why does this happen and can we harvest food from the rainforest without destroying it?

Ecological services

Your home is probably connected to the mains for electricity, water, gas and maybe even cable television and telephones. These are called services and make life in modern Britain easier. Organisms living in the rainforest also depend on services to survive. These are called **ecological services**:

- A plant may depend on an insect to pollinate its flowers and so produce seeds and offspring.

- A bird may need certain kinds of plants to build its nest.

- Many microorganisms provide services for plants by breaking down dead organic matter so that the valuable minerals can be absorbed through their roots.

The brazil nut is a tree that grows in the rainforests of Brazil. No one has yet managed to create a plantation of brazil nut trees – they just fail to grow and produce nuts. Something (or maybe many things) in the rainforest is providing essential ecological services for the brazil nut.

Apple growers in Europe know that keeping a bee hive in the orchard increases the yield of fruit. The bees pollinate the apple blossom. Many orchards produce apples and great honey – so the bees are doubly useful!

FIGURE 1: A French orchard with a heavy crop of apples. Apple growers often keep bees in the orchard to help pollinate the apple blossom. So we can enjoy apples, cider and honey!

QUESTIONS

1. What does the term 'ecological services' mean?
2. Give **two** examples of services a plant may depend on to survive.
3. Suggest something the brazil nut tree needs that it can only get in a rainforest.

...biodiversity ...ecological services

Interdependence

A rainforest is a very complicated ecosystem and the species that live there provide a wide range of ecological services for each other. Loss of one type of organism might lead to problems for another if these services become unavailable.

Biologists use the word **interdependence** to mean the way organisms are linked together by these ecological services. It is different from normal predator–prey relationships where one animal eats another. Here the link is very obvious, but with interdependence and ecological services the link may be much more difficult to see. Scientists have not been able to find out what it is about the rainforest that helps brazil nuts to grow. But we do know that without a rainforest the brazil nut fails.

FIGURE 2: This rainforest flower depends on the ants and the ants depend on the flower.

Minimum critical size of ecosystems

One line of research looks at how much rainforest you need to produce a stable system that provides all of the essential services. Is a patch of rainforest 100 m by 100 m big enough? Or do you need more? The smallest size that provides all of the essential services is called the minimum critical size. Research in the 1980s showed:

- Trees on the edge of a conservation area were much more likely to die than trees in the middle.

- A single isolated area was more likely to fail than smaller areas that were connected by strips of forest.

- Some species needed a minimum amount of undisturbed forest to survive. If these species provided essential ecological services the whole forest failed if they died.

In an attempt to save the rainforest while also allowing farmers and local people to make a living, scientists came up with a plan for 'connected reserves'. Loggers were required to leave strips of forest between conservation areas so that animals could move safely between them.

FIGURE 3: Orangutans are very visible and attract lots of support from environmentalists. But to save these apes, you need to save the whole rainforest because they depend on it for food and shelter.

Biodiversity

Rainforests are some of the richest and most complex environments on the planet. Scientists use the word **biodiversity** to describe the range of organisms living in an area.

- Rainforests have very high biodiversity.

- Apple orchards have low biodiversity.

⋯⋯ QUESTIONS ⋯⋯

4   List some relationships between organisms that are not just predator–prey relationships.

5   What were the main findings of the research on the minimum critical size of ecosystems?

6   How did these findings change the way forests were cleared in Amazonia?

7   What does the word 'biodiversity' mean?

8   Why is a fall in biodiversity worrying?

…interdependence

Managing populations

You will find out:
- Why rabbits are such a problem in Australia
- What factors affect populations of organisms

Billions of bunnies

Rabbits are cute – but they also breed at an incredible rate! Farmers have to keep control of the rabbit populations on their land or the numbers would increase dramatically and would lead to massive losses from their crops. In the UK this is a problem. In Australia it almost became a national disaster!

Little breeders?

- Rabbits have a very high birth rate. A female rabbit can produce 10 young in a litter. Within a day she could be pregnant again! A month later she will produce another litter!

- Many of the young produced early in the season will also be able to breed before the season is out to produce young of their own.

- Rabbits are eaten by foxes and a range of other predators. This **predation** keeps the number down. If the rabbit population rises the foxes breed more as well, so the death rate amongst rabbits increases. Over many seasons this achieves a balance.

- Another factor is that as rabbit populations increase, the chance of disease increases. Lots of rabbits in a small area are more likely to pass infections amongst themselves. This reduces the survival rate.

FIGURE 1: Cute pets or just pests?

FIGURE 2: Giant pandas are an endangered species. They breed very rarely and produce only one cub at a time. How will their population change differ from rabbits?

Tend to increase population	Tend to decrease population
good weather	poor weather
low fox population	high fox population
good food supply	poor food supply
	disease
	overcrowding

QUESTIONS

1. How many young could a female rabbit produce per litter?
2. If a female gives birth every month from March to September how many offspring will she produce?
3. Give **two** factors which tend to reduce the population of rabbits.

...*birth rate* ...*death rate*

Population control (H)

The population of an organism in an area tends to stay roughly constant despite the potential for explosive growth. So, rabbits can breed rapidly but never as rapidly as the simple calculations might suggest. Why?

Local population growth depends on many factors but these can be organised into three main areas:

- **birth rate** – the number of young produced in a given time
- **death rate** – the number of **organisms** that die in the same period
- **population movement** – any movement of organisms into or out of the area.

Birth rate

Birth rate is relatively easy to predict and changes very little. Very poor conditions with reduced food supply will reduce birth rate. Improved food availability has reduced the age of puberty in many human societies worldwide. This means the period when females can be reproductively active is also increased.

Death rate

The death rate is much more easily altered by the environment. Rabbits were introduced into Australia by Thomas Austin. He released a mere 24 rabbits on his property near Melbourne on Christmas Day 1859.

Unfortunately, Australia had few natural predators that would hunt the rabbits so the death rate dropped dramatically. The factors that had controlled rabbit populations in Europe were absent and the population exploded. In 1890, during one of the 'rabbit plagues' 36 million rabbits were discovered on one New South Wales property. Nowadays the cost to Australian agriculture of the cuddly bunny is in excess of £700 million every year!

FIGURE 3: Too much of a good thing? What caused the rabbit population in Australia to rise out of control?

Controlling rabbits is not easy. Rabbits have been poisoned, hunted (with dogs and guns) and even had their warrens dynamited. None of these methods work well. The most successful option was biological control in the shape of a virus disease called myxomatosis. This is a highly contagious disease that spreads rapidly through a rabbit population and causes swellings around the eyes, blindness and eventually death. A Brazilian scientist suggested releasing it in 1918 but the Australian government, in a moment of great foresight, said simply that it 'wouldn't work'! By 1950 the problem was so bad that it was released in the Murray-Darling river basin in South Australia. Within six months the virus that 'wouldn't work' had killed about 95 per cent of the local rabbit population.

Population movement

Population movements can have massive effects on local populations but have no effect on the total population of an organism.

▦ QUESTIONS ▦

4 What are the **three** factors that affect local population size?

5 Why do local populations tend to remain roughly stable?

6 What caused the population explosion of rabbits in Australia in the 19th century?

7 Was the birth rate of rabbits in Australia different from the birth rate of rabbits in Europe at the time?

8 The first use of myxomatosis was phenomenally successful. Why do you think it became less successful in the years that followed?

Weed winners

You will find out:

- What plants compete for
- How weeds compete with valuable crop plants

Weeds not wimps!

Many gardeners talk to their plants! Some believe they grow better with a little bit of TLC (tender loving care). But if treating plants well makes them grow better, why do weeds, which everyone hates and tries to destroy, grow so well? Weeds must be very strong competitors in the plant world!

Competition for resources

Weeds are plants that we don't have a use for or that are growing in the wrong place. Gardeners are always trying to get rid of weeds because they compete with the plants they do want to grow.

Weeds are good competitors because they want the same things from the environment as the gardener's plants. If there is a shortage of these things the weeds will reduce the growth of the useful plants.

There are two main types of **competition**:

- **Interspecific competition** – organisms from different species compete with each other, e.g. poppies in a wheat field, dandelions in a lawn.

- **Intraspecific competition** – members of the same species compete with each other, e.g. lots of lettuces or carrots growing very closely together in a vegetable seedbed.

Intraspecific competition is usually much fiercer. All the plants are the same type and need exactly the same things from the environment. So, gardeners will thin out carrot or lettuce seedlings to give a few strong individuals the chance to grow on.

FIGURE 1: The spaces between the plants in this tiny hillside garden are not wasted – they help to improve the yield of useful vegetables overall by reducing competition between the plants.

QUESTIONS

1. What does the word 'competition' mean in a biological context?
2. What are the **two** main types of competition?
3. Which type is usually fiercer? Why?
4. Why do gardeners sow seeds and then uproot some of the plants that grow before they are mature?

...competition ...interspecific competition

Competition for what?

Animals compete for food, shelter and a mate – **resources**. Since plants produce their own food and do not mate in the same way, what do they compete for?

- Plants need carbon dioxide for photosynthesis. Sugar cane plants growing near the equator are particularly good at getting carbon dioxide from the air. They can grow more quickly than other plants.

- In the UK the light levels are so low that carbon dioxide is not usually a limiting factor. But water can be. Some plants have roots that can extract much more water from the ground than others and so compete more effectively.

- Another way to compete well for limited water is to make sure you make best use of any water you do absorb. Plants like holly and many conifers have leaves covered with a thick waxy cuticle. This reduces evaporation through the leaf.

- Plants need space. Seeds that germinate rapidly crowd out slower-growing species to dominate fresh ground.

FIGURE 2: Bluebells flower in early spring so that they can compete effectively for light.

- In a forest the tallest trees absorb some of the light. They shade the plants below. Very little light reaches the small plants on the forest floor. Bluebells compete in this environment by flowering early in the spring before the trees have produced leaves to shade out the light.

- The increase in yield produced by addition of fertiliser shows just how fierce competition for minerals can be. Of course, weeds are just as capable of benefiting from the increase in mineral nutrients in the soil as crop plants. So adding fertiliser can increase competition.

- Chemical control of weeds relies on herbicides. These kill the weeds but leave the crop untouched. Some work because the weed is such a rapidly growing plant that it takes up more herbicide than the crop. Others work because the broad-leaved weeds take up more herbicide than the narrow-leaved crop plants.

Weeds as killers

A dandelion in the lawn is not a major problem – but an infestation of weeds in your family field may mean the difference between wealth and poverty in some parts of the world. Weeds compete with your food crops to reduce productivity. The graph shows typical figures for some key food crops.

Chemical control of weed growth is possible – but has environmental and financial costs that many people may not be prepared to pay. In many cases the only solution is to hand-weed fields. This encourages larger families to provide more workers which, in turn, can lead to more poverty.

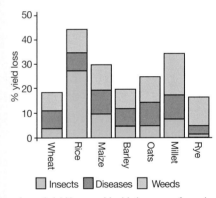

Annual yield loss world-wide because of weeds, diseaes and insects as estimated by FAO, based on data pre-1990.

Source: Freeland, *Food for Life*, British Agrochemical Association

FIGURE 3: Crop losses worldwide due to insects, weeds and diseases.

QUESTIONS

9 List the advantages and disadvantages of chemical weed control and hand-weeding for:

a a potato farmer in Lincolnshire

b a farmer in Tanzania growing food to feed his own family.

QUESTIONS

5 List the factors a plant will compete for.

6 Which of the factors is not usually significant in the UK?

7 List **four** plants and describe their adaptations to their environment.

8 How does addition of a weedkiller affect the competition between weeds and crop plants?

Breathe easy

You will find out:
- How acid gases can damage the environment
- How lichens respond to pollution

The Big Smoke

London used to be called 'The Smoke' because the air was so dirty. Millions of chimneys poured smoke and gases from fires into the air which mixed with fog to produce smog. They were famous the world over – a London 'pea souper' was a smog so dense it looked like pea soup! And then people started dying...

Bad air

Smog is a mixture of smoke and fog. Fog is formed when moisture in cold air condenses into tiny droplets of water – you can imagine them as low-flying clouds. Smoke contains a variety of gases from burning fossil fuels – mainly carbon dioxide, carbon monoxide, sulphur dioxide and tiny particles of carbon. You can see these particles in the smoke or deposited as soot.

London is built in a slight dip in the ground. The air above it does not move easily and so when a smog develops it can remain for some days. The most dangerous smog started on 5th December 1952 and didn't clear for about five days. In that time over 4000 people died above the expected amount.

Most of the deaths were in old people who were already suffering from lung diseases like bronchitis or pneumonia. However, twice the normal number of babies died in that week.

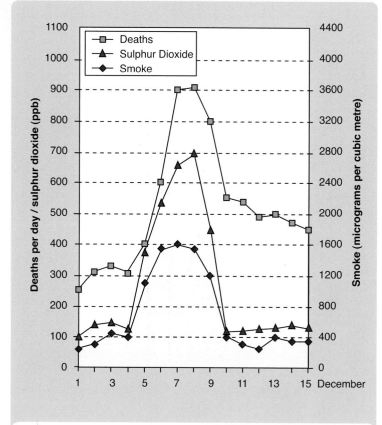

FIGURE 1: Deaths over the first two weeks of December 1952.

QUESTIONS

1 What is smog?

2 What gases does smoke contain?

3 How many extra deaths were recorded during the smog of December 1952?

4 Give **one** piece of evidence that shows the smog was linked to the extra deaths.

...*indicator species* ...*lichens*

Clean Air Acts

The London smog deaths of 1952 forced the government to take action. In 1956 the first Clean Air Act was introduced. This encouraged local councils to set up 'smoke-free zones'. People living in these areas were encouraged to change to smokeless fuels. Grants were given to change from coal fires to gas fires or central heating.

In 1968 the next Clean Air Act encouraged the use of tall chimneys which moved the pollutants higher into the atmosphere well away from people.

We rarely see smog nowadays but pollution, in the form of acid gases, has not gone away. Acid gases include carbon dioxide, sulphur dioxide and nitrogen oxides. These gases are produced by the burning of fossil fuels. The main source of these nowadays is road transport.

Acid gases can:

- reduce the growth of trees, particularly conifers in upland forests
- reduce the productivity of food crops
- increase the level of aluminium in lakes and rivers – aluminium is very toxic and even this small rise can damage fish and the birds that feed on them; some upland lakes are now almost dead because of acid rain
- increase the levels of asthma and bronchitis (a disease of the lungs) in humans.

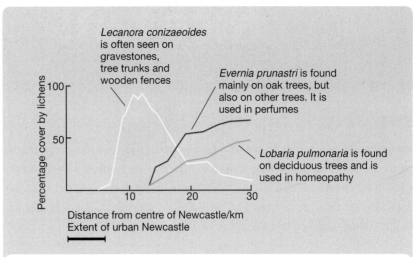

FIGURE 2: This shows the percentage of ash trees that were covered by lichens at increasing distance from Newcastle city centre. What is the link between the growth of these lichens and the presence of acid gases in the atmosphere?

Lichens

Lichens are plants that grow in areas too wet or cold for other plants. Some grow on trees, rocks and buildings. In towns they often grow on gravestones and buildings and look rather like a smudge of orange or grey paint.

Research in Newcastle upon Tyne looked at the growth of lichens and linked this to the presence of acid gases in the atmosphere – **pollution** – as shown in the graph.

FIGURE 3: Two types of lichens growing on a tree trunk. Lichens are very sensitive to air quality.

Indicator species

Lichens are an example of an **indicator species**. They show the first effects of changes in the environment and are often monitored so they can act as early warning signs of potential problems. The environment is a very complex dynamic system which means it is always changing. Monitoring everything is too difficult to do and the results would be too complicated to interpret. This is why indicator species are useful.

QUESTIONS

5 Give **one** piece of evidence that sulphur dioxide is affecting lichen distribution.

6 Which lichen studied is most tolerant of acid gases?

7 Why are indicator species useful in studying complex dynamic systems?

Nice tan!

You will find out:
- What causes skin cancer
- How to protect yourself against skin cancer

Healthy – or not?

Everyone wants a Hollywood tan – but is it healthy? Sunlight is good – but too much causes the skin to age more rapidly and can cause cancer. And the situation is getting worse – pollution has damaged the ozone layer which protects the Earth from dangerous UV light. Should we just stay indoors nowadays?

Cancer alert

In the early 1980s doctors in Scotland began to notice a rise in the number of **skin cancer** patients they were seeing. The cancers, called **melanomas**, tended to appear on areas of the body that were only exposed during the summer. What could be causing this? Some clues began to appear.

- The late 1970s and early 1980s saw the start of cheap flights to the Spanish holiday resorts. The number of Scottish people taking foreign holidays there increased significantly.

- The typical complexion in Scotland is pale. This offers plenty of protection against the pale Scottish sun but burns very easily in the hot Spanish summer.

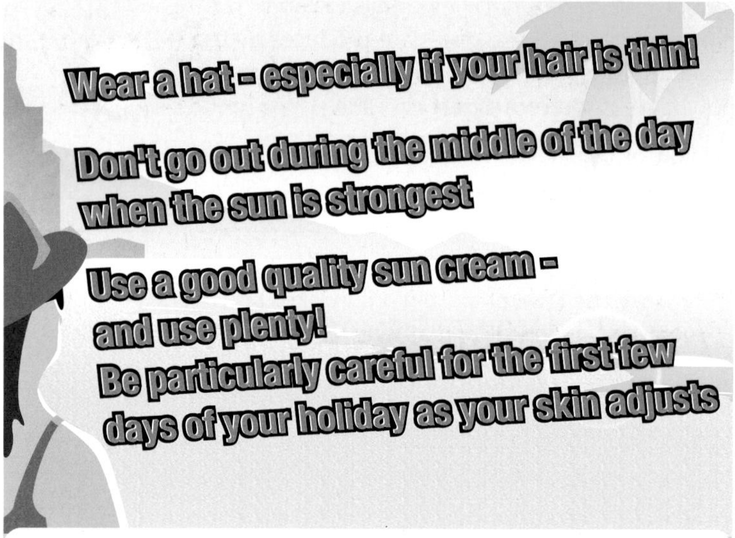

Doctors suggested that people from cooler climates, like Scotland, were at risk if they went to a hot, sunny country like Spain and exposed themselves to bright sunlight. Their skin could not protect them from the dangerous **UV light** and this caused skin cancers.

Doctors offered advice on safe sunbathing and encouraged people to come to see them if they discovered any strange markings on their skin.

Wear a hat – especially if your hair is thin!

Don't go out during the middle of the day when the sun is strongest

Use a good quality sun cream – and use plenty!
Be particularly careful for the first few days of your holiday as your skin adjusts

FIGURE 1: Advice offered by doctors on safe sunbathing.

■ QUESTIONS ■

1. What is a melanoma?
2. Why did the rate of skin cancer rise in the 1980s in Scotland?
3. Why were Scottish people particularly prone to skin cancer compared with local Spanish people?
4. List **four** pieces of good advice to help you avoid skin cancer.

...chlorofluorocarbons   ...melanoma

UV light and skin

Sunlight is certainly a mixed blessing. In many ways it is good for us. Ultraviolet radiation in sunlight drives reactions in our skin that produce the brown pigment melanin – which gives us the tan. Other reactions produce vitamin D which helps to build strong teeth and bones. Some sorts of skin complaints also improve with sunlight. Unfortunately other reactions produce chemicals called free radicals which can lead to cancer and cell damage.

UV light and ozone

Ozone is a gas with the chemical formula O_3. At ground level it is a dangerous pollutant but high in the atmosphere it is useful because it absorbs UV light and acts as a giant 'sunscreen' for the Earth.

The ozone layer in the stratosphere has been around from before life evolved on Earth. It shows natural cycles, but in the 1970s scientists began to detect falls in the concentration of ozone in the ozone layer – and a consequent increase in the levels of UV light reaching the Earth's surface. What was causing this decrease?

Suspicions were raised about a group of chemicals called **chlorofluorocarbons** or CFCs. UV light breaks down CFC molecules to release chlorine which reacts with ozone. Over many years CFCs had been rising through the atmosphere to the ozone layer and destroying it. It was only in the 1970s that it reached such a level that scientist could measure it.

In 1987 the countries that used the most CFCs agreed to phase out the chemicals over the next 30 years. This agreement was known as the Montreal Protocol. Scientists have shown that Montreal will have prevented 19 million cases of skin cancer, 1.5 million cancer deaths and 130 million cases of blindness by 2050. Scientists hope that the ozone layer itself will have recovered by 2050.

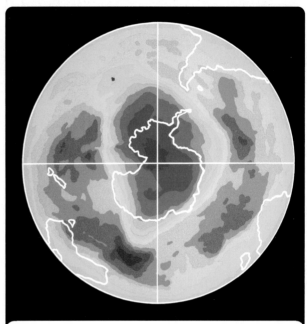

FIGURE 2: The ozone hole over Antarctica was first seen in 1980. It has been growing ever since. The ozone layer in the atmosphere is thinnest over the poles.

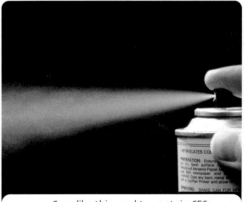

FIGURE 3: Cans like this used to contain CFCs. The use of CFCs was banned after they were found to have damaged the ozone layer.

▦▦▦ QUESTIONS ▦▦▦

5 Give **two** advantages of UV light to health.

6 What is the formula of ozone?

7 Where is the ozone layer?

8 When did scientists begin to detect damage to the ozone layer? How did they detect this damage?

9 What is the Montreal Protocol and when was it agreed?

...ozone   ...skin cancer   ...UV light

Where there's muck

You will find out:
- How sewage can damage the environment
- About biological oxygen demand (BOD) and why it is important

Unfit for bathing!

Some of the rivers in our cities are so polluted that there are signs warning people not to go swimming in them! The danger is not drowning but catching a disease! In fact, things have got much better over the last few years – but you wouldn't catch me drinking water straight from the Thames!

Sources of pollution

Every day we wash millions of tonnes of human waste down the toilet – this has to go somewhere. Normally it is carried to **sewage** works where it is treated and then the waste water is passed into rivers. When all is working well this is not a problem. However, things do go wrong:

- Very dry weather can reduce the flow of water in the rivers. Less water flow means the waste is not diluted so much when it enters the river.

- Sewage works become overloaded by a short-term event. The millions of people who go to Cornwall every summer for a seaside holiday can produce more waste than the sewage systems designed for the local population can handle.

- Sometimes the rain floods the drains and pushes material through the sewage works too quickly. Rain running off fields that have been treated with fertilisers (such as **phosphates** and **nitrates**) or manure can also carry waste into rivers before it can be taken up by plants.

FIGURE 1: A perfect place for a Cornish cream tea – the Jam Pot beach café, Gwithian. But what happens to the scones and strawberry jam after they've been through the holidaymakers?

▥ QUESTIONS ▥

1. What normally happens to sewage flushed down the toilet?
2. Why might a dry summer cause problems for sewage works?
3. Why do Cornwall and Devon have a particular problem with sewage in the summer months?

...biological oxygen demand ...microorganisms

What's the problem with sewage? (H)

Sewage actually encourages the growth of **microorganisms** and these need lots of oxygen. The amount of oxygen needed to keep a watercourse healthy is called the **biological oxygen demand** or BOD. An increase in biological activity leads to an increase in BOD.

Fish are dependent on dissolved oxygen. If the microbes use up all of the oxygen, the fish die. Water plants need oxygen and even though they produce some by photosynthesis they can die if microbes are too active.

Dead bodies decay. This also requires oxygen. Large amounts of dead and decaying materials use up oxygen which kills more living things. Soon all that is left in the watercourse is a black sludge of decaying material and millions of decay organisms.

As time progresses the BOD decreases and the watercourse can recover. Flowing water in a river can bring fresh supplies of oxygen. Some water authorities will also pump oxygen into rivers or ponds to speed up this process.

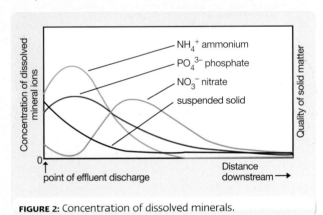

FIGURE 2: Concentration of dissolved minerals.

Table 1: Biological oxygen demand of wastes.

Liquid	BOD mg/l
Treated domestic sewage	20–60
Untreated domestic sewage	300–600
Yard washings from dairy farms	1000–2000
Cattle slurry	10 000–20 000
Milk	140 000

Table 2: Changes in oxygen levels downstream from sewage outlet.

Distance downstream m	Dissolved oxygen mg/l
0	16
10	9
20	5.5
30	5.1
40	6.8
50	8.2
60	10
70	11.2
80	12.4
90	13.2
100	14.5

QUESTIONS

4 Draw a graph to show the level of dissolved oxygen in the river water downstream from the sewage outlet.

5 Explain the shape of the oxygen graph you have drawn.

6 Design a piece of equipment to measure the amount of suspended solids in a sample of water.

7 Ponds are much more likely to be damaged by sewage than fast-flowing rivers. Why?

8 People find it easy to believe that raw sewage is a dangerous pollutant. They find it much more difficult to believe that milk is even more dangerous! Write a short article for a local newspaper explaining how milk can have a disastrous effect on a local pond.

...nitrates ...phosphates ...sewage

Recycle it!

You will find out:
- How degraded land can be brought back into productive use
- How we can avoid doing damage in the first place

Mountains of waste

Every person in Britain produces more than half a tonne of waste every year – that's about the same weight as a small family car! Most of this ends up as landfill. Rubbish is dumped in a large hole in the ground, covered over and left. **Waste disposal** is out of sight, out of mind. But we're running out of holes to fill...

The size of the problem

Material	Potential for recycling
Glass	Very good, reuse of glass is quite easy and saves up to 25 per cent of the energy needed to make fresh glass.
Paper	Easily recycled – almost all of the paper used in newspapers and cardboard is recycled in the UK.
Plastics	Difficult to recycle. Each different type of plastic needs to be treated in a slightly different way. Sorting plastics into different types is a major problem for consumers.
Metals	Technology is straightforward. Over 50 per cent of copper in the United States is recycled. Both copper and lead have a high value so people will collect items for recycling.
Wood	Most wood is not recycled because it cannot be separated from other building materials. Scrap wood is usually burnt on site – even the energy in the wood is wasted.

FIGURE 1: How much of this could be recycled?

In a single year in the UK:

- every family throws away 330 glass bottles and jars
- every person gets through 290 plastic carrier bags
- every family throws away 4 kg of waste paper every week
- the weight of the nappies thrown away is the same as 70,000 double decker buses.

QUESTIONS

1. Which is probably the easiest material to recycle?
2. Which is probably the most difficult to recycle? Why?
3. Should manufacturers be forced to make simple packaging that can be easily recycled?

...incinerator   ...landfill site

Recycle or reuse? (H)

Recycling is not as straightforward as it seems. There are extra energy costs to recycling because it is a much more complex process than simply burning or burying rubbish. So, should we recycle, burn or bury our rubbish? Here are some facts and opinions to think about.

Recycling is all very well – but we need to start reusing instead. Why make a bottle, use it once then destroy it to make another bottle?

Recycling just makes us feel good. It's not even environmentally friendly! Think of the energy used driving to recycling centres, collecting materials, reprocessing them...

Recycling is essential if we are to survive. The **landfill sites** are filling up. They all produce methane as the rubbish decays – and that increases global warming. We have no choice – we must recycle.

Recycled aluminium uses only 5 per cent of the energy needed for new aluminium.

Recycled glass needs 25 per cent less energy to manufacture than new glass.

Britain has a green glass mountain! It exports broken bottles to the continent because there are no uses for them in this country.

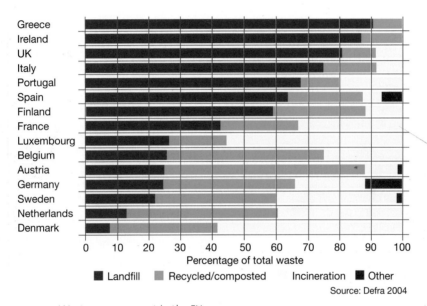

FIGURE 2: Waste management in the EU.

Source: Defra 2004

Percentage of total waste

■ Landfill   ■ Recycled/composted   Incineration   ■ Other

It makes more sense to **incinerate** waste. It's very energy efficient and we can generate power using waste. Modern incinerators have very good filters to stop poisonous wastes getting into the air. It's a win–win situation!

Production of recycled paper uses 80 per cent less water, 65 per cent less energy and produces 95 per cent less air pollution than virgin paper production.

QUESTIONS

4 List the advantages of each approach to tackling rubbish.

5 List the disadvantages of each approach to tackling rubbish.

6 Which countries in the EU use landfill more than the UK?

7 Which country in the EU has the highest rate of recycling or composting of rubbish?

8 Prepare a recommendation for the government about how to deal with our rubbish. It should be under 200 words and include at least one chart and table of data. You may need to do some research on the internet to gather up-to-date facts and figures.

Last chance?

You will find out:

- How humans change the environment
- Why some changes threaten other species
- How use of resources can damage species far away

Dangerously busy?

We seem to have no time nowadays. Everyone is working hard making things, using up resources and producing wastes. This is not always a bad thing – we call it progress. Sometimes, however, the effect we have on the environment is so dangerous that we may be destroying the conditions we need to survive. Are we working the Earth into an early grave?

Extinctions

Extinctions have been happening for as long as life has existed on Earth. Most of the species that have existed are now extinct. It is a natural process driven by evolution as better adapted species replace older ones. However, the rate of extinctions, particularly amongst mammals, has increased dramatically recently. Is this due to human activity?

Only the cute survive

The public collect money for pandas, whales and koala bears but don't seem interested in saving shellfish or some sorts of worms. Birdwatchers will march to protect the habitats of endangered bird species and even ice cream manufacturers are now selling 'Rainforest fruits' ice cream which uses fruits from the rainforest and donates part of the profits to help in conservation. If you're cute or appeal to a special interest group – you survive.

Scientists are no better. Their interest in the obscure or unusual means that 'ordinary' species are lost without anyone noticing. If there is no research grant available then no one cares.

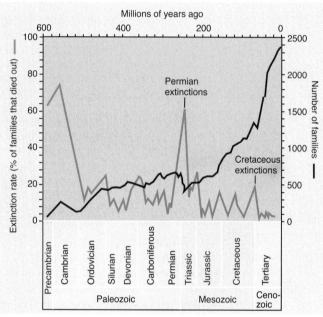

FIGURE 1: Extinctions are a natural part of life on Earth.

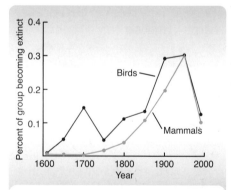

FIGURE 2: Recently the rate of extinctions is rising - at the same time as human impact on the Earth is rising. Coincidence?

▪▪ QUESTIONS ▪▪

1. What does the word 'extinction' mean?
2. Not all extinctions are caused by human activity. Give **two** pieces of evidence to support this idea.
3. What is the biggest known cause of extinction?
4. Why do you think the rate of extinction of mammals and birds has actually started to fall?
5. Which sorts of species are easiest to protect? Why does this cause problems?

...conservation   ...copper

Less from more? (H)

Conservation of plant and animal species is not enough by itself. We also need to look at how we are using up the Earth if we are not to destroy the planet. **Copper** is a crucially important metal. It illustrates one of the problems with human exploitation of the Earth. The highest grade copper ores have been used so modern mines are digging out lower and lower quality ores. This creates two problems:

- More material must be processed – this creates a bigger mine and more environmental damage.

- More energy must be used in the mining and processing of the ore to make copper – this leads to increased global warming.

- Both of these factors increase the impact of the human **population** on the planet.

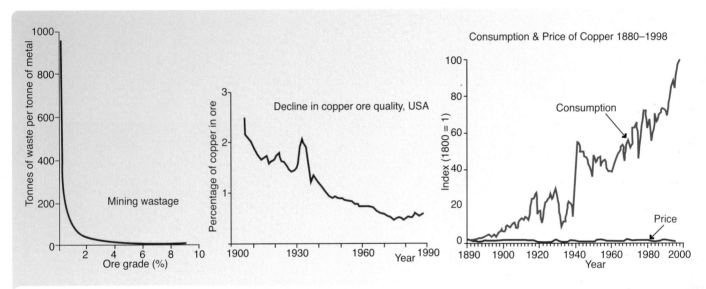

FIGURE 3: The changing use of copper metal over the last few hundred years.

The increase in **global temperature** is threatening these bluebells with extinction. If the trees produce leaves earlier in the year because of warmer weather, the bluebells will not be able to get enough light to grow and reproduce.

FIGURE 4: Bluebells in flower.

QUESTIONS

6 What has happened to copper consumption over the last hundred years?

7 How would the graph be different if the cost of copper had changed at the same rate?

8 Why does a fall in the reserves of copper cause a problem for bluebells?

9 Some environmentalists suggest an increase in the cost of resources like copper and crude oil would be good for the environment. Why do you think they suggest this?

10 Do you agree that more expensive resources might be the only way to save the planet?

...extinction ...global temperature ...population

Unit summary

All organisms are adapted to the area where they live. More extreme environments require more extreme adaptations.

Populations rise and fall in response to changes in the external environment.

Competition between species helps to keep populations under control. The strongest competition occurs between members of the same species.

Human activity has significant effects on the environment. The size of these effects tends to rise with population resource and energy use.

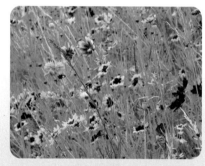

Recycling materials can reduce human impact on the Earth to some extent.

Photosynthesis provides all food across the globe. Farming and food production technologies all seek to maximise the original capture of energy by green plants.

Human impact now occurs on a global scale, e.g. through global warming and ozone layer destruction.

Fertilisers help plants to grow. Sometimes there is a conflict between the use of materials for fertiliser and fuel (e.g. yak faeces in Tibet).

Global warming appears to be caused by a disturbance in the global carbon cycle caused by human use of fossil fuels.

Unit quiz

1 Who first invented tea?

2 Rice, wheat, barley, maize, and oats all belong to which botanical family?

3 Give two differences between plant and animal cells.

4 The molecule needed for photosynthesis is called chlorophyll, chloroplast, chloroquinone or chloral hydrate?

5 A lack of the mineral nitrogen in soil causes what to happen to plants?

6 Active transport requires an energy input by the organism. True or false?

7 Why are fish more efficient converters of food into meat than cows?

8 Which process removes carbon dioxide from the air?

9 Which two processes put carbon dioxide into the air?

10 What is the main greenhouse gas?

11 What caused most deaths in the Irish Potato Famine of the 1840s?

12 What are the three adaptations of the Angler Fish to its life at the bottom of the ocean?

13 What is the difference between coppicing and reforestation?

14 Give three factors that affect the size of a local population.

15 What do plants typically compete for in the UK?

16 What was a 'pea souper'?

17 What is an 'indicator species'?

18 What is the ozone layer?

19 Give one advantage of recycling paper.

20 What does the word 'extinct' mean?

Numeracy activity

The world population is increasing by just over 1 per cent annually – that's about 60 million new mouths to feed every year. Fortunately, food production is increasing at a slightly higher rate so the world has more food now per head of population than 20 years ago. And yet 5 million children die of starvation every year according to UN figures. Why is this?

Famines and disasters occur every year. Unexpected weather can lead to many deaths, particularly in countries without large stores of food or resources to deal with these events. Wars and revolutions are also major causes of food insecurity, and it is in countries with unstable governments that the percentage of the population without adequate food has increased over the last few decades.

Food production per head has increased more in developing countries than in developed countries, but increasingly large amounts of this food is being shipped from poorer countries to richer countries. Crops are selected for export rather than home consumption. The money earned from export crops ensures that the producers get the best land, supplies of fertilisers and so on. So, an increase in food production can lead to a decrease in food availability in the producer countries – particularly for the poorer sections of the population.

QUESTIONS

1 How many children die of starvation every year according to UN figures?

2 Which areas of the world have shown the fastest growth in food production per head of the population?

3 How can an increase in food production mean a decrease in food availability for local people?

4 What factors can create food insecurity? Organise these into two groups: those that are due to 'natural events' over which we have no control and those that are created by the way people behave.

Exam practice questions

1 Animals and plants are composed of cells. There are similarities and differences between animal and plant cells. In the table, tick (✓) boxes to show features that can occur in cells. One feature has been done for you.

Feature	Animal cells	Plant cells
Nucleus	✓	✓
Cell membrane		
Cellulose cell wall		
Cytoplasm		
Chloroplast		
Large vacuole		

[4]

2 The diagram shows the relative numbers of three species of aquatic organisms in a lake.

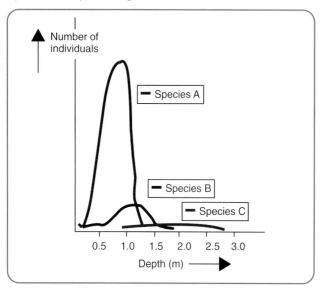

a Species A is a plant (producer). Using information from the graph, give two reasons that support this fact.

....

.... [2]

b In the space below, draw a pyramid of biomass for the three species in the graph. [2]

c A farmer accidentally released some nitrate fertiliser into the lake. Which species of organism is likely to have the highest concentration of nitrate in their tissues? Explain your answer.

....

....

.... [3]

3 Nitrogen is circulated in the environment. This circulation involves several processes. Use words from the box to complete the following sentences about these processes.

> decompose   nitrogen   nitrates   proteins
> ammonium   denitrifying   nitrifying   nitrogen-fixing

Nitrogen in the soil is taken up by plant roots in the form of .... Plants use this form of nitrogen to make .... , which are eaten by animals. When plants and animals die, they .... , and release ammonium compounds. These are broken down by .... bacteria. The bacteria form nitrates, which are released back into the soil. [4]

4 Below are some words about human impacts on the environment. Draw **one** straight line from each word to its description.

Acid rain	Warming of the atmosphere, caused by gases that 'trap' heat
Air pollutant	Caused by certain pollutants, such as sulphur dioxide, which dissolve in rain
Ozone layer	Accumulates in the upper atmosphere, where it traps UV light
Greenhouse effect	Toxic waste substances released into the air

[3]

5 Water is an essential resource for human populations. The graph compares water supply (from rain and snow) with consumption by the human population in a region of Canada.

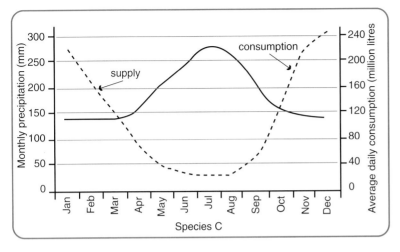

Species C

b During which month was water consumption at its highest?

.... [1]

c Briefly describe **one** way in which humans can increase water supply.

.... [1]

d Briefly describe **one** way in which humans can lower water consumption.

.... [3]

(Total 21 marks)

a When demand for water is high, is the supply of water high or low?

.... [1]

Worked example

The diagram shows the effect of light intensity on the rate of photosynthesis.

a Describe the effect of light intensity on the rate of photosynthesis.

b What light intensity results in a rate of photosynthesis of 3 units?

c Briefly explain why the rate of photosynthesis does not increase at light intensities above 4 units.

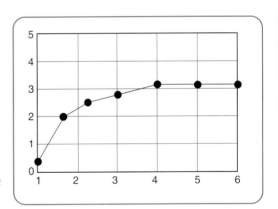

This answer is not complete. At higher light intensities, there is no further increase in the rate of photosynthesis. Avoid simple, short answers when more than one mark is available!

a As the light intensity increases, the rate of photosynthesis also increases.

b 3.5 units

c There is a limiting factor that prevents a further increase in the rate of photosynthesis. For example, there may not be enough CO_2 available for photosynthesis.

This is a very good answer, because it refers to 'limiting factor' and uses an example.

Overall Grade: B

How to get an A

In questions for which there is more than one mark available, a simple statement will not be enough to gain maximum marks.

Chemistry 2a

DISCOVER ELEMENTS!

Believe it or not, this is a periodic table! Each circle contains an element's chemical symbol and atomic number. Elements with similar chemistry occur in the same spoke and some of the different groups are colour coded.

There are millions of different chemical substances. Yet only about 90 elements make up all natural chemicals, and most of the man-made ones too.

Elements react together to make chemical compounds. The properties of these compounds are often very different from the elements from which they are made.

Pa 91
U 92
Np 93
Pu 94
Am 95
Cm 96
Bk 97
Cf 98
Es 99
Fm 100
Md 101
No 102
Lr 103
Rf 104

La 57
Ce 58
Pr 59
Nd 60
Pm 61
Sm 62
Eu 63
Gd 64
Tb 65
Dy 66
Ho 67
Er 68
Tm 69
Yb 70
Lu 71
Hf 72
Ta 73

Sr 38
Ca 20
Mg 12

Sc 21
Ti 22
V 23
Cr 24
Mn 25
Fe 26
Y 39
Zr 40
Nb 41
Mo 42
Tc 43
Ru 44
W 74
Re 75
Os 76
Hs 108
Bh 107
Db

Fr
87

Rn
86

At
85

?
117

Xe
54

I
53

Why do chemical elements react together? How do they do this?

99.5% of the human body is made up of about 13 different chemical elements. These, and tiny amounts of a few others, are all that are needed to make your very own human from scratch!

?
116

Kr
36

Br
35

Ar
18

Cl
17

Po
84

Ne
10

F
9

Na
11

He
2

Li
3

S
16

n
0

O
8

H
1

N
7

P
15

As
33

C
6

B
5

Si
14

Al
13

Ge
32

Sn
50

Ga
31

Pb
82

Zn
30

Ni
28

Cu
29

In
49

Cd
48

Tl
81

Ag
47

Pd
46

Hg
80

?
113

Au
79

Pt
78

Uub
112

Why are some chemical elements found in nature as compounds, whereas others are found as elements?

Rg
111

Ds
110

CONTENTS

Oil matters

You will find out:
- That oil is important to our lifestyle
- That oil supplies may run out in our lifetime
- That carbon can form many compounds

Dependence on oil

Our lives depend on a ready supply of petrol, plastics and many other cruide oil products. Crude oil formed from the bodies of tiny sea creatures that died millions of years ago.

It took a long time to form crude oil, and we are using it up pretty fast! Before the Earth's oil supplies run out, we need to find other sources of energy and the many chemicals we make from oil.

What's the price of petrol?

Lots of people drive cars and are worried about the cost of petrol or diesel. Petrol and diesel are fuels made from **crude oil**.

As oil supplies start to run out, the prices at petrol stations will keep going up and up. This will cause many problems all over the world – can you think of some?

FIGURE 1: A North Sea oil rig.

Many other useful substances are also made from crude oil, such as plastics. Bottles, bags, food wrappings, computer cases, window frames and baths are all made of plastics. How would your life be different if you could not use plastics?

Some new cars can burn **natural gas**, 'biodiesel' made from vegetable oil, or hydrogen gas. These fuels do not come from crude oil and can be made more easily.

In the future we will see many different ways of making energy as the Earth's crude oil runs out.

Looking into the future:

- Coal, oil and gas power stations may close down.
- Our electricity may come from wind, wave, solar or nuclear power.
- We may have to stop burning oil products, so we can use the oil for plastics and other chemicals.

FIGURE 2: Filling up is costing more.

QUESTIONS

1 Why is crude oil important to our lives?
2 What was crude oil formed from?
3 What could happen when oil starts to run out?
4 What other sources of energy could be used?

FIGURE 3: We take plastics for granted.

...*carbon* ...*crude oil* ...*exothermic*

Carbon – an amazing element

Crude oil contains thousands of different compounds, most of which are based around one very special element: **carbon**. How can carbon form so many different compounds?

Carbon is in the middle of the periodic table, in group 4, and can use its four outer electrons to form four covalent bonds. Carbon atoms can make bonds with other carbon atoms, as well as hydrogen, oxygen and many other elements.

All the life on our planet is carbon-based. Every plant and animal, from a small cell to a huge elephant, is made up of complicated carbon compounds.

When tiny creatures in prehistoric seas died, they fell to the bottom. They were covered with sediment, squashed and 'cooked' for millions of years. The complicated compounds in the creatures were broken down over time to simpler ones. These simpler carbon compounds made crude oil and natural gas.

Many people use natural gas in their home for cooking and heating. Natural gas is a compound of carbon called **methane**.

FIGURE 4: Gas is easy to cook with.

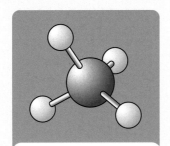

FIGURE 5: Methane contains just five atoms.

Methane contains one carbon atom bonded to four hydrogen atoms. It is the simplest possible **hydrocarbon**. A hydrocarbon is a compound that contains only hydrogen and carbon atoms.

- There are thousands of different hydrocarbons in crude oil.
- Carbon and hydrogen are non-metals so they bond covalently.
- Carbon atoms can bond to other carbon atoms, forming chains and complicated structures.
- There are millions of carbon compounds – these are the basis for life.
- Our bodies, and all plants and animals are made of carbon-based compounds.

> ⬛ **QUESTIONS** ⬛
>
> 5   Why is carbon able to form four bonds?
> 6   Name another element that can make four bonds.
> 7   What is a hydrocarbon?
> 8   What is the simplest hydrocarbon of all?

> **EXAM HINTS AND TIPS**
>
> Life depends on the ability of carbon molecules to form long chains and a huge range of complex molecules.

Hodge Hill School
Bromford Road
Hodge Hill
Birmingham
B36 8HB

Fuels of the future?

Hydrogen is sometimes called the 'fuel of the future' because it is seen as a very 'clean' fuel. Hydrogen gas has the formula H_2 because each molecule contains two atoms.

Hydrogen burns in oxygen to produce only one product, water:

$$2H_2 + O_2 \rightarrow 2H_2O$$

Hydrogen gives off a lot of energy when it is burnt: reactions that give off energy are called **exothermic**.

Many cars in Brazil, and some elsewhere run on pure ethanol because ethanol can be made from sugar cane. When sugar cane grows, it absorbs carbon dioxide from the atmosphere. This is the balanced symbol equation for the combustion of ethanol:

$$C_2H_5OH + 3O_2 \rightarrow 2CO_2 + 3H_2O$$

> ▦ **QUESTIONS** ▦
>
> 9   Why would hydrogen be more environmentally friendly as a fuel than petrol?
> 10 What might be a problem of using hydrogen gas in cars?
> 11 Give an example of an exothermic reaction that is not a combustion.
> 12 Why does burning ethanol made from sugar cane not affect the amount of carbon dioxide in the atmosphere?

What is in oil?

You will find out:

- About two types of hydrocarbons, alkanes and alkenes
- About the four smallest alkanes
- About the structures of some alkenes

Gases at home and away

Most homes have natural gas (methane) pipe to them. People in remote areas, caravans or boats use cylinders of propane gas instead (e.g. 'Calor gas'). Maybe you have a gas barbecue or 'Camping Gaz' stove. Some motor vehicles run on LPG (liquefied petroleum gas) instead of petrol or diesel. It's a mixture of propane and butane.

The alkanes end in -ane

The gases named above all end in the letters -ane. They are members of the same 'family', the **alkanes**.

- Alkanes are hydrocarbons. They contain only hydrogen and carbon atoms, joined by single covalent bonds. Carbon always forms four bonds.
- The four simplest alkanes are methane, ethane, propane and butane.
- If you see a compound ending in -ane, it's probably an alkane (though there are exceptions). It's like a chemistry code, but it's easy to break!

Crude oil contains thousands of different alkanes. They are separated into fractions in a refinery. Each fraction contains a different mixtures of alkanes. As the alkanes get bigger, the fractions get darker and heavier.

Hydrocarbon	No. of carbon atoms	State
methane	1	gas
ethane	2	gas
propane	3	gas
butane	4	gas
octane	8	liquid
paraffin	about 20	thick liquid
bitumen	more than 50	solid

The table shows the formulae of the four smallest alkanes and two ways of drawing their molecules. The carbons are joined by single bonds. Long carbon chains can be built up in this way. Hydrocarbons containing only single bonds are said to be **saturated hydrocarbons**.

FIGURE 1: Gas cylinder fuelling a barbecue.

QUESTIONS

1 What is the smallest alkane?
2 What is methane used for?
3 What is the connection between the number of carbon atoms and the state of the hydrocarbon?

Watch Out 'Saturated' doesn't mean 'wet'. It means alkanes cannot soak up extra atoms. Alkenes can add atoms across their double bond.

...addition   ...alkanes   ...alkenes   ...double bond   ...greenhouse gas

The alkenes end in –ene

Some hydrocarbons have names ending in -ene. They are members of another family called **alkenes**. These are hydrocarbons that contain a **double bond** – that is, two covalent bonds between the same carbon atoms. Crude oil doesn't contain alkenes, but large amounts are produced during refining.

- The simplest alkene is ethene, C_2H_4, with two carbon and four hydrogen atoms. In industry, it is often called ethylene.
- Notice that each carbon still makes four bonds: the double bond is two bonds.
- The next smallest alkene is propene, C_3H_6.
- Hydrocarbons containing double bonds are said to be **unsaturated hydrocarbons**.
- Other types of organic compounds also contain carbon–carbon double bonds They too are described as 'unsaturated'.

ethene

propene

Detecting double bonds

Double bonds can break open easily. This makes alkenes more reactive than alkanes. One such reaction is used to test whether a compound contains a C=C double bond. The test therefore distinguishes between alkenes and alkanes.

- To a sample of the hydrocarbon in a test tube, add a few cubic centimetres of bromine water – an orange-brown solution of bromine in water.
- Stopper the tube and shake well. If the bromine goes colourless, the compound contains a C=C double bond – it is an unsaturated hydrocarbon.
- If the compound is a hydrocarbon, this shows it's an alkene, not an alkane. However, the test works for any substance containing a C=C, such as an unsaturated vegetable oil, not just for alkenes.

This is an **addition** reaction. We say the bromine 'adds across' the double bond, which opens up leaving a single C–C bond. New bonds form between the carbon and bromine atoms. The orange bromine molecules, Br_2, are used up, so the colour disappears.

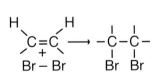

FIGURE 2: Bromine water decolorised by shaking with a gas jar of ethane.

Burning issues

Most of the crude oil extracted ends up being distilled and processed into fuels such as petrol, diesel, kerosene and fuel oil. These fuels are burned to provide heat and motion.

The trouble with burning these hydrocarbons is that the **greenhouse gas** carbon dioxide is given off. Greenhouse gases are causing global warming.

- Hydrocarbons burn in oxygen to produce carbon dioxide and water.
- If there is not enough oxygen present, a poisonous compound called carbon monoxide is formed.
- With even less oxygen, soot (carbon) forms.
- The formula of carbon dioxide is CO_2, and the formula of carbon monoxide is CO. Can you see why they have these names?

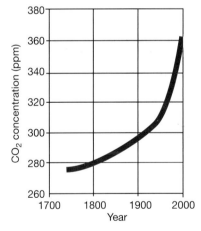

FIGURE 3: Increase in atmospheric carbon dioxide during and since the Industrial Revolution.

⬛⬛⬛ QUESTIONS ⬛⬛⬛

4 Why are the alkenes more reactive than the alkanes?

5 Suggest the name and formula of the next alkene in the series C_2H_4, C_3H_6, ….

6 Why are there fewer hydrogen atoms in ethene, C_2H_4, than in ethane, C_2H_6?

7 How could you tell whether petrol contained any alkenes?

⬛⬛⬛ QUESTIONS ⬛⬛⬛

8 Find out **three** problems that global warming could cause.

9 What product is *always* formed as a product when a hydrocarbon is burnt?

10 Why must gas heaters and cookers be well ventilated?

…saturated hydrocarbons   …unsaturated hydrocarbons

Oils and fats

You will find out:
- About saturated and unsaturated oils and fats
- About polyunsaturated and mono-unsaturated oils

Chips and cheese

We all know how chips are made: they are fried in vegetable oil. Margarine is also made from vegetable oil but there is a big difference. Margarine has to be a solid – though some brands are more solid than others. You may have seen the words 'polyunsaturates' and 'mono-unsaturates' on your tubs of soft margarine. Hard margarines contain 'saturated' fats. So do milk, butter and cheese. But what do these terms mean?

Pingu

Mono or poly?

We have seen that 'saturated' hydrocarbons contain only single bonds. 'Unsaturated' hydrocarbons contain carbon–carbon double bonds. The same applies to oils and fats.

- **Saturated** fats have no C=C double bonds.
- Vegetable oil molecules with one double bond are **mono-unsaturated**.
- Oil molecules with more than one double bond are **polyunsaturated**. ('Mono' means 'one'; 'poly' means 'many'.)

Polyunsaturated oils are thought to be more healthy because they reduce cholesterol, but scientists aren't sure. Body chemistry is very complicated!

FIGURE 1: Margarines often say 'high in polyunsaturates' or 'high in mono-unsaturates'. What is the difference?

Hard or soft?

Saturated fats tend to be solids at room temperature. Animal fats, for example lard and butter, are mainly saturated. Unsaturated fats tend to be liquids, for example, vegetable oils.

- Fats are solid, oils are liquid. Margarines contain both.
- Hard margarines contain more saturated fats. Soft ones contain more unsaturated oils. 'Low-fat' spreads contain less of both, and more water.
- Unsaturated oils are not as bad for you as saturated fats!

The table shows some fats and oils in order of the amount of saturated fat.

FIGURE 2: Butter is a fat, but becomes an oil when it melts.

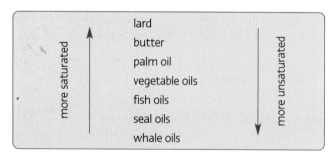

more saturated ↑		more unsaturated ↓
	lard	
	butter	
	palm oil	
	vegetable oils	
	fish oils	
	seal oils	
	whale oils	

'Unsaturated' refers to any compounds with carbon–carbon double bonds – not just oils and fats or alkene hydrocarbons.

Watch Out

▫ QUESTIONS ▫

1. Name **two** foods high in saturated fat, and **two** oils high in unsaturates.
2. What is the difference between mono-unsaturated and polyunsaturated?
3. Which type of fats or oils is supposed to be the least bad for you?

...catalyst   ...hydrogenate   ...mono-unsaturated

Hydrogenated vegetable oils – what are they?

Being unsaturated makes most vegetable oils liquid at room temperature. The double bonds in their carbon chains make the molecules less flexible. They don't fit together so well as the bendy chains in saturated fats. So, they can't hold on to each other so well.

This makes unsaturated molecules easier to separate. They therefore have lower melting points, and are less **viscous** (more runny), than saturated fats.

	Room temperature	State in the refrigerator
Saturates	solid	solid
Mono-unsaturates	liquid	semi-solid
Polyunsaturates	liquid	liquid

FIGURE 3: Why is this cooking oil liquid?

Liquid vegetable oils are good for cooking, but not for spreading on bread. To solve this problem, manufacturers **hydrogenate** vegetable oils to solidify them.

- They heat the oil to about 200 °C, and add small particles of nickel to act as a **catalyst** (see below). They then bubble hydrogen gas through the mixture.
- The nickel causes hydrogen to add across the double bonds. That means the double bonds open up, and an extra hydrogen atom bonds to the carbon atom on each side. This makes the carbon chain saturated.

$$\underset{\text{Unsaturated oil}}{\underset{\text{(liquid)}}{\overset{H}{\underset{H}{C}}=\overset{H}{\underset{H}{C}}}} + H_2 \xrightarrow[\text{and heat}]{\text{nickel catalyst}} \underset{\text{saturated fat}}{\underset{\text{(solid)}}{-\overset{|}{\underset{|}{C}}-\overset{|}{\underset{|}{C}}-}}$$

- Nickel works like lubricating oil in a machine. It makes the reaction faster, but it isn't used up. Substances that help reactions in this way are called catalysts.
- The manufacturers filter the hot mixture to remove the nickel and use it again.
- The saturated fat is used to make foods that need to remain solid at room temperature, such as margarine, chocolate, peanut butter, biscuits and cakes.

Sounds gross? Well it turns out that hydrogenating vegetable oils also helps to keep them from going off. So, hydrogenating vegetable oils is the reason why you can buy your favourite chocolate bar with a 'best before' date over a year away!

FIGURE 4: The oil from sunflower seeds is used as cooking oil and to make margarine.

████ QUESTIONS ████

4   Which have the higher melting points, fats or oils?

5   Which transition metal is used in the hydrogenation process?

6   What kind of products use hydrogenated vegetable oil?

EXAM HINTS AND TIPS

Hydrogenation is an additon reaction – adding a hydrogen molecule across a double bond.

Energy in our diet

- 'Diet' simply means what we eat – we all have a diet, whether or not we are watching what we eat!

- Energy is measured in kilojoules (kJ), or in kilocalories (kcal). Most food labels now have to show how much energy they provide. For example, a Mars bar provides 965 kJ (230 kcal).

- Fats and carbohydrates (including sugars) are the main sources of energy in our diet. Fats, whether unsaturated or saturated, provide about 37 kJ per gram.

- Adult men and women should eat about 10 500 and 8500 kJ a day, respectively from a mixture of the three main types of food – not all from fats or sugars. Most teenagers are still growing and may need more energy than this!

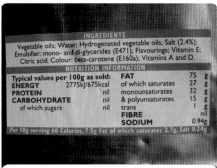

FIGURE 5: Margarine or butter? How can you tell? Not from the energy.

████ QUESTIONS ████

7   What is the third type of food, besides fats and carbohydrates?

8   Is butter more fattening than margarine? Why or why not?

9   How many kilocalories per day should an adult woman eat?

Chemical codes

Simple symbols

Symbols are simple shapes that represent something without using words. They mean the same thing in any language. All over the world, ☦, ☪ and ✡ represent Christianity, Islam and Judaism. Similarly, everyone uses £, € and $ instead of writing 'pounds', 'euros' or 'dollars'. Symbols help people communicate without needing to speak each other's language. The alchemists used chemical symbols, but it was difficult to describe chemical reactions with them.

Compound interest

Alchemists' symbols didn't show what was in a substance. Chemists became interested in finding out what compounds are made of. To show this they needed symbols that they could easily combine into formulae. The symbols we use today were introduced in 1814.

- 114 elements are now known. Each has a number and a symbol. Element number 1 is hydrogen, H; 6 is carbon, C; and 12 is magnesium, Mg.
- Symbols are short versions of the name – but not always in English. Fe, Ag and Pb mean iron, silver and lead – *fer*, *argent* and *plombe* in French.
- The letters are true symbols. They can be used in any language. Even Japanese chemists use O for oxygen, C for carbon and H_2O for water. Their equations look just like ours.

Chemists are interested in making **compounds**. A compound contains two or more elements bonded together. You will learn more about bonding later.

- If a compound contains a metal and a non-metal, for example, MgO, magnesium oxide, the bonding is **ionic**.
- When two non-metals bond together, as in methane, CH_4, or water, H_2O, the bonding is **covalent**.
- The **formula** of a compound tells you what it is made up of.

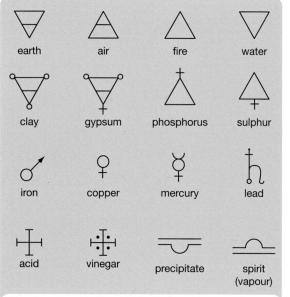

FIGURE 1: A few alchemists' symbols. What else do the iron and copper symbols stand for? Why do you think 'precipitate' and 'spirit' are opposites?

▌▌ QUESTIONS ▌▌

1 What is the symbol for oxygen?
2 Which element has the symbol Fe?
3 What is the chemical formula of water?
4 What is the difference between CO and CO_2?

'*Chemical symbols can be used in any language*'

...addition   ...compounds   ...covalent   ...formula   ...hydration   ...ionic

Breaking the chemical code

What's the best way to describe a midsummer's day? A poem? A picture maybe. What's the best way to describe a chemical reaction? With words? No, because not everyone can read English.

The best way is by writing an equation, using symbols and formula. They're the same in any language, so people across the world can understand them. A **symbol equation** gives lots of information.

- The formulae tell us what substances reacted (the **reactants**) and what substances were made (the **products**).
- Small numbers in the formulae show the composition of each substance.
- Large numbers in front of each formula show how much of one reacts with a certain amount of the other, and how much of each product this gives.

Example: Let's see what this equation means:

$$C_2H_5OH + 3O_2 \rightarrow 2CO_2 + 3H_2O$$

- You probably recognise the formula. The reactants are ethanol and oxygen; the products are carbon dioxide and water.
- Numbers show that each molecule of ethanol:
  - reacts with three molecules of oxygen;
  - produces two molecules of carbon dioxide and three molecules of water.
- Adding state symbols shows that ethanol is a liquid (l), and the rest are gases (g), since combustion produces steam.

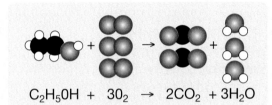

$$C_2H_5OH + 3O_2 \rightarrow 2CO_2 + 3H_2O$$

FIGURE 2: The ethanol combustion equation shown as models. Count the atoms of each type to check that the equation is balanced.

$$C_2H_5OH(l) + 3O_2(g) \rightarrow 2CO_2(g) + 3H_2O(g)$$

A balancing act

Equations must be balanced. There must be the same number of atoms of each element in the products as there were in the reactants: matter cannot be created or destroyed in a chemical reaction!

You have to get the formulae right first. Then balance by writing numbers in front of them. You *must not change* numbers in the formulae themselves. Try the questions below.

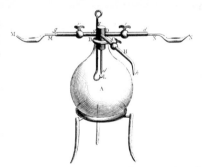

FIGURE 3: An experiment in 1784 when hydrogen was first burnt in air. A 'dew' of pure water formed in the vessel. This proved hydrogen burned to make water.

QUESTIONS

5   Write a word equation for hydrogen burning in oxygen.
6   Write a balanced symbol equation for hydrogen, H_2, burning in oxygen, O_2.
7   Balance the equation: $Na + Cl_2 \rightarrow NaCl$.
8   What do the state symbols (s), (l), (g) and (aq) mean?

Watch Out Whenever you write a symbol equation, count the atoms of each element on both sides to make sure it is balanced.

Adding atoms

Most reactions give two or more products, but some join two substances together to make a single product.

Unsaturated compounds become saturated by 'soaking up' more atoms. These are **addition** reactions – the other reactant adds across the C=C double bond.

- We hydrogenate oils to make margarine.

$$>C=C<(l) + H_2(g) \longrightarrow -\overset{|}{\underset{H}{C}}-\overset{|}{\underset{H}{C}}-(s)$$

- The bromine water test for C=C adds Br_2 instead of H_2.
- **Hydration** is similar. Alkenes don't react with water, but under suitable conditions steam adds across to form an alcohol.

$$>C=C<(g) + H_2O(g) \longrightarrow -\overset{|}{\underset{H}{C}}-\overset{|}{\underset{OH}{C}}-(l)$$

Ethene, from cracking petroleum, gives ethanol (industrial alcohol).

$$C_2H_4(g) + H_2O(g) \rightarrow C_2H_5OH(l)$$
ethene   steam   ethanol

- It needs high pressure, 200 °C and a catalyst to speed up the reaction. Other alkenes give different alcohols.

QUESTIONS

9   Why are hydrations called addition reactions?
10 How are equations for addition reactions different from most?
11 Write a symbol equation for the hydration of propene, C_3H_6. Name the product.

Cracking

You will find out:
- What happens to crude oil at an oil refinery
- What 'cracking' a hydrocarbon involves
- Why 'cracking' is important

There's not enough petrol to go round

Petrol is really important to us. Many millions of people have cars in the UK, and these are needed so that people can carry out their lives. However, crude oil doesn't have enough petrol in it! What do we do? Crude oil is 'cracked' to make smaller molecules, which are used to make more petrol – this process is very important.

A cracking process

The **fractions** of crude oil have lots of different uses. The lighter fractions such as petrol and kerosene contain small **hydrocarbons** and are the most useful to us. To make more of these smaller hydrocarbons, some of the larger hydrocarbons are split up using a special substance called a **catalyst** and high temperature. (These are the 'conditions' for the reaction.) This splitting-up process is called '**cracking**'.

You can think of it being like a cracker that is pulled apart into smaller bits!

Some important features about cracking include the following:

- Cracking is the breaking down of large hydrocarbons into smaller ones.
- Small hydrocarbons such as petrol and methane are good fuels and more useful than the heavier fractions.
- Cracking also produces small molecules called **alkenes** that can be turned into plastics and other petrochemicals.

So you can see that cracking is a very useful process that converts useless heavy fractions into profitable small ones. It makes the oil companies a lot of money!

FIGURE 1: Why is crude oil so much in demand?

FIGURE 2: What's the link between what's happening to this cracker, and what happens to a molecule in the cracking process?

WOW FACTOR!

Oil companies are very rich. They often make *billions*, not millions, of pounds profit every year!

QUESTIONS

1 Why do oil companies crack hydrocarbons?
2 What are the 'conditions' used to 'crack' large hydrocarbons?
3 Find out what is meant by the word 'fraction' used above.

Watch Out When a long chain molecule is cracked, an alkane and an alkene are formed.

...alkenes   ...catalyst   ...cracking

Taking a closer look

There are many examples of cracking, because large molecules can be split up in many different ways. For example, butane can be cracked in at least two ways:

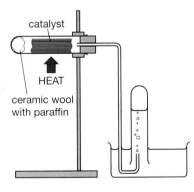

The symbol equation for second example above is:

$$C_4H_{10} (g) \rightarrow CH_4(g) + C_3H_6(g)$$
$$\text{butane} \quad \text{methane} \quad \text{propene}$$

Notice how the number of hydrogen atoms and carbons atoms are the same on each side of the equation. Can you see this is so?

Some important features of cracking include:

■ An alkene molecule containing a double bond is formed, usually ethene. Ethene is a very useful molecule because it can be turned into poly(ethene), a plastic.

■ The 'conditions' used for cracking are high temperature (over 300 °C) and a catalyst (aluminium oxide).

In the laboratory

Cracking can be carried in the laboratory too. Look at the diagram.

Paraffin is an example of a hydrocarbon mixture that can be cracked. Some ceramic wool is soaked in paraffin and then its vapour is passed over heated aluminium oxide (the catalyst). The molecules in paraffin are then broken down to form smaller alkanes and alkenes.

FIGURE 3: This is cracking on a smaller scale!

REMEMBER!

Know your general formulae for alkanes and alkenes: C_nH_{2n+2} and C_nH_{2n}.

QUESTIONS

4 Decane has two more carbon atoms than octane. Write a word equation and symbol equation to show the cracking of decane.

5 How are the cracked gases collected when the process is carried out in the laboratory?

6 What is the name of the catalyst used for cracking?

Catalysts

Catalysts are really special substances. They make a reaction go faster, but at the end of the reaction are still present. It looks as if they haven't done anything!

FIGURE 4: This catalyst makes the reaction go a lot faster. Can you guess what gas is being tested here?

Here are some important features of catalysts:

■ Catalysts, like the one used in cracking, are enormously important in industry because they allow reactions to happen at lower temperatures and pressures than would otherwise be needed. They make reactions cheaper to carry out!

■ Some catalysts are expensive metals, such as platinum, but this is not a problem because the catalyst is not used up, and does not need to be replaced.

■ Catalysts in the body and in biological situations are called **enzymes**.

One important example of a catalyst:

■ Iron catalyses the reaction of hydrogen and nitrogen to make ammonia:

$$N_2(g) + 3H_2(g) \rightarrow 2NH_3(g)$$

QUESTIONS

7 The reaction in Figure 4 is the decomposition of hydrogen peroxide (H_2O_2) to form water and oxygen gas. Write a word equation and balanced symbol equation for this reaction.

8 What is a catalyst?

9 Name the catalyst used in the manufacture of ammonia.

...enzymes ...fraction ...hydrocarbons

Making very long molecules

You will find out:
- How polymers are made from crude oil
- What we mean by polymers and monomers

Saying goodbye to the past!

Over 100 years ago, very few things were made from plastics. Imagine life now without plastics – no credit cards, CDs, DVDs, computers!

Many things that used to be made of 'traditional' materials like wood and metal are now made of plastics.

Molecules like necklaces!

Look at the necklace below. It is made up of many beads all linked together to make a very long chain.

When molecules join together, just like the beads in a necklace, a very long chain molecule can form. These long chain molecules are called **polymers**, as 'poly' means many, and 'mer' means part. Polymers are made by lots of small molecules called **monomers** joining together. All of the monomers have **carbon–carbon double bonds** in them and are therefore **unsaturated monomers**.

- Polymers are long chains with thousands of atoms in them.

- The names of polymers are based on the monomers, for example, poly(ethene) is so called because it is made from ethene. This polymer is sometimes known as 'polythene', and is used for making plastic bags, washing-up bowls, plastic containers and many other everyday items.

- When alkene monomers join together to make a polymer, we call the polymer an **addition polymer**.

Watch Out Monomers that have carbon double bonds in them form addition polymers, and only the polymer is formed. In condensation polymerisation, the polymer and also a small molecule are formed.

FIGURE 1: Think about how much of a modern car is now made with plastics.

FIGURE 2: What would happen if small molecules could be like beads in a necklace?

FIGURE 3: What plastic do you think is used to protect these lettuces?

QUESTIONS

1. What does 'poly' mean in 'polymer'?
2. What is the name of the monomer that makes the polymer called polythene?
3. Find out the meaning of the term 'unsaturated' in the term 'unsaturated monomer'.

REMEMBER!

Polymer chains are very, very long so it is impossible to draw out the whole chain! We therefore draw out the repeat unit of the polymer, or a short section of the chain.

...addition   ...carbon double bonds   ...condensation   ...monomers

Monomers to polymers

How do small molecules join together to make a polymer? The small monomers are unsaturated hydrocarbons, like ethene. Monomers often contain a double bond between two carbons, which breaks open and attaches itself to two other molecules. This process goes on and on, linking more and more monomer molecules, until a huge chain containing millions of atoms is formed.

This is an addition reaction, since the monomers are *adding* on to one another. This kind of polymerisation is called addition polymerisation.

Another common plastic is poly(propene), used for milk crates. It is less flexible than poly(ethene) as it has small side chains.

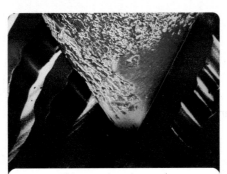

ethene → a strand of poly(ethene)

chloroethene → a strand of poly(chloroethene)

propene → a strand of polypropene

PVC (polyvinyl chloride or poly(chloroethene)) is another common plastic used for making gutters, insulation of electrical wires and window frames.

Teflon®

We can change the properties of a polymer just by changing an atom, or two, in the monomer molecule.

Teflon® is a polymer used for coating non-stick cooking utensils. Its chemical name is poly(tetrafluoroethene), or PTFE. 'Tetra' means 'four' in chemistry – the monomer has four fluorine atoms in each molecule (as well as two carbon atoms).

Teflon® is the 'non-stick' coating used on frying pans and saucepans.

Watch Out When a monomer forms a polymer, the carbon double bond opens up to bond the monomers together. It is therefore not present in the polymer.

FIGURE 4: This amazing picture shows a needle on a record (or vinyl) in a groove, magnified many times. The' vinyl' is made from the polymer called poly(vinylchloride).

WOW FACTOR!

Did you know strands of nylon can now be made that are several times stronger than steel!

Nylon – a different type of polymer

The polymers we have seen until now are addition polymers, made from only one type of monomer (an alkene).

They react by joining together to form a long chain:

A + A + A + A + A → -A-A-A-A-A-

Nylon is one of the most common and useful polymers. It is a **condensation** polymer, made when two different monomers react together:

A+A+A+B+B+B → -A-B-A-B-A-B-

Nylon is made from two monomers that are reactive at both ends. When a condensation polymer such as nylon is made, a small molecule like water or HCl is given off as well – a condensation reaction.

- Condensation polymers are formed from two different monomers.

- These monomers are not alkenes but have reactive groups at each end.

- Nylon is used for some jackets, Velcro®, tights, ropes amongst many other things.

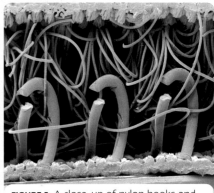

FIGURE 5: A close-up of nylon hooks and loops in Velcro®.

QUESTIONS

4 Give **two** uses for the polymer called poly(chloroethene).

5 Which of these could be a monomer – ethane, methane, propene?

6 Draw the structure of the monomer used to make Teflon®.

QUESTIONS

7 Give **two** common uses of nylon.

8 Why is a 'condensation' polymer like nylon given this name?

Changing materials

You will find out:
- How scientists can alter the properties of polymers
- About problems with getting rid of polymers

Phones that fall apart on their own!

When a mobile phone ends its life, it is normally thrown in a land-fill site, where it can cause pollution in years to come.

What about placing old phones in a special oven and letting the phone take itself apart?

The polymers (plastics) in the phone are special. They can change shape very quickly on heating, and the phone does the rest. The component parts can then be sorted and recycled. Amazing!

FIGURE 1: What properties of polymers make them able to behave like this?

Out with the old, in with the new!

Many things in our lives used to be made of either wood or metal. Buildings were often built with wood, and metal was used for giving the building strength and making guttering for example. But, these days, polymers have taken over from old materials.

Polymers can be designed to have many different properties. This makes them incredibly useful. The polymer can be designed by changing:

- the starting material by modifying the structure of the monomer used

- the reaction conditions such as temperature, pressure, presence of catalysts, etc.

- additives such as **plasticisers**, **preservatives** and **cross-linking agents**. Plasticisers make polymers more pliable or mouldable, and cross-linking agents make the polymer harder and make it less likely to soften on heating.

FIGURE 2: Not much metal or wood here... it is all made of polymers!

Watch Out Polymers are very long chain molecules made when many smaller molecules (monomers) join together.

QUESTIONS

1. Suggest why preservatives are added to some polymers.
2. What property of the polymers used in the mobile phone above enable it to fall apart when heated?
3. Suggest why many wooden objects used to make items kept outside are now made of polymers

...biodegradable   ...cross-linking agents   ...plasticisers   ...preservatives

Choosing the right polymer for the job

Scientists change the properties of polymers by starting with different monomers.

Below are some different polymers with their properties and some uses.

Polymers	Properties	Example uses
poly(ethene)	flexible, cheap, waterproof	shopping bags, dustbins, toys
poly(propene)	stiffer than poly(ethene)	ropes, milk crates
poly(styrene)	can be expanded with gas to insulate heat well	drinks holders
poly(vinyl chloride) (PVC)	waterproof, strong	gutters, raincoats
nylon	stretchy, can be woven	clothing, fibres, ropes, etc.
Perspex™	transparent, rigid	windows, car headlamps

Why is plastic used at all?

Look at the photograph in Figure 3. It shows a scientist holding a polymer film that is able to shows television programmes. The polymer is very light and very thin (only 2 mm). This is a special type of polymer that produces light.

FIGURE 3: Will it be possible to watch your favourite TV programme on a polymer film? It already is!

Most polymers used these days have several advantages over other materials such as wood and metals:

- They can be easily moulded to shape.
- They do not corrode like some metals.
- Unlike wood, they will not be broken down by water or bacteria. But there are problems with plastics too, concerned with getting rid of them:
- Most are not **biodegradable** so do not rot away when buried.
- They give off toxic fumes when burnt.
- There are many different types of plastic, making recycling difficult.

More and more polymers are now designed so that they do rot away naturally, broken down by light or bacteria.

WOW FACTOR!

Polymers can now be designed to do anything: ...light up, vibrate, conduct electricity.

QUESTIONS

4 Give **three** useful properties of polymers
5 What is meant by the term 'biodegradable'?
6 Suggest **one** advantage and **one** disadvantage of disposing of polymers by burning them.

Keeping in shape

Have you noticed that some polymers melt or soften easily when heated, but others do not? This is because there are two general types of plastic – **thermosoftening** polymers (often called **thermoplastics**) contain long chains held together by weak forces between the chains, whereas **thermosetting** plastics have strong covalent bonds between the chains, called 'cross-links'. These different structures explain the different physical properties and uses:

FIGURE 5: Old phones like these are made of bakelite - a thermosetting polymer.

- Thermoplastics soften and melt easily so they can be moulded into different shapes.

- Thermosetting plastics keep their shape when heated. They do not melt but eventually will char and burn.

QUESTIONS

7 In an experiment, a ruler made of a polymer was warmed with a Bunsen burner and found to soften and bend. Is the ruler made of a thermosetting polymer or a thermoplastic polymer?
8 Why do you think thermosetting plastics can become a problem during recycling?
9 Suggest why the presence of cross-links between polymer chains prevents a polymer from melting or softening on heating.

...*thermoplastics* ...*thermosetting* ...*thermosoftening*

Making new compounds

You will find out:

- That amazing chemicals occur naturally in plants
- That scientists can make compounds that also occur naturally

It comes from a tree?

It may seem very odd, but there are many chemicals that are found naturally in plants that can be very helpful to us. The picture below is of a special type of yew tree.

A compound called taxol is extracted from this tree. Taxol can be used to treat various types of human cancer. How amazing!

Making drugs

Drugs are substances that affect our body in a chemical way. This can be in a good way as in **medicines**, or in a bad way for example, alcohol, heroin and amphetamines.

It has been known for over four thousand years that plants and some animal products can be good for our health. If you had a headache in China a thousand years ago, you might chew on some willow bark. This was not just to take your mind off the pain! We now know that willow bark contains a compound very similar to aspirin.

Scientists have analysed the compound in willow bark and know exactly how the atoms in it are bonded together. This means that scientists can work out how to make the molecule.

We take about 40 billion aspirin tablets a year across the world, and there are not enough willow trees to be able to extract this much medicine! Chemists have designed a cheap and easy way to make aspirin in several stages – a **synthesis**.

FIGURE 1: Yew trees have healing properties.

Watch Out A chemical synthesised in the laboratory is exactly the same as the one found naturally. The fact that it is found in nature does not mean that it is somehow better for us than the one made in the laboratory!

WOW FACTOR!

There is concern about destroying rain forests to make way for more agricultural land. Rain forests contain many amazing molecules that we have yet to discover, and many of these may be life savers!

QUESTIONS

1 What is the name of the active compound in yew trees that can treat some cancers?

2 Why might a Chinese person have chewed willow bark in the past?

3 Why it is important that scientists find out ways of making compounds rather than to continuously extract them from their natural source, like a tree?

...analgesic   ...atom economy   ...medicines

The wonder molecule (H)

It has been known for many years that aspirin is a wonder drug. It can cure pain (an **analgesic**), reduce swelling, thin the blood and can even prevent some types of serious illness such as cancer!

Two ways to show the structure of an aspirin molecule are shown below. A molecule of aspirin is made of nine carbon atoms, four oxygen atoms and eight hydrogen atoms.

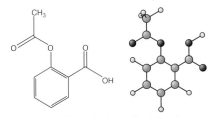

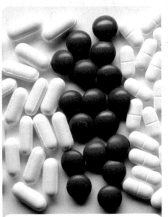

FIGURE 2: Aspirin, ibuprofen and paracetamol – how would our lives be different without these common painkillers?

Some important issues when designing drugs

It is very useful to make compounds that make our lives and others' lives more comfortable. However, there are some issues we need to consider.

- Are any **toxic compounds** involved when making a compound? If there are, is it possible that the compound could be synthesised in a different way?

- How much wastage is there from the reaction? We like to make the most of what our environment offers, so it is important that the chemicals that we use are not wasted. A lot of energy is often required and this would be wasteful. Running our lives by making the most use of the Earth's valuable resources is called **sustainable development**. The **atom economy** of a reaction is given by:

$$\frac{\textbf{Mass of atoms in desired product} \times \textbf{100\%}}{\textbf{Total mass of atoms in reactants}}$$

So the more of the starting atoms that end up in the product, the better will be the atom economy.

- It is possible to *look at other chemical reactions* to help us design new substances, and also to predict what the products of a reaction must be like.

FIGURE 3: This yellow dye has been synthesised.

QUESTIONS

4 What is meant by the term 'analgesic'?

5 Why is it important in a sustainable development to make chemicals with a high atom economy?

6 What is the chemical formula for aspirin?

Staged synthesis (H)

Aspirin is called a 'wonder drug' because it is effective in so many ways. Aspirin does not occur naturally, but is made from a simpler compound called phenol in three stages.

At each stage several 'side-reactions' are possible, which are like paths leading away from the destination of aspirin. If, at each of the three stages, two different products are formed, how many products are possible overall?

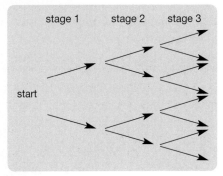

It can be seen that after stage 1, two products are formed, and each of these then forms two products. So at the end of stage 3, there are eight possible products, but often only one product is required.

QUESTIONS

7 What is a disadvantage when making a compound of having lots of stages, one after the other?

8 What would be the atom economy of the reaction above if only one product was required, and all products were formed with equal masses?

...sustainable development ...synthesis ...toxic compound

Weighing it all up

You will find out:
- How to find out the atomic mass of an element
- How to add up the formula mass of a compound

Looking closely at atoms

We know that atoms are very small, too small to be seen. What may not be obvious is that atoms of different elements have different masses: some have very low masses and others have much higher masses.

Chemists use the masses of atoms to calculate the masses' products and reactants in a reaction. This can be very useful.

Weighing up atoms

How much do you weigh? You will probably know how much you weigh in kilograms or in stones. These are two different **units** of mass.

Relative atomic masses, A_r

We compare the masses of atoms with each other. The smallest atoms, hydrogen, have a **relative atomic mass** (A_r) of 1, helium atoms have an A_r of 4, carbon atoms have an A_r of 12, oxygen atoms have an A_r of 16. This means that a hydrogen atom is 12 times lighter than a carbon atom, whereas an oxygen atom is 16 times heavier than a hydrogen atom.

FIGURE 1: These are real atoms seen with an electron tunnelling microscope.

Relative formula masses (M_r)

Compounds contain more than one element chemically bonded together. The relative formula mass of a compound is found by adding up the atomic masses. Remember that methane has the formula CH_4. This means it contains one carbon atom and four hydrogen atoms. Add up the individual masses of these: C = 12, H = 1.

M_r for CH_4 = 12 + (4 × 1) = **16**. The **relative formula mass** of methane is 16.

Another example: Water has the formula: H_2O. The relative formula mass of water is (2 × 1) + 16 = **18**.

FIGURE 2: We all know our weight, but what about the weight (or mass) of atoms?

QUESTIONS

1 Why are the relative atomic masses atoms of different elements not the same?
2 Calculate the relative formula mass of carbon dioxide, CO_2.
3 What is the relative formula mass of CaO (Ca has an A_r of 40)?

WOW FACTOR!

The number of atoms in only 1 g of hydrogen gas is enormous. It is 600 000 000 000 000 000 000 000 atoms, or $6 × 10^{23}$ of them!

...*empirical* ...*expected yield* ...*percentage yield*

It's all in a formula! (H)

How do we know that a chemical formula is correct or not? How do we know that water has the formula H_2O and calcium carbonate is $CaCO_3$?

A chloride of titanium has a total mass of 5.00 g. It is found that there is 1.26 g of titanium in the compound. What is the simplest, or **empirical**, formula for the compound? (A_r data: Ti = 48, Cl = 35.5)

	Titanium	Chlorine
Mass	1.26 g	5.00 g – 1.26 g = 3. 74 g
Divide by the A_r for each element	1.26/48 = 0.0263	3.74/35.5 = 0.105
Divide each by the smallest number	0.0263/0.0263 = 1	0.105/0.0263 = 4

So the empirical formula is $TiCl_4$.

Making equations work for you

If you are using a recipe from a cookery book, it usually tells you how many servings you will end up with, as well as how much of each ingredient to use. Symbol equations can be just as useful – you can use them to work out what mass of product you will get for a certain amount of each reactant.

Example question: How much magnesium oxide will be made from burning 100 g of magnesium? (A_r for Mg = 24 and O = 16)

■ Write a word equation:

magnesium + oxygen → magnesium oxide

■ Write a balanced symbol equation:

$$2Mg(s) + O_2 (g) → 2MgO(s)$$

■ So two 'lots' of magnesium give two 'lots' of magnesium oxide.
■ Convert into relative masses gives:

2 × 24 g of magnesium give 2 × (24 + 16) g of magnesium oxide

So 48 g of magnesium give 80 g of magnesium oxide

■ The 1 g line: 1 g of magnesium gives 80/48 g of magnesium oxide. (If 1 g of magnesium oxide was *required*, the mass of magnesium needed would be 48/80 g.)

■ So 10 g of magnesium will give 10 g × 80/48 = 16.7 g

FIGURE 3: Magnesium burns in oxygen to form magnesium oxide. But how do we work out the mass of magnesium oxide that may form?

■■■■ QUESTIONS ■■■■

Consider the burning of 26.0 g of methane in excess oxygen:

$$CH_4(g) + ...O_2(g) → CO_2(g) + ...H_2O(l)$$
(A_r data: C = 12, H = 1, O = 16)

4 Balance the equation above by placing numbers in the spaces provided.
5 Calculate the mass of carbon dioxide formed from 1.00 g of methane.
6 Hence calculate the mass of carbon dioxide formed from 26.0 g of methane.

Watch Out An empirical formula is another name for the simplest formula a compound has. Hydrogen peroxide has the chemical formula: H_2O_2, but its empirical formula is HO.

Yields of reactions (H)

In chemistry we cannot guarantee that all the reactants of a reaction react together in the right way. A measure of the amount of product that is actually formed as a proportion of the theoretical maximum mass is called the **percentage yield**. It is calculated by dividing the actual yield by the **expected yield** (or theoretical yield) and multiplying by 100:

$$\% \text{ yield} = \frac{\text{actual yield (in grams)} \times 100}{\text{expected yield (in grams)}}$$

For example, in the reaction shown:

$$CaCO_3 → CaO + CO_2$$
(A_r data: Ca = 40, O = 16, C = 12)

If calcium carbonate is heated for ten minutes, not all of it may have decomposed into calcium oxide and carbon dioxide. If 100 g of calcium carbonate is used, and 45 g of calcium oxide is formed, what is the percentage yield?

Mass of calcium oxide expected

$$= \frac{(40 + 16)}{[40 + 12 + (3 \times 16)]} \times 100 = 56.0 g$$

$$\% \text{ yield} = \frac{45 g}{56 g} \times 100 = 80.4\%$$

■■■■ QUESTIONS ■■■■

7 If 54 g of calcium oxide was made in the reaction above, what would the % yield be?

8 Aspirin is made by a complicated synthesis, involving lots of steps. If the expected mass of aspirin to be made is 800 kg, and the mass of pure aspirin actually made is 320 kg, what is the % yield?

When the oil runs out

You will find out:
- That we rely on oil for more than just energy
- What we mean by 'sustainable development'

Life in mid-21st century

What will life be like when you approach retirement in 50 years' time? At the moment, we depend on crude oil for much of our energy, and for petrochemicals that provide many everyday materials. But oil is finite. So what happens when it runs out? How will you manage? Just possibly, you may have moved to the Moon or Mars – but there's no oil there either!

Not just fuels

About 80% of our energy comes from fossil fuels – coal, oil and gas. But they don't just give energy. **Petrochemicals** from crude oil provide:

- polymers, from throw-away plastic bags to long-life window frames
- beauty products, detergents and medicines to keep us clean and healthy
- dyes, inks, paints and pigments to brighten our lives
- insecticides, weed-killers and other farm chemicals.

Using oil for fuels means there's less for making these things. Once burned, it's gone for ever. Experts think oil will run out in about 40 years. That's within your lifetime! What can scientists do about it?

The alternatives

Using alternative energy, for example wind and tidal energy, will save oil for petrochemicals, but oil will still run out. We need alternative *chemical sources*, not just energy.

- Agriculture – we already make alcohol and biodiesel. These and other chemicals from plants could be used as **renewable** raw materials.
- Recycling – metal ores are also **finite**. They too will run out sooner or later. We can't grow more metals, so we must re-use what we've got.
- New processes – chemists are developing methods to make better use of raw materials and energy.

FIGURE 1: Will your children's bedroom still look like this? Without petrochemicals the room would be almost empty, and much less colourful.

Experts think oil will run out within your lifetime!

FIGURE 2: There was once a mountain here. Now it's a copper mine 4 km wide and 750 m deep. How much bigger will it get before the ore runs out?

QUESTIONS

1 Why is oil important apart from providing various fuels?
2 **a** Name **two** chemical products made from plants.
   b Why do we describe products from plants as 'renewable' materials?
3 Why should we encourage recycling?

WOW FACTOR!

Making aluminium from its ore needs 20 times as much electricity as recycling used aluminium.

...atom economy   ...finite   ...petrochemicals   ...recycling

Sustainable development

Advances in science and technology have improved our lives in many ways, but there are also major problems.

- New technology needs new materials, like polymers and lightweight alloys.
- As their use increases, finite raw materials are used up faster. Where will we get them in the future?
- We need to plan **sustainable development**. 'Sustainable' means 'able to keep going'. Using up the Earth's resources faster and faster is clearly *not* sustainable. When they're gone, they're gone.

Imagine a forest. You cut down trees for timber. Eventually there's none left. But, if you plant more each year, and limit the number cut down, that's sustainable.

Chemicals from crops

Many polymers are made from ethene, obtained by cracking oil. One alternative may be to grow sugar and ferment it to make ethanol. Dehydrating ethanol (removing H and OH) gives ethene:

$$C_2H_5OH \rightarrow C_2H_4 + H_2O$$

Waste not, want not

Conservation isn't just about wildlife and pollution. We must conserve raw materials so they last longer. **Recycling** helps. The more we re-use materials, the less we need to mine minerals, or use oil, to make new supplies.

FIGURE 3: Triangular recycling code on a margarine tub. '5 PP' means the tub is made from poly(propene).

- Recycling glass saves sand, limestone and sodium carbonate, and uses less energy. Using scrap metals saves ores, coke, and for aluminium, huge amounts of electricity.
- Recycling plastics is tricky. There are many types, each with different properties. We need to use the right one for each purpose. Mixed plastics waste isn't much use.
- Code numbers marked on items show the type of plastic. Unfortunately, at present there's no public system for collecting these separately.
- Sorting materials from scrap cars is even more difficult, but it must be done.

WOW FACTOR!

From 2006, when a car is scrapped at least 85% of its parts must be recycled.

FIGURE 4: Plastic parts being removed from a car for recycling.

Improving processes

To make resources last longer, chemists research ways to use them economically.

'**Atom economy**' means the percentage of reactants that end up as useful product. The rest form wasteful, unwanted by-products.

Ibuprofen pain-reliever used to be made by a six-stage process, with a 40% atom economy. Now a 77% three-stage synthesis is used. This produces only about one-fifth as much waste for each tonne of Ibuprofen. Can you work out why?

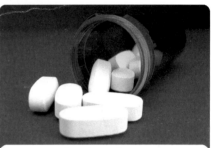

FIGURE 5: Making Ibuprofen now uses up less raw materials and reagents than it used to.

A simple example:

Chloromethane is made by the reaction:

$$CH_4 + Cl_2 \rightarrow CH_3Cl + HCl$$

- Relative formula mass, M_r:

  $$CH_4 = 16; \quad Cl_2 = 71; \quad CH_3Cl = 50.5$$

- Atom economy

$$= \frac{\text{mass of atoms in desired product}}{\text{total mass of atoms in all reactants}} \times 100\%$$

$$= \frac{M_r \text{ of desired product}}{\text{total } M_r \text{ of all reactants}} \times 100\%$$

$$= \frac{50.5}{87} \times 100 = 58\%$$

- It is low since half the chlorine is unused.

QUESTIONS

4 Why is forestry sustainable, but not refining crude oil?

5 How could polythene be made from sugar? What would be the advantages?

6 Why are plastic bottles more difficult to recycle than metal drinks cans?

7 Suggest how to separate valuable aluminium cans from cheap steel ones.

QUESTIONS

8 Why do we want high atom economy?

9 What is the difference between atom economy and percentage yield?

Plastics with a purpose

SELF-CHECK ACTIVITY

CONTEXT

Farrah lives for her surfing. As much of her summer as she can is spent catching waves and her favourite beach is Fistral in Newquay. Her board is a 6' 7" short board, made from a foam former with layers of GRP (glass reinforced plastic).

The material at the centre of a surfboard is polyurethane foam, which is then treated with layers of GRP (glass reinforced plastic, sometimes known as fibre glass) that are added to build it up and to put a good finish on it. There will be several layers of GRP on the board.

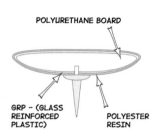

POLYURETHANE BOARD

GRP – (GLASS REINFORCED PLASTIC)

POLYESTER RESIN

The later layers are of a material called polyester resin, which is a thermosetting plastic. It gives a very strong finish, which is important for the hard use that a surfboard gets.

Every so often Farrah's board gets damaged, sometimes on a submerged rock or sometimes as a result of a collision. The damaged areas are called 'dings'. The dings can be fixed by adding polyester resin.

About 20 miles from Fistral is the Eden Project, a unique venture with huge biomes, each producing a climate suitable to grow plants from very different parts of the world. Eden has been described as the world's biggest greenhouse – but it's not made of glass. Each of the panels is covered with a thermoplastic called ETFE (Ethylene TetrafluoroEthylene) – sometimes known as 'cling film with attitude'. In fact, the panels are covered with three layers, and the layers are inflated, so the panels bulge slightly. They're much lighter than glass, so the supporting structure is thinner. In fact, the air inside the biomes weighs more than the biomes themselves.

STEP 1

What is the difference between a thermoplastic and a thermosetting plastic?

STEP 2

What does 'poly' – as in polyester – mean?
What does this suggest about the arrangement of molecules in polyester?

Polyester resin is very strong.
- What is it about the arrangement of molecules that makes it strong?
- Why does this make it suitable for surfboards?
- Why does this mean that it cannot be re-formed by the application of heat?

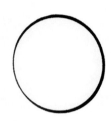

Draw and label diagrams to show how the way the molecules are arranged in ETFE and polyester resin gives them their properties.

Maximise your grade

These sentences show what you need to include in your work to achieve each grade. Use them to improve your work and be more successful.

Grade	Answer includes...
F	Have some idea about terms, including thermoplastic, thermosetting plastic and polyester.
	Explain terms, including thermoplastic, thermosetting plastic and polyester.
	Apply these ideas to the two uses in this piece of work.
	Offer some ideas as to how the arrangement of molecules in thermoplastics and thermosetting plastics gives them their respective properties.
C	Explain how the arrangement of molecules in thermoplastics and thermosetting plastics gives them their respective properties.
	Compare and contrast the arrangements of molecules in thermoplastics and thermosetting plastics.
A	Compare and contrast the arrangements of molecules in thermoplastics and thermosetting plastics to explain the similarities and differences in properties.
	Compare and contrast the arrangements of molecules in thermoplastics and thermosetting plastics to explain the similarities and differences in properties with particular detail and clarity.

- How are the properties of ETFE different to those of polyester resin?
- How are they the same?

Atoms

You will find out:
- That atoms make up everything in the Universe
- That atoms are very small and cannot be seen with the naked eye

'Seeing' atoms

It may not be obvious, but everything around us is made of small particles that we cannot see called **atoms**. The air, water, trees, cars, buildings and even people are made up of particles that are so small they cannot be seen.

Although atoms cannot be seen with the naked eye, a special device called a scanning electron tunnelling microscope allows us to see atoms by 'feeling' the surface of a substance. Figure 1 shows a picture of some atoms that spell the letters 'IBM' – how clever!

FIGURE 1: 'IBM' in atoms!

What are atoms?

Atoms are very small; however, they make up everything that we see. It is therefore very important that we try to understand the world of the atom and what it is like to be that small. There are some important facts about atoms:

- Atoms are the building blocks of everything.
- They make up everything in the Universe from the incredibly small to the absolutely massive.
- Atoms are very difficult to break apart, or split – they are very tough. The word atom comes from the Greek word '*atomos*' meaning indivisible or difficult to break down.

What do atoms look like?

Many clever experiments were carried out over a hundred years ago which showed that atoms are made up of even smaller particles called **protons**, **neutrons** and **electrons**. The neutrons and protons exist inside a central part of the atom called the **nucleus**. The electrons fly around the nucleus, like bees around a honeypot. Figure 2 shows the protons, neutrons and electrons present in an atom.

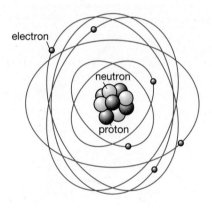

FIGURE 2: The structure of an atom.

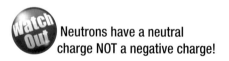

Neutrons have a neutral charge NOT a negative charge!

QUESTIONS

1 What is the name of the instrument that can be used to 'see' atoms?
2 What is the name of the central part of the atom?
3 What is the name for the particles in an atom that orbit the nucleus?

WOW FACTOR!

An atom is so small that if 10 million of them were lined up in a queue, the length of the queue would measure only one millimetre. Look at your ruler to see how small a millimetre is!

...atom   ...electron   ...neutron   ...nucleus   ...proton

A closer look at subatomic particles

Protons, neutrons and electrons are called **subatomic** particles since they make up atoms. To understand how atoms behave, we have to understand some things about these particles.

Some facts that are interesting to know are:

- The nucleus of an atom contains protons and neutrons.
- Protons have almost the same mass as a neutron, and also have a positive charge.
- Neutrons have a neutral, or zero, charge.
- Electrons have a very small mass – about 1/2000th of a proton or a neutron.
- Electrons have a negative charge and orbit the nucleus.

Some of this information is summarised in the table below.

Name of particle	Relative mass	Relative charge
Proton	1	+1
Neutron	1	0
Electron	1/2000	−1

An amazing experiment

An inventive scientist called Millikan carried out an ingenious experiment to determine the charge of an electron. This is very difficult to do because electrons cannot be seen, and their charge is very small.

In this experiment, small oil drops made in an atomiser were squirted into a container, and there they were given a negative charge by firing electrons at each drop. Then the oil drop was held suspended in mid-air by changing the voltage across two plates until the drop stayed in the same place. The measurements were then used to calculate a value for the charge of the electron. Amazing!

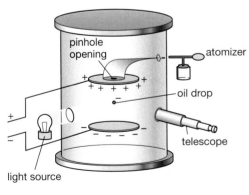

FIGURE 3: Millikan's experiment.

Watch Out Relative mass means when one thing is compared with another. Protons and neutrons have about the same mass, and so their relative mass is both 1.

QUESTIONS

4 If the mass of a proton is 1, what is the mass of an electron?
5 What is the name of the famous scientist who worked out the charge of an electron?
6 Where in the atom is most of the mass found?

More about electrons

Electrons are very small and move around the nucleus very quickly. What is very strange about electrons is that they can have only certain energies when they orbit the nucleus. We sometimes say that electrons that have the same energy are found in the same **shell** of an atom. There are many different shells around the nucleus.

- The first shell which is closest to the nucleus holds a maximum of two electrons.
- The second and subsequent shells, up to and including atomic number 20, can hold a maximum of 8 electrons.

An atom of potassium has 19 electrons and these move around the nucleus so that there are 2 electrons in the first shell, 8 in the second shell, 8 in the third shell and 1 in the outer shell.

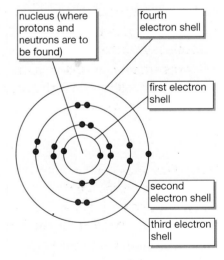

FIGURE 4: A potassium atom.

QUESTIONS

7 How many electrons does a potassium atom have?
8 Insert the missing words in 'Electron .... contain electrons which all have the same ....'.
9 A potassium atom is 2, 8, 8, 1. What do you think this means?

...relative mass   ...relative charge   ...shell   ...subatomic

A closer look

You will find out:

- How to work out the numbers of subatomic particles in an atom
- What is meant by isotopes
- How to work out the average relative atomic mass

Making food safe

Food will not last forever. It goes 'off' because there is bacteria in food that make the food go mouldy after a certain time.

It is possible to irradiate food with a special type of radiation called gamma radiation. This kills the bacteria and makes the food last longer. The gamma rays come from a **radioactive** substance called an isotope.

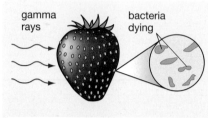

FIGURE 1: Irradiated food lasts for longer.

What makes atoms different from each other?

Everything may be made up of atoms, but atoms are not all the same. Atoms of certain elements are all very similar, but they are different from atoms of other elements. How can this be?

When we look at a periodic table and find an element of our choice, we see that there are two numbers written near to the symbol of the element:

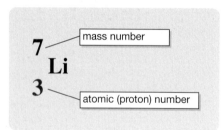

- The smaller number is called the **atomic number**, and this number is always equal to the number of **protons** in the nucleus of an atom. So there are three protons in the nucleus of a lithium atom.

- The atomic number also tells us the number of **electrons** in an atom. The number of electrons is equal to the number of protons for an atom. So an atom of lithium has three electrons, as well as three protons.

- The larger number is called the **mass number**, and it is equal to the total number of protons and **neutrons** in the nucleus. So for lithium, since we already know the number of protons is three, there must be seven minus three neutrons, which is four neutrons.

QUESTIONS

1. An atom has an atomic number of 11 and a mass number of 23. How many protons, neutrons and electrons are in the atom?

2. An atom has 12 protons and 12 neutrons. What is its mass number?

3. How many electrons are there in an aluminium atom, if there are 13 protons and 14 neutrons present?

WOW FACTOR!

The atomic number is a special number that identifies an element. This number is sometimes called the proton number, which tells us exactly what it means.

...atomic number   ...electron   ...isotopes   ...mass number   ...neutrons   ...protons

The same or not the same?

What we know so far:

- Atoms of different chemical elements contain different numbers of protons in the nucleus – this number is called the atomic number or proton number of that element.
- The atomic number tells us the number of protons as well as the number of electrons. In an atom, the numbers of these particles are always equal to each other.
- The mass number tells us the total number of protons and neutrons in an atom.

FIGURE 2: How old is this grave?

Look at Figure 2. It shows an archaeologist looking at a very old grave that he has just excavated. He may want to know how old the grave is. How will he find this out?

Carbon atoms are present in all living things. However, there are three main types of carbon atom, and they are all slightly different.

The following table shows the number of protons, neutrons and electrons in each type of carbon atom.

$$^{12}_{6}\text{C} \qquad ^{13}_{6}\text{C} \qquad ^{14}_{6}\text{C}$$

FIGURE 3: Carbon

Number of subatomic particles	Carbon-12	Carbon-13	Carbon-14
Protons	6	6	6
Neutrons	6	7	8
Electrons	6	6	6

These atoms are all carbon since they have the same atomic (or proton) number of 6. However, they differ in the number of neutrons in each atom. Atoms of this type are called **isotopes**.

Carbon-14 is radioactive. As it releases its radiation, it changes into another element and the time it takes for half of the carbon to do this is about 5300 years. So, if we know how much carbon-14 is left in the grave, we know how old the grave is. This is called carbon dating.

RADIOACTIVE ISOTOPE

An iodine isotope, iodine-131, can be used to treat thyroid cancer. It is a radioactive isotope and is injected into the body where it then destroys the cancer.

QUESTIONS

4 What are isotopes?

5 There are two isotopes of chlorine (atomic number = 17) of mass numbers 35 and 37. What is the difference between these two atoms in terms of the numbers of subatomic particles present?

6 What is the name of the isotope of carbon used in carbon dating?

ISOTOPES

Isotopes differ in the number of neutrons that are found in the nucleus. The number of protons is the same.

Comparing masses (H) of atoms

When we consider an element such as boron, we see that it has two isotopes. However, these isotopes do not occur in equal amounts. It is known that 18.7% of boron is boron-10 and 81.3% is boron is boron-11.

We can calculate a value for the **relative atomic mass** (r.a.m.) of the element using the **relative abundance** (different abundance) of each isotope.

Average r.a.m.

$$= \left(\frac{18.7}{100 \times 10}\right) + \left(\frac{81.3}{100 \times 11}\right)$$

$$= 1.87 + 8.94 = 10.8$$

When we look at some periodic tables, most r.a.m. values are whole numbers. However, chlorine is often written as 35.5. This is because 75.5% of chlorine is 35-Cl and 24.5% of chlorine is 37-Cl. The average value for the r.a.m. is therefore:

$$\left(\frac{75.5}{100 \times 35}\right) + \left(\frac{24.5}{100 \times 37}\right)$$

$$= 26.4 + 9.07 = 35.5$$

QUESTIONS

7 To which atoms are all other atoms compared when measuring a relative atomic mass?

8 Why is chlorine's relative atomic mass often written as 35.5 rather than a whole number?

9 Two isotopes of an element have mass numbers of 6 and 7 of relative abundance 20% and 80% respectively. What is the average relative atomic mass of the element?

Patterns with electrons

You will find out:

- How electrons are arranged around the atomic nucleus
- About electronic configuration
- Why elements in the same group of the periodic table often react in similar ways

Violent chemistry

Potassium is a metal with a mean reputation. It belongs to a group of elements in the **periodic table** called the **alkali metals**.

Potassium can react with other elements, and often does so explosively. Figure 1 shows what may happen if a chemical reaction is carried out using potassium.

Potassium is so reactive because of the way its electrons are arranged.

Electrons in shells

We already know that electrons move around the nucleus in defined orbits called **electron shells**.

- Each shell contains electrons of the same energy.
- A maximum number of electrons are allowed in each shell.

FIGURE 1: Potassium reacts violently with water.

Shell number	Maximum number of electrons allowed
1st shell	2
2nd shell	8
3rd shell	8

Electrons enter the first shell. When this is filled, they then enter the second shell, and so on. For example, an atom of aluminium has 13 electrons – these enter the shells as 2, 8, 3 – two in the first shell, eight in the second shell, and three in the outer electron shell.

We say that aluminium has an **electronic configuration** of 2, 8, 3.

Carbon has an atomic number of 6. This means that it has six electrons in total. Two of these electrons are added to the inner shell and the remaining four are added to the outer shell.

REACTIVE METALS

The alkali metals are seriously reactive. They all react in a similar way because they have one outer electron each.

QUESTIONS

1. How many electrons are allowed in the second electron shell of an atom?
2. What is the electronic configuration of an element having 17 electrons?
3. An element has an electronic configuration of 2, 8, 8, 2. What is its atomic number?

Watch Out The atomic number tells us the number of electrons, but only for atoms.

...alkali metals   ...electronic configuration   ...electron shell

A link with the periodic table

The periodic table is a very important part of chemistry. It brings all of the chemical elements together and places them onto a chart. This sounds very simple, but the position of an element in the periodic table is of crucial importance.

Look at the periodic table in Figure 2.

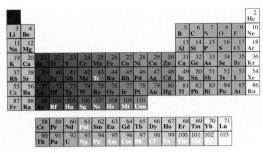

FIGURE 2: The periodic table.

It is made up of chemical elements arranged in a special way.

Elements are placed into groups, all of which react in a similar way.

Some families, or groups, are given names.

Group number	Name of element family
1	The alkali metals
2	The alkaline earth metals
7	The **halogens**
0	The **noble gases**

Let us write down the electronic configurations of the first ten elements. See if you can spot a special link between the position of an element in the periodic table and the electronic configuration.

Name of element	Atomic (proton) number	Electronic configuration
Hydrogen	1	1
Helium	2	2
Lithium	3	2, 1
Beryllium	4	2, 2
Boron	5	2, 3
Carbon	6	2, 4
Nitrogen	7	2, 5
Oxygen	8	2, 6
Fluorine	9	2, 7
Neon	10	2, 8

Can you see that the number of outer electrons is the same as the group number in which the element is found? For example, oxygen has an electronic configuration of 2, 6 and it is group 6 of the periodic table.

QUESTIONS

4 What is the name of the chemical elements in group 7 of the periodic table?

5 How many outer electrons would elements in group 2 be expected to have?

6 An element has 14 electrons. In which group of the periodic table would the element be found?

What explains the similarity? (H)

Let is think about the elements in group 1 of the periodic table: lithium, sodium, potassium and others. Why do these elements react in a similar way? Let us write down their electronic configuration and we will see something special.

Lithium 3 2, 1

Sodium 11 2, 8, 1

Potassium 19 2, 8, 8, 1

Can you see that all of these elements have one electron in their outer shell. This is why they all react in a similar way.

If we look at two of the elements in group 7 (the halogens), we also see a pattern.

Fluorine 9 2, 7

Chlorine 17 2, 8, 7

They both have seven outer electrons. This explains why they have similar chemical behaviour.

QUESTIONS

7 What is the link between the group in which an element is to be found in the periodic table and its electronic configuration?

8 Why do the elements in group 8 of the periodic table (the noble gases) react in a similar way?

9 An atom has five protons and six neutrons in its nucleus. In which group of the periodic table would the element be found?

...halogens   ...noble gases   ...periodic table

Beautiful patterns in nature

You will find out:

- How Mendeleev and Newlands contributed to the periodic table
- How the modern periodic table differs from early versions

Nerves on silicon

The amazing photograph shows **nerve** cells growing on a **silicon chip**. The neurons are linked by a long *axon*, which is responsible for passing signals from one cell to another. The signals take the form of electrical impulses, which means that it may be possible for nerve cells to be linked in a circuit with electronic chips.

This could be used to replace damaged tissue, for example, in the eyes of people who have retina problems. Silicon is an element in group 4 of the periodic table. We can use the periodic table to find other elements that may behave like silicon.

FIGURE 1: A nerve attached to a silicon chip.

The periodic table

Many people were involved in the putting together of the periodic table, but the so-called father of the table was a Russian man called Dmitri **Mendeleev**.

Mendeleev's table uses similar ideas to those of John **Newlands** (discussed on the next page). The major advance of Mendeleev's table was:

- *all* elements in each group behaved in a similar way

- and, most amazingly, he left spaces for elements that were yet to be discovered.

Mendeleev therefore found a way of classifying (putting into classes) the chemical elements. The modern periodic table is built on Mendeleev's table and his table is now considered to be one of the most remarkable ideas in the whole of science.

FIGURE 2: Mendeleev – the 'father' of the periodic table.

Watch Out Remember that elements in the same group of the periodic table have similar chemical properties.

QUESTIONS

1   What is the name of the Russian scientist who is sometimes called the 'father of the periodic table'?
2   How did the Russian's periodic table take account of yet-to-be-discovered elements?

WOW FACTOR!

There are only 92 naturally occurring elements. The human body contains about 13 different chemical elements.

...atomic number   ...Mendeleev   ...nerve   ...Newlands

Amazing minds

John Newlands was an English scientist who lived in the 19th century. In 1869 he read an important paper to the Chemical Society in London.

He said that if the elements were arranged in order of their **relative atomic masses** (atomic weight as it was known), any one element had properties that were very similar to those of elements eight places in front of it and eight places behind it in the list.

Newlands called this his 'Law of Octaves'. It was like in music where each note sounds similar to another note that is eight notes above or below.

A sample of his octaves is shown below.

H		Li	Be	B	C	N	O
F			Na	Mg	Al	Si	P	S
Cl			K	Ca	Cr	Ti	Mn	Fe
Co and Ni	Cu	Zn	Y	In	As	Se

Newlands' idea was not accepted by the scientific community. Some people said that he should arrange the elements in order of first letter instead – it was about as meaningful!

What was wrong with Newlands' idea?

- It assumed that all elements had been discovered.
- Sometimes there were elements placed into one group that were very different.

Despite all of the criticism that was fired at Newlands' periodic table, many people today now see him as a great scientist. What an amazing idea it was to arrange the elements in the way he did: nobody had thought of doing this before.

Today, when we look at the periodic table, we see that the idea of placing elements into groups according to their chemical behaviour is a most important idea. John Newlands was the first to call an arrangement of elements of this type a periodic table.

FIGURE 3: John Newlands.

The modern-day periodic table

The periodic table that scientists use today is shown in Figure 5.

There are some important things to notice about this periodic table.

- The elements are not arranged in order of the relative atomic mass number, as early scientists would have done: they are arranged in order of **atomic number**.
- If elements were to be arranged in order of relative atomic mass, then some elements would need to be swapped around, such as potassium and argon. Argon is a highly unreactive gas, whereas potassium is a highly reactive metal – they are very different elements. It would be silly to put argon in potassium's group because argon does not react with anything. Similarly, potassium is very reactive and should not be in argon's group.

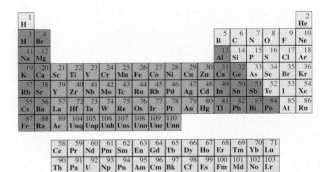

FIGURE 4: The modern periodic table.

QUESTIONS

3 What is the name given to Newland's arrangement of the elements?

4 Give **one** reason why some scientists thought that Newland's idea was bad science.

QUESTIONS

5 In what order are elements arranged in a modern periodic table?

6 Why shouldn't the position of potassium and argon be swapped around in the periodic table?

Reactivity

You will find out:
- Why the noble gases are so unreactive
- Why the alkali metals are so reactive
- How electronic structure can be used to explain reactivity

A violent reaction

Sodium and chlorine are highly reactive elements. When hot sodium is placed into a gas jar of chlorine, a violent chemical reaction takes place and a new substance called sodium chloride is formed.

Why are some elements such as sodium and chlorine reactive, whereas other elements such as gold and platinum very unreactive?

Lights and Las Vegas

The photograph shows Las Vegas in the USA at night time.

Notice all the bright and colourful lights. Similar scenes may be seen in Piccadilly Circus in London and in other big cities. How are these lights made to be so colourful?

Each of the lights is filled with an unreactive gas. This gas may be helium, neon or argon, and the amazing thing is that when 240 volts pass through the gas, the gas glows a certain colour.

Why are the noble gases so unreactive? The noble gases are found in group 0 of the periodic table. There are six members of this group: helium (He), neon (Ne), argon (Ar), krypton (Kr), xenon (Xe) and radon (Rn).

The **electronic configurations** for the first three noble gases are:

	Atomic number	Electronic configuration
Helium	2	2
Neon	10	2, 8
Argon	18	2, 8, 8

Notice how each element has a full, or complete, outer shell of electrons. This is probably what makes the noble gases so unreactive.

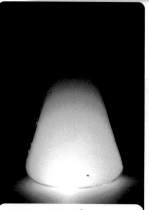

FIGURE 1: Lots of energy is released when sodium reacts with chlorine.

FIGURE 2: How are coloured lights like these made?

▌ QUESTIONS ▐

1 In which group of the periodic table are the noble gases to be found?
2 What do all noble gases have in common with their electronic configurations?

Watch Out The **noble gases** are all unreactive because they have complete outer **electron shells**.

...alkali metal   ...attractive force   ...electronic configuration   ...electron shells

Elements of high reactivity

Although the noble gases are extremely unreactive, many other elements are considerably more reactive. Elements in group 1 of the periodic table are a family of elements of extreme reactivity.

There are six **alkali metals**: lithium, sodium, potassium, rubidium, caesium and francium. Lithium, sodium and potassium are so reactive that they are stored under paraffin to stop them reacting with the oxygen and water vapour in the air.

They are all extremely reactive metals, but they do differ in their reactivity on moving down the group.

When the alkali metals are added to water, a reaction occurs to produce a solution of the metal hydroxide and hydrogen gas.

As the group is descended, the metals become more reactive. Why is this?

Here are the electronic configurations of lithium, sodium and potassium.

	Atomic number	Electronic configuration
Lithium	3	2, 1
Sodium	11	2, 8, 1
Potassium	19	2, 8, 8, 1

FIGURE 3: Sodium reacting with water.

When alkali metals react, they lose their outer electron in order to leave a complete outer electron shell. The reason why potassium does this quicker than lithium is that:
- the outer electron in potassium is further away from its **nucleus**. This means it is easier to remove.
- there are two extra electron shells in potassium that '**shield**' or '**screen**' the outer electron being removed – this reduces the attraction between the outer electron and the positive **nuclear charge** and so it is easier to remove the electron.

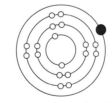

A lithium atom showing one outer electron to be removed

A potassium atom showing the outer electron. Notice how the extra electron shells in this atom that make it easier to remove the outer electron

FIGURE 4: Lithium and potassium atoms.

Watch Out The alkali metals become more reactive going *down* the group, whereas non-metals, such as the **halogens**, become more reactive going *up* the group.

Watch Out Distance of the electron from the nucleus and the number of electron shells are both important ideas when explaining reactivity of elements.

Salt makers

The halogens are found in group 7 of the periodic table. They include fluorine, chlorine, bromine, iodine and astatine.

The halogens react with metals to form compounds called salts. This is where the name halogen comes from: 'salt maker'.

When halogen atoms react, they do so by gaining one electron. They do this because they have seven outer electrons and need one more electron to complete their outer shell.

Fluorine is the most reactive in the group because the electron being added is very close to the nucleus, and so the **attractive force** is greater.

However, iodine is less reactive because the added electron is added a long way from the nucleus because there are more electron shells.

FIGURE 5: Chlorine, bromine and iodine at room temperature and pressure.

QUESTIONS

3 Name **three** metals in group 1 of the periodic table.
4 Why are the group 1 metals placed together in the same group?
5 What happens to the reactivity of the group 1 metals on descending the group?

QUESTIONS

6 Why are the halogens so called?
7 How many outer electrons do halogens have?
8 What happens to the reactivity of the halogens as the group is descended?

...halogen   ...noble gases   ...nuclear charge   ...nucleus   ...screen   ...shield

Ions

You will find out:
- What is meant by the term 'ions'
- How ions are formed
- How to work out the formula of a compound given the charges present

Ions in space

The photograph shows the Orion Nebula (M42). This is known as an **emission nebula** and is found in the constellation of Orion. Ultraviolet **radiation** removes electrons from hydrogen atoms in the nebula, which then emits the red light seen; hence the name 'emission nebula'. A nebula is a cloud of gas and dust in space, many light years across. The Orion is brighter than any other nebula.

What are ions?

You should be familiar with atoms. They are neutrally charged particles, because they have the same number of positively charged protons as negatively charged electrons.

Consider a sodium atom. It has a mass number of 23 and an atomic number of 11. There are therefore 11 protons, 11 electrons and 12 neutrons.

Number of protons = 11   total proton charge = 11 × +1 = +11
Number of electrons = 11   total electron charge = 11 × −1 = −11
Number of neutrons = 12   total neutron charge = 12 × 0 = 0

Total overall **electrical charge** = +11 − 11 = 0

FIGURE 1: The Orion nebula produces red light which is caused by ions of a high energy.

When metals react with non-metals, something special happens to the outer electrons. When sodium reacts with chlorine, an electron moves from the sodium atom to the chlorine atom – this happens because each particle formed then has a complete outer shell of electrons.

	At the start of the reaction		At the end of the reaction	
	Sodium	Chlorine	Sodium	Chlorine
Electronic configuration	2, 8, 1	2, 8, 7	2, 8	2, 8, 8

The sodium and chlorine particles formed are called **ions**, because the number of protons and electrons in each particle is now not the same.

After reaction	Number of protons	Number of electrons	Overall charge
Chlorine	17	18	17 − 18 = −1
Sodium	11	10	11 − 10 = +1

QUESTIONS

1 Why do atoms have zero electrical charge?
2 The fluoride ion has the **formula** F⁻. Why is this particle charged?

WOW FACTOR!

Sodium is a dangerous metal that may explode. Chlorine is a highly toxic gas that was used to kill people in the First World War. However, sodium chloride is ordinary table salt and contains only sodium and chlorine! How can this be?

...electrical charge ...electrostatically   ...emission nebula   ...formula

Making ions

When an alkali metal reacts with a halogen, an electron is transferred from the metal to the non-metal atom. When this happens, ions are formed.

> An ion is an atom or a molecule that has had electrons either added or removed. It is therefore charged.

Figure 2 shows what happens when hot sodium is added to a chlorine gas.

Figure 3 shows what happens to the atoms when they react. Notice how an electron moves from the sodium atom and moves to the chlorine atom.

The ions formed can be written as Na^+ and Cl^- ions and are called the sodium ion and chloride ion respectively. Since there are as many sodium ions as chloride ions formed, the formula of sodium chloride is NaCl.

The ions formed attract each other **electrostatically**, since they have opposite charges. The forces that hold the ions together are called **ionic bonds**.

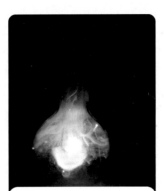

FIGURE 2: A reaction between sodium and chlorine gas.

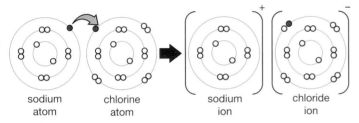

| sodium atom | chlorine atom | sodium ion | chloride ion |

FIGURE 3: How chlorine and sodium atoms change when they react.

What about other reactions?

How about when magnesium ribbon burns in air?

	Atomic number	Mass number	Electronic configuration
Magnesium	12	24	2, 8, 2
Oxygen	8	16	2, 6

- The magnesium atom loses its outer two electrons and these go to the oxygen atom.
- The magnesium atom forms a magnesium ion, Mg^{2+}, and the oxygen atom forms an oxide ion, O^{2-}.
- The ions will attract each other using ionic bonds since they are oppositely charged.

The formula of magnesium oxide is MgO since one magnesium atom needs one oxygen atom for the reaction.

▥▥▥ QUESTIONS ▥▥▥

3 What is an ion?

4 Why are the sodium ions attracted to the chloride ions in sodium chloride?

5 Calcium has the atomic number 20, and fluorine has the atomic number 9. Predict the charges on the calcium and fluoride ions, and hence the formula for calcium fluoride.

Cracking the code

When we know the ions present in a compound, we can easily work out its formula. Some common ions are shown in the table.

Positive ions	Negative ions
Sodium, Na^+ Potassium, K^+ Lithium, Li^+	Chloride, Cl^- Fluoride, F^- Bromide, Br^-
Calcium, Ca^{2+} Magnesium, Mg^{2+}	Oxide, O^{2-} Sulphide, S^{2-}
Aluminium, Al^{3+}	Hydroxide, OH^-
Copper, Cu^{2+}	Carbonate, CO_3^{2-}
Iron, Fe^{2+} or Fe^{3+}	Sulphate, SO_4^{2-}
Ammonium, NH_4^+	Nitrate, NO_3^-

So for example, if we wanted to work out the formula for calcium chloride, we write out the appropriate ions:

$$Ca^{2+} \qquad Cl^-$$

Then we swap the charges round, so the 2 from Ca^{2+} moves to Cl, and the 1 from Cl moves to Ca. This gives the formula:

$$Ca^{2+} + 2 \!\!\times\!\! Cl^- \rightarrow CaCl_2$$

The formula for aluminium sulphate is $Al_2(SO_4)_3$ since the ions are Al^{3+} and SO_4^{2-}. When they are swapped, they make:

$$2Al^{3+} \!\!\times\!\! 3SO_4^{2-} \rightarrow Al_2(SO_4)_3$$

▥▥▥ QUESTIONS ▥▥▥

6 Why does a calcium ion have a charge of +2 when a sodium ion has a different charge of only +1?

The atomic numbers of calcium and sodium are 20 and 11 respectively.

7 Using the table above, what are the formulae for

a sodium sulphate

b calcium carbonate

c aluminium chloride

d ammonium sulphate?

Substances made of ions

You will find out:
- How ionic substances have special properties
- About evidence for the existence of ions
- Some useful everyday applications of ions

Melting rocks

Rocks are all around us. The whole Earth is made up of rocks. About 85% of all rocks are what is called igneous rocks. This means that the rocks were once upon a time molten, or liquid rock, and probably came from a volcano millions of years ago!

Rocks do not melt very easily. However, at a temperature of about 1200 °C, a rock will melt. Rocks have such a high melting temperature because they are made up of ions.

Looking at substances made of ions

Figure 2 shows a salt crystal, otherwise known as sodium chloride, NaCl.

If we were to magnify this crystal millions of times, we would see the particles that make it up.

Sodium chloride is a compound of a metal and a non-metal. It is therefore made up of ions. Figure 3 shows a crystal of sodium chloride. The green balls are chloride ions, and the yellow balls are sodium ions.

We know that the sodium and chloride ions are strongly attracted to each other, but the ions are attracted to each other throughout the whole structure. This type of structure is called a **giant ionic structure**:

- *giant* – because the ions are strongly attracted throughout the structure
- *ionic structure* – because ions make up the crystal.

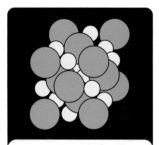

FIGURE 3: Crystal of sodium chloride.

All compounds made up of a metal and a non-metal are made up of ions. They also exist as giant ionic structures.

Ionic structures that consist of equal numbers of positive ions and negative ions are called **binary salts**. Binary salts will have the general formula of AB since the number of ions of A is the same as the number of ions of B.

FIGURE 1: Lava flows like this are made of molten rock.

FIGURE 2: A salt crystal made up of millions of ions!

▪▪ QUESTIONS ▪▪

1. What is the chemical formula for sodium chloride?
2. What is the name of the particles that make up sodium chloride?
3. What is the name of the structure of sodium chloride?

WOW FACTOR!

Lightning often results in the formation of many negatively charged ions in the air. This makes the air smell fresh and clean, and is even supposed to make us feel happier!

...Acinetobacter infection   ...bacteria   ...binary salts   ...electrical conductivity

How do we know that ions exist?

It is very important in science that we always question what people say. This is because people do not always tell the truth, or what they say may be based on weak evidence.

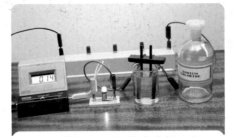

FIGURE 4: Why does the bulb light up?

So what is the evidence that ions exist?

It is very easy to carry out an experiment in which a beaker of pure water is connected, via two graphite **electrodes**, to an electrical power pack. A light bulb is placed into the circuit.

When the power pack is switched on, the bulb does not light up. Why? It is because water does not contain any charged particles – it is made up of water molecules and these do not have an electrical charge. Therefore, there are no charged particles to carry the electrical current.

What happens when we add salt to the water in the beaker? This time, the bulb lights up! Why is this? It is because whatever is in the salt, the particles in it carry electricity. The particles in sodium chloride must therefore be charged, and these are the ions that we have already mentioned.

What else do ionic substances do?

Ionic substances have particular properties that can be explained by the fact that these substances are made up of ions.

Property	Explanation in terms of ions
Good electrical conductors when molten and when dissolved in water	Ions are free to move and carry or conduct the electrical charge. This will make the substance conduct electricity.
Poor electrical conductors when solid	There may be charged ions present, but they are fixed in position in their lattice, and so cannot move and carry the charge.
Regular crystal shape	The ions are arranged in a pattern, or lattice. This will form a regular crystal structure that repeats itself.
High melting and boiling points	The oppositely charged ions are strongly attracted to each other. This means that it is difficult to separate the ions from each other, and so the substance has a high melting point.

Watch Out Solutions and molten substances containing ions conduct electricity because *ions* can carry the charge (not electrons).

ELECTRICAL CONDUCTIVITY

For *electrical conductivity* to take place, *charged particles* must be present and they must be able to *move*.

Air ionisers wipe out hospital infections

Repeated airborne infections of the **bacteria** *Acinetobacter* in an intensive care ward have been eliminated by the installation of a negative air **ioniser**.

The ionisers produce negative air ions that collide with suspended particles and give them a charge. The scientists believe charged particles aggregate and fall out of the air, thereby disinfecting the atmosphere and stopping the transmission of infection.

'We don't fully understand how it is working, but we suspect it is damaging or killing the bacteria', said a scientist. 'But if the ionisers are cleaning the air in this way, we would expect to find more precipitation of *Acinetobacter* on surfaces and this is exactly what we found.'

Acinetobacter infections are often very difficult to treat as the bacterium is resistant to many antibiotics. It poses no real threat to healthy humans but can cause serious infections in people with weakened immune systems.

By Natasha McDowell in *New Scientist* 18 February 2003.

QUESTIONS

7 Suggest how the ioniser produces negatively charged particles in the air.

8 What is the meaning of the term 'suspended particles'?

9 Why are *Acinetobacter* infections difficult to treat?

QUESTIONS

4 Why does pure water not conduct electricity?

5 Potassium fluoride, KF, has a high melting temperature. Explain, using the ideas of particles, why this is so.

6 Why do sodium chloride crystals all have the same cubic shape?

Ions and electricity

You will find out:
- That important substances are made with electricity
- The meaning of the term 'electrolysis'
- How to predict which product forms at which electrode

Bubbles!

We have all discovered that soap can be used to keep us clean. Soap is very good at making bubbles too!

How is soap made though? Various fats and oils from plants can be mixed with a chemical called sodium hydroxide. Sodium hydroxide is very important as it can be used to make lots of things that we see around us every day. Sodium hydroxide, in industry, is made by passing electricity through a solution of sodium chloride, or seawater (brine).

FIGURE 1: Making bubbles with soap!

A scientist and genius

Michael Faraday (1791–1867) was an English chemist and physicist. He was considered a great experimentalist in both chemistry and physics. In 1832 Faraday produced his Laws of Electrolysis. These laws predict how chemicals will behave when electricity is passed though them.

When electricity is passed through some chemicals, new substances are formed.

The breaking down, or **decomposition**, of a substance using electricity is called **electrolysis**.

How is an electrolysis carried out?

Figure 3 shows how to carry out an electrolysis of acidified water.

Electrical energy from the battery is used to break down the chemicals in the beaker, in this case water (with a small amount of dilute sulphuric acid). Notice that gases are being formed, and these are collected in the test tubes. The gases can be tested and are found to be oxygen and hydrogen.

FIGURE 2: Michael Faraday – a great scientist.

FIGURE 3: How to electrolyse water.

QUESTIONS

1 How is sodium hydroxide made industrially?
2 What are the names of the two gases formed when acidified water is electrolysed?

...anion ...anode ... cathode ...cation

How does an electrolysis work?

You should already know the following:

- Compounds that contain metals are made up of **ions**.
- Ions are free to move when the substance is molten, or when dissolved in water. This means that the substance *will* conduct electricity.
- Ions are not free to move when the substance is solid. This means that the substance will *not* conduct electricity.

When electricity is passed though a molten compound called lead bromide, $PbBr_2$, the compound conducts electricity. As it does so, it gets broken down to form the elements that make it up: lead and bromine.

There are a few things to learn about the electrolysis:

- The electrodes have a charge. The negatively charged electrode is called a **cathode**, and the positively charged electrode is called the **anode**.
- The ion of opposite charge to the electrode is attracted to it. So the positively charged lead ion, called an **cation**, moves to the cathode, and the negatively charged bromide ion, called a **anion**, moves to the anode.
- Electrons move through the wires, and ions move through the molten liquid – this is how the circuit is completed and the liquid conducts electricity.
- When the ions reach the electrode surfaces, a chemical change then takes place:

lose electrons

At the anode: bromide ions ⟶ bromine molecules

gain electrons

At the cathode: lead ions ⟶ lead atoms

> ### CHEMICAL CHANGE
> Electrolysis involves the breaking down of a substance using electricity. It is a chemical change.

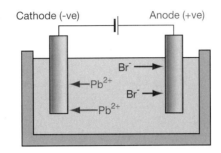

FIGURE 4: What happens when molten lead bromide is electrolysed?

> ### REMEMBER
> In some hospitals, the radioactive tracer technetium-99 is produced artificially in a small nuclear reactor. Remember PANCake – Positive Anode Negative Cathode

QUESTIONS

Fill in the gaps.

3   When a molten compound is electrolysed, ... are able to move and conduct the charge?

4   An ionic compound will *not* conduct electricity when in the ....state because the ions are unable to .... This is because they are .... in their ....

5   Why do ions have electrons removed at the surface of an anode?

> ### Watch Out
> When an ion moves towards the cathode, it is called a cation; when it moves to the anode, it is called an anion.

Predicting the reaction (H)

When a molten salt is electrolysed, we can predict what will form, and at which electrode, when it is being electrolysed.

Consider electrolysing molten sodium chloride, NaCl. What will form when it is electrolysed? Only two things can form: sodium and chlorine (they are the only two elements present).

At which electrode will they form?

- Sodium ions are positively charged, and so these will move to the negatively charged electrode (the cathode). When they reach the surface, the ions gain an electron to form sodium atoms:

$$Na^+ + e^- \rightarrow Na$$

Equations of this type, with electrons written into them, are called ionic half equations.

- Chloride ions are negatively charged, and these will move to the positive electrode (the anode). When they arrive at the surface, they have electrons removed, and form chlorine molecules:

$$Cl^- - e^- \rightarrow Cl$$

Then: $Cl + Cl \rightarrow Cl_2$

Or, as an overall ionic half equation:

$$2Cl^- - 2e^- \rightarrow Cl_2$$

QUESTIONS

6   What are the names of substances formed when molten potassium iodide is electrolysed?

7   At which electrode will each of the substances mentioned in question **6** form?

8   Write ionic half equations to show these elements forming at each electrode.

... decomposition   ... electrolysis   ...ion

We live in a metallic world

You will find out:
- Metals are useful and have special properties
- Why metals behave the way they do
- Metals may be mixed together to make mixtures called alloys

Forever gold

Gold is one of the most precious of metals. It is a beautiful metal to look at and is often used in jewellery.

However, gold has some amazing properties as a metal and has many uses other than being used just for making rings, bracelets and earrings! It is also used to make coins, in dentistry, coating space satellites, photography, and in treatment for arthritis and cancer!

FIGURE 1: Gold is a very beautiful and useful metal.

Metals for mobiles

Most of us own a mobile phone. Many use them every day and probably upgrade them annually! We take this amazing technology for granted, and yet when we look at how many substances are needed to make a phone, particularly metals, we realise how complicated a device it really is.

Typical metals and their use in a mobile phone are as follows:

Aluminium	metal **alloy** in dial mechanism, transmitter and receiver
Beryllium	alloy in dial mechanism
Cadmium	colour in yellow plastic housing
Cobalt	magnetic material in receiver
Germanium	transistors in Touch-Tone dial mechanism
Gold	electrical contacts
Mercury	colour in red plastic housing

FIGURE 2: Technology like this requires some amazing properties in the various metallic elements that are used to make the components.

How do metals work?

Metals are made up of a **close-packed arrangement** of particles. This type of structure is called a **giant metallic structure**.

These particles could be considered to be atoms; however, each atom is known to lose some **electrons** which then roam around the structure. This explains why metals conduct electricity well. So a metal is really made up of **ions** surrounded by mobile electrons.

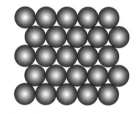

FIGURE 3: Metals are made of millions of particles packed together very closely.

> **Mixtures of metals are called alloys.**

📖 QUESTIONS 📖

1. Give **three** uses for gold.
2. What is mercury used for in a mobile phone?
3. Metals are made up of a close-packed arrangement of .... through which .... can move. These mobile particles explain why metals are very good ....

...alloy   ...close-packed arrangement   ...electrical conductor

Amazing uses for amazing metals

We have already mentioned gold. However, it is an excellent **electrical conductor** and is used for making electrical contacts on a lot of electrical equipment, such as cameras and musical equipment.

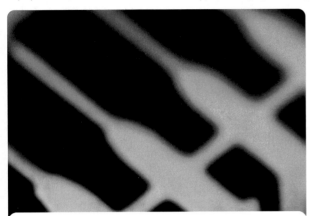

FIGURE 4: Gold contacts are used here because gold is an excellent electrical conductor.

In a nuclear power plant, a nuclear reaction takes place in the reactor. It gets very, very hot.

The heat generated by the reactor is absorbed by sodium metal (which is a liquid when used in this way). The liquid sodium then passes through water in which it travels in metal tubes to stop it from coming into contact with the water. The water then turns into steam and passes through turbines to produce electrical power. Why is sodium used in this way? The reason is that it is a very good heat, or thermal, conductor.

Explaining properties of metals

As the above two examples illustrate, metals have some special properties.

Property	Explanation
Excellent electrical conductors	Metals have mobile electrons that can move within the metallic structure. The electrons carry the electrical charge.
Excellent thermal conductors	The particles are bonded together tightly. This means that heat energy can move through the metal quickly.
High melting/boiling points	The strength of the structure also means that it is very difficult to separate the particles, since positively-charged ions will be attracted to the negatively charged electrons.
Malleable (can be hammered into thin sheets)	Metal particles form layers in which many ions are packed together. It is easy for one layer to slide over another.

▶▶▶ **QUESTIONS** ◀◀◀

4 What is the meaning of the term 'malleable'?
5 Why mustn't very hot liquid sodium be allowed to come into contact with water?
6 The strength of the bond between which two types of particles explains why metals have a high melting temperature?

WOW FACTOR!

Tungsten is a metal with the highest melting temperature of all metals: 3410 °C.

Mixing it!

Atoms of different metal elements have different sizes, so mixtures cannot form such regular arrangements as single atoms. This produces some useful effects.

- Mixtures of metals are called alloys.
- Examples of alloys are brass and bronze.
- Brass is an alloy of copper and zinc.
- Bronze is an alloy of copper and tin.

FIGURE 5: This trombone is made of brass – an alloy of copper and zinc.

Each metal has its own set of special properties. This means that when metals are mixed together, the final alloy can have properties that are very different from the original metals.

Solder is a mixture of lead and tin. The melting temperature of solder is much lower than the melting point of tin or lead!

▶▶▶ **QUESTIONS** ◀◀◀

7 What is an alloy?
8 Name **two** metals used to make the alloy called solder.
9 Name **two** alloys that both contain copper.

...electrons   ...giant metallic structure   ...ions   ...malleable

Unit summary

Concept map

The modern day periodic table has all elements arranged in order of atomic number, not atomic mass.

Elements in the same group of the periodic table have similar chemical properties.

Group 1 are called the alkali metals, group 7 are called the halogens and group 8 are called the noble gases.

The elements in the early periodic tables consisted of elements arranged in order of the atomic mass.

The periodic table

The alkali metals react by losing their outer electron to form a ion with a +1 charge. The alkali metals are very reactive metals.

Metals may be mixed together to make alloys. Alloys often have different properties from the metals making them.

Metals have high melting and boiling points, as well as being malleable and hard. They are also very good electrical conductors.

The halogens react by gaining one electron to for a negatively charged ion with a −1 charge. The halogens are a reactive group of non-metals.

Atoms are made of subatomic particles called neutrons, protons and electrons.

Electrons are negatively charged, protons have a positive charge and neutrons have a neutral (zero) charge.

Atoms are very small and cannot be seen with the naked eye.

Atoms

The number of outer electrons is the same as the group in which the element is found in the periodic table.

The average relative atomic mass can be calculated by adding up the percentage abundance of an isotope multiplied by the relative atomic mass for each isotope.

Isotopes are atoms that have the same number of protons but different numbers of neutrons.

The reactions of a particular element are determined by the outer electron structure.

Elements in the same group have similar chemical properties because they have the same number of outer electrons.

Unit quiz

1 What are the relative mass and relative charge of:
   a) a proton
   b) an electron?

2 How are the electrons arranged around the nucleus of an atom?

3 Aluminium has an atomic number of 13 and a mass number of 27. How many protons, neutrons and electrons are there in an atom of aluminium?

Questions **4-8** involve the following information.

- Fluorine has nine neutrons in its nucleus, and nine electrons.
- Fluorine reacts with sodium to form a compound of formula NaF_x where x is a whole number.
- Sodium has an atomic number of 11.

4 What is the electronic configuration of a fluorine atom?

5 How many protons are in an atom of fluorine?

6 What is the mass number of fluorine?

7 Suggest, in terms of electron transfer how fluorine may react with sodium.

8 What is the value of x in the formula NaF_x?

9 What are meant by 'isotopes'?

10 Give **two** physical properties expected of a compound made up of ions.

11 In modern periodic tables, elements are arranged in order of their .... number.

Questions **12-15** are about the following experiment.

- Solid lead(II) bromide was heated and electricity passed through the molten compound.
- It was found that a dark grey solid formed at the cathode and an orange gas was formed at the anode.

12 What is the decomposition of a compound using electricity known as?

13 What is the electrical charge on:
   a) a cathode
   b) an anode?

14 What are the names of the substances formed at:
   a) the cathode
   b) the anode in the reaction?

15 Molten lead(II) bromide conducts electricity because .... are free to move and carry the electrical charge.

Numeracy activity

Sir Humphry Davy: British inventor, chemist and philosopher

Pure sodium was first isolated by Humphry Davy in 1807 through the electrolysis of caustic soda (NaOH). Barium was first isolated by Davy in 1808 through the electrolysis of molten barium oxide (BaO).

In 1809, Humphry Davy invented the first electric light. Davy connected two wires to a battery and attached a charcoal strip between the other ends of the wires. The charged carbon glowed making the first arc lamp. He also later invented the miner's safety lamp in 1815. Humphry Davy's achievements:

- Discovered the medical properties of nitrous oxide or laughing gas.
- Boron compounds have been known for thousands of years, but the element was not discovered until 1808 by Davy, Gay-Lussac and Thenard.
- Performed the first electrochemical decompositions, isolating potassium, sodium, barium, strontium, calcium and magnesium.
- Invented the first electric light and the miner's safety lamp.

QUESTIONS
1 Name **five** elements discovered by Humphry Davy.
2 Name **two** other scientists that discovered the element: boron.
3 What is meant by the term 'electrochemical decompositions'?

Exam practice

In **Q1–9** choose the best answer to each question.

1 When a large alkane is broken down into smaller fragments what do we call the process?
 A Fraction
 B Cracking
 C Distillation
 D Unsaturation [1]

2 Select the correct formula for propene:

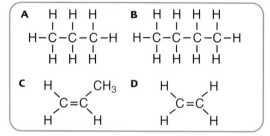

[1]

3 Select the correct statement:
 A Breakdown of a large alkane can make a saturated alkene and an unsaturated alkane.
 B Breakdown of a large alkane can make an unsaturated alkane and an alkene.
 C Breakdown of a large alkane can make unsaturated alkenes only.
 D Breakdown of a large alkane can make an unsaturated alkene and a saturated alkane. [1]

4 What is the relative formula mass of $NaHCO_3$?
 A 84
 B 42
 C 6
 D 156 [1]

5 Which of these is *not* a property of metals?
 A High melting point and boiling point
 B Malleable
 C Hard
 D Good insulator [1]

6 Which of these statements best describes the structure of atoms?
 A They have a nucleus containing electrons and protons.
 B All atoms of the same element have the same number of protons.
 C All atoms of the same element have the same number of neutrons.
 D Atoms have a nucleus containing only protons. [1]

7 Which is the *best* description of the properties of an ionic compound?
 A They have high melting and boiling point.
 B They have high melting and boiling points and can conduct electricity.
 C They have high melting and boiling points and conduct electricity when molten.
 D They have high melting and boiling points and are insoluble in water. [1]

8 Given that a sulphide ion is S^{2-} and a sodium ion is Na^+, what is the formula of sodium sulphide?
 A NaS_2 **C** NaS
 B Na_2S **D** $2NaS$ [1]

9 What is the correct electron arrangement for ?
 A 2,9   **C** 2,8,9
 B 2,8,8,1   **D** 2,7 [1]

10 What is it about the carbon atom that means that carbon is the basic element of life?

.... [2]

11 Describe a simple test to distinguish between an alkane and an alkene.

.... [2]

12 a Complete this chart to show the similarities and difference between thermosetting and thermosoftening plastics.

Type of plastic	Does it contain long chains?	Does it contain cross-linking?	Waste be can recycled	Does it soften on heating?
Thermoplastic				
Thermosetting				

[4]

b Give an example of
 i Thermosetting plastic ....
 ii Thermoplastic............... [2]

c Ethene is a monomer in the formation of poly(ethene). Draw a section of the polymer showing three monomer units. [1]

13 a Explain what you understand by each of these terms used to describe oils:

i Saturated

....

ii Monounsaturated

....

iii Polyunsaturated

.... [3]

b Polyunsaturated oils are far less viscous than saturated ones and can be processed in order to make them into spreadable solids. What is the name of this process?

.... [1]

(Total 23 marks)

Worked example

Atom economy can be calculated using this equation:

$$\text{atom economy} = \times 100\%$$

The compound $C_4H_2O_3$ can be synthesised in different ways, for example:

$$C_6H_6 + 4\tfrac{1}{2}O_2 \rightarrow C_4H_2O_3 + 2CO_2 + 2H_2O$$

a i Calculate the relative formula mass of $C_4H_2O_3$ [1]
ii Calculate the relative mass of all of the CO_2 formed [1]
iii Calculate the formula mass of all of the water formed [1]

b i Use the equation above to calculate the atom economy for this reaction [3]
ii Why is it important to consider the atom economy of the various synthetic routes? [1]

c Another way of evaluating a synthetic route is to calculate the % yield of a reaction.
i If 36.0 kg of C_6H_6 is reacted, what is the maximum theoretical yield of $C_4H_2O_3$ that can be formed? [3]
ii If 24.2 kg of $C_4H_2O_3$ is formed then what is the % yield of the reaction? [3]

Correct answer. It is sensible to show the working.

a i $C_4H_2O_3 = (4 \times 12) + (2 \times 1) + (3 \times 16) = 98$
ii $2CO_2 = 2 \times (12 + 32) = 88$
iii $2H_2O = 2 \times (2 + 16) = 34$

b i atom economy = 0.441
ii It is important to know the atom economy because it tells you what mass of chemicals you need to react.

b i One slip in the calculation. The atom economy is a percentage and the calculation should have been $\times 100\%$. The student forgot to multiply by 100. The answer should have been 44.1%. Only 1 mark lost, though.
b ii The student has not understood the idea of atom economy. It gives you an idea of the proportion of the reactants that is being 'useful' and what proportion is wasted. This is important for sustainable development as it avoids waste.

c i $C_6H_6 + 4\tfrac{1}{2}O_2 \rightarrow C_4H_2O_3 + 2CO_2 + 2H_2O$
72 g would give 98 g
So 72 kg would give 98 kg
And 36 kg would give 49 kg
ii % yield = $\times 100 = 202\%$

c i has been done very clearly and very well. In **c ii** the student should have spotted that 202% yield was impossible and looked for the error in the calculation. The calculation is upside down. % yield = $\times 100\%$. This gives $\times 100\% = 49.4\%$.

Overall Grade: B

How to get an A

This student seemed to know what they were doing with the calculations but was making silly mistakes. Could they have avoided this? I would say they could have. You must always check your final answer and make sure it makes sense. Provided you have worked clearly you will be able to work back and spot your mistakes.

Chemistry 2b

DISCOVER FIREWORKS!

Fireworks are usually made from a mixture of an oxidising agent, a reducing agent, a colouring agent, binders and regulators.

Have you ever wondered how fireworks work? What are the component parts of fireworks? What elements and chemical compounds cause fireworks to explode? What chemical compounds are responsible for the colours of fireworks?

Oxidisers produce the oxygen to burn the mixture in a firework. They can be nitrates, chlorates or perchlorates.

Reducing agents burn, using oxygen from the oxidisers, and they produce hot gases. Two examples of reducing agents are sulphur and charcoal (carbon). These react with the oxygen to form respectively sulphur dioxide and carbon dioxide.

Before the 19th century, only various yellows and oranges could be produced by burning steel and charcoal. Chlorates, an invention of the late 18th century and an industrial product of the 19th century, added basic reds and greens to the pyrotechnist's repertoire. Good blues and purples were not developed until recently.

CONTENTS

Metallic behaviour

You will find out:

- About some useful properties of metals
- Why most metals are so hard and dense
- How metals conduct electricity

Valuable metals

The most valuable metals are not necessarily the most expensive. Even the cheapest, iron and steel, are valuable because we couldn't manage without them. Steel is used to make many things, including cars, ships, bridges, frames in large buildings, and fridges. You'd be in the dark without aluminium power lines, copper wiring and tungsten light bulb filaments.

Why are metals so useful?

Metals have the right properties for a wide range of uses. They are:

- good conductors of heat and electricity
- usually hard and **dense**, with high melting and boiling points
- **malleable** (can be bent to shape without breaking, and keep this shape)
- **ductile** (can be pulled out into thin wires).

Some are better than others for particular jobs. Here are some examples.

Metal	Properties	Uses
Aluminium	light (low density)	aircraft; overhead power cables
Copper	good electrical conductor good heat conductor	electrical wiring; boilers; bottom of saucepans
Magnesium	strong and light	racing car wheels
Stainless steel	does not corrode (rust)	cutlery; saucepans; sinks
Steel	malleable and strong	car bodies
Titanium	strong, light, unreactive	mountain bikes; body joints

Some unreactive metals occur in the ground as the metal itself, like gold and silver. Most metals occur as an ore. An ore is a compound of the metal, e.g. haematite is an ore of iron because it contains iron oxide.

FIGURE 1: 'Let there be light!' This image represents tungsten in the Visual Elements periodic table.

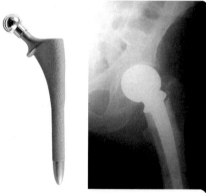

FIGURE 2: Replacement titanium hip joint and X-ray of it in position.

WOW FACTOR!

Gold is so dense that a block the size of a 330 ml cola can would weigh over 6 kg!

QUESTIONS

1. Which metal would you use to make railings? Explain your choice.
2. Which **two** properties are needed for overhead power cables?
3. Give **two** properties that metals have and non-metals do not have.
4. What is the difference between 'malleable' and 'flexible'?

...alloy ...conductivity ...delocalised ...dense ...ductile

How do metals conduct?

Metals have high electrical **conductivity**. They can carry an electric current – whether tiny from a watch battery, or huge through a lightning conductor. So, how do metals do it?

- An electric current is electrons moving through the metal.
- These are outer-shell electrons – those that the metal passes to a non-metal in ionic bonding. This leaves the metal as a positive ion.
- When there's no non-metal to take them away, the electrons stay nearby.
- The result is a regular pattern (called a **lattice**) of positive metal ions (+), with a 'sea of electrons' (–) around them. The negative electrons attract the positive ions. They are the 'glue' that holds the metal lattice together.
- This method of holding metal atoms together is called **metallic bonding**.
- The electrons in the sea no longer belong to particular atoms. They are free or '**delocalised**' and can move through the lattice.
- Moving electrons = electric current. So the metal conducts.

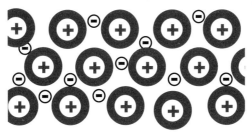

FIGURE 3: Regular lattice of metal ions surrounded by a sea of electrons.

Not just conduction

Metallic bonding explains other properties as well as conduction. The strong attractions between ions and electrons hold the metal atoms tightly together.

- Closely packed atoms give high density.
- The bonding makes metals difficult to break apart, so they're strong and hard.
- It needs lots of heat energy to separate the atoms to let them flow and vaporise. So metals have high melting and boiling points.
- The layers can slide over each other, but still be held together by electrons. So metals bend and stretch without breaking. They're malleable and ductile.
- The ions and delocalised electrons can vibrate, passing heat energy through the lattice. So metals also conduct heat well.

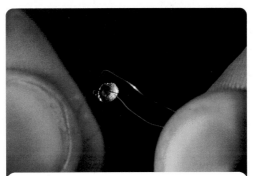

FIGURE 4: Copper is ductile. Pulling it through the tiny hole in this diamond makes extremely thin wire.

The 'middle' metals

The metals in the middle of the periodic table are the **transition metals**. They are nearly all 'typical' metals – hard, dense, shiny and not very reactive, unlike sodium, magnesium and aluminium, for example.

You will know some transition metals already such as iron, copper, zinc, gold and silver.

Sc 21	Ti 22	V 23	Cr 24	Mn 25	Fe 26	Co 27	Ni 28	Cu 29	Zn 30
Y 39	Zr 40	Nb 41	Mo 42	Tc 43	Ru 44	Rh 45	Pd 46	Ag 47	Cd 48
	Hf 72	Ta 73	W 74	Re 75	Os 76	Ir 77	Pt 78	Au 79	Hg 80

Let's have a look at some uses of the less common transition metals. An **alloy** is a mixture of metals.

- Chromium – makes steel alloys stainless.
- Vanadium – makes steel alloys very hard.
- Nickel and Cadmium – in NiCad batteries.
- Tungsten – used for light bulb filaments.
- Titanium – in low-density alloys for military aircraft.

Many transition metals are used as catalysts.

- Nickel is used in the manufacture of margarine.
- Platinum is used in catalytic converters in car exhaust systems.

FIGURE 5: The SR-71 Blackbird is built mainly from titanium alloy.

QUESTIONS

5 What do we mean by a 'sea of electrons'?

6 What happens to these electrons when a metal conducts electricity?

7 Why doesn't a sheet of steel break when bent into the shape of a car body?

8 Suggest why diamonds are used to 'draw' out thin wires.

QUESTIONS

9 Why is tungsten used to make filaments for light bulbs?

10 What are the properties of a typical transition metal?

11 Find out which **three** transition metals are magnetic.

Simple structures

You will find out:

- About the forces between molecules
- Why covalent substances do not conduct electricity
- Some facts about the Group 7 elements

Seaside wonders

Beaches are wonderful places – literally 'full of wonders'. Sand, sea and air all contain oxygen, but one is a solid, one is a liquid and the other is a gas. Have you ever wondered why? And why doesn't the sea dissolve the sand? If you leave a bowl of sea water in hot sun, salt appears and the water disappears. How? Let's think about these problems.

What's the difference?

Why is air a gas, water a liquid and sand a solid?

- A gas is a substance that is above its boiling point. Oxygen and nitrogen boil at nearly −200 °C. So air is a gas at normal temperatures.

- A liquid is above its melting point, but below its boiling point. So water is liquid at temperatures between 0 °C and 100 °C.

- A solid is below its melting point. Chocolate may melt on a hot day (around 35 °C, but sand won't. Its melting point is nearly 2000 °C.

So what makes the melting and boiling points of oxygen, hydrogen oxide (water) and silicon oxide (sand) so different?

- Gases are made up of **molecules** containing a few atoms. Molecules in the air (nitrogen, N_2, and oxygen, O_2), have only two. These small, light molecules need little energy to move around. They easily separate from each other to become a gas at low temperatures.

- Water molecules, H_2O, are very small. Most liquid molecules are a bit bigger, like ethanol, C_2H_5OH, and sulphuric acid, H_2SO_4. It takes more energy to get them moving. So their melting and boiling points are higher.

- Heavier molecules, like sulphur, S_8, need even more energy. You must heat sulphur to 113 °C to separate the molecules and melt it.

- It takes an awful lot of energy to melt sand. That's because each grain is one *giant* molecule, similar to diamond.

- Salt also has a giant structure. Water can evaporate easily, but salt cannot. So, warming evaporates salt water, leaving salt crystals behind.

FIGURE 1: An empty beach, full of wonders.

FIGURE 2: At what temperature do icicles melt?

Watch Out Melting and boiling points increase with molecular mass, but also depend on how strongly the molecules are held together.

QUESTIONS

1 What is a molecule?
2 What happens to molecules as the temperature increases?
3 Why do substances with heavier molecules have higher melting points?

...*conduction* ...*covalent bond* ...*diatomic* ...*halogens* ...*inter-molecular forces*

Small and simple

All gaseous or liquid non-metals and their compounds have **simple molecular structures**. So do solids with low melting points.

- Their atoms are grouped into individual molecules, containing a small number of atoms – up to about 10 for gases, 30 for liquids.
- The atoms in each molecule are held together by strong **covalent bonds**.

Generally, gas molecules have fewer atoms than liquids, while solids have more. However, it's not that simple. Why is butane, C_4H_{10}, a gas, but water, H_2O, a liquid? And why is decane, $C_{10}H_{22}$, a liquid, but iodine, I_2, a solid?

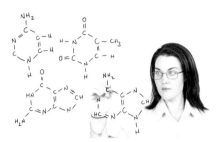

FIGURE 3: Some not-so-simple molecular structures.

Two main factors determine a substance's melting and boiling points – and thus whether it's a solid, liquid or gas at room temperature:

- **relative molecular mass**, M_r – which depends not only on the number of atoms, but also on their atomic masses;
- **inter-molecular forces** between one molecule and the others around it.

Molecules attract each other. These inter-molecular forces vary, but they're much weaker than covalent bonds. However, we still need to add energy to overcome the force of attraction.

FIGURE 4: Why is water's boiling point so high compared with other small molecules?

Warming a solid gives the molecules energy. They move more. When they have enough energy to flow, the solid breaks up and melts. Molecules still attract each other in the liquid. More heat overcomes these attractions. The molecules break free, separate completely and become gas. The liquid boils.

The heavier the molecules (the higher M_r) and the stronger the inter-molecular forces, the more energy is needed. Water has small molecules, but particularly strong inter-molecular forces.

Covalency and conduction

Covalent compounds, whether simple molecules or giant covalent structures like sand, do not conduct electricity. **Conduction** needs either electrons or ions that are free to move. Covalent compounds have neither.

Graphite is an exception. Find out why on page 165.

QUESTIONS

4   Give **three** examples of substances with a simple molecular structure.
5   What are the forces between molecules in liquids and gases called?
6   How could you tell whether a substance has a simple molecular structure?

Salt makers

The elements of Group 7 are called the **halogens**, from the Greek for 'salt maker'. You will have come across some halogen salts, called 'halides': sodium chloride, sodium fluoride (in toothpaste) and potassium iodide, for example.

The halogens are non-metals with simple molecular structures – pairs of atoms known as **diatomic** molecules (F_2, Cl_2, Br_2, I_2), just like dydrogen and oxygen.

Their physical properties show clear trends down the group.

Halogen	State	M_r	Density /g cm^{-3}	mp /°C	bp /°C
Fluorine	gas	38	0.0016	−220	−188
Chlorine	gas	71	0.0030	−101	− 34
Bromine	liquid	160	3.12	− 7	59
Iodine	solid	254	4.93	114	184
Astatine	?	420	?	?	?

The larger and heavier the molecules, the stronger the inter-molecular forces will be.

- Pulling heavier molecules closer together increases the density.
- Stronger attractions between heavier molecules means more heat energy is needed to move and separate molecules. So melting and boiling points increase.

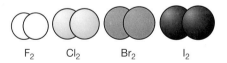

F_2 Cl_2 Br_2 I_2

FIGURE 5: Relative sizes of halogen molecules, and colours when gaseous.

QUESTIONS

7   From information in the table, predict the data for astatine.
8   Draw a dot and cross diagram to show the bonding in fluorine.
9   Find out a use of each halogen from fluorine to iodine.

Bonding

You will find out:
- How atoms are held together by bonds
- How covalent bonds are made by sharing electrons
- Why bonds hold atoms together

The unreactive elements

Mendeleev's periodic table didn't include helium, neon or the rest of that group. They exist in the air around us, but weren't discovered until the 1890s because they are invisible gases and don't form compounds. They are called the 'noble gases' because they won't join in reactions with common elements. They're so unreactive they don't even pair up with each other.

FIGURE 1: 'Neon' signs. Only electricity can brighten up the noble gases.

Sticking together

Why is diamond so hard? Why does glue hold things together? Why do two hydrogen atoms and one oxygen atom stick together to form a water molecule? The answer in each case is that atoms come together and share some of their electrons. This sharing forms a bond between the atoms.

The reason **noble gases** don't react is also the reason that other elements do.

- Noble gases are unreactive because they have the most stable arrangement of electrons.

- Their **outer shell** has a 'full set' of eight electrons (two for helium).

- When other atoms react they try to copy this stable structure by filling or emptying their outer shell, to leave a full set.

FIGURE 2: Chemical bonds work like glue. They hold things together, but can be pulled apart again.

Atoms bond together either by passing electrons from a metal to a non-metal (**ionic bonding**), or sharing electrons (**covalent bonding** between two non-metals).

Understanding bonding means knowing about the electrons in the outer shell. Remember, elements in Group 1 have one electron in their outer shell, elements in Group 2 have two electrons in their outer shell and so on up to Group 7 elements which have seven electrons in their outer shell.

QUESTIONS

1. Which group of elements are very stable and unreactive?
2. Name **two** elements in Group 7.
3. When two non-metals bond together, what type of bonding is there?
4. How many electrons do elements in Group 7 have in the outer shell?

WOW FACTOR!

There are about 67 million million million million covalent bonds in 1 litre of water.

...covalent bonding   ...double bond   ...group number

Sharing electrons

Atoms have electrons orbiting in shells around the nucleus. If you look at the periodic table, the **group number** tells you the number of electrons in the outer shell. Only the noble gases – neon, argon, etc. – in Group 0 have a full set of eight in their outer shells. Other non-metal atoms get a full set by sharing electrons in a covalent bond.

- If an atom has seven electrons in the outer shell, like fluorine, it needs to share one more. It makes one covalent bond.
- If an atom has four electrons in its outer shell, like carbon, it needs to share four more. It makes four covalent bonds.
- The number of bonds a non-metal atom makes is the number of electrons it needs to share to fill its outer shell.

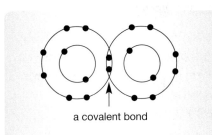

FIGURE 3: Two fluorine atoms sharing a pair of electrons. Count the electrons in each outer shell now. Are they full sets?

The formula for methane is CH_4. Figure 4 shows the covalent bonds holding these five atoms together.

Count the electrons in each outer shell now. Remember that the first shell can hold only two electrons, so hydrogen forms only one bond.

- Two non-metal atoms can share electrons to make a covalent bond.
- The shared electrons are then counted as part of both of the outer shells.

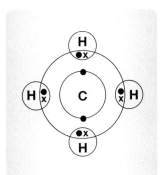

FIGURE 4: Dot and cross diagram of methane.

Why do bonds hold atoms together?

When two atoms share a pair of electrons between them, the atoms are held together by the 'covalent bond'. Why is this?

- The positive nuclei of both atoms are attracted towards the shared electrons, which are negative.
- It's like two people (the atoms) pulling on a short rope (the electrons) and not letting go!

FIGURE 5: A covalent bond is like these two people. The pull holds them together.

When one is not enough

Whenever you see carbon in a compound, it makes four bonds in order to fill its outer shell. Those bonds could be four single bonds, or two **double bonds**... Can you think of another possibility?

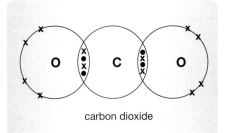

FIGURE 6: In CO_2 carbon makes two double bonds.

- A single covalent bond is a shared pair of electrons.
- A double bond is two shared pairs of electrons.

Some hydrocarbons contain double bonds: the alkenes (ethene, propene, etc.). So does oxygen gas, O_2.

The alkenes are more reactive than hydrocarbons with a single bond (the alkanes) because the double bond is reactive. It can break open and form two new bonds to other atoms.

...ionic bonding   ...noble gases   ...outer shell

Carbon footballs

You will find out:

- That many discoveries in science have happened by chance
- About carbon 'buckyballs' – molecules in the shape of a football

Discovery by accident

Some very important discoveries in science have been made purely by chance! In 1791 Luigi Galvani reported that frog legs hanging on a wire near a metal railing twitched when the wind made the legs touch the railing. He decided to find out why. This was the beginning of the science of electric currents.

A joint British and American discovery

In 1985, scientists including Harry Kroto discovered a new form of carbon by chance. People had known about **diamond** and **graphite** for centuries. The new form was a great surprise.

- It turned out to be C_{60}: 60 carbon atoms bonded in the shape of a football. Molecules are far too small to see. It took five years to prove that this was the correct structure.

- In 1996 Harry Kroto shared the Nobel Prize for Chemistry with his two American co-discoverers.

- C_{60} was named **buckminsterfullerene** after the architect Buckminster Fuller. He designed buildings made up of hexagons and pentagons. The molecules are often called 'buckyballs'.

- Buckminsterfullerene is pure carbon, just like graphite and diamond. What would burning buckminsterfullerene produce?

- Possible future uses of C_{60} and other **fullerenes** (enclosed carbon molecules) include catalysts, lubricants and superconductors. A superconductor is a substance that conducts electricity with no resistance at all.

FIGURE 1: 'Chance favours the prepared mind.' Galvani was ready and able to investigate his chance discovery.

FIGURE 2: Buckminsterfullerene has 60 carbon atoms and 90 bonds connecting the atoms.

QUESTIONS

1 Why do you think buckminsterfullerene might be a good lubricant?
2 How many bonds does each carbon make in buckminsterfullerene?
3 Is buckminsterfullerene closer in structure to diamond or graphite?

LUCKY DISCOVERIES

There's a fun word that means making lucky discoveries by chance. It is 'serendipity'.

Nanotubes

Scientists have also recently discovered long tubes of carbon atoms, like a sheet of graphite rolled up.

- This is a new form of the element carbon, just like 'buckyballs'.

- **Nanotubes** are extremely small: it would take well over 1 million of them rolled up to be the size of a human hair.

- Nanotubes have lots of useful properties: they are extremely strong – many times stronger than steel, weight for weight.

- Some of them are good electrical conductors.

- Nanotubes are thought to have many possible uses in the future, from making super-strong 'nanoropes' and fibres, to making tiny wires.

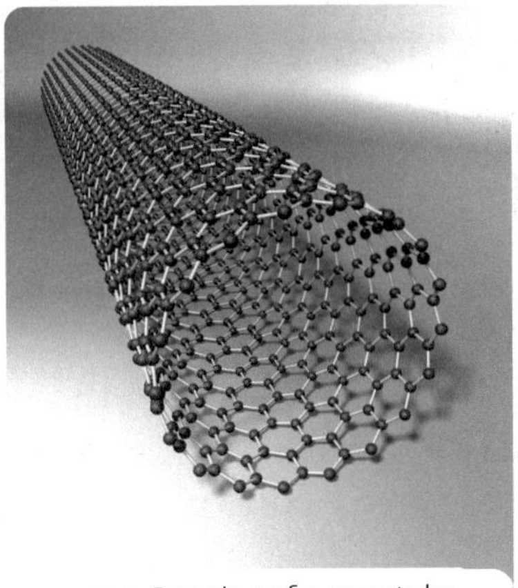

So watch out for news about 'nanotubes' in the next few years, and remember – they are just another form of pure carbon.

FIGURE 3: Drawing of a nanotube. The carbon atoms are arranged in hexagonal layers, as in graphite.

ANOTHER BALL

As well as buckyballs and nanotubes, there is an oval-shaped gullerene, C_{70}, like a carbon rugby ball.

Organic chemistry

The element carbon occurs as graphite, diamond, buckyballs and nanotubes. There are also millions of compounds containing carbon that have been discovered. There is more to the chemistry of carbon than all the other elements put together!

So why does carbon form so many compounds? Life on Earth is based around the carbon atom. Carbon-based compounds form a large branch of chemistry called Organic Chemistry. '**Organic**' means that it deals with living things, like plants and animals.

But why is carbon such a special element?

- Carbon can form four bonds – most other elements cannot form as many.

- Carbon forms very strong bonds with hydrogen, oxygen, nitrogen... and many other elements.

- Carbon can easily form chains of itself; for example, the hydrocarbon octane contains eight carbons in a row.

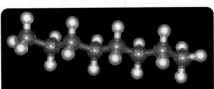

FIGURE 4: Octane is a hydrocarbon with the formula C_8H_{18}.

Making diamonds

Diamonds used in cutting tools are not mined any more, but are made artificially. They are manufactured in a press from graphite heated with a metal at a temperature of up to 1500 °C and a pressure of 50 000 atmospheres. Under these extreme conditions the graphite structure breaks apart and reforms into diamond, because diamond is slightly denser. Actually, anything that contains carbon can be turned into diamonds – it's even been tried with peanut butter!

FIGURE 5: Peanut butter can be turned into diamond!

QUESTIONS

7   Is diamond an element or a compound? What would be its formula?

8   Is there a chemical difference between 'natural' and 'artificial' diamonds?

9   Why are diamonds so expensive if they can now be created in a few hours?

QUESTIONS

4   What is the branch of chemistry concerned with carbon compounds?

5   Can you find another element in the periodic table near carbon that also makes four bonds?

6   Draw the structure of dodecane, the straight chain hydrocarbon with 12 carbon atoms. How many hydrogen atoms does it have?

...graphite   ...nanotubes   ...organic

Strong stuff

You will find out:

- That diamond and graphite are forms of carbon and contain covalent bonds between carbon atoms
- That diamond and graphite are giant covalent structures

Diamonds are forever

Diamond is the hardest material on Earth. It is a form of the element carbon that has been formed under great pressure in the Earth's crust. Diamonds are crystals. Pure ones have no colour – you can see through them and they sparkle in the light.

Diamonds are used to cut metals and grind through rock. We need to look at the structure of diamond to explain its hardness.

Do diamonds burn?

Scientists used an expensive way to find out what **diamonds** are made from: they burnt some in oxygen! They got only one product: carbon dioxide. This proved that diamonds are pure carbon. Here are the equations:

FIGURE 1: A cut and polished diamond.

Word equation: **diamond + oxygen → carbon dioxide**

Symbol equation: C + O_2 → CO_2

You probably have a more common type of carbon in your pencil case. Pencil 'lead' contains **graphite**, another form of pure carbon. Different forms of the same element are called **allotropes**.

Can you melt a diamond?

If you try to melt a diamond or pencil lead with a Bunsen burner, you won't succeed! They both have melting points over 3500 °C. This is because they both have giant structures. A giant structure is one where the bonds extend right through the material. There are no separate molecules.

- Carbon forms only covalent bonds. Diamond and graphite have **giant covalent structures**.

- They both have very high melting points because the bonds are strong.

- Instead of melting, they turn straight from a solid to a gas. This is called subliming.

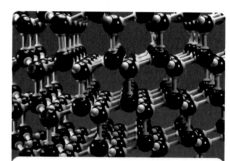

FIGURE 2: A model of the giant structure of diamond. Every carbon atom is bonded to four others around it.

EXAM HINTS AND TIPS

Allotropes are elements with their atoms arranged differently – like diamond and graphite, or oxygen, O_2, and ozone, O_3.

QUESTIONS

1 What is the word for different forms of the same element?
2 Give **one** property that diamond and graphite have in common.
3 Give **one** way in which diamond and graphite are different.
4 Sublime means 'wonderful', but what do we mean by 'graphite sublimes'?

...allotropes ...delocalised ...diamond

Layers upon layers

The graphite in pencils is soft – when you write, layers rub off onto the paper. Diamond, however, is used to drill through rock and is the hardest naturally – occurring substance. Both are forms of pure carbon, so why do they have such different properties? The answer lies in their structures.

- Carbon always forms four bonds, as in CH_4, methane. In diamond, each carbon atom has four strong covalent bonds to other carbon atoms in a **tetrahedral** arrangement. (A tetrahedron is a shape with four faces.)

- This 3-D network of strong bonds through the whole crystal makes the structure very rigid. This is why diamond is so hard.

- Graphite has a layered structure. Each carbon atom has three bonds to other carbon atoms, forming flat layers of hexagons, like honeycomb. These are strong covalent bonds.

- The fourth bond, between the layers, is much weaker. This is why the layers can slide easily over one another. Graphite can be used as a lubricant between two metal moving parts. It doesn't flow away like oil does.

- The bonding between the layers is made from **delocalised** electrons, similar to the 'sea of electrons' in metals. So, graphite is able to conduct electricity.

To melt diamond or graphite, you need to break all the strong covalent bonds. This takes a great deal of energy, so both allotropes remain solid up to 3500 °C.

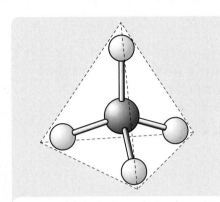

FIGURE 3: A tetrahedron – 'tetra-' means 'four' in chemistry.

FIGURE 4: The carbon atoms form strong layers in graphite.

Diamond	Graphite
Atoms arranged tetrahedrally	Atoms in hexagonal layers
Strong bonding throughout structure	Weak forces between layers
Extremely hard and rigid	Layers slide and rub off easily
Sublimes above 3550 °C	Sublimes above 3650 °C
Does not conduct electricity	Good electrical conductor

QUESTIONS

5 Explain why graphite is used in pencils.

6 In diamond, how many bonds to other atoms does each atom form?

7 What kind of symmetry does the structure of diamond have?

8 Why does graphite conduct electricity, but not diamond?

Conduction

Substances can conduct electricity if they have charged particles that are able to move. These particles are either ions or electrons.

Substance	Particle doing the conducting of electricity
graphite	electrons between the layers
metals	electrons
molten ionic compounds	ions
ionic compounds dissolved in water	ions

- An electric current is the movement of charged particles through a conductor.
- Graphite is a good conductor of electricity.
- Most non-metals do not conduct electricity because they do not have any electrons or ions which are free to move.
- Some metals conduct electricity particularly well because they have lots of free electrons. Copper, silver and gold are used for electrical connections where low resistance is important.
- Solid ionic compounds do not conduct because the ions are unable to move.

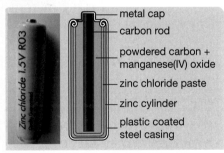

metal cap
carbon rod
powdered carbon + manganese(IV) oxide
zinc chloride paste
zinc cylinder
plastic coated steel casing

FIGURE 5: A 'battery' contains three types of conductor: zinc metal, a graphite rod and an ionic electrolyte.

QUESTIONS

9 Which allotrope of carbon has the lowest electrical resistance?

10 Name the particles that move and conduct in salt water.

11 Can hexane (a liquid) conduct electricity? Why or why not?

12 Do you think graphite conducts electricity well in all directions?

...giant covalent structure   ...graphite   ...tetrahedral

Medicines?

You will find out:

● About the scientific method used to test new discoveries and ideas

● About homeopathic medicine and the debate – does it work?

Therapies

Most of us will use some form of medicine for different problems. We may use paracetamol for a headache, antiseptic cream for a graze, and anaesthetic during an operation! All these treatments are conventional medicines – scientifically proven to have a helpful effect on our bodies.

The scientific method

What is science?

Chemistry began as alchemy in the Middle Ages. Alchemists tried to turn lead into gold and to find cures for all illnesses, including death! We now know they were looking for things that can't be found. Modern scientists look for cancer treatments and cures for the common cold. Perhaps these will be found in your lifetime.

FIGURE 1: Many of us take some kind of medicine regularly.

Over the last 200 years, science has developed ways of looking at the world and increasing our knowledge. There are five main stages to the modern **scientific method**: observation (noticing things); identification (finding out what things are); description (writing down their properties); investigation (conducting experiments to find out more), and explanation (coming up with a theory that fits the facts).

What is a scientific approach?

Scientists try to work out why things behave as they do. They make up theories and test them by doing experiments, then repeating them. They also discuss their results with other scientists all over the world. This is what the internet was set up for!

- New medicines must be tested for several years before they're allowed to be used. Doctors must be sure the medicines work and cause no harm. They need to study lots of chemistry and biology at university!

- New medicines that are found to be safe go through 'trials'. Different groups of patients try a medicine to see how well it works.

- Many illnesses still have no cures. Medicine is not perfect.

PENICILLIN

The antibiotic medicine penicillin was discovered accidentally. Mould fell into a Petri dish and killed the bacteria growing in it.

QUESTIONS

1 What were the aims of alchemists in medieval times?

2 How has scientific communication changed from 1800 until now?

3 What has to happen when someone invents a new medicine?

...alternative medicine   ...homeopathy

Strange cures

Medical treatments that do not take a science-based approach are called **alternative medicine**. One of the most popular is **homeopathy**. Homeopathic remedies are natural remedies made from plant, animal and mineral extracts.

- Homeopathy works by treating 'like with like'. ('Homo' means 'same'.)

- An 18th century German doctor discovered that taking a poisonous substance called quinine produced the same symptoms as malaria.

- He developed the theory that a poison that has a similar effect to a disease can be used to treat that disease, as long as it's taken in very small amounts.

- Tonic water contains quinine, and was popular in India as it was thought to guard against malaria. Quinine does have some anti-malarial effects but cannot cure or prevent malaria completely.

FIGURE 2: Quinine gives tonic water its bitter taste.

Many doctors are puzzled by the apparent effectiveness of homeopathic remedies. People all over the world take arnica (extracted from a herb) to relieve bruising, or apis mel (extracted from honey bees) for bee stings. However, these 'medicines' have not been proved to have any positive effects. Their claimed effects cannot be explained scientifically. The arguments are still going on about whether these treatments are effective or just **placebos**. A placebo is a treatment that has an effect only because the patient believes it does!

Homeopathy states that an illness may be cured by using diluted doses of a substance that causes symptoms similar to the illness.

Other alternative therapies include acupuncture, herbal medicine, aromatherapy and using wrist bracelets made of copper or other metals.

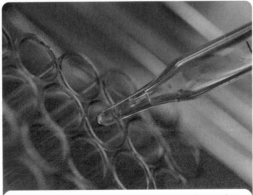

FIGURE 3: Preparing homoeopathic medicines by diluting many times.

'Many doctors are puzzled by the apparent effectiveness of homeopathy'

Dilution factors (H)

Homeopathic remedies are highly diluted.

- One drop of quinine solution shaken vigorously with 99 drops of 80 per cent alcohol solution makes a 1 centesimal (1c) potency.

- One drop of 1c diluted with 99 drops of alcohol and shaken makes a 2c potency, and so on. 2c is very dilute (0.01 per cent), but some treatments call for 10c or even 30c potency.

- 30c is 100^{30} (=10^{60}) times less concentrated than the original solution.

- This is so dilute that in a 30c solution there will not be any molecules of quinine.

- Conventional medicine says that if there are no molecules of quinine present, it can't work. Homeopathic practitioners say that the solution retains some kind of 'memory' of the quinine molecules. They also claim that the more diluted the solution, the more effective it is!

QUESTIONS

7 How many times more dilute is a 6c solution than a 2c solution?

8 If there are 1×10^{23} molecules of quinine in the original sample that is mixed, how many molecules would be left in a 10c solution?

9 Why do you think the solutions are shaken vigorously at each stage?

QUESTIONS

4 What is the idea behind homeopathic medicines?

5 Why is it difficult to prove the effectiveness of some medicines like pain killers?

6 What would be needed to prove the effectiveness of a homeopathic remedy?

...placebo   ...scientific method

Modelling molecules

You will find out:

- Molecules have a 3-D shape which cannot easily be drawn on paper
- Molecules can be understood better with computer models

Shape matters

Have you ever wondered why ice floats, and non-stick pans don't stick? Some everyday chemicals have peculiar properties. When you freeze a liquid it usually becomes denser and sinks – but not water. You can glue most materials – but not Teflon®. Do you fancy caraway chewing gum? The flavouring chemical is the same as spearmint, except that the molecules are mirror images. All these oddities are due to the shapes of molecules.

The shape of molecules

Everyone knows the formula of water is H_2O, but how are the atoms connected together?

- Each hydrogen atom is joined to the oxygen with a single **covalent bond**.

- The bonds are at an angle to one another, giving water a V shape.

- When water freezes into ice, this V shape makes the molecules join up in open hexagons. You can see this hexagonal symmetry in snowflakes.

- This open 'honeycomb' shape means there's more space between ice molecules. So its density is low.

A molecule's shape depends on how its atoms are arranged – and their size. Molecules aren't flat. They're 3-D, and difficult to draw on paper. Hydrocarbons are often drawn as in Figure 3.

There are two problems with such diagrams. In real butane molecules the carbon atoms are not in a straight line; and the **bond angles** (the angles between the C–H bonds) are over 100°, not 90° as shown.

FIGURE 1: Models representing the shape of water molecules.

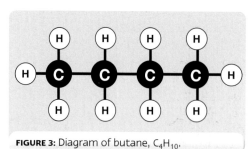
FIGURE 3: Diagram of butane, C_4H_{10}.

FIGURE 2: Hexagonal shapes of some snowflake crystals. No two snowflakes are exactly the same!

QUESTIONS

1. What kind of bonding holds the atoms in a water molecule together?
2. What shape is a water molecule, H_2O?
3. Why do huge icebergs float?
4. Why is it difficult to draw the shapes of molecules properly on paper?

...ball-and-stick models   ...bond angles   ...computer graphics

Molecules in 3-D   (H)

The best way of seeing the shape is to make models. There are two main types.

- **Ball-and-stick models** show the positions of atoms and the bonds in between. In the butane model you can see that the atoms are not really in straight rows.

- **Space-filling models** indicate the overall shape of the molecule. They show the atoms as overlapping spheres, so you can't see the bonds.

Models are colour-coded: black = carbon, white = hydrogen, red = oxygen.

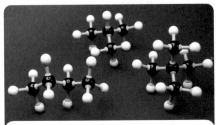

FIGURE 4: Models of three hydrocarbons. Butane, C_4H_{10}, is front left.

FIGURE 5: Space-filling models of two isomers of C_4H_{10} – the two molecules on the left of figure 4.

Right- and left-handed molecules

Is your left hand the same as your right? Does your left hand fit your right glove? Your hands may look the same, but they are mirror images.

Some molecules are mirror images of each other, like your hands. This causes surprising effects. For example, one chemical tastes of spearmint. The same atoms rearranged as the mirror molecule taste of caraway.

Left- and right-handed molecules affect your body differently in other ways too – not just taste. When making a medicine, scientists must make sure that it is the correct handed version, or it may have the wrong effect on your body.

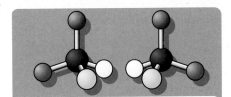

FIGURE 6: Mirror image molecules. The four coloured balls may represent single atoms or different groups of atoms.

IT helps

Computer graphics have helped molecular modelling in recent years. We can now draw diagrams that look like 3-D models. Even better, we can make the image of the molecule rotate, so we can look at it from different angles.

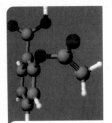 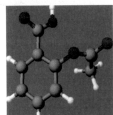 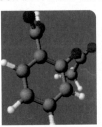

FIGURE 7: Rotating model of aspirin, $C_9H_8O_4$. Carbon atoms are shown grey.

QUESTIONS

5   What are the advantages of using models rather than paper drawings?

6   Why do you think molecular models are colour-coded?

7   Why does it matter that some molecules have left- and right-handed forms?

What's the angle?

Methane has tetrahedral symmetry, but what is the angle between the bonds?

Covalent bonds repel each other as far as possible. In 3-D this turns out to be $109.5°$, not $90°$.

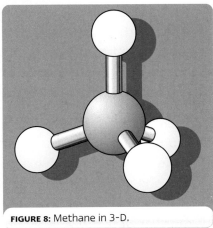

FIGURE 8: Methane in 3-D.

What is the angle between the C–H bonds in ethene?

$$H \diagdown \underset{H \diagup}{\overset{\diagup H}{C=C}} \diagdown H$$

Ethene

There are only three groups of electrons repelling each other around the carbon atom (two single C–H bonds and one C=C double bond). The maximum bond angle possible is therefore $120°$.

The molecule is flat, or planar: all the atoms are in the same plane.

QUESTIONS

8   CO_2 is called a 'linear molecule'. What do you think the bond angle is?

9   Why do covalent bonds coming out of the same atom repel each other?

10   If there are six bonds repelling each other, what would the bond angle be? (Hint: think of the x, y and z axes on a graph in Maths.)

Chemical structures

SELF-CHECK ACTIVITY

CONTEXT

Andy likes science; he is part of a team of pupils that visit classes of younger pupils to work with them to develop their understanding of science. He likes using models and analogies to explain ideas and thinks he has come up with a good one to explain why conductors conduct electricity and insulators don't.

The model goes like this. All materials are made of atoms; sometimes the atoms are joined up to make molecules. Atoms have a nucleus that consists of protons and neutrons, and they also have electrons. The number of electrons has to be the same as the number of protons in order to make the atom neutral. It's the electrons that are really crucial in this model.

Andy then sets out a number of plastic Petri dishes in a row. He says that each of these represents an atom. The atom needs exactly the right number of electrons. If it has too many the extra ones will be repelled. If it doesn't have enough it will attract more until it does.

He then gets some marbles and puts some in each dish. To fill the dish, without any being stacked up on top of others, takes exactly thirteen. The marbles represent the electrons in the atom.

Andy then says that in order for a current to flow along this wire, extra electrons have to arrive at one end, displace electrons from the first dish to the second, from the second dish to the third, and so on. This is conduction.

He now gets the Petri dish lids and puts them on the dishes, enclosing the marbles. Now if more marbles are supplied at one end, the others can't move along. In this model, electrons can't be transferred. This is insulation.

CHALLENGE

STEP 1

Draw a diagram of the row of Petri dishes set up to model conduction and label it to show what the object represent.

STEP 2

Now draw the model and label it as it is set up to model insulation.

STEP 3

Do you think Andy has come up with a good model?
- Explain how it explains conduction and insulation well.
- Now explain the shortcomings of the model.

STEP 4

One of Andy's friends comes up with some other features that the model might be able to show. Explain, perhaps using diagrams, how you could use or develop the model to show that:
- wires are not just one atom wide
- atoms of different materials have different numbers of electrons
- atoms also have protons and neutrons (though they don't flow)
- some materials are better conductors than others.

Maximise your grade

These sentences show what you need to include in your work to achieve each grade. Use them to improve your work and be more successful.

Grade	Answer includes...
F	Have some idea of subatomic particles.
	Know that protons, electrons and neutrons are subatomic particles.
	Know that the number of protons is equal to the number of electrons in an atom.
	Have some idea about mobile electrons as charge carriers.
C	Explain that in a conductor the electrons are less tightly bound in to an atom than they are in an insulator.
	Use and explain a model to show various features of conduction.
A	Manipulate and evaluate a model to show various features of conduction.
	Manipulate and evaluate a model to show various features of conduction and explain it in a clear and convincing way.

Hot and cold reactions

You will find out:
- What is meant by an exothermic reaction
- Why many reactions that produce heat can be useful
- What is meant by an endothermic reaction

5th November

It is that time of year when the night sky comes alive with beautiful colours and loud explosions.

A firework is filled with special chemicals, some of which are very dangerous. When these chemicals react, they produce new substances, but they also produce lots of **energy** in the forms of heat, light and sound.

FIGURE 1: 5th November – a display of chemical magic!

Exothermic and endothermic reactions

FIGURE 2: The thermite reaction – look at the heat energy produced by this reaction!

Reactions that get warm, or hot, are called **exothermic reactions**. This means that they give out heat energy to the surroundings.

Another example of an exothermic reaction is a famous process known as the **thermite** reaction. This involves a mixture of aluminium and iron oxide reacting and producing a lot of heat energy.

In the laboratory, we can see whether a reaction is exothermic by using a thermometer and taking some measurements. We could add some zinc powder to some copper sulphate solution, and record the **temperature** change.

Some typical results are shown below from an experiment that was carried out twice. These are known as **replicate readings**.

FIGURE 3: This is how we may record a temperature change in a reaction.

	Initial temperature (°C)	Final temperature (°C)	Temperature change (°C)
Try 1	21.5	29.5	8.0
Try 2	21.5	30.5	

QUESTIONS

1. What is meant by an exothermic reaction?
2. Give an example of an exothermic reaction.
3. What was the temperature change in try 2 in the experiment?
4. Suggest one reason why the temperature changes are different in the experiments.

Watch Out Heat energy always passes from a hot body to a colder one, never the other way around.

...endothermic reaction   ...energy   ...exothermic reaction   ...initial temperature

Cool reactions

When plants grow, they need energy, and this is absorbed from the sun. The process of using sunlight to help plants grow is called **photosynthesis**. We can write an equation to show photosynthesis:

Word equation: **water + carbon dioxide → glucose + oxygen gas**

Symbol equation: $6H_2O(l) + 6CO_2(g) → C_6H_{12}O_6(aq) + 6O_2(g)$

Photosynthesis is an example of an **endothermic reaction**. This is when the reaction takes heat energy in.

Endothermic reactions in the laboratory

We can carry out a reaction in the laboratory to show a very interesting endothermic reaction. It involves the reaction between two solids called barium hydroxide and ammonium thiocyanate.

When these two solids are added together, they react, and, as they do so, they absorb heat energy. If we touch the conical flask, it feels very cold since heat energy is being absorbed from our hands.

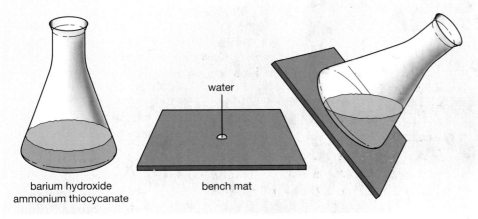

FIGURE 4: An endothermic reaction in action.

We can add some water to a bench mat, and put the flask on it. We can then turn the flask upside-down and the flask has stuck to the mat! How can this happen?

- The water molecules lose energy and this energy passes into the endothermic reaction taking place in the flask.
- As the water molecules lose energy, they slow down until they eventually stop. Ice is then formed.
- The ice then 'glues' the flask to the bench mat.

Anyone for coffee?

You may have seen a self-heating coffee cans in some shops. They are very clever. At the push of a button, the coffee starts to heat itself up until it is hot enough to drink.

In the base of the can is a white solid called calcium oxide. When this mixes with water, a fast and exothermic reaction takes place. This heat energy then passes into the water in the coffee and the coffee gets hot.

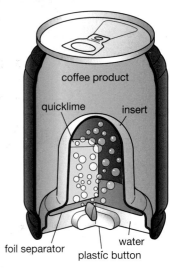

FIGURE 5: Can you see how the heat energy from the reaction heats up the coffee?

The exothermic reaction taking place is:

Calcium oxide + water → calcium hydroxide

$$CaO(s) + H_2O(l) → Ca(OH)_2(aq)$$

QUESTIONS

5   What **two** chemicals are required for photosynthesis to take place?

6   Give an example of an endothermic reaction other than photosynthesis.

7   Why does it feel cold when you touch an endothermic reaction?

QUESTIONS

8   Which **two** chemical substances react together to produce heat energy in a self-heating coffee can?

9   Why must the reaction be *fast* as well as exothermic?

The source of the fire

You will find out:

- What keeps atoms together
- Why heat energy is needed to break chemical bonds
- Why some reactions are exothermic and others endothermic

Lighting the fire

We are all familiar with lighting a fire. Coal, wood and gas can all burn to produce heat energy. However, substances such as these do not catch fire on their own: they need a source of energy to start the fire.

Many chemical reactions need energy to start them. Why is this?

FIGURE 1: A coal fire needs heat energy to start it.

Looking at the microscopic world

When we want to understand why chemical reactions happen, we need to use our imaginations so that we can visualise the particles that chemicals are made of. We know that chemical substances are made up of atoms, and atoms are held together by **chemical bonds**.

For example, let us consider a hydrogen **molecule**. This is made up of two hydrogen atoms joined together by a single **covalent bond**.

FIGURE 2: A hydrogen molecule.

What holds the atoms together in this molecule? Think about the types of particle in this molecule.

Hydrogen has an atomic number of 1 and a mass number of 1. This means that a hydrogen atom has:

- one proton, which is positively charged
- one electron, which is negatively charged and
- no neutrons, which have no charge at all.

If we bring two protons together, they will repel each other because they have the same charge.

What happens when we place two electrons in between the two protons? The electrons behave as a kind of atomic 'glue' and bind the protons together.

We have now made a hydrogen molecule, and we can see that the two atomic nuclei are held together because of the electrons that are forming the covalent bond.

It is important to understand that atoms are held together in molecules by chemical bonds. These bonds are **electrostatic attractions** between the protons in each nucleus and the electrons in the covalent bond.

▌▌ QUESTIONS ▌▌

1. Give the names of **three** substances that are often burnt to produce heat.
2. What holds hydrogen atoms together in a molecule?
3. How many protons and electrons are there in a hydrogen molecule?

Watch Out Breaking bonds requires heat energy, so it is endothermic. Making bonds is exothermic and releases heat energy.

...*chemical bond*   ...*covalent bond*   ...*electrostatic attraction*   ...*endothermic*

The role of the molecule

Look at Figure 3. It shows a model of a molecule of methane, CH_4.

FIGURE 3: A methane molecule.

- This molecule consists of one carbon atom and four hydrogen atoms covalently bonded together to form a methane molecule.
- The carbon and hydrogen atoms are bonded together strongly, so it is very difficult to pull the atoms from the molecule.
- To break a bond means that we are going to have to overcome the attractive forces between the atoms. This means that energy is required to break chemical bonds. We also know that when heat energy is absorbed, we call this an **endothermic** reaction.
- The opposite is also true: when bonds are made, heat energy is released. This is an **exothermic** reaction.

So remember:

BENDOMEX – Breaking bonds is Endothermic. Making bonds is Exothermic

Working out a heat change

When chemicals react together, they may either release heat energy (they are exothermic) or absorb heat energy (they are endothermic). The heat change in a reaction is measured in kilojoules (kJ).

Consider what happens when hydrogen and oxygen are mixed together and the mixture ignited. A massive explosion occurs!

Word equation: **hydrogen gas + oxygen gas → water**

Symbol equation: $2H_2(g)$ + $O_2(g)$ → $2H_2O(g)$

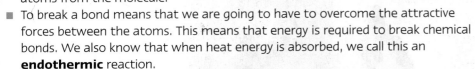

We then need to know the energies of the bonds. They are as follows:

$E(H–H) = 436\,kJ$; $E(O=O) = 496\,kJ$ and $E(O–H) = 463\,kJ$.

- The total 'break' energy is the *energy needed* to break all of the bonds on the left hand side:

  $2 \times E(H–H) + E(O=O) = (2 \times 436) + 496 = 1368\,kJ$

- The total 'make' energy released when the bonds on the right hand side are formed is:

  $4 \times E(O–H) = 4 \times 463\,kJ = 1852\,kJ$

- The total energy change will then be equal to the 'break' energy minus the 'make' energy. This is equal to:

  $1368\,kJ – 1852\,kJ = –484\,kJ$

The negative sign means that heat energy is left over, and this means that the reaction is exothermic.

QUESTIONS

4 How much energy is absorbed or released in the following changes?
   a $H_2(g) \rightarrow 2H(g)$
   b $H_2O(g) \rightarrow 2H(g) + O(g)$

REMEMBER

The heat energy required to break a bond is the same as the heat released when the bond forms. The only difference is the sign.

Why are some reactions exothermic and others endothermic? (H)

Whether heat is absorbed or released in a reaction depends on the balance between the bond-breaking energy and the bond-making energy.

In an exothermic reaction, more heat energy is released on forming new bonds in the products than the heat energy taken in to break reactant bonds. We can draw an **energy level diagram** to show this.

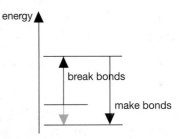

In an endothermic reaction, more heat energy is taken in to break reactant bonds than the heat energy given out when new bonds are formed.

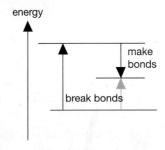

QUESTIONS

5 Bond breaking .... heat energy whereas bond making .... heat energy.

6 In a reaction, stronger bonds are present in the reactants than in the products. Will the reaction be exothermic or endothermic?

...energy level diagram ... exothermic ...molecule

Fast and slow reactions

You will find out:

- What is meant by reaction rate
- That reaction rate may be changed
- How to analyse graphs

Flammable gas

Hydrogen gas has the chemical formula H_2. It is the lightest gas known, and is also the most common element in our Galaxy. Hydrogen has the ability to react with oxygen quickly, and the reaction also releases lots of heat energy.

Hydrogen can be made in many ways, and some of these ways may be helpful if hydrogen becomes the new fuel of the future.

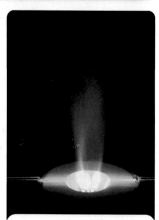

FIGURE 1: What is formed when hydrogen burns?

Watch Out The rate of reaction is always greater at the start of a reaction. The rate decreases with time.

Rates of reaction

An explosion is a very fast reaction in which lots of hot gases are produced. On the other hand, rusting can be a very slow reaction. A car may take as long as five years to show signs of rusting.

The speed at which a chemical reaction happens is called the **rate of reaction**.

There are many ways that we can change the speed or rate of a chemical reaction. These include changing:

- the **temperature**
- the **surface area** of a solid
- the **concentration** of any solutions used.

We can show how these factors affect the rate of the reaction in the laboratory by carrying out experiments. The quantity that we are changing is called a **variable**.

- We have to make sure that the factor that we want to investigate (temperature, surface area or concentration) is the only thing that varies.
- We must control all the other variables so that they do not change.
- We must find a way of monitoring the reaction so that we can record how a quantity changes with time.
- A graph can then be plotted so that the relationship between the variable and the reaction rate can be found.

FIGURE 2: Rust is formed by a slow chemical reaction.

QUESTIONS

1. Why is hydrogen highly flammable when in the air?
2. Name three factors that affect the rate of a chemical reaction.
3. When investigating how temperature affects the rate of a reaction, why must all other variables be kept constant?

CONCENTRATION

Concentration is a measure of the number of particles in a certain volume of liquid.

...concentration   ...data logger   ...gradient   ...intensity   ...rate of reaction

Changing surface area (H)

We can carry out a reaction between marble chips and hydrochloric acid. The word and symbol equations for this reaction are as follows:

Calcium carbonate + hydrochloric acid → calcium chloride + water + carbon dioxide gas

$$CaCO_3(s) + 2HCl(aq) \rightarrow CaCl_2(aq) + H_2O(l) + CO_2(g)$$

We can set up the following apparatus.

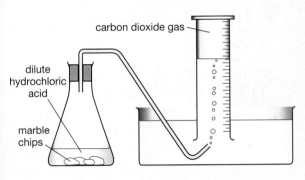

FIGURE 3: Apparatus for the reaction of marble chips and hydrochloric acid.

We then monitor how the volume of carbon dioxide gas varies with time and plot a graph. We then repeat the experiment. This time we take the same mass of marble chips but make sure that the chips are a lot smaller. This means that they have a larger **surface area**.

The typical graphs produced from this experiment are as follows.

They show that the rate of reaction is faster as the surface of the marble chips increases.

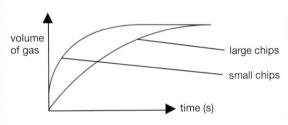

FIGURE 4: Rate of reaction.

Changing concentration

A reaction takes place between sodium thiosulphate solution and dilute hydrochloric acid. In this reaction, sulphur is formed.

We can monitor this reaction by using a light sensor connected to a **data logger**.

As the sulphur is formed, sulphur reduces the light **intensity** falling on the sensor, so this value falls with time. The data logger can then be linked to a computer and the data imported into **spreadsheet** software such as *Excel*. A graph can then be plotted of light intensity with time. The experiment is then repeated using a different concentration of either solution

Looking at graphs

When we carry out an experiment in which data are collected and a graph is plotted, we then have to interpret the information in the graph.

A typical graph of the mass or volume of product with time is as follows.

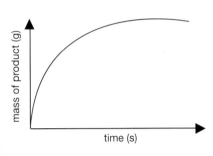

FIGURE 5: How mass of product increases with time.

The graph is steeper at the start of the reaction. This means that it is faster at this stage.

We can measure the **gradient** of a curve by drawing a **tangent** to the curve at a certain time, and then measuring its gradient.

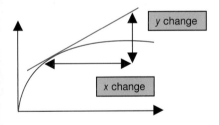

FIGURE 6: How to measure the gradient of a curve.

The gradient of the line is equal to the rate of reaction, that is:

$$\textbf{Rate} = \frac{\textbf{y change}}{\textbf{x change}}$$

QUESTIONS

4 Give the name of a piece of apparatus that can be used to measure the volume of a gas.

5 How do the graphs above show that the rate of reaction is greater for the reaction in which the surface area was greater?

6 Suggest why sulphur formation reduces the light intensity falling on the light sensor.

QUESTIONS

7 What happens to the mass of product with time in Figure 5?

8 What happens to the rate of the chemical reaction with time in Figure 5?

...spreadsheet   ...surface area   ...tangent   ...temperature   ...variable

Particles and rate

You will find out:

- What is meant by the collision theory
- About the idea of colliding particles
- How temperature affects the rate of a reaction

A firework reaction

When a mixture of iron oxide and aluminium is ignited, a very exciting reaction takes place called the thermite reaction.

Reactions like this one are fast, but others can be slow. Why can reactions be so different?

FIGURE 1: Look how fast this reaction is!

Using particles to help explain things

We know that everything is made up of **particles**. When we see a chemical reaction take place and we need to explain why a chemical reaction behaves in the way it does, it is important that we can use our imaginations to visualise things that we cannot see.

The collision theory

The **collision theory** says that the following things happen in order for chemicals to react:

- Particles must collide with each other.
- Particles must collide with sufficient energy.

An experiment to think about

Let us consider a reaction between magnesium and dilute hydrochloric acid. The word and symbol equations for the reaction are:

magnesium + dilute hydrochloric acid → magnesium chloride solution + hydrogen gas

$$Mg(s) + 2HCl(aq) \rightarrow MgCl_2(aq) + H_2(g)$$

Let us think about how the rate of this reaction is affected by increasing the **concentration** of the acid.

As the concentration increases, the rate of reaction is found to increase. We know this because the volume of gas varies with time according to Figure 2.

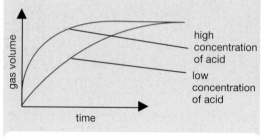

FIGURE 2: How gas volume varies with time.

(graph axes: gas volume vs time; curves labelled "high concentration of acid" and "low concentration of acid")

■ QUESTIONS ■

1 Give an example of a fast chemical reaction.
2 What **two** things must happen if particles are to react?
3 Using Figure 2, how do we know that the high concentration experiment was faster than the low concentration?

PARTICLES

For particles to react together, they must a) collide and b) collide with enough energy.

...collision theory   ...concentration   ...kinetic energy

Explaining things using particles

Why does the *concentration* of a solution increase the rate of reaction between dilute hydrochloric acid and magnesium?

There are more particles per unit volume in a concentrated solution than a dilute solution. This means that there are more collisions every second taking place between the particles in the solution and the magnesium.

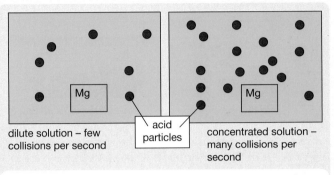

FIGURE 3: How concentration affects the rate of reaction.

Also, since there are twice as many acid particles per unit volume in the concentrated solution, we would expect the number of collisions per second to double also. This means that if we plotted a graph of concentration against rate, we would expect a straight line.

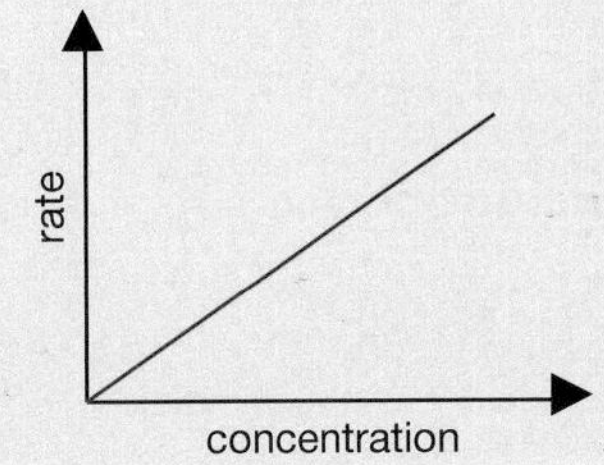

Why does the *surface area* of a solid affect the rate of reaction between dilute hydrochloric acid and magnesium?

FIGURE 4: How rate of reaction varies with concentration.

Just imagine breaking the piece of magnesium up into bits before it is added to the hydrochloric acid solution. What difference would this make?

There will be more collisions between the acid particles and the surface of the magnesium ribbon per second, so the rate of reaction will be faster. This is because the magnesium has a larger surface area.

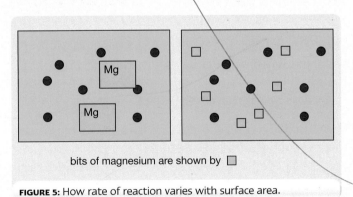

bits of magnesium are shown by □

FIGURE 5: How rate of reaction varies with surface area.

Watch Out An increase in **temperature** affects both the number of collisions taking place per second, but more importantly, the combined energy of the collision.

Fast and slow particles (H)

Particles move when they are dissolved in a solution, or when they are in the gas phase.

The moving energy (**kinetic energy**) of particles depends on the temperature: the higher the temperature, the greater will be the particles' moving energy.

If we carry out a reaction between zinc and dilute sulphuric acid, hydrogen gas is given off as bubbles.

FIGURE 6: Zinc reacting with sulphuric acid.

If we increase the temperature of the acid by warming it up with a Bunsen flame before adding the zinc, the reaction is a lot faster.

This is because the acid particles are moving with a greater kinetic energy and collide with the surface of the zinc harder and more frequently. This means that more particles will collide, resulting in new products being formed. This type of collision is called a **successful collision**.

The rate of the reaction is therefore greater at the higher temperature.

IIII QUESTIONS IIII

4 Explain why a dilute solution reacts more slowly then a concentrated solution.

5 Why does a sugar lump dissolve more slowly in a cup of tea than powdered sugar?

IIIIII QUESTIONS IIIIII

6 When the temperature is increased, particles move with a ....

7 What is meant by a successful collision?

...particle ...successful collision ...temperature

Catalysts

You will find out:

● About catalysts and enzymes

● Why enzymes and catalysts are so useful

● About a new drug that can reduce heart attacks

Whiter than white

When we wash clothes, washing powder is used to make sure that the clothes are as clean as possible.

Amazingly, dirty clothes can be cleaned at temperatures as low as 40 °C. This is because an **enzyme** has been added to the washing powder. Enzymes are **catalysts** that break down dirt and grease very quickly.

FIGURE 1: Washing powder can wash clothes at low temperatures – all because of enzymes!

Watch Out Enzymes are complicated chemical substances, and are found in living things. However, they are not living themselves.

What are catalysts?

Hydrogen peroxide solution will slowly decompose at room temperature to produce water and oxygen gas:

Hydrogen peroxide solution → water + oxygen gas

$$2H_2O_2(aq) \rightarrow 2H_2O(l) + O_2(g)$$

A substance called manganese dioxide added to the hydrogen peroxide solution makes the oxygen gas form more rapidly. Manganese dioxide is called a catalyst.

FIGURE 2: Adding manganese dioxide to hydrogen dioxide makes the production of oxygen quicker. The gas can be tested for with a glowing splint.

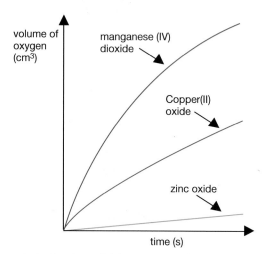

volume of oxygen (cm³)

manganese (IV) dioxide

Copper(II) oxide

zinc oxide

time (s)

FIGURE 3: Rates of reaction with different catalysts.

A catalyst is a chemical substance that increases the rate of a reaction, but is still present at the end of the reaction.

Figure 2 shows the above reaction taking place (on the left), and what happens when a glowing splint is added to the container (on the right).

Investigating catalysts

We can add a certain mass of a catalyst such as manganese dioxide to some hydrogen peroxide solution. We monitor how the oxygen gas is produced over time. We can do this for different catalysts and draw a graph like the one on the left from the results.

■■ QUESTIONS ■■

1 What is a catalyst?

2 Which gas is being tested in Figure 2 by adding a glowing splint?

3 Using Figure 3, which of the three substances is the better catalyst? Explain your answer.

Watch Out The amount of product in a catalysed reaction is the same as when the catalyst is not present. A catalyst only changes the rate at which the product is formed.

...*amylase* ...*atherosclerosis* ...*carbohydrase* ...*catalyst* ...*cholesterol* ...*enzyme*

Reducing heart attacks

Many thousands of people die of heart attacks in the UK every year. A diet high in fat, sugar and salt contributes to heat attacks. Smoking is also known to increase the chances of suffering a heart attack.

It has recently been discovered that a new class of compounds called '**statins**' can decrease the chance of a heart attack by about 30%.

Statins work by lowering the level of **cholesterol** in the blood by reducing the production of cholesterol by the liver. Statins block the enzyme in the liver that is responsible for making cholesterol.

Cholesterol is critical to the normal function of every cell in the body. However, it also contributes to the development of **atherosclerosis**, a condition in which cholesterol-containing **plaques** form within the arteries. These plaques block the arteries and reduce the flow of blood to the tissues the arteries supply. When plaques rupture, a blood clot forms on the plaque, thereby further blocking the artery and reducing the flow of blood. This may result in a heart attack or stroke.

FIGURE 4: Statins can reduce the chances of heart attacks.

What are enzymes?

- Enzymes are biological catalysts.
- They belong to a class of chemicals called **proteins**. These are very complicated molecules and often contain hundreds of atoms in each molecule.
- Enzymes often work fastest between 35 and 40 °C. This temperature is a lot lower than those needed with most other 'normal' catalysts.

Enzymes are very useful in our lives. Some names and uses of enzymes include the following.

- **Pectinase** breaks down insoluble pectin polysaccharides and so is used to clarify fruit juices.
- **Amylases** break down carbohydrates and **lipases** break down fats.
- Enzymes are used in genetic engineering and penicillin production.
- **Carbohydrases** are used to convert starch syrup into sugar syrup.
- **Invertase** is used to make the sugar for soft-centred chocolates.

WOW FACTOR!

Enzymes make reactions in living things happen at a faster rate. This means enzymes are crucial to life.

QUESTIONS

4 Explain briefly how statins prevent heart attacks.

5 Give **three** substances in food that are known to increase the chances of suffering from a heart attack.

6 What is an enzyme?

7 What is the name of the enzyme used to make chocolates with soft centres?

Russia: Torpedo blast sank *Kursk*

FIGURE 5: The nuclear submarine Kursk.

A senior Russian naval officer said a torpedo explosion sank the nuclear submarine *Kursk* in August 2000 in the Barents Sea, killing all 118 people aboard. A Vice-Admiral said a small explosion was followed by a large one in the torpedo area of the submarine.

United States officials say that there were two explosions on board the submarine, the first equivalent to that of a torpedo warhead.

The *Kursk* was carrying torpedoes powered by a liquid hydrogen peroxide fuel, a substance tried by Britain's Royal Navy in the 1960s but rejected for being too unstable. It is believed that a torpedo may have misfired on the *Kursk*, and exploded in the tube.

Certain metals such as platinum and silver are known to catalyse the decomposition of hydrogen peroxide. A leak from a torpedo could have come into contact with a catalytic surface. This could have caused the explosion.

QUESTIONS

8 What is the name of the chemical that was used to power torpedoes in the *Kursk*?

9 What is the name of the gas formed when the fuel decomposes?

10 Why did the Royal Navy reject the use of the **propellant** in its submarines?

...*invertase* ...*lipase* ...*pectinase* ...*plaque* ...*propellant* ...*protein* ...*statin*

Reactions going both ways

You will find out:

- What is meant by a reversible reaction
- How a reversible reaction may come to chemical equilibrium
- How tooth decay is an example of chemical equilibrium

Heating copper sulphate

We are all familiar with the effect of heat on **hydrated** copper sulphate crystals. The crystals lose their water and white **anhydrous** copper sulphate forms.

However, we also know that if we add water to white copper sulphate powder, it turns blue again! This reaction seems to be able to go both ways. It is called a **reversible** reaction.

FIGURE 1: Heating blue copper sulphate crystals gives a white powder.

Bubbles of gas

When we drink a fizzy drink, we notice that there are lots of gas bubbles present. These gas bubbles are carbon dioxide.

These drinks are made fizzy by passing carbon dioxide gas under **pressure** into the solution in the bottle. The carbon dioxide gas then dissolves to form a weak acid called carbonic acid.

$$\text{carbon dioxide} + \text{water} \rightarrow \text{carbonic acid solution}$$

$$CO_2(g) + H_2O(l) \rightarrow H_2CO_3(aq)$$

When we open a fizzy drink, we notice that carbon dioxide gas bubbles form from the solution. This is the reverse of the process happening above.

$$\text{carbonic acid solution} \rightarrow \text{carbon dioxide} + \text{water}$$

$$H_2CO_3(aq) \rightarrow CO_2(g) + H_2O(l)$$

This means that carbon dioxide can dissolve in water to form carbonic acid, but carbonic acid can also decompose to form carbon dioxide gas.

This is therefore a reaction that goes both ways. It is called a reversible reaction.

We can write the above reaction like this:

$$CO_2(g) + H_2O(l) \rightleftharpoons H_2CO_3(aq)$$

The double-headed arrow means a reversible reaction.

FIGURE 2: Bubbles of carbon dioxide in a fizzy drink.

QUESTIONS

1 Give an example of **two** reactions that are reversible.
2 What is the chemical formula for carbonic acid?
3 What is the meaning of 'anhydrous' in anhydrous copper sulphate?

...anhydrous   ...chemical equilibrium   ...dynamic chemical equilibrium

Equilibrium (H)

Imagine a bucket that is being used to collect rainwater. However, the bucket has a small hole in it! As the rain enters the bucket, the rainwater also comes out of the hole.

It is observed that the level of the water remains the same in the bucket. What does this means about the rate at which the water enters the bucket and the rate at which it leaves the bucket?

It means that the water is entering the bucket at the same rate as it leaves the bucket. This is called a state of **equilibrium**.

 A state of chemical equilibrium is a special point in the reaction in which the forward and reverse rates are equal to each other.

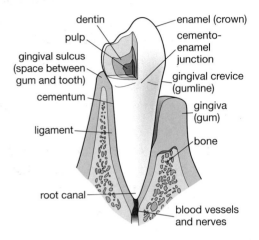

- In a chemical reaction that is **reversible**, a state of **chemical equilibrium** can happen.

- In a bottle of fizzy drink (with the top on), there is a state of chemical equilibrium.

The forward and reverse reactions are both occurring at the same time:

$$CO_2(g) + H_2O(l) \rightleftharpoons H_2CO_3(aq)$$

When a reaction has come to equilibrium, the amounts of reactants and products are *not* equal to each other. However, the rate of the forward reaction is equal to the rate of the reverse reaction.

When the rate of the forward reaction is equal to the rate of the reverse reaction, we call this a state of **dynamic chemical equilibrium**. The reaction is then written with a different sign between the reactants and the products. The reversible sign changes to an equilibrium sign.

So the equilibrium taking place in a bottle of fizzy drink is:

$$CO_2(g) + H_2O(l) \rightleftharpoons H_2CO_3(aq)$$

WOW FACTOR!

Reactions that are at chemical equilibrium are everywhere. Some of these reactions take fractions of a second to come to equilibrium, others can take many years!

Watch Out What is equal about a reaction at equilibrium? It is the rates of the forward and reverse processes.

QUESTIONS

4 What do $\rightleftharpoons$ and $\rightleftharpoons$ mean?

5 What is the meaning of a dynamic chemical equilibrium?

6 Explain why a fizzy drink may not come to chemical equilibrium if the top is removed from the bottle.

Decaying teeth

Tooth enamel consists of a substance called hydroxyapatite.

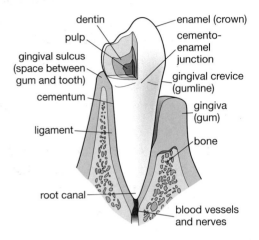

Labels: dentin, pulp, gingival sulcus (space between gum and tooth), cementum, ligament, root canal, enamel (crown), cemento-enamel junction, gingival crevice (gumline), gingiva (gum), bone, blood vessels and nerves

FIGURE 3: The structure of a tooth.

Dissolving hydroxyapatite is called demineralisation, and its formation is called remineralisation. In the mouth there is an equilibrium between these two processes which is established even with healthy teeth.

Hydroxyapatite $\rightleftharpoons$ calcium ions + phosphate ions + hydroxide ions

When sugar ferments on teeth, hydrogen ions (H^+) are produced – these make the saliva acidic.

These hydrogen ions upset the equilibrium between demineralisation and remineralisation by combining with hydroxide ions to form water.

Removal of hydroxide ions causes more hydroxyapatite to dissolve, resulting in tooth decay. Fluoride helps prevent tooth decay by replacing the hydroxide ions in hydroxyapatite. The resulting chemical compound is very resistant to acid attack.

QUESTIONS

7 What is the chemical name for tooth enamel?

8 Which ion is present in the acidic saliva?

9 Which ion does the hydrogen ion remove from the chemical equilibrium?

...equilibrium ...hydrated ...pressure ...reversible

Affecting the balance

You will find out:
- How the thickness of an egg shell can be explained
- What is meant by a clathrate
- How the equilibrium position is affected by changing conditions

Chickens and their eggs

The shell of a chicken's egg is made of a chemical called calcium carbonate. It is important that the shell is thick enough to stop the egg cracking and spoiling.

We know the amount of calcium carbonate in an egg shell can be affected by many things. An understanding of chemical equilibrium may help us understand what affects the amount of calcium carbonate in an egg shell.

Free-range chickens and shell thickness

To make an egg, a chicken needs to combine calcium ions and carbonate ions. This results in the formation of calcium carbonate.

Calcium ions + carbonate ions → calcium carbonate

$$Ca^{2+}(aq) + CO_3^{2-}(aq) \rightarrow CaCO_3(s)$$

Calcium ions are obtained from various foods by the chicken, but what about the carbonate ions?

Carbon dioxide is produced when a chicken **respires**. This gas is in equilibrium with a special acid in the blood called carbonic acid.

Carbonic acid forms carbonate ions when dissolved in water.

carbon dioxide + water ⇌ carbonic acid ⇌ hydrogen ions + carbonate ions

$$CO_2(g) + H_2O(l) \rightleftharpoons H_2CO_3(aq) \rightleftharpoons 2H^+(aq) + CO_3^{2-}(aq)$$

- If the chicken is free-range, it is able to move and run about more than if it is kept in a small cage.
- This means that it produces more carbon dioxide gas as it respires.
- The carbon dioxide is removed from the equilibrium above, and this causes more carbonic acid to be used up.
- However, the carbonic acid is made from carbonate ions. Therefore, carbonate ions are used to make more carbonic acid.
- Therefore, the egg shell becomes thinner.

FIGURE 1: Chickens like these lay lots of eggs. Egg shells are made of calcium carbonate.

FIGURE 2: What factors affect the thickness of the shells on these eggs?

Watch Out When the conditions of an equilibrium are changed, a new equilibrium mixture is formed. The rates of the forward and reverse processes will again be equal when the new equilibrium is formed.

QUESTIONS

1 What is the shell of a chicken's egg made of?
2 Which gas does a chicken produce when it respires?
3 Why does a chicken kept in a cage generally produce an egg with a thicker shell?

...clathrate ...concentration ...equilibrium position

The Bermuda Triangle

The Bermuda Triangle or Devil's Triangle is a mysterious region in the North Atlantic Ocean in which more than 50 ships and 20 planes have disappeared during the past 200 years. The map shows where the Bermuda Triangle is.

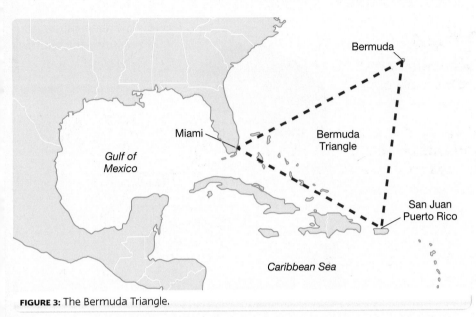

FIGURE 3: The Bermuda Triangle.

Many ships in this region have failed to send radio signals and have disappeared mysteriously. The most notable was the loss of the US nuclear submarine *Scorpion* in May 1968. In December 1945 five bombers on a routine training mission were lost. A rescue mission also vanished in this triangle. So far more than 1000 people have lost their lives in this area.

Chemical cages

It is known that, at the bottom of the Bermuda Triangle, methane gas is found trapped in ice 'cages' called **clathrates**.

These clathrates may burn when the methane gas within them is released. Methane gas is in equilibrium with the solid clathrate:

$$CH_4(g) \rightleftharpoons CH_4(s)$$

This reaction is exothermic.

If there is some volcanic activity on the ocean floor, the reverse reaction will take place. This means that the **equilibrium position** has shifted to the left hand side. This causes methane to be produced, which may rise to the surface of the ocean and might potentially destroy a ship. Could this be true?

FIGURE 4: How is ice able to 'store' methane?

QUESTIONS

4   What other substance is required in order for methane to form a clathrate?

5   Why is the snowball on fire in Figure 4?

6   What would happen to the above equilibrium if the temperature was decreased? Explain your answer.

Watch Out The equilibrium position indicates the relative amounts of products and reactants present at equilibrium. If there are more products, the equilibrium position has moved to the right, and vice versa.

Shifting equilibrium position

Three factors may affect the position of an equilibrium:

- **concentration**
- **temperature**
- **pressure** (in a gas phase reaction).

Consider the general equilibrium:
$A(g) \rightleftharpoons 2B(g)$

Forward reaction is endothermic.

- Concentration: when the concentration of A increases, the equilibrium position moves to the right. If the concentration of A decreases, the equilibrium position moves to the left-hand side.
- Temperature: since the forward reaction is endothermic, the reverse process must be exothermic. On increasing the temperature, the reaction decreases the temperature by using its endothermic route. The equilibrium position moves to the right-hand side.
- Pressure: there are two volumes of gas on the right-hand side (high pressure) and one volume of gas (low pressure) on the left-hand side. If the pressure is increased, the side with the lower volume of gas is formed. This means that equilibrium moves to the left-hand side.

QUESTIONS

7   Consider the ozone gas/oxygen equilibrium:
$3O_2(g) \rightleftharpoons 2O_3(g)$, the reaction is endothermic

What happens to the equilibrium position when:

a The temperature is increased?

b The ozone is removed as soon as it is formed?

c The pressure is decreased?

Ammonia

You will find out:
- What ammonia is used for
- How ammonia is made using the **Haber process**
- How temperature and pressure affect the yield

Eating to stay alive

Every day, one in five of the world's population – some 800 million people – go hungry. There are often many reasons why people are not able to eat enough food, and a lot has to do with a lack of money.

Sometimes, the soil is not fit to grow plants in. **Ammonia** is a substance that we can make **fertilisers** from, which enable plants to grow better.

FIGURE 1: Is it not a human right that everybody should have enough to eat?

What is ammonia?

Ammonia is a gas at room temperature. It has a pungent smell and can irritate the eyes and lungs. It is a compound of nitrogen and hydrogen and has the chemical formula NH_3.

Ammonia exists as a molecule at room temperature and pressure containing four atoms – three are hydrogen and one is nitrogen.

- Ammonia gas has many uses in our lives.
- The major use of ammonia and its compounds is as fertilisers.
- Ammonia is also used in large amounts in the Ostwald process for the synthesis of nitric acid; in the Solvay process for the synthesis of sodium carbonate; and in the synthesis of numerous organic compounds used as dyes, drugs, and in plastics; and in various metallurgical processes

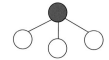

FIGURE 2: An ammonia molecule.

The fountain experiment

Ammonia is an extremely soluble gas in water. In Figure 3, ammonia gas is in the round-bottomed flask and has dissolved in a small amount of water. A **partial vacuum** is then created. Atmospheric pressure pushes the water up the glass tube into the flask to make a fountain.

FIGURE 3: The fountain experiment.

■■ QUESTIONS ■■

1. What is the chemical formula for ammonia gas?
2. Give **two** uses for ammonia gas.

WOW FACTOR!

Fritz Haber worked out that there was enough gold in 1 cubic mile of seawater to make a lot of money. Unfortunately, extracting the gold proved to be too expensive!

...ammonia   ...catalyst   ...equilibrium   ...fertiliser

The Haber process   (H)

The Haber process is a method of producing ammonia developed in the First World War. The Germans needed nitrogen for making their explosives. When the Allies blocked the trade routes going to and from Germany, the Germans had no access to sodium nitrate and potassium nitrate, their only sources of nitrogen.

The chemist Fritz Haber developed the Haber process which takes nitrogen from the air and combines it with hydrogen to form ammonia gas.

The equation for this reaction is:

$$N_2(g) + 3H_2(g) \rightleftharpoons 2HN_3(g)$$

The heat change, ΔH, is −92 kJ/mol.

Figure 5 shows the stages involved in making ammonia using the Haber process. Notice the conditions used:

- temperature = 400–450 °C
- pressure = 200 atm
- **catalyst** is iron.

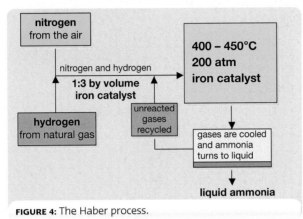

FIGURE 4: The Haber process.

How does pressure affect the yield of ammonia?

Look at the graph below. It shows how the yield of ammonia is affected by an increase in pressure and temperature.

At a particular temperature, the **percentage yield** of ammonia increases with increasing pressure. Why is this? Look at the reaction:

$$N_2(g) + 3H_2(g) \rightleftharpoons 2NH_3(g)$$

- There are four volumes of gas on the left hand side and only two volumes on the right hand side.
- On increasing the pressure, the **equilibrium** position moves to the left hand side, which results in a decrease of the pressure.
- This means that the equilibrium position moves to the right hand side to reduce the pressure.
- So more ammonia forms at a higher pressure.

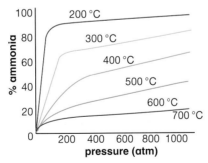

FIGURE 5: How the yield of ammonia is affected by pressure and temperature.

WATCH OUT

In the reaction $N_2(g) + 3H_2(g) \rightleftharpoons 2NH_3(g)$, there are 4 volumes of gas on the left hand side (1 from the nitrogen and 3 from the hydrogen). On the right hand side there are 2 volumes of ammonia.

Temperature effects

We know that the reaction is:

$$N_2(g) + 3H_2(g) \rightleftharpoons 2NH_3(g)$$

and the heat change, ΔH, is −92 kJ/ mol.

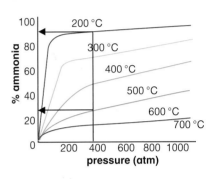

FIGURE 6: Working out the effects of temperature changes.

Take any pressure, say 400 atm. Look at the graph in Figure 6 to see the pressure line 400 atm. How does increasing temperature affect the yield of ammonia?

At 200 °C, the percentage yield of ammonia is about 90%, whereas at 500 °C, the yield is only 30%. Why is this?

- The forward reaction is exothermic, since ΔH is negative.
- This means that the forward reaction produces heat.
- As the temperature increases, the reaction uses its endothermic route to reduce the temperature.
- This means that the reverse process will take place.
- The percentage yield of ammonia therefore decreases with increasing temperature.

▦▦ QUESTIONS ▦▦

3 Is the production of ammonia exothermic or endothermic? How do you know?

4 What happens to the yield of ammonia as the pressure increases?

5 Consider the following equation:

$$2A(g) + B(g) \rightleftharpoons 3C(g)$$

What effect, if any, does increasing the pressure have on the equilibrium position? Explain your answer.

▦▦ QUESTIONS ▦▦

6 Using the graph, what is the percentage yield of ammonia at 500 °C and 1000 atm?

7 Why isn't a *very* low temperature used to increase the yield of ammonia?

Growing organically

You will find out:

- What is meant by organic food
- The disadvantages and advantages of using organic fertilisers
- What is meant by GM foods

Are you an organic food fan?

Organic produce is made without the use of artificial chemicals, such as weed-killers and **pesticides**. Organic foods also exclude GM (**genetically modified**) ingredients, as well as artificial colours or flavours.

Organic foods are available in nearly all supermarkets in the UK. Sales of organic food have been increasing for the past five years.

FIGURE 1: Taste good?

What is organic food?

In one way all food is organic, because it has come from plants or animals. However, for some 50 years the word 'organic' has been used to describe food grown without **artificial fertilisers** or pesticides. It is also important to make the most of **natural fertilisers** and ensure that the life of the soil is maintained.

Some facts about organic farming in the UK:

- Although organic farming affects the **environment** less than conventional farming, it does mean that yields are lower from organic systems. So, more land is needed to grow a given amount of food. Organic foods are more expensive because of this.
- UK organic farmers currently provide around 50% of the organic produce on sale in this country. The rest is imported to meet additional consumer demand or because the produce cannot be grown here; for example bananas.
- Consumers have different reasons for choosing organic foods. The environmental benefits, enhanced animal welfare and lower pesticide levels left in food are some of these reasons. Better taste is also mentioned. Many consumers also perceive them as more natural and healthier. However, current research has yet to show conclusively any significant difference, in terms of food safety and nutrition, from food produced non-organically.

Watch Out Chemicals are everywhere. Don't assume that just because a chemical is 'natural' that it is better for you than a chemical that is artificial!

FIGURE 2: These potatoes are grown organically.

QUESTIONS

1. What is meant by a food that is sold as being 'organic'?
2. Give **two** advantages and **two** disadvantages of organic foods.
3. What proportion of UK organic food is grown in the UK?

WOW FACTOR!

The word 'organic' has lots of different meanings. In chemistry, it means a molecule containing carbon. These molecules used to be removed from living organisms.

...artificial fertilisers ...environment ...genetically modified

Organic or manufactured fertilisers?

Most people are concerned about the environment, and this means that there has been interest in the use of organic fertilisers. As a result, there is a debate about the qualities of organic versus manufactured fertilisers.

FIGURE 3: Liquid manure or sludge being injected into a field of stubble.

Watch Out The GM food debate, organic foods issues and whether fertilisers should be organic or artificial are all questions that need accurate scientific evidence before any conclusions can be formed.

There are advantages and disadvantages about the use of each fertiliser type. Here are some thoughts.

- Organic fertilisers are normally made from various animal and plant by-products, such as poultry feathers, manures and treated sewage sludge. These materials require soil micro-organisms to break down the substances into chemicals that plants can use. This slow release is good for some plants, but not all. Approximately half or less of the nitrogen is released for crop use the first year.

- Organic fertilisers are comparatively low in nutrient content so they require significantly larger volumes when being used.

- Manufactured nitrogen fertilisers are normally made from petroleum or natural gas. Chemicals are released into the ground which vary in release time from a few days to a few weeks, giving a quick response after fertiliser application. Costs are comparatively low to moderate.

- Manufactured fertilisers are relatively high in nutrient content, therefore only small amounts are required. If too much fertiliser is used, this causes leaves to become yellow or brown. On sandy soils, too much fertiliser can leach into groundwater and this may cause other problems.

- Both types of fertiliser will pollute our groundwater, lakes and streams when spilled onto roads, paths, etc., although neither will pollute when correctly applied to lawns and garden soils.

QUESTIONS

4 Give **three** examples of organic fertilisers.

5 Give **one** advantage and **one** disadvantage of using an organic fertiliser instead of an artificial fertiliser.

6 Give the name of a chemical element that is important for plant growth.

GM food

Genetic engineering is used to take genes and segments of DNA from one species, e.g. fish, and put them into another species, e.g. tomato. Once the different segments of DNA have been isolated, they can be studied, multiplied and spliced (stuck) to any other DNA of another cell or organism. It makes it possible to break through the species barrier and to shuffle information between completely unrelated species. For example, it is possible to splice the anti-freeze gene from flounder into tomatoes or strawberries, an insect-killing toxin gene from bacteria into maize, cotton or rape seed, or genes from humans into pigs.

FIGURE 4: A genetically produced tomato.

- What are the *benefits*? Genetically modified foods (GM foods) offer a way to quickly improve crop characteristics such as yield, pest resistance or herbicide tolerance, often to a degree not possible with traditional methods. Further, GM crops can be manipulated to produce completely artificial substances, from the precursors to plastics to consumable vaccines.

- What are the *risks*? The power of genetic modification techniques raises the possibility of human health, environmental and economic problems, including allergic responses to new substances in foods, the spread of pest resistance or herbicide tolerance to wild plants, and inadvertent toxicity to wildlife.

QUESTIONS

7 What is meant by the term 'pest resistance' in the first bullet point?

8 Why would it be an advantage for some products from GM crops to be 'from precursors to plastics to consumable vaccines'?

9 What is the meaning of the term 'inadvertent toxicity' in the second bullet point?

...natural fertilisers ...organic ...pesticide

Unit summary

Concept map

Sometimes, a reversible reaction can form a special state called chemical equilibrium.

When a reaction has reached chemical equilibrium, the rates of the forward and reverse rates of reaction are equal.

When a reaction is at equilibrium, the amounts of product and reactant are not equal.

Some reactions can proceed in the forward and reverse directions. These are called reversible reactions.

Reversible reactions and equilibria

Reactions at equilibrium have an equilibrium position. This is a measure of the relative amounts of products and reactants at equilibrium.

Exothermic reactions produce heat energy, endothermic reactions absorb heat energy.

The thermite reaction is an example of an exothermic reaction.

Photosynthesis is an example of an endothermic reaction.

Endothermic reactions involve weaker bonds forming in the products than those that need to be broken in the reactants.

Energy in chemistry

Exothermic reactions involve stronger bonds forming in the products, than those that need to be broken in the reactants.

For a reaction to take place, collisions must take place between particles of sufficient energy

Temperature, concentration of a reactant, and the surface area of a solid reactant all affect the reaction rate.

Reaction rates

Collisions that result in the chemical reaction are called successful collisions. Those that do not result in a reaction are ineffective collisions.

Catalysts are substances that make a reaction of faster, but at the end of the reaction, are chemically unchanged. Enzymes are biological catalysts found in living things.

Unit quiz

1 What is meant by the term 'exothermic'?

2 The breaking of bonds is .... and the making of bonds is ....

3 Explain, in terms of the strength of chemical bonds, from where the heat energy in a chemical reaction comes.

4 Give an example of:
   a) an exothermic reaction
   b) an endothermic reaction.

5 Explain, using ideas of forces, why heat energy is needed to make water boil.

6 Name **three** factors that affect the rate of a chemical reaction.

7 What is the meaning of the term 'concentration'?

8 Explain, using ideas of particles, why increasing the surface area of a solid increases the rate of a chemical reaction.

9 Explain what is meant by the term 'catalyst'.

10 Why does increasing temperature increase the rate of a chemical reaction?

11 'A catalyst does not affect the yield of a product in a reaction'. What does this statement mean?

12 Give **three** uses for enzymes.

13 What is meant by a reversible reaction?

14 What is the name of the industrial process used to manufacture ammonia?

15 The production of ammonia involves a 'dynamic chemical equilibrium'. What is the meaning of this term?

16 Write an equation to show the equilibrium that exists between ammonia gas and its constituent elements (including state symbols in your answer).

17 Why does an increase in pressure increase the yield of ammonia in the above process?

18 Give a use for the ammonia formed in the process.

19 Give **one** advantage and **one** disadvantage of using organic fertilisers instead of synthetic chemical fertilisers.

20 Why is a moderately high temperature used in the process even though a low temperature should produce the highest possible yield of ammonia?

Numeracy activity

Ethanol

Ethanol, CH_3CH_2OH, is an alcohol, a group of chemical compounds whose molecules contain a hydroxyl group, $-OH$, bonded to a carbon atom. Ethanol melts at $-114.1\ °C$, boils at $78.5\ °C$, and has a density of $0.789\ g/cm^3$ at $20\ °C$. Its low freezing point has made it useful as the fluid in thermometers for temperatures below $-40\ °C$, the freezing point of mercury, and for other low-temperature purposes, such as for antifreeze in automobile radiators.

Ethanol has been made since ancient times by the fermentation of sugars. Simple sugars are the raw material.

Zymase, an enzyme from yeast, changes the simple sugars into ethanol and carbon dioxide. $C_6H_{12}O_6 \rightarrow 2CH_3CH_2OH + 2CO_2$

In the production of beverages, such as whiskey and brandy, impurities supply the flavour. Starches from potatoes, corn, wheat and other plants can be used in the production of ethanol by fermentation. Starches must first be broken down into simple sugars. An enzyme released by germinating barley, diastase, converts starches into sugars. The first step in brewing beer from starchy plants is called malting.

QUESTIONS
1 What is the chemical formula for ethanol?
2 In what physical state (solid, liquid or gas) will ethanol be at:
   a) $-220\ °C$ b) $0\ °C$?
3 Give the names of **two** enzymes that are mentioned in the passage.

Exam practice

Exam practice questions

In **Q1-6** choose the best answer to each question.

1 **1** Which of the following is not a form of carbon?
 A Buckminsterfullerene
 B Diamond
 C Methane
 D Graphite [1]

2 Simple molecular substances...
 A are ionically bonded.
 B have high melting and boiling points.
 C are good conductors of electricity.
 D are covalently bonded. [1]

3 Metals conduct electricity because...
 A their ions are free to move.
 B they have a giant structure of atoms.
 C layers of atoms can slide over each other.
 D they have relatively free electrons. [1]

4 Which is the correct statement about exothermic reactions?
 A They take in heat energy.
 B An example is combustion of fuels.
 C Bond breaking is exothermic.
 D They are accompanied by a decrease in temperature. [1]

5 A reaction will not be speeded up by...
 A increasing the concentration of a solution.
 B adding a catalyst.
 C increasing the temperature.
 D decreasing the surface area of a solid. [1]

6 Which statement is true about the exothermic reaction $N_2 + 3H_2 \rightleftharpoons 2NH_3$?
 A Increasing the temperature will decrease the yield of ammonia.
 B Decreasing the pressure will increase the yield of ammonia.
 C Increasing the concentration of nitrogen will decrease the yield of ammonia.
 D Changing the temperature will affect the rate of reaction but not the yield of ammonia. [1]

7 **a** **i** What do you understand by the term 'enzyme'?

 .... [1]

a **ii** What is the importance of enzymes in biological systems?

 .... [2]

8 Describe and explain the trend in the boiling point of the halogens (Group 7) as you go down the group.

 ....

 .... [2]

9 Complete this table which compares the similarities and differences between the bonding in the two forms of carbon: graphite and diamond.

	Diamond	Graphite
Is the bonding ionic or covalent?		
How many other carbons is each carbon bonded to?		
Are the melting and boiling points high?		
Is the structure giant?		
Is it hard or soft?		
Does it conduct electricity?		

[6]

10 What are the advantages of the following?

 a Using simulation software to represent models of molecules

 .... [1]

 b Using an artificial fertilizer rather than using organic farming methods

 .... [1]

 c Using a datalogger to obtain data during an experiment on rates of reaction

 ....

 .... [2]

 (Total 21 marks)

Mia wants to study the effect of surface area of a solid on the rate of reaction. She set up the apparatus shown below. Look carefully at all the information on the diagram and then answer the questions.

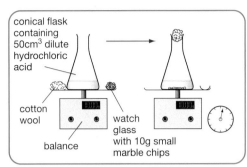

conical flask containing 50cm³ dilute hydrochloric acid

cotton wool

watch glass with 10g small marble chips

balance

a The marble chips contain calcium carbonate ($CaCO_3$). Complete this word equation to show what happens when the marble chips react with the hydrochloric acid.

Hydrochloric acid + calcium carbonate → .... + carbon dioxide + water   [1]

b Complete this symbol equation for the reaction. Remember to include state symbols.

$2HCl (aq) + CaCO_3(s) →$ ....   [3]

c What measurements must Mia make?   [2]

Once she has completed the first experiment she needs to change the size of the marble chips. Give three things she must keep constant to make this a fair test.   [3]

d Here are the results of the two experiments:

Time/minutes 0 0.5 1.0 1.5 2.0 2.5 3.0 3.5 4.0 4.5 5.0 Small marble chips Loss in mass/g 0.00 0.66 1.14 1.50 1.72 1.88 2.00 2.10 2.16 2.20 2.20 Large marble chips Loss in mass/g 0.00 0.26 0.48 0.68 0.88 1.08 3.00 1.41 1.56 1.61 1.84

i Draw a graph to show these results.   [4]

ii What do expect the total mass loss, in the experiment with large chips, will be if the experiment was left for another 3 minutes.   [1]

Correct answers to **a** and **c** but the student has not sorted out her symbol equations. This answer would score zero marks. The correct answer is:
$2HCl (aq) + CaCO_3(s) → CaCl_2(aq) + CO_2(g) + H_2O(l)$
Since calcium is in Group 2 and chlorine in Group 7 this makes the formula for calcium chloride $CaCl_2$. The numbers must be shown as subscripts. The only large numbers are the numbers put in to balance the equation. No state symbols were added.

a *Calcium chloride*

b $2HCl (aq) + CaCO_3(s) → CaCl + CO_2 + H_2O$

c *Mia has to measure the time and the mass*

d i

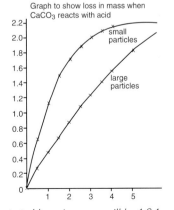

Graph to show loss in mass when $CaCO_3$ reacts with acid

small particles

large particles

No, eventually the total loss in mass will reach the same total in both experiments (2.2 g).

ii *The total loss in mass will be 1.84 g.*

Overall Grade: B

How to get an A

You must practise writing out formulae using the exam data sheet to help you. Do what the question asks. If it asks for state symbols then you should give them.

DISCOVER SPEED!

This car is the Thrust SSC. In October 1997 it became the first vehicle to travel faster than the speed of sound along the ground.

Thrust SSC's official record speed is just over 763 mph (nearly 1228 km/h, just over 341 m/s)

The speed of sound is 331 m/s in air at 0°C, but increases with temperature. Runs were made in the morning when it was colder so that the speed needed to 'go supersonic' was not so high.

To break a land speed record you have to make two runs in opposite directions within one hour of each other. Thrust SSC managed this with time to spare!

CONTENTS

How fast?

You will find out:

- How to calculate speed
- The difference between speed and velocity
- How to calculate average velocity

Which way to go

You have used the idea of **speed** before to describe the motion of many different objects. But speed is not the whole story. If you have two trains on the same piece of track travelling at the same speed, one other factor is very important: that they are both travelling in the same **direction**. The word 'velocity' is not just an old-fashioned word for speed, it means speed in a particular direction.

FIGURE 1: It is vital to keep track of what trains are where.

Distance, speed and velocity

Speed is the measure of how fast you are going – how much ground you are covering every second. The table shows you some different speeds.

Object	Speed in m/s	Speed in km/h
Human sprinter	10	36
Racehorse	19	68
Formula 1 racing car	100	360
Dolphin	11	40
Jet fighter	694	2500

- If you have a high speed, you cover a lot of ground each second.
- Speed can be calculated from:

$$\text{speed} = \frac{\text{distance}}{\text{time}}$$

- Most journeys are not done at constant speed, so when we calculate speed from the equation above we are really calculating the **average speed** for the journey.
- We measure speed in metres per second, m/s.
- Other units, such as km/h, may be more suitable for journeys from one place to another.
- If you want to give the velocity of something, you must give its direction as well as its speed, e.g. 20 m/s west.
- If two objects are moving in opposite directions, we can represent this by giving one of the velocities a negative value.

FIGURE 2: A top-class sprinter can cover more than 10 m in a second!

QUESTIONS

1. John's journey to school takes 10 minutes and is 3.6 km. What is his speed in km/minute?
2. What is John's speed in m/s? (3.6 km = 3600 m and 10 minutes = 600 s)
3. Alice runs round the athletics track. She does 400 m in 1 minute 20 seconds. What is her speed in m/s?
4. At one point Alice is running due west at 6 m/s. Later she is running due east at 4 m/s. How could we write her velocities to show that they are in opposite directions?

Velocity is speed in a given direction

...*average speed* ...*average velocity* ...*direction* ...*displacement* ...*distance*

Vector quantities

Velocity and displacement are not the only vector quantities. Any quantity that has a direction as well as size is a vector quantity. Quantities that only have size are called **scalar** quantities.

Speed, velocity and displacement

The picture shows a small section of a map of Cardiff.

Imagine you want to travel from the southeast corner of Eyre Street to the northwest corner of Cameron Street. There are several ways you could go but none of them is a straight line. You will have to walk further than the actual distance between the two points. The distance in a straight line between your starting point and ending point is called your **displacement**. Displacement is how much your position has changed at the end of the journey.

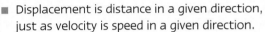

FIGURE 3: A map of part of Cardiff – maybe you live near here!

- Displacement is distance in a given direction, just as velocity is speed in a given direction.

- Quantities such as displacement and velocity, which have direction as well as size, are called **vector** quantities.

- These two vector quantities are related by the equation:

$$\text{Average velocity} = \frac{\text{displacement}}{\text{time}} \quad \text{or} \quad v = \frac{s}{t}$$

- For motion in a straight line, distance travelled is the same as the size of the displacement, and speed is the same as the size of the velocity.

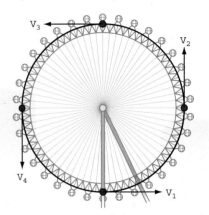

FIGURE 4: A change of direction is a change of velocity.

- We say that scalar quantities only have **magnitude** (size).
- Vector quantities have magnitude and direction.
- Scalar quantities include mass, density, volume, temperature, energy, speed and distance.
- Vector quantities include displacement, velocity, acceleration, force.
- Vector quantities can be represented by drawing arrows that point in the direction of the quantity and have a length proportional to the magnitude of the quantity.

QUESTIONS

5 Simon walks 400 m west, turns a corner and walks 300 m north. It takes him 5 minutes 50 seconds. What total distance does he travel?

6 Is the size of his displacement
 a the same as the answer to question **5**?
 b more than the answer to question **5**?
 c less than the answer to question **5**?

7 What is Simon's average speed?

8 The size of Simon's displacement is 500 m. What is the size of his average velocity?

QUESTIONS

9 Is 'area' a vector or scalar quantity?

10 Draw an arrow to represent a velocity of 10 m/s south.

11 Using the same scale as in question 10, draw an arrow to represent a velocity of 5 m/s north.

12 Explain why a car going round a corner can have a constant speed but a changing velocity.

Faster and faster

You will find out:
- What is meant by the idea of acceleration
- How an object can be accelerating without changing its speed
- How to calculate acceleration

Going faster, faster

The fastest dragsters are capable of completing 0.25 of a mile (396 m) from a standing start in under 4.5 s, travelling at about 530 km/h or 148 m/s at the highest **speed**. The initial acceleration is such that the cars reach over 50 m/s within 20 m of the start line in about 0.8 s.

Acceleration

Anything that has been still and starts moving has accelerated: its speed has increased from 0 m/s to some higher value. The dragster described above reaches 530 km/h in 4.5 s. That is an average **acceleration** of about 118 km/h per second; compare this with a normal family car which might accelerate from 0 to 100 km/h in around 10 s. Of course, a car does not have to be stationary to start accelerating; any increase in speed is an example of an acceleration.

- Acceleration measures the rate of change of speed: how much the speed increases each second.

- Acceleration can be measured in kilometres per hour per second.

- Notice that units of time are mentioned twice in these units, kilometres per *hour* per *second*.

- The standard (Système International or SI) unit of acceleration is m/s^2, this is said as 'metres per second per second' or 'metres per second squared'.

- A bigger change of speed in a certain time means a bigger acceleration.

- The shorter the time for a given change of speed the bigger the acceleration.

FIGURE 1: A top fuel dragster.

A top fuel dragster accelerates at about 118 km/h per second

QUESTIONS

1 If a Ford Focus accelerates from 0 to 100 km/h in 10 seconds, how much does its speed increase each second?

2 Michael and Maurice run a sprint race. Michael reaches 9 m/s after 3 s and Maurice reaches 8.5 m/s after 3 s. Who has the greater acceleration?

3 Charlene's car does 0–100 km/h in 8 seconds and Simon's car does 0–100 km/h in 9.5 seconds. Which has the greater acceleration?

4 Two cyclists are timed. Paul's speed increases from 0 to 20 m/s in 5 s and James' speed increases from 0 to 15 m/s in 3 s. How could you work out which had the greater acceleration?

...acceleration ...deceleration ...distance

Calculating acceleration

Acceleration measures the rate of change of speed. We can write:

$$\text{acceleration} = \frac{\text{change in speed}}{\text{time}}$$

to calculate acceleration for objects whose speed is changing.

However the definition of acceleration is that acceleration is equal to the rate of change of **velocity**.

Acceleration should be calculated from the equation:

$$\text{acceleration} = \frac{\text{change in velocity}}{\text{time}}$$

which can be written in time as:

$$a = \frac{(v - u)}{t}$$

FIGURE 2: They're off!

- a stands for acceleration, v stands for final velocity, u stands for initial velocity and t stands for time taken for the change.
- This equation assumes that the velocity has been changing at the same rate all the time. If this is not true, the equation gives you the *average* acceleration.
- Velocity is usually measured in m/s, time in s and acceleration in m/s^2.
- If the object is slowing down, then v is less than u and the answer for acceleration comes out as a negative number. A **negative acceleration** is the same as a **deceleration**.
- If the object is moving in a straight line, then the change in velocity is the same as the change in speed.
- Velocity is speed in a particular direction, so any change in the direction of movement is a change in velocity even if there is no change in speed.
- This means that if an object is changing its direction of motion it is accelerating.
- The equation acceleration = change in velocity/time is true whether the change in velocity is a change in magnitude, in direction or both, but the calculation where there is a change in direction is difficult.

▪▪▪ QUESTIONS ▪▪▪

5 What is the difference between speed and velocity?

6 A train moves away from a station along a straight track, increasing its velocity from 0 to 20 m/s in 16 s. What is its acceleration in m/s^2?

7 The train moves round a gentle curve maintaining the same speed. What is true about
   a the distance travelled per second?
   b its velocity?
   c its acceleration?

8 The train approaches a station travelling at 20 m/s. It slows to a stop in 12 seconds. What is its acceleration?

Watch Out You have to calculate acceleration only for motion in a straight line, but remember that a change in direction is also an acceleration.

Using acceleration

If you know the acceleration of an object, you can calculate other quantities relating to its motion.

- Calculate time for change from

$$t = \frac{(v - u)}{a}$$

- Calculate final velocity from $v = u + at$.
- Calculate initial velocity from $u = v - at$.
- The average velocity is equal to:

$$\frac{(u + v)}{2}$$

so it is possible to calculate **distance** travelled during the acceleration from:

$$\frac{t(u + v)}{2}$$

FIGURE 3: Is this rally car accelerating?

▪▪▪ QUESTIONS ▪▪▪

9 Maria pedals harder on her bike, accelerating from 8 m/s to 11 m/s in 1.5 s. What is her acceleration?

10 A rally car accelerates from 100 km/h to 150 km/h in 5 s. What is its acceleration in
   a km/h/s?
   b m/s^2?

11 Calculate the time required for a motorbike to accelerate from 15 m/s to 30 m/s with an acceleration of $2 m/s^2$.

12 Calculate the distance the motorbike will travel while it accelerates.

...negative acceleration   ...speed   ...velocity

Getting the picture

Keeping track

When you are travelling from one place to another, you start off, accelerate to the **speed** you want to travel at, and decelerate to a stop at the end of your journey. Of course, it is very unlikely that you will complete the journey at a constant speed: there are corners, junctions, traffic lights and other motorists making even the simplest journey quite complicated. We can use a **velocity-time graph** to picture how motion changes during a journey.

FIGURE 1: Constant speed of 0 m/s!

The steeper the slope of the line, the greater the magnitude of the acceleration.

Velocity variations

A graph shows when an object is moving or stationary, when its velocity is constant, and when it is speeding up or slowing down.

- A velocity time graph will have its x-axis labelled 'time' or 't'.
- The y-axis will be labelled 'velocity' or 'v'.
- A constant velocity is shown as a horizontal line
- If an object is not moving it has a constant velocity of 0, shown as a horizontal line along the x-axis.
- If an object is increasing its velocity (accelerating), this will give a line sloping upwards.
- If the velocity is decreasing (decelerating), this will give a line sloping downwards.
- If the sloping line is straight, then the **acceleration** is constant.
- The steepness of the line is proportional to the acceleration. A steep line means that there is a large velocity change per second, so the acceleration is large. A shallower line would mean a lower acceleration.

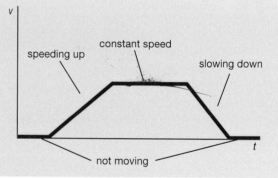

FIGURE 2: A velocity-time graph.

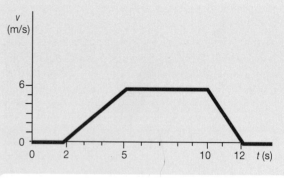

FIGURE 3: Velocity-time graph for calculations.

▪▪ QUESTIONS ▪▪

1. In the velocity–time graph above, what is the object doing between 0 and 2 s?
2. What is happening between 2 s and 5 s?
3. When is it travelling at a constant speed?
4. What is happening between 10 and 12 s?

...acceleration   ...gradient   ...negative acceleration

A slippery slope

In the velocity–time graphs on the opposite page, you can tell which acceleration is greater, the positive acceleration (where the velocity is increasing) and the **negative acceleration** (where the velocity is decreasing) just by looking at the graph. The steeper the slope of the line, the greater the magnitude (or size) of the acceleration. The acceleration can be calculated from the slope or **gradient** of the line. Look at Figure 4.

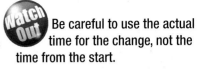
Be careful to use the actual time for the change, not the time from the start.

■ Gradient = vertical increase/horizontal increase.
■ Choose two points on the slope you want to measure
■ Draw lines across to the y-axis to find what velocities they represent. Examples: on the diagram v_1 and v_2 or v_3 and v_4.

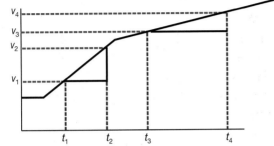

FIGURE 4: Calculating gradients.

■ Work out the increase in velocity. Examples: on the diagram $(v_2 - v_1)$ or $(v_4 - v_3)$
■ Draw lines down to the x-axis to find out what times the points represent. Examples: on the diagram t_1 and t_2 or t_3 and t_4.
■ Work out the time taken for the change. Examples: on the diagram $(t_2 - t_1)$ or $(t_4 - t_3)$.
■ Calculate the gradient from increase in v/change in t. Examples: on the diagram $(v_2 - v_1)/(t_2 - t_1)$ or $(v_4 - v_3)/(t_4 - t_3)$.

There and back again

This graph shows some of the motion of a bouncing ball. The ball is released and accelerates as it falls. It hits the ground and rebounds, decelerating on the way up. After reaching the top of its bounce it accelerates downwards again.

■ The gradient of the sloping parts of the graph is the same each time. This shows that the acceleration is always the same.
■ The values of velocity switch between positive and negative values. This is because the ball is changing its direction, and a velocity in the opposite direction is shown as a negative value.

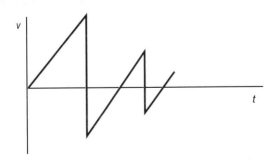

FIGURE 5: Velocity–time graph for a bouncing ball.

A change of pace

The graphs you have met so far have shown accelerations that have remained the same for a period of time: these are constant or uniform accelerations. This graph shows the motion of a car as it accelerates from a stop to its highest speed.

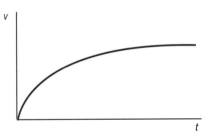

FIGURE 6: Velocity–time graph for non-uniform acceleration.

■ The gradient of the line is changing, showing that the acceleration is changing.
■ The line starts off steep and gets less steep until it is horizontal..
■ This shows that the acceleration is decreasing to zero.

QUESTIONS

9 What would the graph of an increasing acceleration look like?

10 Sketch the velocity–time graph for a car that accelerates uniformly from rest. It travels at a constant velocity and then decelerates with a decreasing negative acceleration.

11 Sketch the velocity–time graph for an object that is accelerating with a decreasing acceleration. It then experiences a greater but decreasing negative acceleration.

QUESTIONS

5 Calculate the two accelerations shown in Figure 3.
6 Explain why the gradient of a line on a velocity–time graph gives the acceleration.
7 In Figure 5 which direction does the velocity have a positive value, going down or going up?
8 Where on the graph has the ball reached the top of its bounce?

Forcing the pace

You will find out:

- An acceleration always has a force causing it
- How to work out the acceleration caused by a particular force
- What is meant by momentum and how to work it out

Another big bang?

Hopefully not, but with huge trucks racing round a track there is the possibility of some nasty bumps. Of course this isn't the form of racing with the highest velocities and greatest accelerations, but it may have the largest masses. Mass matters, as you are about to find out.

FIGURE 1: Racing trucks have large masses.

The use of force

It is possible, if you are a 'World's Strongest Man' competitor, to pull a truck (see Figure 2). Not surprisingly the truck's acceleration will be very small compared with that produced by its engine. This is because **acceleration** depends on **force**: the greater the force applied, the greater the acceleration, and the smaller the force applied, the less the acceleration.

Mass matters

If you have ever got held up behind a big lorry, you will know that it can maintain a good speed on a fairly straight and level road, but will take a long time to get going again if it has to stop or slow down. Lorries have big engines that provide a large driving force, but have a lower acceleration than the average family car. This is because of their **mass**, which is much greater than the mass of a car. More mass means less acceleration.

FIGURE 2: Pulling power – would you like to be this strong?

There are three important points about mass and acceleration:

- If there is an acceleration there must be a force to cause it.
- For a particular mass, the greater the force, the greater the acceleration. In fact, however the force changes, the acceleration changes in a similar way: twice the force, twice the acceleration.
- For a particular force, the greater the mass being accelerated, the lower the acceleration. In fact, if you have twice the mass you get half the acceleration.

▌▌ QUESTIONS ▌▌

1. If two objects have the same mass but different forces acting on them, what can you say about their accelerations?
2. Why do cars with larger engines generally take less time to get from 0 to 100 km/h?
3. Why are racing cars made as light as possible?
4. Andrew and Peter are going to have a race on their bikes. Andrew can apply more force to the pedals than Peter. What else would you have to know to work out who would have the greater acceleration?

Force = mass × acceleration

...*acceleration* ...*force* ...*mass*

Finding the force

You have seen that acceleration changes as the force changes. We say that acceleration is directly proportional to force. Doubling the force on a particular mass will double its acceleration, ten times the force will give ten times the acceleration and so on. On the other hand, it is also true that doubling the mass acted on by a particular force will halve its acceleration and ten times the mass will give one-tenth of the acceleration. We say that acceleration is inversely proportional to mass.

FIGURE 3: Accelerating, soon to be decelerating.

- We can write acceleration is proportional to force as $a \propto F$, where a is the symbol for acceleration and F is the symbol for force.

- We can write acceleration is inversely proportional to mass as $a \propto 1/m$ where m is the symbol for mass.

- These can be combined as $a \propto F/m$.

- Rearranging this gives $F \propto ma$.

- The unit of force, the newton, is chosen so that a force of 1 N causes a mass of 1 kg to accelerate at 1 m/s^2.

- This means that we can write the equation for force, mass and acceleration as:

$$F = ma$$
force = mass × acceleration

- As we have seen, force is measured in newtons (N), mass in kilograms (kg) and acceleration in metres per second squared (m/s^2).

- Acceleration and force are both **vector** quantities. The acceleration is always in the same direction as the force causing it.

- The equation $F = ma$ can be used to calculate acceleration or mass:

$$a = F/m$$
$$m = F/a$$

- A useful short cut from combining the equation $F = ma$ and the equation for acceleration $a = \left(\dfrac{v - u}{t}\right)$, gives:

$$F = m\left(\frac{v - u}{t}\right)$$

Use this to calculate force directly from information about velocities.

QUESTIONS

5   What force is required to accelerate a 1000 kg car at 6 m/s^2?
6   What force is acting if a 60 kg bungee jumper is accelerating at 10 m/s^2?
7   What acceleration will be given to a 20 g (0.02 kg) bullet if the gun applies a force of 500 N?
8   What is the mass of a lorry that decelerates at 5 m/s^2 due to a braking force of 100 000 N?

Momentum   (H)

The brakes used to stop a bicycle would not be much use on a car, and a lorry needs even better brakes. This is because a car has more speed and more mass than a bike and a lorry has much more mass than a car. The mass and velocity of an object are combined in the idea of **momentum**.

FIGURE 4: Bike brakes – these wouldn't be much use on a car!

- Momentum is a measure of how hard it is to change the motion of an object.
- Momentum is calculated from

Momentum = mass × velocity
= mv

- Mass is measured in kilograms (kg) and velocity in metres per second (m/s).
- Momentum is measured in kg m/s (kilogram metres per second)

WOW FACTOR!

European truck racing has a speed limit of 160 km/h (100 mph). It's just too dangerous otherwise: there would be too much momentum.

QUESTIONS

9   What is the momentum of a 58 g tennis ball travelling at 40 m/s?
10 What is the momentum of a 2000 kg car travelling at 25 m/s?
11 A plane of mass m increases its velocity from u to v. Write an equation for its change in momentum.
12 Compare the equation from question **11** with $F = m(v - u)/t$. What is the change in momentum equal to?

...*momentum*   ...*vector*

The lawman

You will find out:

- That Isaac Newton described three laws of motion
- What is meant by 'resultant' force
- How to use Newton's laws to work out how things move

There are laws and laws

The laws which have to be obeyed in the UK are made by Oarliament, and you can be prosecuted and punished in some way if you break them. But it is possible to break them. The laws of physics, including Newton's laws, are different. You and all other objects have no choice about obeying them. These are laws which describe how things are, rather than rules about how things ought to be.

FIGURE 1: Newton – the lawman!

Lawman 1: The beginning

Newton's first law can be written like this:

> If the **resultant force** acting on a body is zero, it will remain at rest or continue to move at the same speed in the same direction.

The statement contains the following ideas.

Resultant force

FIGURE 2: Balanced forces?

- In a tug of war both sides are pulling hard, but in opposite directions. There may not be much movement because the forces cancel each other out.
- If several forces act on an object some may add together if they are in the same direction, and some may cancel out if they are in opposite directions.
- The resultant force is the 'left-over' force when all forces have been added up or taken away.

Remain at rest

- 'Rest' means not moving.
- 'It will remain at rest' tells you that if there is no resultant force on an object that is stationary, it won't start moving.

Same speed in the same direction

- 'Same speed in the same direction' is sometimes written as 'constant motion' or 'uniform motion'.
- No change in speed or direction means no change in velocity, which means there is no **acceleration**.

FIGURE 3: Toy truck

- If any object is moving at a constant speed in a straight line then there is no resultant force on it. Any forces acting are cancelling each other out.
- Forces that completely cancel each other out are called 'balanced forces'.

ᴵᴵ QUESTIONS ᴵᴵ

1 A plane is flying at a steady speed of 100 m/s due North. What can you say about the forces acting on it?
2 What is the resultant force on the toy truck in Figure 3?
3 What can you say about the toy truck's acceleration?
4 A satellite is orbiting Earth at a constant speed. Is there a resultant force on it?

...acceleration ...action

Lawman 2: Maximum force

Newton's second law leads to something familiar. The law can be stated as follows:

The acceleration of an object is directly proportional to the resultant force acting on the object, is in the same direction as the resultant force, and is inversely proportional to the mass of the object.

This law is summed up in the equation you have already met:

$$F = ma$$

Notice that F is the net or resultant force acting on the object.

First and second law

Newton's first law is really just an example of the second. If the resultant force, F, acting on an object of mass m is zero, then:

$$F = 0 = ma$$

and the acceleration is zero. If acceleration is zero there is no change in velocity so the object keeps moving at the same speed in the same direction.

This last idea, that you did not need a force to *keep* something moving, only to *change* its movement had been very controversial in the time of Galileo. At that time, scientific ideas were taken largely from the writings of Aristotle. Aristotle had stated that a force was necessary for an object to keep moving. This, of course, fits well with everyday experience where frictional forces act against motion. Galileo challenged Aristotle's conclusions, basing his ideas on observation and experiment. Newton built on the work of Galileo to formulate his laws.

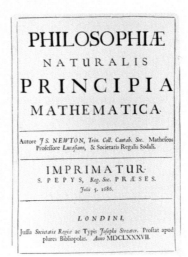

FIGURE 4: Newton's Philosophiae Naturalis Principia Mathematica or The Mathematical Principles of Natural Philosophy.

FIGURE 5: Going faster than the limit is breaking the law.

Lawman 3: Opposition

Newton's third law is often quoted, you may have heard of it. The law states:

*To every **action** there is an equal and opposite **reaction**.*

- The idea is that if you push a door with a force of 5 N ('the action'), the door pushes back on you with a force of 5 N in the opposite direction ('the reaction').
- This should cause the door to move, not you, because you are probably heavier than the door and the frictional forces on you are greater.
- Another example: the Earth pulls you with a force we call your weight. This might be about 600 N. You also pull the Earth with a force of 600 N, but the mass of the Earth is so large, your force has no measurable effect.

▨▨▨▨ QUESTIONS ▨▨▨▨

9 An engine pulls 10 trucks. The force the engine exerts on the first truck is 5000 N. What force does the truck exert on the engine?

10 The total mass of the trucks is 100 tonnes (100 000 kg). What is their acceleration?

11 What did you have to assume to be able to answer question **10**?

12 If there was a frictional force of 1000 N acting on the trucks what would be the acceleration?

▨▨▨▨ QUESTIONS ▨▨▨▨

5 A 10 kg sledge is pulled with a force of 50 N. What is its acceleration?

6 Calculate the maximum mass of a bungee-jumper who can use a cord which applies a force of 2000 N and needs to produce a deceleration of 25 m/s^2.

7 A pram is being pushed with a force of 20 N and moving with constant velocity. What can you say about the frictional forces on it?

8 During experiments with a forcemeter, Mandeep notices that she has to apply a force of 2 N to keep a book steadily moving across a table. 'Aristotle was right!' she says. Explain why this force is needed.

Falling down

You will find out:
- How to 'lose weight'
- That all objects fall with the same acceleration due to gravity
- How air resistance affects the way objects fall

What goes up...

However good you are at going up, eventually you will fall back to the ground. The force of gravity pulls you down. In fact it pulls you 'down' wherever you are on the Earth; in other words you are actually being pulled towards the centre of the Earth.

Weighty matters

Two quantities that often confuse people are **mass** and **weight**. The confusion happens because outside the science laboratory we use the word 'weight' when we are really talking about mass.

- Mass measures the amount of material that is in an object and is measured in kilograms.
- To change your mass you need to lose or gain more material in your body. People on a diet are really trying to lose mass.
- Weight measures the force of gravity on an object.
- Weight is measured in newtons.
- Your weight changes as you go to different places on Earth as gravitational force varies slightly. You weigh very slightly less at the equator than at the poles (and not because you aren't wearing so much!).
- Your weight would be different on the Moon or on another planet because the gravitational force is different.

If you are on Earth, and you hang different masses on a newtonmeter (or spring balance) you will find that each kilogram is pulled downwards by a force of about 10 N. We say that the weight of a mass of 1 kg is 10 N.

When you jump from a diving board or from a plane if you are parachuting, your weight is the force that pulls you down.

- If your mass is 50 kg, your weight will be 500 N. 500 N is the force causing you to accelerate downwards.
- From $F = ma$ you can work out that your acceleration is 500 N/50 kg = 10 m/s².
- Whatever your mass, your acceleration is 10 m/s². This is called the **gravitational acceleration** and it is given the symbol 'g'.

FIGURE 1: 'Mass loss' not 'weight loss'.

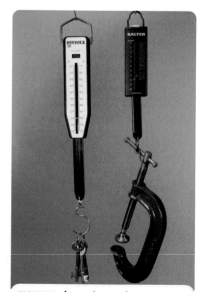

FIGURE 2: A newtonmeter measures weight.

⊪ QUESTIONS ⊪

1 What is the weight of a person whose mass is 60 kg?
2 What acceleration will they have if they are falling?
3 What is the weight and acceleration of someone whose mass is 30 kg?
4 Why is the acceleration always the same?

...air resistance   ...drag   ...gravitational acceleration

The real story

Your weight is the force of gravity on you and it is the force that accelerates you downwards when you fall or jump. Weight, W, can be calculated from:

$$W = mg$$

where m is your mass and g is the gravitational acceleration. Gravitational acceleration, g, is about 9.8 m/s^2, though the value 10 m/s^2 is often accurate enough for use in calculations.

Weight, and the acceleration it causes, are not the whole story of what happens to you while you are falling. If it were, then you would see all objects fall in exactly the same way when they are dropped. But if you drop a brick and a feather at the same time from the same height, the brick will hit the ground first.

- The brick and feather both have the same acceleration due to gravity.

- But there is another force acting: the force of **drag**, also called **air resistance** or fluid friction.

- Experiments done in a vacuum show that heavy and light objects will fall with the same acceleration if there is no air.

- Drag always acts against the direction of motion.

- At the beginning of a fall, the weight is much greater than the drag so the object will accelerate.

FIGURE 3: No air, no difference: when an astronaut on the moon dropped a hammer and a feather, they reached the ground together!

 Be careful of saying that drag slows things down. What is usually happening is that it reduces acceleration and limits top speed.

It's terminal (H)

The force of drag on an object falling through air is not constant:

- Drag increases as speed increases.
- The resultant downwards force on the object = weight – drag.
- The acceleration at any instant = (weight – drag)/mass.
- As drag increases (weight – drag) becomes less so the acceleration is less.
- Eventually drag becomes equal to weight, the resultant force becomes zero and so does the acceleration.
- The object continues to fall at a constant speed, called the '**terminal velocity**'.

Opening a parachute provides more drag. This slows the parachutist until the drag force has dropped to be equal to the weight again. This is now at a lower and hopefully safer terminal velocity.

QUESTIONS

Use $g = 9.8$ m/s^2 in these questions

9a How fast will you be travelling 1 s after jumping from a plane?

b If drag is equal to $0.15 \times v^2$, what will be the magnitude and direction of this force after 1 s?

c What will be the magnitude and direction of the resultant force on you? Assume your mass is 60 kg.

d What will be the magnitude and direction of your acceleration at this time? How will the increase in velocity change each second?

QUESTIONS

Use $g = 9.8$ m/s^2 in these questions

5 If your mass is 50 kg what is your weight?

6 If you jump out of a plane how fast will you be falling after 0.5 s?

7 What have you had to ignore to calculate the value in question 6?

8 If the drag force on you is 8 N, what is the resultant force acting on you?

It all adds up

You will find out:
- How to deal with several forces acting on an object
- How we can model changes in motion using spreadsheets

Far too many forces

Newton's first law tells us that a plane flying at a steady speed in a straight line has no **resultant force** on it. That does not mean it has no **force** at all on it, just that the forces on it are balanced. In fact, there is the thrust of the engines pushing forwards, the drag due to the air pushing backwards, its weight pulling downwards and the lift generated by the wings pushing upwards.

Free bodies

Many different forces can act on an object.

Working out the effect of forces is easier if we forget about the background and concentrate on the object itself. We can draw a diagram called a **free-body diagram**.

- The object can be represented by a simple shape.
- The forces are drawn as arrows.
- The direction of each arrow shows the direction the force is acting in.
- The length of the arrow represents the magnitude of the force.

The free-body diagram for the plane could look like Figure 2.

- You can see that weight and lift cancel out so the vertical forces are balanced.
- You can see that thrust is larger than drag, so the resultant force will be forwards.
- The plane will be accelerating forwards.

Use Figure 3 to answer the questions below.

FIGURE 1: No resultant force but four forces altogether.

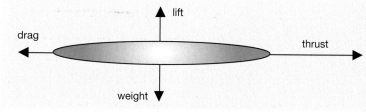

FIGURE 2: The free-body diagram for a plane.

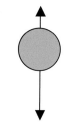

FIGURE 3: The free-body diagram for a falling object.

▟ QUESTIONS ▙

1. What forces do the arrows represent?
2. Which direction will the resultant force be in?
3. Describe the motion of the object.
4. Draw a free-body diagram for a mass hanging on a string (it is not moving).

...force   ...free-body diagram   ...resistance

Computing a solution

The rules for combining forces to find the effect on an object's motion are fairly straightforward, but doing the calculations can be just a bit dull! This makes this sort of work ideal for doing on a computer.

Here's an example. A parachutist falls for a while before opening their 'chute. During this time they accelerate because of the force of gravity on them, but there is also the force due to air **resistance** acting upwards. This force increases as velocity increases, until it becomes equal to their weight and they reach terminal velocity.

A **spreadsheet** can be used to calculate the resultant force, acceleration and velocity at very small time intervals, to create an approximation of how the motion changes.

You need to put in:

- The mass of the parachutist. For a real parachutist this could simply be measured with bathroom scales.
- A value for the acceleration due to gravity. This does vary from place to place, but using $g = 9.8\,\text{m/s}^2$ is sufficiently accurate.
- The initial velocity (usually 0 m/s).
- The constant, k, in the equation for drag $F_D = kv^2$. This depends on the density of the air, the cross-sectional area of the parachutist, and the shape of the falling object. A good value for k is 0.15.

The table shows a section of a spreadsheet used to do this calculation as the parachutist approaches their terminal velocity of just over 58 m/s.

Time (s)	Velocity (m/s)	Acceleration (m/s²)	Drag (N)
13.3	57.95	0.41	470.06
13.4	57.99	0.39	470.73
13.5	58.03	0.38	471.38
13.6	58.06	0.37	472.01
13.7	58.10	0.35	472.61

---- QUESTIONS ----

Use $g = 9.8\,\text{m/s}^2$, mass of 50 kg, 0.15 for the value of k.

5 Calculate the velocity 0.5 s after jumping out of the plane.

6 Calculate the drag force after 0.5 s.

7 Calculate the resultant force and the acceleration after 0.5 s.

8 Calculate the speed at 1.0 s (using your acceleration value from question 7).

Forces in two dimensions

Forces don't always act in the same or opposite directions. This sledge is being pulled at a constant velocity on level ground.

FIGURE 4: What forces act on the sledge?

The free-body diagram for this would be:

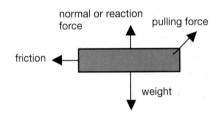

normal or reaction force

pulling force

friction

weight

FIGURE 5: Free-body diagram for a sledge.

- There is no resultant force if there is no change in velocity.
- This means that all the horizontal forces cancel out, and all the vertical forces cancel out.
- The pulling force is at an angle to the horizontal so it contributes a bit to the vertical forces and a bit to the horizontal forces.
- The pulling force can be split into two components: a horizontal component we call P_H and a vertical component we call P_V.

Use the free-body diagram to answer these questions.

---- QUESTIONS ----

9 One force acts downwards. What is it?

10 Two forces act upwards. What are they?

11 One force acts backwards. What is it?

12 One force acts forwards. What is it?

Take a brake

You will find out:
- What is meant by the stopping distance for a car
- How stopping distance is worked out
- What factors affect stopping distance

A little extra help

The Space Shuttle needs to use a parachute to stop safely on its runway. If you are travelling very fast and need to stop quickly, then you need a big deceleration. A big deceleration needs a big force to make it happen.

FIGURE 1: A parachute is needed to stop the Shuttle.

Thinking, braking, stopping

Cars don't need parachutes, but they do need to be able to stop quickly. It is important that brakes are properly maintained and that drivers know how to minimise the distance they need to come to a halt.

- The distance your car will travel between when you see a problem and when the car is stationary is called the **stopping distance**.

- The stopping distance is made up of two parts: the thinking distance and the braking distance.

- The **thinking distance** is the distance the car travels *before* you apply the brakes: it is the distance you travel while you are reacting to the problem.

- The **braking distance** is the distance the car moves between the brakes being applied and its coming to a halt.

- **Stopping distance = thinking distance + braking distance**.

When you are learning to drive you will be expected to know these distances for different speeds.

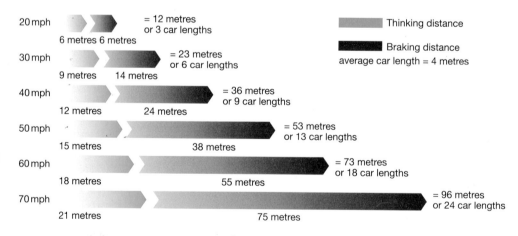

20 mph	6 metres 6 metres = 12 metres or 3 car lengths
30 mph	9 metres 14 metres = 23 metres or 6 car lengths
40 mph	12 metres 24 metres = 36 metres or 9 car lengths
50 mph	15 metres 38 metres = 53 metres or 13 car lengths
60 mph	18 metres 55 metres = 73 metres or 18 car lengths
70 mph	21 metres 75 metres = 96 metres or 24 car lengths

Thinking distance

Braking distance
average car length = 4 metres

FIGURE 2: Minimum stopping distances for a car.

QUESTIONS

1. What happens to the thinking distance as speed increases?
2. What happens to braking distance as speed increases?
3. Do you see any difference in the way these change with speed?
4. What happens to stopping distance as speed increases?

...braking distance   ...reaction time

Stay safe

Both thinking distance and braking distance are increased by increasing speed.

FIGURE 3: A safe space between two cars may be longer than you think!

Watch Out You need to double the gap between you and the car in front if the road is wet, and leave an even bigger gap if it is icy.

Thinking distance

- During the time you take to react, the car will have travelled a certain distance.
- As speed = distance/time it is also true that distance = speed × time.
- This means that if your speed is greater, you go further while you are reacting.

Of course you may not be at your most alert: the factors listed below will make your **reaction time** longer and your thinking distance longer:

- If you have been drinking *alcohol* or taking *drugs*.
- If you are *tired* or *unwell*.
- If you are *distracted* by your passengers or by talking on the mobile phone.

Braking distance

Brakes can provide only a certain maximum deceleration even when they are working properly. As acceleration = change in velocity/time, it is also true that time = change in velocity/acceleration. This means that if your speed is higher, it will take a longer time for you to stop. But your average speed during that time is also higher.

So braking distance is increased by higher speed in two ways. In fact, doubling your speed will make your braking distance four times as long.

If the effectiveness of your brakes is reduced in some way your braking time and distance will increase further:

- if the brakes are *not properly maintained*
- if there is reduced friction between tyres and road due to *wet* or *icy conditions*
- if your car is heavily loaded, as deceleration will be reduced if mass is increased.

QUESTIONS

5 You are travelling at 15 m/s. You see a problem ahead. Your reaction time is 0.5 s. Work out your thinking distance.

6 What would your thinking distance be if you were travelling at 30 m/s?

7 The mass of your car is 1000 kg. The force your brakes can apply is 10 000 N. What is your deceleration? (Refer back to 'Falling down' if you need reminding about force.)

8 Using the deceleration you worked out in question **7**, how many seconds will it take you to stop if your speed is:
   a 15 m/s   **b** 30 m/s?

Stopping short

Many of the ideas we have met in this topic come together in working out stopping distances:

- **Stopping distance = thinking distance + braking distance.**

- **Thinking distance = reaction time × speed.**

- **Braking distance = braking time × average speed during braking.**

- **Average speed during braking = (speed of travel + 0)/2.**

- **Braking time = (speed of travel − 0)/braking deceleration.**

- **Braking deceleration = braking force/mass of vehicle.**

QUESTIONS

Use these values to answer the questions below:

Speed of travel = 20 m/s

Reaction time = 0.4 s

Braking force = 10 000 N

Mass of car = 1500 kg

9 What is the thinking distance?

10 What is the deceleration?

11 Work out the braking time and braking distance.

12 Work out the stopping distance.

...stopping distance   ...thinking distance

Safe inside

You will find out:

- What safety features cars have to limit the damage to you
- How to assess how effective these are
- About the physics behind these safety features

Accidents happen

Your car may be properly maintained and you may be driving in the highest state of alertness, but you may still be involved in a **collision** one day. It is worth checking what features your car has to protect you if you do have an accident, as this may make all the difference to what happens to you.

FIGURE 1: Accidents can happen!

The protectors

Modern cars have several features designed to protect you from the worst effects of a collision.

You are required by law to wear **seatbelts** when sitting in a car in the front seats and the back seats. They stop you continuing forwards if there is a collision. If you are thrown forwards without a seatbelt you will be injured or killed. If you are in the back of the car without a seatbelt, you may injure or kill the person in front of you. Seatbelts will be permanently stretched by a small amount if they are used in a collision.

Airbags are designed to inflate almost instantly if there is a collision, preventing you from hitting the dashboard.

FIGURE 2: Activated airbags – these protect people in an accident.

- Some cars have side airbags to protect you in the case of a side impact.

- Airbags inflate with considerable force. Babies, small children and frail people should not sit where there are airbags.

Crumple zones are built into the structure of the car in the front or rear bodywork and in some cases in the doors: areas outside the passenger compartment. They are designed to collapse slowly in case of a collision. This absorbs some of the energy of the collision protecting those inside the car. They are designed so that the damage happens outside the area where the people are.

▌▌ QUESTIONS ▌▌

1 Why should you wear seatbelts wherever you sit in the car?

2 Which fact above explains why seatbelts should be replaced if the car has been involved in a collision?

3 Why shouldn't you sit too close to the steering wheel if you have a driver's airbag?

4 Crumple zones are deliberately made weaker than other parts of the car. Why is this better than having all parts of the car equally strong?

WANT TO KNOW MORE?

Go to http://www.dft.gov.uk/ to find information about using airbags.

...airbag *...collision* *...crumple zone*

Is it worth it?

Many people do not wear their seatbelts and do not choose their next car on the basis of its safety features. Is there evidence that these features actually make a difference? Here are some facts and figures about seatbelts.

Seatbelts

Wearing seatbelts in the front of cars was made compulsory in January 1983. This caused the number of people wearing them to increase from 40% in December 1982 to 93% in February 1983 and this level has remained about the same since.

- The Department for Transport states that wearing seatbelts saves over 2200 lives per year in the UK.
- These statistics are estimates, as figures of seatbelt wearing are not collected at accidents.
- A study in Canada supports these figures, finding 11 690 lives saved over 11 years (the population of Canada is just under 33 million, the population of the UK is 60 million). Again this is based on estimates.
- About 15 people each year are killed by impacts from rear seat passengers who were not wearing seatbelts.

The graph shows the fatality rates for road accidents and other forms of transport from 1980 to 2003.

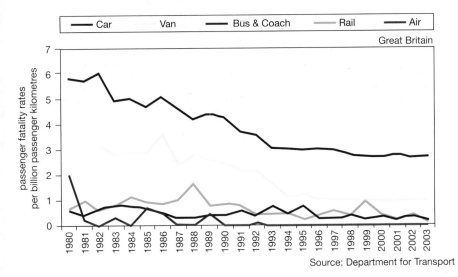

FIGURE 3: This graph compares the safety of different forms of transport.

WANT TO KNOW MORE?

Go to http://www. publications. parliament.uk to find a House of Lord's discussion on seatbelt statistics

Forward momentum (H)

Newton's second law can be written in terms of **momentum**:

$$Ft = mv - mu$$

or

Force × time = change of momentum

What is this telling you?

- In a collision you have a certain amount of momentum to lose.
- This depends on your mass and the velocity before the collision.
- You can lose it due to a large force operating for a small time or a smaller force operating for a longer time.
- The second option is less painful.

Safety features such as crumple zones, airbags and seatbelts make use of the effect of prolonging the time the person takes to come to a halt.

QUESTIONS

9 Seatbelts stretch slightly in a collision. How does this reduce the force on the wearer?

10 Airbags inflate very quickly then deflate slowly. How does this reduce the force on the user?

11 Crumple zones deform during the collision. How does this reduce the force on the occupants of the car?

12 Find out about other safety features to look out for in choosing a car.

QUESTIONS

5 Do you think most people feel that wearing seatbelts is a sensible idea in the front of a car? What evidence supports your answer?

6 The percentage of people wearing seatbelts in the rear of a car is not as high. What fact above would you use to try to convince people that they should 'belt up' in the back?

7 What evidence is there that wearing seatbelts has made a difference to road safety?

8 There is some concern that the rate of seatbelt wearing among young drivers and their friends is lower than it should be. Design a leaflet aimed at people your age to remind them that seatbelts are a good idea.

Take a chance?

You will find out:

- About some of the risks that people take
- How we can measure the size of a risk
- About some of the factors that decide whether people will take risks or not

Crazy or what!

People jump out of planes. They do it deliberately. They do it freely; nobody makes them. They pay for the privilege. Some people take part in BASE jumping, jumping from objects such as **B**uildings, **A**erials, **S**pans and the **E**arth, which may be illegal as well as dangerous. Why? If you are involved in any sort of dangerous sport (and that may include more sports than you would think), then perhaps you can give an answer yourself.

FIGURE 1: Having fun?

Won't catch me doing that!

Most people regard sharks as dangerous; however, it has been suggested that falling coconuts kill more people each year than sharks.

If you try to find out what is the most dangerous sport, there is no definite agreement because there are many different ways of measuring the risk. It is possible to make a case for fishing being the most dangerous sport in the UK, in terms of the number of people killed while doing it. Anglers drown and catch their rods in electricity cables. Of course many more people go fishing than take part in, say, motor sport, horse riding or boxing.

We are not very good at **assessing risk**.

- Some things scare us more than others, even if they are unlikely to happen.
- Some disasters are widely reported in the media.
- Some risks we are very used to and do not recognise their danger.

It is important to have a way of measuring risk to compare how dangerous particular activities are. For sports there are many different ways of measuring the risk.

- The total number of deaths. This puts many sports that lots of people do high on the list.
- The number of injuries treated in hospital. This puts certain sports at the top of the list: those that are likely to cause injuries but not necessarily deaths, and in which lots of people participate, such as football.
- The number of deaths as a percentage of people attempting them. This puts sports such as BASE jumping high on the list: not many people attempt it, but if anything goes wrong you are likely to die.

FIGURE 2: How dangerous?

QUESTIONS

1 Why might coconuts be more dangerous than sharks?
2 It is possible to reduce your risk from sharks or coconuts to zero. How?
3 Why is it hard to compare the dangers of BASE jumping and fishing?
4 Many people believe that they are much more likely to be a victim of crime than is actually the case. Why do you think that is?

...assessing risk *...choice*

Rate the risk

People about to do something that might be dangerous, such as parachuting, want to have some idea of how dangerous it is.

The British Parachute Association (BPA) makes several points in answer to the question 'How safe is sport parachuting/skydiving?'

- It isn't safe, not completely.
- They measure risk with two figures, injuries per 1000 jumps and fatalities per 100 000 jumps.
- There are four methods of taking your first jump and they have very different levels of risk.
- The riskier methods are the better preparation for solo jumping: for becoming a skydiver in your own right.
- One method of doing a jump is the tandem jump where you are strapped to an instructor.
- For tandem jumps, between 1990 and 2004, out of 153 382 jumps there was one fatality, a rate of 0.7 per 100 000 jumps.
- Another method, accelerated freefall (AFF), requires the jumper to freefall, open their parachute and control their own descent and landing. They do have two instructors jumping with them to tell them what to do.
- For AFF jumps in the same period, out of 6360 jumps there was 1 fatality, a rate of 15.7 per 100 000 jumps.

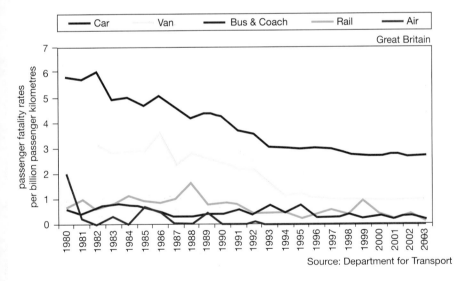

FIGURE 3: Which is safest?

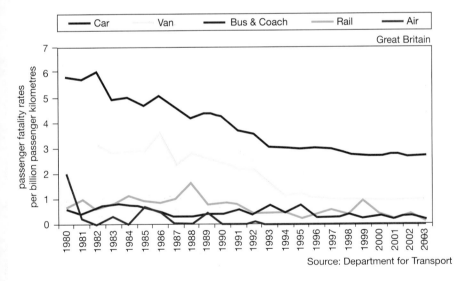 legend: Car — Van — Bus & Coach — Rail — Air — Great Britain. Y-axis: passenger fatality rates per billion passenger kilometres. Source: Department for Transport

QUESTIONS

5 Which method of taking your first jump, tandem or AFF, is safer?

6 Do you think the statistics comparing these two methods are reliable? Explain your answer.

7 Why would people attempt AFF even though it appears to be more dangerous?

8 Why do you think that the BPA does not measure injury rates and fatality rates against the same number: both per 1000 jumps?

WANT TO KNOW MORE?

About parachuting and its risks?
Visit http://www.bpa.org.uk/

It's a matter of choice

Every year over 3000 people die in road accidents in the UK. It is unlikely that anybody will avoid making a car journey as a result of hearing the figures. A rail crash or a passenger plane crash will be reported nationally and may result in people changing their travel plans as a result.

The graph opposite shows how dangerous different forms of transport are.

- The data are shown as fatalities per billion passenger kilometres.
- Cars are shown to be more dangerous than rail or air travel.

Our perception of risk often doesn't match the reality. Why?

Familiarity

- Cars are part of many people's experience practically from birth.
- Trains and planes may be used less frequently.

Control and choice

- People feel in control in their car. They can choose what risks to take.
- In other forms of transport they depend on others' judgements in operation and maintenance.

QUESTIONS

9 What is the safest form of transport per billion passenger kilometres?

10 Roughly how many times more dangerous is car travel than rail travel?

11 Can you think of examples where many people underestimate the risk?

12 Can you think of examples where people overestimate the risk?

Risky business

SELF-CHECK ACTIVITY CHALLENGE

CONTEXT

Look at this list of objects or activities that contain a certain element of risk:

- firefighting
- rock climbing
- nuclear power
- sunbathing
- terrorism

It is often difficult trying to assess the likelihood of something happening to you. Sometimes figures are quoted that are averages, but these may not help. For example, the probability of being killed on the roads in Britain was 1 in 20 000 in the year 2000. However, that rises or falls dramatically according to personal circumstance – someone driving as part of their work has a significantly greater likelihood of being killed on the roads than someone who works at home on a computer.

The likelihood of being killed in an air accident is around 1 in 11 000 000 (the journey to and from the airport is much riskier than the flight). However, when air disasters do occur they are often spectacular and produce national headline news stories in a way that car accidents rarely do and this influences perception.

Do you think generally that we worry about the right things? Can you think of something that has been in the news and has caused a lot of debate that wasn't really that big a deal? Are they things that you think we should be more concerned about than we are?

STEP 1

Look at the list and put the objects and activities in order according to which you think is the most risky. How do you decide whether one of the objects and activities is more risky than another? Are you influenced by how likely it is to affect you? Are you influenced by whether you have any control over it? Working in a small group, share your ideas and try to reach agreement to put the list in order of risk.

STEP 2

Look at the items in the list you think you know more about and discuss them within the group. How do you know about them? Is it from common sense, from your education or another source? Does knowing more make them more or less worrying? Are you more influenced by the scale of a disaster or by its likelihood? Does an understanding of what an accident in a nuclear power station can do make it more or less worrying? Does something being more likely make it more or less worrying?

Look at your results from step 1 and plot the objects and activities on a graph like this.

Unknown risk

Dread

Look at ones that are in the top right quadrant. Why are you more worried about these? Does ignorance of the effects make them more worrying?

Look at ones in the bottom right quadrant. Does knowledge make those more worrying?

Maximise your grade

These sentences show what you need to include in your work to achieve each grade. Use them to improve your work and be more successful.

Grade	Answer includes...
F	Place objects or activities into order according to which is the most dreadful.
	Explain why objects or activities were put in that order.
	Suggest how some of those objects or activities are known about by the person doing the task.
	Offer some rationale as to what makes objects or activities more or less dreadful.
C	Offer some rationale as to what kind of information source carries more credibility.
	Offer some idea as to how the nature of knowledge affects the perception of a hazard.
A	Reflect on how the nature of knowledge affects the perception of a hazard
	Reflect on how the nature of knowledge affects the perception of a hazard with particular clarity and insight.

STEP 4

Some people are worried about mobile phones and the health risk. Where on the graph would you put mobile phones?

Get to work!

You will find out:

- How work and energy are connected
- That work depends on force and distance
- How to calculate the amount of work being done

On the job

Who is doing the most work? These men would probably argue about this; the construction worker would talk about the physical effort, difficulties with weather, penalties for not finishing the work on time. The office worker might mention long hours, the mental demands of the job, perhaps having to take work home, competition with colleagues for promotion, tight deadlines for completing work. In science, as you will see, it is quite easy to answer this question.

Work and energy

Everything that happens requires a transfer of energy.

- A car journey requires energy to be transferred from the chemical energy in the fuel to **kinetic energy** of the car.
- The car may have to go uphill, so some energy is being transferred to **gravitational potential energy**.
- When the car needs to slow down or stop, the driver will apply the brakes, turning kinetic energy into heat energy.

Only some **energy transfers** are counted as doing work. These transfers are ones that involve something being moved by a **force**. Our construction worker is doing work when he lifts things up and carries them from place to place, and when he moves himself around the site. The office worker is doing work as he picks things up from his desk and moves them around, and if he leaves his chair to fetch something from the filing cabinet or go to another part of the building. Nothing is moved when he is sitting thinking, so this does not count as work.

- If nothing is moved, no work is done.
- If something is moving with no forces acting on it, as might be possible in space, then no work is being done.
- The greater the force required to move an object a certain **distance**, the more work is done.
- The greater the distance moved for a certain force, the more work is done.

FIGURE 1: Working hard?

FIGURE 2: Working harder?

FIGURE 3: Who does the most work?

QUESTIONS

1. Is the construction worker or the office worker doing most work?
2. Jack and Jill went up the hill. Jack's weight is 500 N and Jill's is 450 N. Who does the most work?
3. Wayne and Shane are competing in a strongest man contest and have to carry heavy loads as far as they can. Wayne carries his further than Shane. Who does the most work?
4. Explain why, however long you have been sitting writing, you have hardly done any work at all.

...distance   ...energy transfer   ...force   ...gravitational potential energy

Work it out

Work is the amount of energy transferred by a force, when the object acted on by the force moves a certain distance. You do work every time you move something or move yourself from place to place.

■ Work, like energy, is measured in **joules** (J).

■ Work measures the amount of energy 'spent' making a particular movement happen. It does not measure the amount of energy that may be contained within the object doing the work.

■ Work only applies to energy transformations where a movement occurs due to an applied force.

■ **Work done** is defined by the equation:

Work done (J) = force (N) × distance moved in the direction of the force (m)

■ This can be written as:

$$W = Fs$$

where W represents work, F represents applied force and s represents the distance moved in the direction of the force.

It is important to be clear what is meant by 'distance moved in the direction of the force'. For example, if you are climbing a flight of stairs the force you apply is equal to your weight in newtons. Weight acts vertically. But, in climbing the stairs you are moving vertically and horizontally. In the calculation to find the work done ($W = Fs$), s will be the vertical distance moved, which is equal to how high the stairs are.

FIGURE 4: A competition tractor pulling a sledge.

Watch Out It is important to remember that s is the distance moved in the direction of the force, which might be different from the overall distance travelled.

More force, more work

In a tractor-pulling contest the tractor pulls a sledge which gets harder to pull the further it goes.

■ For constant force the work done Fs is equal to the area under a force distance graph as shown in Figure 7.

■ For a steadily increasing force this is still true, but the area is now a triangle. The average force is half the maximum force, so work done = $\frac{1}{2} F_{max}s$, and the area of the triangle is $\frac{1}{2}$ base × height.

■ Where the force changes in a non-uniform way, the work is still equal to the area under the graph, but now you might have to count squares!

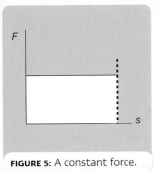

FIGURE 5: A constant force.

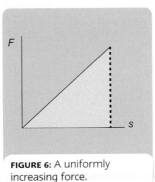

FIGURE 6: A uniformly increasing force.

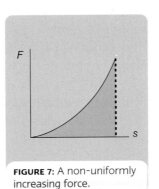

FIGURE 7: A non-uniformly increasing force.

▮▮▮▮ QUESTIONS ▮▮▮▮

5 Chloe is stacking bags of flour on a shelf. Each bag has a **mass** of 1.5 kg, and the shelf is 1.2 m high.

  a What is the weight of each bag (take $g = 10\,\text{m/s}^2$)?

  b How much work does she do to stack each bag on the shelf?

  c If there are 20 bags, how much work does she do altogether?

6 Jack is climbing a flight of 20 stairs. Jack's weight is 600 N. Each step is 15 cm high.

  a How much work does Jack do as he climbs each step?

  b How much work does he do to reach the top?

▮▮▮▮ QUESTIONS ▮▮▮▮

7 Amanda pushes a wheelbarrow up a 5 m long ramp onto a surface 1.6 m higher than her starting level. The weight of the barrow is 300 N.

  a How much work has been done in raising the barrow 1.6 m?

  b The force she needed to push the barrow along the ramp is 100 N. How much work did she do?

  c Why are these numbers different?

  d Why are ramps useful?

...joule ...kinetic energy ...mass ...work done

People power

You will find out:
- How to relate power to work and energy
- How to calculate power
- How to use the equation for power to calculate other quantities

One man went to mow...

It is possible, and in many places necessary, to plough a field by hand, with oxen or horses. There are many advantages to using animals to do the work and one big disadvantage: it takes a long time. In Britain, the introduction of tractors meant that one person could do much more work in the same time, so fewer people were needed. The **power** of the tractor and other large-scale machines is what has made the difference.

Pulling power

The idea of 'work' in science is about how much energy is changed from one form to another. The **work done** by a team of horses is the same as that done by a tractor, if they both plough the same field using the same plough. The difference comes in how long it takes them to do it: the tractor will complete the field much more quickly than the horses. The rate at which work is done is called **power**. You can compare power by seeing how long it takes to do a certain amount of work, or by seeing how much work is done in a certain **time**.

- The more work done in a certain time, the greater the power.
- The less time it takes to do a certain amount of work, the greater the power.
- Power is measured in **watts** (W), named after the engineer James Watt.
- A power of 1 watt means that 1 **joule** of work is being done each **second**.
- Larger values of power can be measured in **kilowatts** (kW). 1 kW = 1000 W.
- Very large values can be measured in **megawatts** (MW). 1 MW = 1 000 000 W.

FIGURE 1: Oxen and tractors can do similar things, but the tractor will do them faster!

▐ QUESTIONS ▐

1 How many joules of energy are transferred each second by a motor if its power is 200 W?

2 How many watts are in 4.5 kW?

3 Peter and Paul walk home from school together up a hill. Peter is heavier than Paul.
   a Who does the most work?
   b Who is producing the most power?

4 Zara is peddling on an exercise bike. Her power is 15 W.
   a How many joules of work does she do each second?
   b How many joules would she transfer in 10 s?

...energy transfer ...force ...joule ...kilowatt ...megawatt

Working out

Power measures the rate of **energy transfer**, which is how many joules are transferred per second. In the case of a **force** causing a movement, power is the rate of doing work. If a motor has a power output of 100 W, then it can do work at a rate of 100 J each second. In one second it will have done 100 J of work, in 2 seconds 200 J, in 10 seconds 1000 J and so on.

- 1 watt = 1 joule per second.
- From this it is possible to see that the equation to calculate power is:

$$\text{Power} = \frac{\text{work}}{\text{time}}$$

- Symbols can be used to represent these quantities, and the equation for power can be written as:

$$P = \frac{W}{t}$$

where P represents power, W represents work and t represents time.

- If the power is known this equation can be used to calculate work done from:

$$\textbf{Work} = \textbf{power} \times \textbf{time}$$

- In symbols, the equation for work becomes $W = Pt$
- The time taken to do work can be calculated from:

$$\text{Time} = \frac{\text{work}}{\text{power}}$$

- In symbols, the equation for time becomes $t = W/P$.

Power is the rate of doing work.

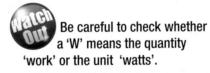
Be careful to check whether a 'W' means the quantity 'work' or the unit 'watts'.

Horsepower

When figures are given for the power of motor vehicles, the measurements are not given in watts but in horsepower. This term was invented by James Watt, who found that a horse could lift 150 pounds a height of 220 feet in 1 minute.

FIGURE 2: Two horsepower!

The calculation below shows how Watt's measurements relate to the SI units we use now.

- 1 pound (lb) is equal to 0.45 kg.
- 150 lb = 67.5 kg.
- The weight of this is 675.0 N (taking $g = 10$ m/s^2).
- 1 foot (ft) = 0.304 m.
- 220 ft = 66.88 m.
- Work done = 675.0 N × 66.88 = 45 144 J.
- Power = 45 144 J/60 s = 752.4 W.

The horsepower is taken now as being equal to 746 W.

QUESTIONS

5 A crane lifts a load of 5000 N up 20 m.
  a How much work is done?
  b If it takes 10 s what is the power in i) watts ii) kilowatts
6 What is the power in each of these cases?
  a 200 J of work done in 5 s?
  b 5000 J of work done in 2 s?
  c 0.3 J of work done in 6 s?
7 Calculate the work done by a 75 kW tractor in 20 s.
8 Calculate how long it would take the tractor to do 300 kJ of work.

QUESTIONS

9 What quantities (not units) did Watt measure?
10 A one horsepower (746 W) horse raises a load of 500 N a height of 10 m. How long would you expect it to take?
11 Two horses are pulling a cart. If they have to pull it for 5 km in 50 minutes, what is the maximum load they can pull?

...power   ...second   ...time   ...watt   ...work done

Going up

You will find out:

- What is meant by potential energy
- How to recognise examples of potential energy and potential energy transfers
- How to calculate potential energy

Potentially exciting

When you were very young, playing on a slide probably seemed a really exciting activity. In many ways a big roller coaster uses the same principles on a bigger scale: you gain height slowly to lose it again very quickly. This lesson looks at the **energy** you have when you are high up: **gravitational potential energy**.

Showing potential

If you know what you are doing, you can perform all sorts of spectacular movements on your way down from a diving board. A diver standing on a board has gravitational potential energy because of their position in the Earth's gravitational field.

- The higher up you are, the greater your **potential energy**.
- The greater your **mass**, the greater your potential energy.
- Potential energy is measured in **joules** (J).

If you jump from a 10 m diving board, the potential energy you have is converted to kinetic energy.

- As you accelerate your kinetic energy is increasing.
- Because you are falling, your height above the water is decreasing and therefore your potential energy is decreasing.
- As you reach the water, the potential energy you had because of being higher up has all been converted into kinetic (or movement) energy.

The idea that energy changes from one form to another, and does not just appear or disappear, is called the law of **conservation of energy**. This law states that energy is never created or destroyed, but can be transformed from one kind of energy to another, or transferred from one object to another. This allows us to say that the kinetic energy at the bottom of the dive is equal to the potential energy at the top of the dive. In fact, when you move, some energy is converted to heat because of frictional **forces**.

FIGURE 1: A drop in gravitational potential energy.

FIGURE 2: Diving makes use of gravitational potential energy.

▪▪ QUESTIONS ▪▪

1. Christopher and Craig are preparing for a synchronised dive. They are both standing on the 10 m board. Christopher has a greater mass then Craig. Who has the most potential energy?

2. Would Christopher have more potential energy standing on a 5 m high board or on a 10 m high board?

3. If we ignore frictional forces, what can you say about Christopher's potential energy at the top of his dive and his kinetic energy as he reaches the water?

4. If we do take frictional forces into account what can you say about Christopher's potential energy at the top of his dive and his kinetic energy as he reaches the water?

WOW FACTOR!

Divers may add to their energy at the start of their dive by jumping up higher and using spring boards instead of fixed boards.

...conservation of energy   ...distance   ...energy   ...force

What's your potential?

To see how to calculate the gravitational potential energy of an object we use the equation for calculating **work done**:

Work done (J) = force × distance moved in the direction of the force

Imagine a crane lifting an object of mass 500 kg up 10 m.

- The force needed is equal to the weight of the object.
- Weight equals mass times gravitational field strength:

Weight = 500 kg × 10 N/kg = 5000 N

FIGURE 3: Lifting an object increases its gravitational potential energy.

- The **distance** moved in the direction of the force is the height the object has risen = 10 m.
- In this case

work done = 5000 N × 10 m = 50 000 J

- Looking back at how the calculation was done:

Work done (J) = mass (kg) × gravitational field strength (N/kg) × height (m)

- Because of conservation of energy, the work done on the mass is equal to the gravitational potential energy gained, so we can write:

potential energy transferred = mass × gravitational field strength × change in height

- In symbols this can be written as:

PE = m × g × h

or simply PE = mgh, where m is the mass of the object, g is gravitational field strength and h is the height the object is lifted.

- Remember that m × g is equal to weight so we can also write:

PE = weight × change in height

Watch Out Be careful to notice if you have been given mass or weight in a question.

▮▮▮ QUESTIONS ▮▮▮

Take g = 10 N/kg.

5 Calculate the potential energy you gain by climbing a flight of stairs 5 m high if your mass is 60 kg.

6 How much potential energy do you give to a box of mass 8 kg if you lift it onto a 1.5 m high shelf?

7 A diver runs along a 10 m board and jumps up 1 m above the height of the board before dropping to the water below. If the mass of the diver is 50 kg, how much kinetic energy does she have as she reaches the water?

8 What happens to this energy after the dive is completed?

Potential conflict?

Energy is measured in joules. This unit is named after James Prescott Joule, an English scientist and inventor who lived and worked during the nineteenth century. His work is fundamental to our understanding of energy and energy changes. He was a dedicated experimenter, so much so that he spent part of his honeymoon in the Alps trying to measure the temperature at the top and bottom of a waterfall to record the transformation of kinetic energy into heat.

FIGURE 4: James Prescott Joule.

- Joule calculated that one pound of water (0.454 kg) would have to fall through 772 ft (235.306 m) to raise its temperature by 1°F (0.560 °C).
- Our modern value for the amount of energy needed to raise the temperature of 1 kg of water by 1 °C is 4200 J.

▮▮▮ QUESTIONS ▮▮▮

9 Joule calculated how far water would have to fall (235.306 m) to raise its temperature by 0.56 °C. Calculate how far it would have to fall to raise its temperature by 1 °C.

10 Calculate the potential energy transferred if 1 kg of water drops through the height calculated from question **9**. Use g = 9.8 N/kg.

11 How does Joule's value compare with the accepted value of 4200 J/kg °C?

...gravitational potential energy   *...joule*   *...mass*   *...potential energy*   *...work done*

Energy on the move

You will find out:
- What affects the amount of kinetic energy an object has
- How to calculate kinetic energy
- Why kinetic energy can be calculated in that way

A need for speed

It's easy to see that a plane taking off from an aircraft carrier has a lot of kinetic (movement) energy, but what about the aircraft carrier itself? The ship is moving more slowly, but has a much greater mass. We use the ideas of the **work done** to get an object moving, and **conservation of energy**, to determine how much **kinetic energy** an object will have.

FIGURE 1: Moving objects have kinetic energy.

Getting moving

Kinetic energy is the energy something has because it is moving. In the case of cars, buses and trains, that energy will have been transferred to them by the work done by the driving force of their engines. The law of conservation of energy tells us that the kinetic energy gained by an object is equal to the work done on it by the force that causes it to accelerate. This helps us to see which objects are going to have greater kinetic energy.

FIGURE 2: The car has kinetic energy.

- It takes more work to accelerate an object to a higher **velocity** than it does to accelerate it to a lower velocity.

- This means that the faster an object is moving, the greater its kinetic energy.

- If two different objects are accelerated to the same velocity, then the one with the greater mass will need more work done on it.

- So if there are two objects moving with the same velocity, the one with the greater mass has the greater kinetic energy.

- Kinetic energy is measured in joules (J).

▦ QUESTIONS ▦

1 The kinetic energy of a car is increasing. How is the car moving?

2 Andrew is rolling a large snowball round his garden. The snowball's kinetic energy is increasing. What are two possible reasons for this?

3 A child of mass 20 kg sits at the top of a 1.5 m high slide.
   a How much potential energy does the child have? (Use $g = 10$ N/kg)
   b How much kinetic energy will the child have at the bottom of the slide?

4 A catapult is used to project a small ball. The catapult applies an average force of 30 N for a distance of 10 cm (0.1 m).
   a How much work, in joules, is done on the ball?
   b How much kinetic energy will the ball have?

...acceleration ...conservation of energy ...distance

Kinetic calculations

The kinetic energy (KE) gained by an object is calculated from the equation:

Kinetic energy = $\frac{1}{2}$ mass × (velocity)^2

In symbols this is written as

$$KE = \frac{1}{2}mv^2$$

where m is the mass of the object and v is its velocity.

- Mass is measured in kilograms (kg).
- Velocity is measured in metres per second (m/s).
- Kinetic energy is measured in joules (J).

Kinetic energy and braking distances

The braking distance for a car is the **distance** it moves after the brakes are applied before it comes to a halt. The brakes have a maximum force they can exert in order to stop the car; the braking distance is the minimum distance the car can be stopped in with the brakes applying their maximum braking force.

Velocity		Braking distance
10 m/s (about 23 mph)	7.7 m	
15 m/s (about 34 mph)	17.3 m	
20 m/s (about 45 mph)	30.8 m	
25 m/s (about 57 mph)	48.2 m	
30 m/s about 68 mph)	69.3 m	
35 m/s (about 79 mph)	94.4 m	
40 m/s (about 90 mph)	123.3 m	

FIGURE 3: Minimum braking distances for a car.

- The work done, W, is equal to the braking force × braking distance ($N = Fs$).
- Using the principle of conservation of energy, the work done in stopping the car is equal to the change in kinetic energy.
- We write $Fs = \frac{1}{2}mv^2$.
- As for a particular set of brakes there is a maximum braking force, so the braking distance depends on the square of the velocity the car is travelling at.
- This means that doubling the velocity will require four times the braking distance.

QUESTIONS

5 A lorry of mass $m = 25\,000$ kg is travelling at a velocity $v = 20$ m/s.

  a Calculate v^2.

  b Calculate mv^2.

  c Calculate $\frac{1}{2}mv^2$.

  d What unit is the answer measured in?

6 What is the kinetic energy of a free fall parachutist of mass 70 kg falling with a terminal velocity of 60 m/s?

7 What is the kinetic energy of a bullet mass 20 g (0.02 kg) travelling at 100 m/s?

8 What is the kinetic energy of a 10 g (0.01 kg) snail travelling at 2 mm (0.002 m) per second?

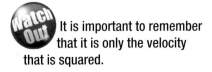

Watch Out It is important to remember that it is only the velocity that is squared.

Want to know why?

Where does the equation for kinetic energy come from?

- An object accelerates from 0 to v m/s in time t seconds.
- Its acceleration a is equal to v/t.
- The force F acting to cause this acceleration $= ma = mv/t$.
- While this **acceleration** is happening, the object moves a distance s.
- s is equal to average speed × t $= (v/2) \times t = \frac{1}{2}vt$.
- The kinetic energy gained by the object is equal to the work done on it $= Fs$.

$$Fs = \frac{mv}{t} \times \frac{1}{2}vt = \frac{1}{2}mv^2$$

QUESTIONS

9 What principle is being applied in saying that the kinetic energy gained by the object is equal to the work done on it?

10 Calculate the kinetic energy of an oxygen molecule of mass 5.3×10^{-26} kg, travelling at 450 m/s.

11 a What is the speed of 60 kg diver who drops from a 10 m board, just before she hits the water. (Take $g = 9.8$ N/kg)

  b Why do you not need to know the diver's mass?

Keeping accounts

You will find out:
- About different types of energy
- How to use the principle of conservation of energy
- How to calculate amounts of electrical energy

Shaken or stirred?

James Joule showed that water could be heated by stirring it. In one experiment he used a paddle wheel to stir the water in a copper container. The wheel was driven by falling weights, so that the amount of **work done** could be accurately measured. His experiments laid the foundation for our understanding of **conservation of energy**.

FIGURE 1: Joule's paddle wheel.

Types of energy

- Sound energy is energy carried through materials by longitudinal waves.
- **Electrical energy** is the energy carried by an electric **current**.
- Heat energy is energy carried by infra-red radiation.
- Light energy is energy carried by electromagnetic waves at frequencies detected by our eyes.
- Elastic potential energy is energy stored because of a change of shape of an object.
- Chemical energy is energy that is stored in substances and can be released by a chemical reaction.
- Nuclear energy is energy that can be released because of changes in the nuclei of atoms.

Time for a change

Every process requires a transformation of energy from one form to another or a transfer of energy from one object to another.
- A candle transforms chemical energy to light and heat energy.
- A light bulb transforms electrical energy to light and heat energy.
- A catapult converts elastic potential energy to kinetic energy.
- The Sun transforms nuclear energy to light and heat energy.
- A wind turbine transfers kinetic energy from the air to the kinetic energy of the turbine and to electrical energy.
- A car engine converts chemical energy to heat and the heat energy to kinetic energy.
- A solar cell converts light energy to electrical energy.

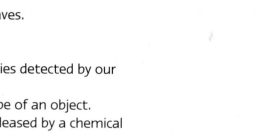

FIGURE 2: Chemical energy being transformed into light energy.

▣ QUESTIONS ▣

1 In a toaster, what form of energy is:

   a the input to the toaster?   **b** the output from the toaster?

2 Name a device that converts electrical energy into kinetic energy.

3 Name a device that:

   a converts electrical energy into sound energy

   b converts sound energy into electrical energy.

4 Name **two** devices that, working together, could transform light energy into electrical energy and electrical energy into kinetic energy.

...conservation of energy   ...current   ...electrical energy   ...energy transfer

Equal energy

The law of conservation of energy applies to all types of energy changes.

- A falling object is transforming gravitational potential energy to kinetic energy.
- The kinetic energy just before the object hits the ground will be equal to the reduction in **potential energy** due to the reduction in height.
- The energy does not vanish when the object hits the ground. It will be dissipated as heat among particles in the ground and the object itself.

Electrical energy

When an object is being lifted up, kinetic energy is being transformed into gravitational potential energy. Kinetic energy must come from somewhere; another form of energy must be transformed into kinetic energy. One way of lifting a load is with an electric motor.

- An electric motor will have a **voltage** (potential difference) of V volts across it and a current of I amperes flowing through it.
- It will lift the load in a time of t seconds.
- The voltage V multiplied by the current I is equal to the **power** P being supplied to the motor:

$$P = V \times I$$

- Power measures the rate of **energy transfer** so:

$$\text{power (watts)} = \frac{\text{energy transferred (joules)}}{\text{time (seconds)}}$$
$$P = E/t$$

where E is the electrical energy transferred in time t.

- The equation for power can be rearranged:

$$\text{energy transferred} = \text{power} \times \text{time}$$
$$E = P \times t$$

- If energy transferred = power × time, and power = voltage × current, then:

$$\text{electrical energy transferred} = \text{voltage} \times \text{current} \times \text{time}$$
$$E = V \times I \times t$$

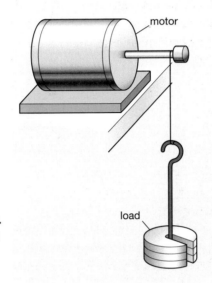

FIGURE 3: Electrical energy being transformed into gravitational potential energy.

Another Joule of an achievement

One of the energy transfers investigated by James Prescott Joule was the energy transfer between electrical energy and heat. As a result of his measurements he arrived at what is now known as Joule's Law.

- A steady current I flows in a conductor.
- The resistance of the conductor is R.
- The current flows in the conductor for a time t.

Joule found that the heat Q produced in the conductor is given by the equation:

$$Q = I^2 \times R \times t \qquad \textbf{Joule's law}$$

where Q is measured in joules, I in amperes, R in ohms and t in seconds.

QUESTIONS

7 What is the heat produced if a current of 0.5 A flows through a resistance of 470 Ω for 20 s?

8 How much current would have to flow to produce 400 J of heat each second in a resistance of 100 Ω?

9 Show that, if the energy output is heat (E = Q), the equations E = VIt and Q = I²Rt are the same (HINT: remember how resistance is calculated).

QUESTIONS

Use g = 10 N/kg.

5 A motor lifts a 2 kg load up a height of 0.8 m.
   a How much work has it done?
   b How much potential energy (in joules) is gained by the load?
   c How much electrical energy will be supplied to the motor?

6 The motor in question **5** draws a current of 2 A from a 12 V supply while lifting another load. It takes 5 s to lift the load 1.5 m.
   a How much electrical energy is supplied to the motor while lifting the load?
   b What is the weight of the load?
   c What is the mass of the load?

On a roll

You will find out:

- How a roller coaster works
- What happens on a roller coaster
- What is happening to an object moving in a circle

Up and down and round and round

Not everybody enjoys roller coasters and other theme park rides. Some people don't like the height of some of the rides, though you might be higher up in a tall building. Some people don't like the **speed** they travel, though you might be travelling faster in the family car on the motorway. So why are they exciting or terrifying?

What's going on?

A traditional form of roller coaster might be like the one in the diagram. There are big changes in the **resultant force** acting on you (and on your stomach!) on different parts of the roller coaster.

- The car is winched up to the top of the first hill.
- Work is done on the car by the **force** pulling it up the slope.
- The car gains **gravitational potential energy** as its height increases.
- After reaching the highest point on the ride the car will be allowed to travel down the first slope.
- As its height reduces, its **potential energy** will be transformed to **kinetic energy** and its speed will increase.
- As it travels up the second slope, some of that kinetic energy is transformed to gravitational potential energy and the car will be decelerating.
- This potential energy will be transformed back into kinetic energy as the car travels down the other side of the second slope.
- The same energy changes happen as the car travels over the final hill.
- When the car has returned to the lowest level of the ride, it will have its maximum kinetic energy and its highest **velocity**.
- At the end of the run, brakes will be applied to transform the car's kinetic energy into heat and the car will be brought to a halt.

On real roller coasters some kinetic energy is transformed into heat during the ride because of friction. This is why the hills have to get smaller.

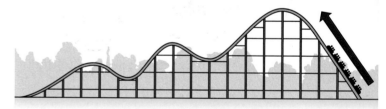

FIGURE 1: What goes up, must come down – but how?

QUESTIONS

1. What can you say about the work done by the force pulling the car up the first slope and the potential energy the car has at the top?

2. On the roller coaster in the diagram above, the kinetic energy the car has after it has come down the first drop will be less than the potential energy it had at the top. Why?

3. On a real roller coaster the kinetic energy at the end just before the brakes are applied will not be equal to the potential energy at the start. Why not?

4. Why do the hills need to get smaller as you go along the roller coaster?

WOW FACTOR!

The fastest roller coaster in the world is the Kingda Ka in New Jersey in the USA. Its speed is about 205 km/h.

...centripetal force   ...constant speed   ...gravitational potential energy

In the loop (H)

On some rides you go upside-down at some point in the journey, but you do not fall out of the car. The reason for this is that it takes a force to make you and the car go round in a circle.

FIGURE 2: Why won't you fall out?

- Remember that according to Newton's first law, an object will move with **constant speed** in a straight line unless acted on by a resultant force.

- In other words, if you are not moving at constant speed, or not moving in a straight line, there must be a resultant force acting on you.

- Moving round a circle is clearly not moving in a straight line even though it may be at constant speed.

- This means that a resultant force is needed to keep you moving in the circle.

- At the top of the loop you might expect to fall out of the car because of the force of gravity (your weight) pulling you down.

- In fact your weight, and some push from your seat, is needed to keep you moving round in the circle.

- The car needs to be moving at high enough speed to make sure that the force needed to keep you going round in the circle is greater than your weight.

The same effect lets you swing a bucket full of water in a vertical circle without getting wet, as long as you swing the bucket fast enough.

An object moving in a circle at constant speed has a resultant force acting on it

Centripetal force (H)

It is important to understand that an object moving in a circle at constant speed has a resultant force acting on it:

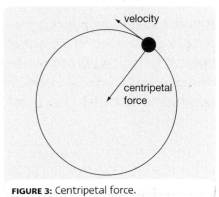

FIGURE 3: Centripetal force.

- An object moving in a circle is constantly changing its direction of motion.

- This means that its velocity is changing even if its speed is constant.

- If its velocity is changing, then it is accelerating.

- If it is accelerating, then there is a resultant force acting on it.

- The force causing an object to move in a circle is directed towards the centre of the circle and is called a **centripetal** force.

QUESTIONS

8. What is the difference between speed and velocity?

9. How can an object travelling at constant speed be accelerating?

10. What would an object moving in a circle do if the centripetal force was suddenly removed?

11. The Earth moves in a (nearly) circular orbit round the Sun.

   a. Draw a diagram showing the Sun, the Earth, Earth's orbit and the direction of the force acting on the Earth.

   b. What provides the centripetal force in this case?

QUESTIONS

5. What is meant by the term 'resultant force'?

6. Why does motion in a circle require a resultant force?

7. Draw a diagram of an object moving in a circle. Mark on arrows at two points on the circle to show which way the object is moving at that point.

A new idea

You will find out:
- Some of the contributions Einstein made to science
- Creativity is essential for producing new ideas
- How experimental evidence is used to test new ideas

The world's most famous

Albert Einstein has become perhaps the world's best known example of a scientist, but when he started to make his discoveries he wasn't working in a university, and did not even have particularly good qualifications.

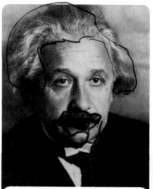

FIGURE 1: Albert Einstein (in case you didn't know).

A bit of background

By any standards Albert Einstein had an interesting life.

- He was born in Germany in 1879, but later moved to Switzerland and trained as a teacher of maths and physics in Zurich, becoming a citizen of Switzerland in 1901.
- Owing to his less than outstanding record as a student he failed to get a job in a university and began working in the patent office in Berne.
- In his spare time he thought about some of the problems in physics that needed explaining.
- In 1905 he published three papers based on his ideas that changed physics completely. One of these outlined the special **theory of relativity**.
- Following this he worked at several universities, ending back in Germany in 1914 and taking German citizenship again.
- He was awarded the Nobel Prize for physics for 1921.
- Owing to rising anti-Semitism in Germany, in 1933 he emigrated to the United States.
- In 1939 he warned President Roosevelt that the Germans were intending to develop an atomic bomb, which resulted in the Americans working on this themselves.
- He became a citizen of the United States in 1940.
- Following the Second World War, he worked to stop the development of nuclear weapons.
- In 1952 he was offered the presidency of Israel, but declined.
- He died in 1955.

FIGURE 2: Not so famous then!

QUESTIONS

1 What difficulties did Einstein face during his life?
2 How many countries was he a citizen of?
3 Give **two** ways he was rewarded for his achievements.

...energy   ...gravity   ...light   ...mass

Think about it

When Einstein developed his special theory of relativity, he was not working in a major university with access to the resources of such an institution. It was a good thing that he was able to do 'thought experiments' in his head.

- He thought about experiments on **light** that had been done by other scientists but that could not be adequately explained by the theories of the time.

- He thought about an experiment that showed that the **speed of light** was the same however the person measuring it was moving.

- He thought about the fact that two objects dropped in a gravitational field fall with the same acceleration regardless of their **mass**, and wondered why **gravity** should be like that.

- From these thoughts he produced theories that changed our understanding of the nature of light, mass, **energy** and gravity, and showed that Newton's laws could not fully describe every sort of motion.

Einstein's work is a clear example of the creative thought that is needed to make discoveries in science. Progress in science requires scientists to generate ideas and solutions to problems, and devise experiments that can test if these ideas are correct. It is not the case that random experiments are carried out that automatically produce new ideas.

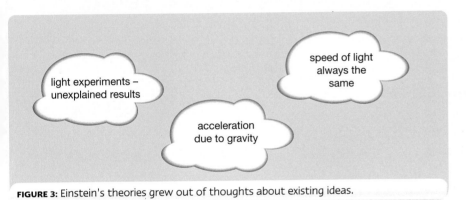

FIGURE 3: Einstein's theories grew out of thoughts about existing ideas.

WANT TO KNOW MORE?

Galileo did thought experiments as well. See http://www.pbs.org/wgbh/nova/galileo/expe_fobj_2.html

Science in the skies

In 1915 Einstein published the General Theory of Relativity which provided a whole new way of looking at gravity. It was possible in 1919 to test this theory.

- Einstein predicted that light should be bent by a gravitational field.

- The light from stars in a direction close to the Sun should be deflected and the apparent positions of the stars would be changed.

- This could be tested during the solar eclipse in 1919. The Sun's light was blocked out and the starlight passing near the Sun could be observed.

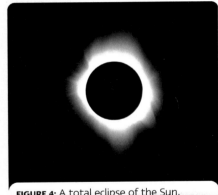

FIGURE 4: A total eclipse of the Sun.

- It was found that the apparent positions of the stars were changed from where they appeared to be when the Sun was in a different part of the sky.

- This result was an important piece of evidence in support of Einstein's theory.

QUESTIONS

4 Why was it a good thing that Einstein did 'thought experiments'?

5 State **one** thing he thought about.

6 State **one** thing we have changed our ideas about as a result of Einstein's work.

7 How is scientific thought creative?

QUESTIONS

8 Why would bending of light make the stars appear to be in a different place?

9 Why did this have to be done when there was a solar eclipse?

...speed of light   ...theory of relativity

Pass the test

You will find out:

- About the reasons for the opposition to Einstein's ideas
- About some of the predictions of the theory of relativity
- About evidence that supports relativity

Time for a change

When Galileo suggested that objects of different **mass** would fall with the same **acceleration** it seemed to contradict people's experience of how objects behave. There is no definite record to show that Galileo did drop balls of different masses from the leaning tower of Pisa, but there is now plenty of evidence to support this idea. Einstein's **theory of relativity** also makes predictions that seem to be very strange.

Opposition to Einstein

The theory of relativity makes predictions that are different from the predictions made by Newton's laws. Newton's laws were the established description of how all objects moved and had proved good enough for practical calculations of motion. Several factors would have made it hard for other scientists to accept Einstein's ideas straight away:

- They required the currently accepted theory to be discarded. Newton's laws provide good approximations for the motion of objects moving at speeds much slower than the **speed of light**, but are no longer considered to be a correct description of motion.

- Einstein's theories made predictions that seemed to go against common sense, as well as against established scientific theories.

- Einstein was not a recognised member of the scientific community at the time that he published his ideas.

There was a great deal of opposition to the theory of relativity in Germany and Einstein's lectures on the subject in 1920 in Berlin were disrupted by demonstrations. A factor that probably increased this opposition was the fact that Einstein came from a Jewish family and was famous at a time when anti-Semitism was already a force in Germany.

In the end, scientific theories must be supported by experimental evidence. The existence of evidence that supports relativity causes it to be almost universally accepted today.

FIGURE 1: The site (allegedly) of a famous experiment by Galileo.

Einstein's predictions went against common sense and scientific theory

---

■■ QUESTIONS ■■

1 What are Newton's laws?
2 What sort of motion do Newton's laws describe well?
3 What sort of motion don't they describe well?
4 What caused Einstein's theories to be accepted eventually?

...*acceleration* ...*energy* ...*light* ...*mass* ...*speed of light*

Weird science

Some of the predictions made by Einstein as part of the theory of relativity seem very strange because they do not fit with our experience of how things behave.

- Nothing can travel faster than the speed of light: you can't just keep accelerating until you are going faster than the speed of light.

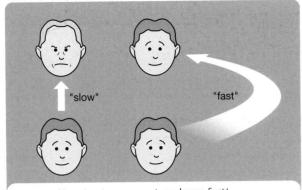

FIGURE 2: How to stay young: travel very fast!

- The speed of light is the same whatever the speed of the object giving out the light.

- Time measurements are different for a moving clock compared with a stationary clock. Time will run more slowly for the moving clock. This is called **time dilation**.

- Distance measurements are different for a moving object: lengths on a moving object are shorter than on a stationary object.

- If a twin goes on a spaceship travelling at a speed close to the speed of light, then he will be younger when he returns than his twin brother who stayed on Earth.

- That mass is a form of **energy**: the famous equation $E = mc^2$ is about this idea. The equation gives the amount of energy E represented by a mass m where c is the velocity of **light**.

WOW FACTOR!

GPS positioning satellites carry atomic clocks and make use of relativity calculations to keep these synchronised.

QUESTIONS

5 Why is it strange that the speed of light is the same whatever the speed of the object emitting it?

6 Which point above is an example of time dilation?

7 Light, sound, mass: why is it strange to include mass as a type of energy?

Testing the theory   (H)

Relativity has been supported by many pieces of evidence:

- Using the theory, Einstein was able to explain some features of the orbit of Mercury that could not be explained before.

- Some types of cosmic rays would normally last only a short time before decaying into other sorts of particle. They are seen to last longer when travelling at high speeds, supporting the idea of time dilation.

- If an atomic clock is carried on a very fast plane it is seen to run slower than a clock that remains stationary on the ground. This experiment was first performed in 1971 and produced results that supported the predictions of relativity.

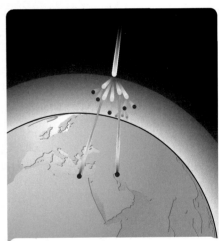

FIGURE 3: Muons produced in the upper atmosphere only last long enough to reach Earth's surface due to time dilation.

QUESTIONS

8 How much energy would you get if you could convert all the mass of an apple (0.1 kg) into energy? Take the velocity of light $c = 3 \times 10^8$ m/s.

9 Muons are particles produced in the upper atmosphere by cosmic rays. They should not last long enough to reach the surface of the Earth, but are detected there in large numbers. How does this support relativity?

Unit summary

Concept map

Average velocity = displacement/time
$v = s/t$

momentum = mass × velocity

Stopping distance = thinking distance + braking distance

Airbags, seatbelts and crumple zones protect passengers in the case of a collision.

A falling object is acted on by weight and air resistance, when these forces balance terminal velocity is reached.

Acceleration can be found from the gradient of a velocity–time graph.

Velocity is speed in a given direction and is a vector quantity.

As fast as you can

Forces acting on a body can be represented by a free-body diagram.

Acceleration = change in velocity/time $a = (v - u)/t$

Force = mass × acceleration
$F = ma$

Newton's laws
- A body will accelerate in the direction of a resultant force with an acceleration proportional to the force and inversely proportional to its mass.
- If the resultant force acting on a body is not zero, it will accelerate in the direction of the resultant force.
- When two bodies interact, the forces they exert on each other are equal and opposite and that these are known as action and reaction forces.

Work done is equal to energy transferred.

Kinetic energy = ½ × mass × (velocity)^2
$KE = ½ × mv^2$

Potential energy transferred = mass × acceleration of free-fall × change in height
$PE = m × g × h$

Electrical energy = voltage × current × time
$E = V × I × t$

Work done = force × distance moved in the direction of the force
$W = F × s$

Roller coasters and relativity

The principle of conservation of energy: energy cannot be created or destroyed, but can be transformed from one kind of energy to another, or transferred from one object to another.

Power = work done/time taken
$P = W/t$

An object moving in a circle at constant speed must be accelerating due to its direction changing.

There must be a resultant force acting on an object which is moving in a circle in order to bring about this acceleration.

Scientists may be reluctant to accept new theories, such as Einstein's relativity, when they overturn long-established explanations.

Einstein's theory of relativity is believed because its predictions were tested successfully.

Some scientific theories, such as Einstein's theory of relativity, require creative imagination.

Unit quiz

1 Write down the equation that relates acceleration, change in velocity and time.

2 What is weight measured in?

3 Draw a free-body diagram for an object falling at its terminal velocity.

4 What is meant by the phrase 'resultant force'?

5 List **four** factors that could increase the thinking distance for a vehicle.

6 List **four** factors that could increase the braking distance for a vehicle.

7 Describe one safety feature in a car and explain how it works.

8 Cars are a relatively dangerous way to travel. Why do you think people do not worry more about this danger?

9 Write down the equation that relates work, force and distance.

10 Write down the equation that relates power, work and time.

11 A child of mass 30 kg slides down a 2 m high slide. Take g = 9.8 N/kg.
   a) How much potential energy has the child lost when she reaches the bottom of the slide?
   b) If all the potential energy is transformed into kinetic energy what will be her speed at the bottom of the slide?

12 A motor connected to a power supply draws a current of 2 A from a 12 V power supply.
   a) How much electrical power is supplied to the motor?
   b) How much energy is transferred to the motor in 10 s?

13 An object is moving in a circle at a constant speed. What can you say about:
   a) its velocity
   b) its acceleration
   c) The force acting on it?

14 Explain why:
   a) Einstein was a surprising person to produce a significant scientific theory
   b) his theory of relativity was difficult for many scientists to accept
   c) the theory was eventually accepted.

Numeracy activity

This table shows the velocity of a runner at different times during part of his journey.

Time (s)	0	2	4	6	8	10	12	14	16	18	20
Velocity (m/s)	0	3	6	6	6	7	8	8	8	2	0

QUESTIONS

1 Draw a velocity–time graph to show these results.

2 Describe what is happening to the velocity in each of the following time intervals
   a) 0–4 s
   b) 4–8 s
   c) 8–12 s
   d) 12–16 s
   e) 16–18 s

3 The acceleration at each time represented on the graph can be found from the gradient at that point. Calculate the acceleration at:
   a) 3 s
   b) 9 s.

Exam practice

Exam practice questions

1 The diagram shows two forces acting on a rocket just before it is launched.

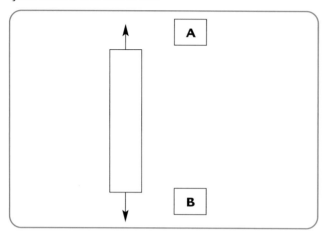

a Write down the names of forces A and B:

Force A ....

Force B .... [2]

b What can you say about the magnitude of upwards and downwards forces:

Just before the rocket is launched

....

Just after the rocket is launched

.... [2]

c The thrust caused by the engines is 2000 kN. If the rocket accelerates at 15 m/s^2, calculate the mass of the rocket.

.... [4]

2 The table gives some information about the stopping distance of a car.

Speed	Thinking distance	Braking distance	Stopping distance
10 m/s	10 m	15 m	
15 m/s	15 m	25 m	
20 m/s	20 m	35 m	

a Complete the last column of the table showing the total stopping distance. [2]

b The thinking distance is the distance travelled in the driver's reaction time. Calculate the reaction time using information from the table. [3]

c One traffic calming measure slows down the speed of a driver by 5 m/s. However, it is a distraction and doubles one driver's reaction time. Calculate the effect that this measure has on the driver's overall stopping distance if they would have been travelling at 20 m/s without the scheme in place. [ ]

d Explain what happens to the kinetic energy of the car as it brakes. [2]

3 Bungee jumpers jump off high objects. They are attached to an elastic cord, which is designed to stop their fall before impact with the ground.

a A bungee jumper, mass of 60 kg, is standing on a bridge 50 m high. Calculate their initial potential energy. [3]

b How much work does the rope do if it stops the jumper after they have fallen 40 m? [2]

c Answering in terms of forces, explain why the bungee jumper initially accelerates and then slows down coming to a momentary halt at the bottom of their jump. [4]

d A skydiver will eventually reach a steady speed as they fall. Explain why and state the name given to this speed. [3]

(Total 30 marks)

Power

An electric motor is used to raise a container onto a ship. The container weights 2000 kg and is lifted by 10 m.

a Calculate the power of the motor if it completes the lift in 30 seconds. [3]

b Why is the power of the motor likely to be higher than this figure? [1]

c Workers who have done the same job over many years may have accidents. So may people working in a new job. Explain why both sets of workers are still be at risk. [2]

Always give answers to a sensible number of decimal places (e.g. 2 d.p.). The students has lost 1 mark by forgetting to change a mass of 2000 kg = a weight of 20 000 N.

a Power = work done/time taken = 2000 × 10/30 = 666. 6666666666 W

b Energy is wasted as heat/sound

c The workers are working there every day and forget to look.

The pupil gets 1 out of 2 marks. Experienced workers get over-familiar and can forget simple safety precautions; new workers do not know all the risks they may be taking.

This is correct – full marks.

Overall Grade: C

How to get an A
Remember to answer all parts of a question. Make sure that you show your working when doing calculations.

Physics 2b

DISCOVER STORMS!

There are people known as 'storm chasers' whose hobby is to pursue storms, tornados, hail and lightning – often with a view to capturing stunning photos like these. Storm chasers are most active in May and June across the Great Plains of the United States and Canada, when severe weather conditions are frequent.

Storms are created when a centre of low pressure develops, with a system of high pressure surrounding it. This combination of opposing forces can create winds and result in the formation of storm clouds, such as the cumulonimbus.

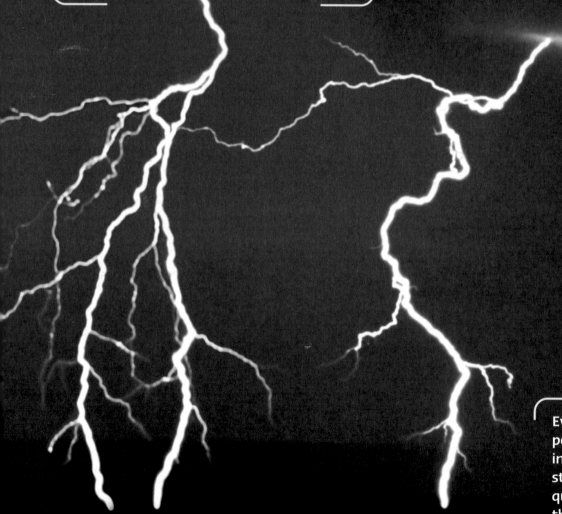

Every year, nearly 2000 people worldwide are injured by lightning strikes, and between a quarter and a third of these are fatal strikes. The danger comes from the electricity, heat and the mechanical energy which these generate.

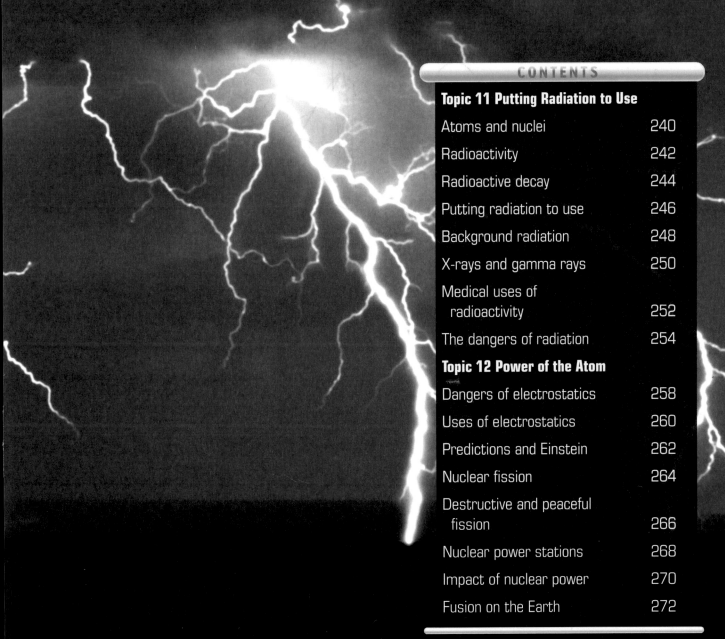

A bolt of lightning can reach 28 000 kelvins (around 28 000 degrees Celcius) in a split second. This is about five times hotter than the surface of the sun.

CONTENTS

Atoms and nuclei

You will find out:
- About the structure of the atoms
- About the composition of the nucleus
- About isotopes

Where do we find atoms?

All matter is made up of atoms.

Atoms are extremely small and cannot be seen directly. However, scientists can now use powerful microscopes to see individual atoms.

FIGURE 1: Everything you see in this picture is made up of atoms.

The structure of the atom

The ancient Greeks believed that the atom was the smallest particle that made up everything. In fact, the name 'atom' comes from the Greek word *atomos* meaning 'uncuttable'. However, the discovery of the **electron** in 1897 by Sir J. J. Thomson shattered the idea of the indivisible atom.

Scientists now believe in the nuclear model of the atom. The atom is quite small, but the **nucleus** is even smaller. In fact the nucleus is about 100 000 times smaller than the atom itself! Within the nucleus there are two types of particles: **protons** and **neutrons**. The protons and neutrons are collectively known as the **nucleons**. The electrons orbit round the positive nucleus.

The proton has a positive charge, the neutron has no charge and the electron has a negative charge. The nucleus is very small. It is also massive because it contains the majority of the mass of the atom.

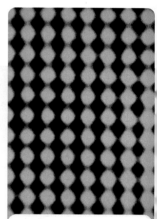

FIGURE 2: These atoms of gold are about 0.000 000 2 mm in diameter!

Vital statistics of the particles of the atom

Particle	Relative mass*	Relative charge*
Neutron	1	0
Proton	1	1
electron	$\frac{1}{1840}$	−1

(*mass and charge compared with that of the proton)

For a neutral atom, the number of electrons is equal to the number of protons. Removing electrons from the atom or adding extra electrons to the atom makes it acquire a net charge. It is then called an **ion**.

FIGURE 3: Sir J. J. Thomson discovered the electron and hence showed that the atom must be 'divisible'.

ⅲⅲ QUESTIONS ⅲⅲ

1. Why is the nucleus of an atom positive?
2. Name two types of particles within the nucleus.
3. What is the common name for neutrons and protons?
4. A neutral atom has six protons and five neutrons within the nucleus. How many electrons orbit the nucleus?

WOW FACTOR!

Most of matter is empty space. For the Earth, all its protons, neutrons and electrons would fit inside a small concert hall – the rest of the space is vacuum!

...*atomic number* ...*atoms* ...*electron* ...*isotope* ...*mass number* ...*neutron*

How do we represent nuclei?

There are more than one hundred different types of atoms. The simplest atom is that of hydrogen that has one proton and one orbiting electron. On the other extreme, a particular atom of uranium has 238 nucleons tightly packed within the nucleus and 92 electrons whizzing round the positive nucleus.

What is the best shorthand for representing different nuclei? The nucleus of an atom may be represented as follows:

$$_Z^A X$$

where X is the chemical symbol for the element, Z is the **proton number** or **atomic number** – the total number of protons within the nucleus and A is the **mass number** or **nucleon number** – the total number of protons and neutrons within the nucleus.

The number of neutrons is the difference between the nucleon number and the proton number:

number of neutrons = A – Z

Here are some examples of nuclei:

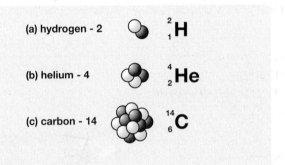

(a) hydrogen - 2 $_1^2 H$

(b) helium - 4 $_2^4 He$

(c) carbon - 14 $_6^{14} C$

FIGURE 4: (a) $_1^2 H$ – one proton and one neutron; (b) $_2^4 He$ – two protons and two neutrons; (c) $_6^{14} C$ – six protons and eight neutrons.

EXAM HINTS AND TIPS

Isotopes must have the same number of protons – hence the proton, or atomic number, will be the same.

QUESTIONS

5 The nucleus of uranium-235 has 235 nucleons and 92 protons. How many neutrons are there in the nucleus of a uranium-235 atom?

6 The chemical symbol for boron is B. How would you represent a boron nucleus that has five protons and six neutrons?

7 A carbon-14 nucleus is represented as: $_6^{14} C$. What is the proton (atomic) number and the nucleon (mass) number for this nucleus? How many neutrons are there in the nucleus of carbon-14 atom?

What are isotopes? (H)

Are all the atoms of gold the same? The simple answer is no! There are several different sorts of gold atoms. They all have 79 protons within the nucleus but the number of neutrons is different. These different sorts of gold nuclei are known as the **isotopes** of gold.

The isotopes of an element are nuclei that have the same number of protons but different number of neutrons. For a particular element, this means that the nuclei have the same proton number but different nucleon numbers.

The isotopes of hydrogen are:

$$_1^1 H \qquad _1^2 H \qquad _1^3 H$$

All neutral atoms of hydrogen have one proton and one orbiting electron, but the number of neutrons within the nucleus is different. All the isotopes of hydrogen have the same chemical properties.

Most of the oxygen we inhale (99.8%) is oxygen-16. Each atomic nucleus has eight protons and eight neutrons. However, we also inhale small amounts of oxygen-17 and oxygen-18. All three of these isotopes have the same number of protons within the nucleus, but the number of neutrons is different.

QUESTIONS

8 What is the same for all the isotopes of a particular element?

9 One of isotopes of nitrogen is nitrogen-14, which may be represented as $_7^{14} N$. How would you represent an isotope of nitrogen that has eight neutrons?

10 Explain whether or not the following are isotopes: $_{92}^{232} U$ and $_{91}^{233} Pa$

Radioactivity

You will find out:
- About radioactivity
- About ionisation
- About the properties of alpha particles, beta particles and gamma-rays

Is everything around us radioactive?

Most of the things around us are stable because the atomic nuclei remain unchanged. However, for a radioactive material its nuclei are unstable.

RADIOACTIVE MATERIALS

The radiation emitted by unstable nuclei

The nuclei of unstable atoms split up or disintegrate and emit either a particle (alpha and beta – see later) or a short burst of electromagnetic radiation.

When a radioactive nucleus emits radiation, it becomes much more stable.

WOW FACTOR!

We, too, are slightly radioactive. During our lifetime, some billion nuclei will decay in our body!

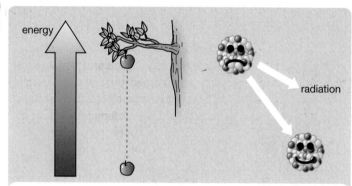

energy

radiation

FIGURE 1: The apple drops to ground in an attempt to become more stable. In a similar manner, a radioactive nucleus emits radiation to become more stable.

Radioactivity is not affected by external conditions such as pressure and temperature!

The three types of radiation are: **alpha particles**, **beta particles** and **gamma rays**. Alpha (α) particles are helium nuclei emitted from within the radioactive nucleus. An alpha particle consists of two protons and two neutrons. Beta (β) particles are electrons that emerge from within the nucleus itself. They are not the orbiting electrons of the atom! Gamma (γ) rays are electromagnetic waves of extremely short wavelengths.

▋▋ QUESTIONS ▋▋

1. Why do radioactive nuclei emit radiation?
2. Name the part of the atom where the alpha particles come from.
3. Is it true that the beta particles are the orbiting electrons of the radioactive atoms?
4. What are gamma rays?
5. Name the two radiations that are particles.

...alpha particle   ...beta particle   ...daughter nuclei

Ionisation (H)

All three radiations emitted from radioactive materials cause **ionisation**. They are referred to as **ionising radiation**. Ionisation is the process of removing electrons from atoms or molecules by collisions, thus creating positive ions.

Alpha particles are slow-moving helium nuclei. Because they are massive and carry a large positive charge, they are very good ionisers. Beta particles are fast-moving electrons and because they are not too massive and carry only a small negative charge, they are not as good ionisers as alpha particles. Gamma rays carry no charge and therefore are very poor ionisers.

Radiation properties

Figure 2 shows alpha particles emitted from a radium source. Each track shows the path of a single alpha particle. The alpha particles are good ionisers and therefore they do not travel too far in air. In fact, a few centimetres of air or thin paper will stop the majority of the alpha particles.

You can use a Geiger–Müller (GM) tube or a photographic film to investigate the penetration ability of the three radiations.

The table below summarises the main properties of the three radiations.

FIGURE 2: Tracks left by alpha particles emitted from a radioactive source.

Radiation	What is it?	Charge compared with a proton	Speed m/s	Ionising property	What is it stopped by?
α particles	Helium nuclei ($^4_3$He)	+2	~10^7	Very strong	Thin paper or a few centimetres of air
β particles	Electrons	−1	~10^8	Medium	A few millimetres of aluminium
γ rays	Electro-magnetic waves	0	3×10^8	Weak	A few centimetres of lead

|||| QUESTIONS ||||

6 What is ionisation?
7 Why would it be safe to work a few metres away from an alpha-emitting source?
8 Name the radiation that can be stopped by a few centimetres of lead.

The nucleus after beta or alpha decay

What happens when a radioactive nucleus emits either an alpha particle or a beta particle? The nuclei left behind (known either as **daughter** or **residual nuclei**) have a different atomic number and therefore the element has changed. Many centuries ago, it was a dream of alchemists to change ordinary metals into gold. This may be possible with some radioactive substances but you may have the problem of having radioactive gold!

In alpha decay, two protons and two neutrons are removed from the nucleus. The proton number decreases by 2 and the nucleon number decreases by 4. An americium-241 nucleus will change to a nucleus of neptunium-237. This decay may be represented by the equation:

$$^{241}_{95}\text{Am} \rightarrow {}^{4}_{2}\text{He} + {}^{237}_{93}\text{Np}$$

americium nucleus   alpha particle   neptunium nucleus

In beta decay, one neutron within the nucleus changes into a proton and an electron. The electron is emitted as a beta particle and the proton remains within the nucleus. The proton number increases by one but the nucleon number remains the same. A carbon-14 nucleus will change into a nucleus of nitrogen-14. This decay may be represented by the equation:

$$^{14}_{6}\text{C} \rightarrow {}^{0}_{-1}\text{e} + {}^{14}_{7}\text{N}$$

carbon nucleus   electron (beta particle)   nitrogen nucleus

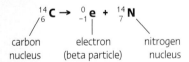

9 Explain why the nucleon number for an alpha particle is 4.
10 A uranium-235 ($^{235}_{92}$U) nucleus decays by alpha emission into a nucleus of thorium. How many protons and neutrons are there in the nucleus of thorium?
11 In beta decay, what happens within the nucleus of the atom?

Radioactive decay

You will find out:
- About half-life
- How nuclei decay over time
- About the random nature of nuclear decay

Do all nuclei decay at the same rate?

Some radioactive atoms decay very quickly, whereas other atoms can take a considerably longer time to decay. Describing radioactive atoms in terms of their half-lives is helpful in describing how fast or slow they decay.

Half-life

The **half-life** of an isotope is the average time taken for half the number of active nuclei to decay or disintegrate.

The half-life depends on the type of isotope and can range from 10^{-16} s to 10^{10} years! Here are some examples:

Isotope	Half-life
Beryllium-8 ($^{8}_{4}$Be)	3×10^{-16} seconds
Radon-219 ($^{219}_{86}$Rn)	3.9 seconds
Hydrogen-3 ($^{3}_{1}$H)	12.3 years
Carbon-14 ($^{14}_{6}$C)	5700 years
Thorium-232 ($^{232}_{90}$Th)	1.4×10^{10} years

The radiation from radioactive sources can be very dangerous and they can remain active for many years. This is why it is necessary to store radioactive sources in lead-lined containers.

FIGURE 1: Radioactive sources are kept in lead-lined containers.

WOW FACTOR!

Lead-204 has a half-life 10 000 000 times longer than the age of our universe.

QUESTIONS

1. How many radioactive nuclei remain after a time equal to one half-life?
2. A sample of wood has 5000 nuclei of the carbon-14 isotope. Use the table above to predict the number of carbon-14 nuclei left after a period of 5700 years.

EXAM HINTS AND TIPS

The fraction of active nuclei left after n half-lives is $\frac{1}{2^n}$

...activity ...chance ...count-rate

Activity of a source

The **activity** of a source is the total number of nuclei decaying per second. The activity is measure in becquerels (Bq). Each decay will release a single alpha or beta particle. In school laboratories, radioactive sources have a typical activity of about 200 000 disintegrations per second or 20 000 Bq.

The **count-rate** is the number of alpha or beta particles detected by a Geiger–Müller (GM) tube per second. The count-rate is a **fraction** of the source activity.

The activity of a radioactive material depends on the amount of material and the half-life of the isotope. Having a large amount of radioactive material means that there are more nuclei decaying in a given time, and so the activity is greater. A radioactive material with a short-lived isotope will have a large activity because the nuclei are decaying quicker.

As radioactive nuclei decay, the number of active nuclei decreases. The activity of the source and the measured count-rate also decrease with time.

The number of active nuclei, the activity of the source and the measured count-rate *all* halve in a time period of one half-life.

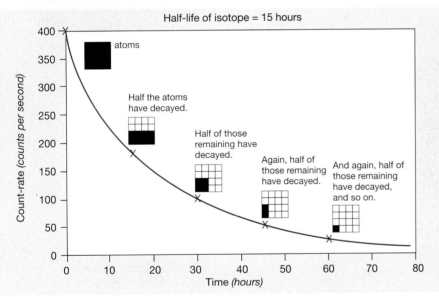

FIGURE 2: The number of active nuclei is halved after a time of one half-life.

The randomness of decay

Radioactive decay is described as a **random** process. This means that it is impossible to **predict** when a *particular* nucleus in a sample will decay. However, each nucleus has the same chance of decaying in a given time. Hence, it is possible to predict how many nuclei in a very large population of radioactive nuclei will decay in a given interval of time.

The behaviour of radioactive nuclei can be compared with rolling a large number of dice. If you roll 6000 dice at the same time, then there is a good **chance** that 1000 dice will show a six.

FIGURE 3: Radioactive nuclei behave just like dice.

You can observe the random nature of radioactive decay by using a GM counter to measure the alpha particles emitted from a radioactive source over a 30 s period. You will end up with 'counts' that show statistical variation such as:

210 199 202 209 205 211 200

▓▓▓ QUESTIONS ▓▓▓

3 What is meant by the activity of a radioactive source?

4 The count-rate from a radioactive source decreases from 4000 counts per second to 2000 counts per second in a time of 24 days. What is the half-life of the isotope?

5 The activity of a radioactive sample is 5200 disintegrations per second. The half-life of the isotope is 90 s. What is the activity from the sample after 90 s and after 180 s?

▓▓▓ QUESTIONS ▓▓▓

6 How do radioactive nuclei decay?

7 A radioactive material has 10 000 active nuclei. The isotope has a half-life of 30 s. How many of the active nuclei and daughter nuclei are there:

   a after a time of 30 s?

   b after a time of 60 s?

...half-life   ...predict   ...random   ...stable

Putting radiation to use

You will find out:
- About the benefits of radioactivity
- How gamma rays are used for treating food
- About smoke detectors
- About radioactive dating (carbon-dating)

Radioactivity is dangerous but it does have its uses

There is no doubt that radiation from radioactive materials can be dangerous. However, there are many safe uses of radiation in industry, hospitals and the home.

Uses of radioactivity

Here are just some of the uses of **radioactivity**:

- **Irradiating** fresh fruit such as strawberries helps to prolong their shelf-life. The gamma rays kill off the microbes, bacteria and insects in foods even after the food has been packaged. Some people believe that this alters the taste of the food. Irradiating fresh food in this way is safe because it does not make the food itself radioactive!

- In paper mills, the thickness of paper is controlled by measuring the amount of beta particles transmitted through the paper.

- In industry, gamma rays are used to check the quality of welding or detecting cracks in metals such as aeroplane wings.

- In hospitals, gamma rays from particular cobalt atoms are used in the treatment of cancer (see page 'Medical uses of radioactivity').

- In hospitals, radioactive atoms can be injected into patients to examine the insides of their bodies (see page 'X-rays and gamma rays').

- The water industry uses radioactive atoms to detect leaks in underground pipes. A radioactive material emitting beta particles (known as a **tracer**) is fed into the pipe and a radiation detector such as a GM detector is used above the ground to detect increased levels of radiation. A great deal of time and money are saved using this technique.

- A weak source containing radioactive americium is used in domestic **smoke detectors**.

FIGURE 1: Strawberries stay fresh for longer when exposed to gamma rays.

FIGURE 2: A must in all homes – a smoke detector.

QUESTIONS

1. What type of source is used to monitor the thickness of paper?
2. Name the radioactive substance used in smoke detectors.
3. Explain why irradiating strawberries with gamma rays prolongs their life.
4. Name **two** uses of beta sources.

WOW FACTOR!

Radioactive plutonium can produce 200 W of power – enough for a space probe to explore the Solar System.

...ionisation ...ions irradiation ...smoke detectors ...radioactive dating

More details on smoke detectors

Many homes are now fitted with smoke detectors. These have undoubtedly saved many lives. How does a smoke detector work?

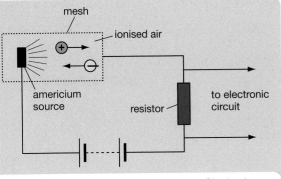

FIGURE 3: A smoke detector works because of ionisation.

Most smoke detectors have a weak source of americium-241 isotope. Americium-241 is an alpha emitter. As we have already seen, alpha particles are the most ionising radiation. The radioactive source ionises the air and this produces charged **ions**. The charged ions are attracted towards the positive and negative electrodes and this in turn produces a small current in the circuit and in the resistor. The resistor is connected to an electronic circuit that monitors the size of the current. When smoke or other invisible products of combustion enter the smoke detector, it absorbs the alpha particles. Hence less current due to **ionisation** is produced. The electronic circuit detects this drop in current and this triggers the alarm.

The half-life of the americium-241 isotope is 460 years – so the smoke detector will continue to work as long as you regularly change the battery!

QUESTIONS

5 Name the type of radiation emitted by the radioactive source used in smoke detectors.

6 What do the alpha particles do to the air inside the smoke detector?

7 Explain why it is not sensible to have a smoke detector that has a radioactive source with isotope half-life of a few months.

Radioactive dating

The isotope of uranium-238 ($^{238}_{92}$U) has a very long half-life of 4500 million years. This type of isotope is found in very small amounts in rocks. This isotope of uranium decays slowly into the stable isotope of lead-206 ($^{206}_{82}$Pb). By measuring the number of uranium nuclei and the number of lead nuclei it is possible to determine the age of ancient rocks formed during the creation of the Solar System and our own Earth. Another isotope used in dating ancient rocks is thorium-232 which has a half-life of 14 000 million years.

Radioactive dating also uses the isotope of carbon-14 ($^{14}_{6}$C) to date objects. The half-life of carbon-14 is 5700 years. All living things absorb carbon-12 and carbon-14 in photosynthesis. The ratio of carbon-14 atoms to carbon-12 atoms in living material is about $1:10^{12}$. When a living thing dies, this ratio starts to decrease. By measuring the actual ratio of carbon-14 atoms to carbon-12 atoms it is possible to estimate the age of ancient relics. The main problem with carbon dating is that the number of atoms of carbon-14 is very small. This introduces a significant **uncertainty** in the dating process.

Carbon dating can be used to date bone, cloth, wood and paper. The Turin shroud was alleged to be the cloth used to cover Christ when he was brought down from the cross. Many scientists believe the shroud to be a fake because carbon dating places it in the fourteenth century!

FIGURE 4: Carbon dating was used to date the Turin shroud.

QUESTIONS

8 Name **two** isotopes used to date ancient rocks in our Solar System.

9 The current ratio of carbon-14 atoms to carbon-12 atoms in living wood is about $1:10^{12}$. Estimate the age of a piece of wood found in a cave for which this ratio is one-quarter of the current ratio. (The half-life of carbon-14 is 5700 years.)

Background radiation

You will find out:
- About background radiation
- About the origin of background radiation
- About the dangers of radon gas

Radiation is all around us

What happens when you switch on a Geiger–Müller counter in the laboratory? It shows random 'clicking', even though there are no obvious sources of radioactivity close to the counter. The radiation it detects comes from a variety of sources. This radiation is referred to as the **background radiation** and human beings have been exposed to this ever since they walked the Earth.

Rocks emit radiation

A simple experiment can be carried out to show that some rocks, such as granite, emit radiation.

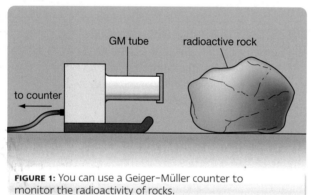

GM tube   radioactive rock

to counter

FIGURE 1: You can use a Geiger–Müller counter to monitor the radioactivity of rocks.

The experiment involves two Geiger–Müller counters. One of them is placed at the back of the laboratory and the other is placed very close to a large block of granite. The counters are reset and then record the counts for a time period of about 40 minutes. The counter placed close to the granite records more counts than the counter at the other side of the laboratory. Why? Both counters record the counts from the background radiation, but the one close to the granite also records the extra counts from the rock itself. The count-rate from the granite is normally about 1.2 times greater than the background count-rate. The activity levels are quite small and do very little harm to us. Humans are used to low-level exposures to background radiation. However, great damage is possible from high levels of radiation from radioactive sources (see page 'The dangers of radiation').

Cosmic rays come from outer space and the Sun.

FIGURE 2: Background radiation has been around for a very long time.

■■ QUESTIONS ■■

1 The background count-rate in a particular science laboratory is 12 counts per minute. What is the background count-rate in counts per second?

2 A rock is found to be radioactive. Is it true that all the atoms within the rock are radioactive?

Watch Out Human beings have always been exposed to radiation from the Earth and space.

...artificial sources   ...background radiation   ...cosmic rays

The origin of background radiation (H)

Most of the background radiation is from natural sources, but human beings cause some. Here is a list of the **natural sources** that contribute towards the background radiation:

- The Sun and outer space. Some of the energetic particles such as protons, electrons and neutrinos from the Sun and outer space (known as **cosmic rays**) penetrate the Earth's atmosphere and reach human beings. The danger from cosmic rays increases with altitude because there is less atmosphere for the rays to penetrate. Mountaineers and people flying in planes have a greater exposure to cosmic rays than people at sea level.
- Rocks such as **granite**. Some parts of the United Kingdom have rocks and building materials that emit radiation.
- Food. Almost all the food we eat will have some radioactive isotopes. As a result, our own bodies emit low levels of radiation. Shellfish, tea, coffee and Brazil nuts have higher than average levels of radioactivity.

Here is a list of **artificial sources** that contribute towards the background radiation:

- Nuclear power stations.
- Fallout from previous nuclear explosions or accidents.
- Radiation from equipment or waste from hospitals.
- Individual radiation exposure from dental or chest **X-rays.**

FIGURE 3: The testing of a nuclear bomb contributes towards the background radiation.

The pie chart in Figure 4 shows the main contributors to the background radiation in the United Kingdom:

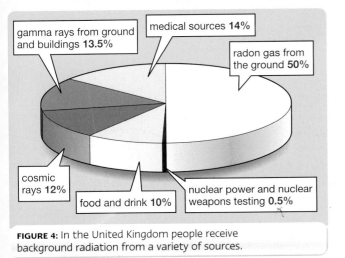

gamma rays from ground and buildings **13.5%**

medical sources **14%**

radon gas from the ground **50%**

cosmic rays **12%**

food and drink **10%**

nuclear power and nuclear weapons testing **0.5%**

FIGURE 4: In the United Kingdom people receive background radiation from a variety of sources.

The dangers of radon gas (H)

Some rocks emit radiation. Granite contains radioactive isotopes of uranium and thorium. The by-product of the decay of these radioactive isotopes is radioactive **radon gas**. Excessive exposure to the radiation from radon gas can cause lung cancer.

Radon gas rises from ground that contains granite. Radon gas is particularly dangerous if it remains trapped in the walls of buildings or under the floorboards. Not every town in the United Kingdom is exposed to the dangers of radon gas. Cornwall and some parts of Scotland have significant amounts of granite and it is here that the dangers from radon gas are greater.

The dangers from the radiation from radon gas can be minimised by adequately ventilating any inhabited rooms and using ventilation bricks with holes to allow airflow through the walls (especially cellars).

WOW FACTOR!

Receiving a dental X-ray is equivalent to an exposure to background radiation over a period of a week.

...granite   ...natural sources   ...radon gas   ...X-rays

X-rays and gamma rays

You will find out:

● About the properties of X-rays and gamma rays
● About the origin of gamma rays
● About the origin of X-rays

X-rays

Wilhelm Röntgen discovered X-rays in 1895. He quickly established that X-rays could penetrate matter and he took the world's first X-ray photograph of his wife's hand.

Many of us have had at least one X-ray photograph of our bodies. X-ray photographs are an invaluable tool for doctors in identifying broken bones and for dentists to check for fillings or the formation of teeth.

FIGURE 1: German physicist Röntgen discovered X-rays.

Similar properties of X-rays and gamma rays

Like visible light and radio waves, X-rays and gamma rays are **electromagnetic waves**. All electromagnetic waves are transverse waves, can travel through vacuum, consist of vibrating electric and magnetic fields and travel at the same speed c of 300 000 000 m/s in vacuum.

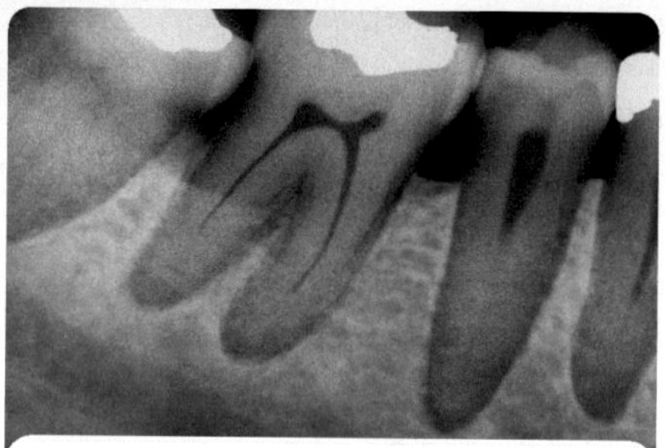

The speed c of electromagnetic waves is given by:

$$c = f\lambda$$

where f is the frequency in hertz (Hz) and λ is the wavelength in metres (m).

FIGURE 2: A false-colour dental X-ray photograph.

X-rays have wavelengths of about 10^{-10} m, about 5500 times shorter than the wavelength of visible light. Gamma rays have even shorter wavelengths of about 10^{-15} m.

Electromagnetic spectrum

wavelength (m)

| 10^{-12} | 10^{-10} | 10^{-8} | 10^{-6} | 10^{-4} | 10^{-2} | 1 | 10^2 | 10^4 |

| 10^{20} | 10^{19} | 10^{18} | 10^{17} | 10^{16} | 10^{15} | 10^{14} | 10^{13} | 10^{12} | 10^{11} | 10^{16} | 10^{9} | 10^{8} | 10^{7} | 10^{6} | 10^{5} | 10^{4} |

frequency (Hz)

X-rays — gamma — ultraviolet — visible light — infra-red — microwaves — radiowaves

FIGURE 3: X-rays and gamma rays are part of the electromagnetic spectrum.

QUESTIONS

1 State **two** similar properties of X-rays and gamma rays.

2 What is the typical ratio of wavelength of X-rays : wavelength of gamma rays?

3 Calculate the frequency of
  a gamma rays of wavelength 1.0×10^{-15} m
  b X-rays of wavelength 1.0×10^{-10} m.

X-rays and gamma rays are electromagnetic waves.

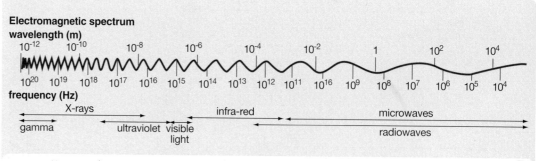

... cancer   cobalt-60   ...electromagnetic waves   ...gamma rays   ...ionising radiation

X-rays and gamma rays are both ionising radiations

Both X-rays and gamma rays are **ionising radiations**. The shorter wavelength gamma rays cause greater ionisation effects than X-rays. Both types of waves can knock off electrons from atoms and molecules. Hence X-rays and gamma rays will both affect photographic film. Exposure to either X-rays or gamma rays can cause permanent damage to tissues and cells. They are both extremely dangerous and can result in **cancer**. This is why radiographers, dentists and doctors working with these ionisation radiations wear film badges to monitor the exposure they receive over a period of time.

Are X-rays and gamma rays emitted from similar sources? No! Gamma rays are emitted from unstable radioactive nuclei (e.g. **cobalt-60**) whereas X-rays are emitted when high-speed electrons hit a target metal in an X-ray machine. Television screens produce a small amount of X-rays because electrons striking the screen produce the picture. The intensity of the X-rays is quite weak and so we need not be too concerned.

FIGURE 4: Many of us will have had an X-ray photograph taken in hospital.

One of the most important applications of X-rays is taking photographs.

The exposure to X-rays has to be kept to the minimum because of the damage X-rays can cause. X-rays will pass through soft tissues but are easily absorbed by bones. Hence they are ideal for identifying broken bones. To diagnose the function of the large intestines (soft tissues), an X-ray photograph is taken after the patient has drunk a mixture containing barium (barium meal) – barium is very good at stopping X-rays.

X-rays and gamma rays are both ionising radiations.

FIGURE 5: An X-ray photograph of a patient after taking a barium meal

...target metal   ...X-rays   ...X-ray tube

The origin of X-rays

Figure 6 below shows the main components of an **X-ray tube**.

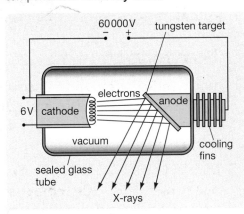

FIGURE 6: An X-ray tube.

A high voltage of 60 000 V is applied between the cathode and anode. The cathode has a hot filament from which the electrons are easily removed. These electrons are accelerated to high speeds towards the positive anode. At the anode, the electrons hit the target metal, (tungsten). The electrons collide with the **target metal** atoms and this makes some of the atoms emit X-rays with a range of wavelengths.

The target metal has to be water-cooled to ensure it does not melt!

X-rays are also produced in space by high-density stars and interacting galaxies. The X-rays are produced by the bombardment of high-speed electrons with the material in space. Astronomers have successfully used X-rays photographs to identify the presence of black holes.

FIGURE 7: An X-ray image of the centre of our Milky Way.

QUESTIONS

4 What type of radiation are X-rays and gamma rays?
5 Suggest why gamma rays are more dangerous than X-rays.
6 What technique is used to diagnose the function of the large intestines?

QUESTIONS

7 How are X-rays produced in an X-ray tube?
8 What is the main energy transfer of the kinetic energy of the colliding electrons in an X-ray tube?

Medical uses of radioactivity

You will find out:

- About sterilising equipment
- About the medical applications of radioactivity

Radioactivity and medicine

Radioactive nuclei emit harmful ionising radiations in the form of alpha particles, beta particles and gamma rays. In spite of the obvious dangers, gamma rays have been successfully used in hospitals for treating some cancers and to diagnose the function of vital organs such as the kidney and the brain.

Sterilising instruments

As you have already seen, the life of fruit can be prolonged by irradiating it with gamma rays. The gamma rays have sufficient energy to kill off **bacteria** within the fruit. In hospitals, metal instruments used by surgeons can be boiled to remove the germs but this cannot be done when sterilising plastic syringes or bandages. Bandages and syringes can be sealed in plastic bags and then exposed to intense gamma radiation. The equipment and package both become sterile. This **sterilisation** process minimises the risks of infection spreading.

Gamma radiation kills bacteria such as *Staphylococcus*, including MRSA (methicillin-resistant *Staphylococcus aureus*) and *Escherichia coli* (*E. coli*) that can seriously harm the health of patients in hospitals.

FIGURE 1: These syringes have been sterilised by gamma radiation.

FIGURE 2: The E. coli bacterium can be destroyed by gamma radiation.

◼ QUESTIONS ◼

1. What is the source of gamma rays or gamma radiation?
2. Name **two** items in hospitals that gamma rays are used to sterilise.
3. What do gamma rays destroy during the sterilisation process?

GAMMA RAYS

A high dose of gamma rays can be extremely dangerous.

...bacteria   ...cancer   ...half-life   ...isotope

Radiotherapy

We have already seen one beneficial use of gamma rays in destroying bacteria when sterilising hospital equipment. In **radiotherapy** (also known as radiation therapy) gamma rays can also be used in the treatment of **cancer**.

The most common radioactive source used in radiotherapy is cobalt-60. The isotope of cobalt-60 has a half-life of 5.3 years. Doctors carefully direct a number of gamma ray sources from different directions on to the cancerous tissues to destroy the cancer cells. Each source emits a weak beam of gamma rays. Where the gamma beams cross, the energy from the combined beams is intense enough to destroy the cancerous cells. This procedure also destroys some healthy tissues surrounding the cancerous region and can make the patient very ill, but radiotherapy can stop the growth of the cancer or at least slow down its growth.

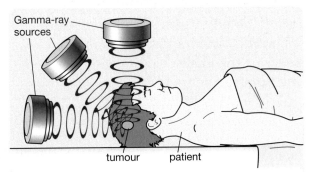

FIGURE 3: In radiotherapy, several gamma sources are targeted towards the cancerous region.

Radioactive tracers in medicine

Radioactive **tracers** (also known as radionuclides) help doctors to check the insides of our bodies. A small amount of radioactive substance emitting gamma rays is injected into the patient. Gamma rays are not as ionising as alpha particles or beta particles and so cause less damage to the cells. A radioactivity material emitting alpha particles would be extremely dangerous if injected into a person!

The gamma rays are detected outside the body by a gamma camera connected to a computer that coverts the counts from the gamma camera into a high-quality image that doctors can use to check the function of certain organs.

To investigate the function of the kidneys, the isotope used as a tracer is iodine-123. The **isotope** of iodine-123 has a **half-life** of about 13 hours. A very short time after being injected into the patient, the radioactive iodine is absorbed from the bloodstream by the kidneys and after about 20 minutes it should be passed with the urine into the bladder. However, if one or both of the kidneys is not functioning properly, then the kidneys will retain the iodine and this will be clearly displayed by the picture from the gamma camera.

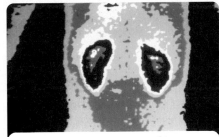

FIGURE 4: A gamma ray scan of two healthy human kidneys.

QUESTIONS

4   What organ is iodine-123 used to investigate?

5   Why are radioactive tracers always gamma-emitting sources?

6   Explain why radioactive tracers must have a short half-life.

7   The radioactive isotope iodine-123 has a half-life of 13 hours. What fraction of the iodine nuclei are still active after 26 hours?

What other radioactive tracers are there?

To investigate the function of the kidneys, the radioactive tracer used is iodine-123. Are any other tracers used in medicine? The answer is a simple yes.

The table below shows some of the most common radioactive tracers used in hospital, their half-lives and some of the medical uses.

Tracer	Half-life	What is it used for?
Technetium-99	6 hours	Lung function Heart function Bone growth Blood flow in the brain
Xenon-133	2.3 days	Lung function
Iodine-123	13 hours	Kidney function Thyroid function
Iodine-131	8 days	Kidney function Thyroid function

QUESTIONS

8   Name the radioactive tracer that can be used to check the function of the brain.

9   Explain **one** advantage of using technetium-99 rather than xenon-133 when checking the function of the lungs.

10 Explain why an injection containing a radioactive tracer has a limited shelf life.

The dangers of radiation

You will find out:
- About the dangers of radiation
- How the Earth's atmosphere and magnetic field protect us

How did scientists discover the dangers of radiation?

Early pioneering researchers into radioactive materials and the radiation they emitted were unaware of the dangers. Many scientists such as Marie Curie touched radioactive materials with their bare hands and sadly paid the price by developing leukaemia (cancer of the white blood cells). It is truly amazing that after more than one hundred years Marie Curie's notebooks remain radioactive!

Taking precautions

It is worth reminding yourself that the following ionising radiations are dangerous:

- alpha particles (radiation)
- beta particles (radiation)
- gamma rays (radiation)
- X-rays.

The radioactive sources used in schools are weak and should not create too much danger if used sensibly and carefully. What further precautions can we take to minimise the dangers posed by the ionising radiations from radioactive sources? Here are some useful **safety** tips when using radioactive sources in the school laboratory:

- Always point the radiation from the radioactive sources away from yourself and other people.
- Never ever handle radioactive sources with your fingers. Use special holders or tongs to hold radioactive sources.
- Remove radioactive sources from their lead-sealed containers only when carrying out experiments.
- Always wash your hands after carrying out experiments with radioactive sources.
- Do not eat food or drink in the laboratory when using radioactive sources.
- Cover any scratches or cuts with plaster while conducting experiments.

FIGURE 1: Marie Curie developed leukaemia from working with radioactive materials.

WOW FACTOR!

Some cosmetic products in the 1910s were made from radioactive radium because it made the face 'glow'.

QUESTIONS

1. Name **four** ionising radiations.
2. Why is it sensible to store radioactive sources in lead-lined containers?
3. Why is it safe to pick up a radioactive source using a long holder or tongs?

...atmosphere   ...cancer   ...DNA   ...magnetic field

The dangers of ionising radiation

Early scientists experimenting with radioactive sources were not conscious of their dangers. It is through their mistakes and our better understanding of the properties of the ionising radiations that we can protect ourselves from their dangers.

All ionising radiations carry sufficient energy to damage individual cells in our bodies. If the damage is sufficiently great, then the cell cannot repair itself and will die. Ionising radiations also damage the **DNA** (deoxyribonucleic acid) of the cell. Changes in the genetic material of the cell (**mutations**) cause the cells to change or reproduce uncontrollably, leading to **cancer**.

Alpha particles are easily stopped by skin. Large doses of alpha radiation can lead to skin cancer. However, it is very easy to minimise the dangers of alpha particles by wearing plastic gloves and keeping the source at a distance from the body – remember that alpha particles are stopped by a few centimetres of air. Sources emitting alpha particles can be particularly dangerous if inhaled or swallowed.

Gamma rays and beta particles can penetrate the skin and therefore can cause internal damage to our bodies. Excessive doses of ionising radiation can cause permanent damage to cells. This can lead to radiation sickness where victims lose their hair and vomit uncontrollably.

Watch Out All ionising radiations damage cells and the DNA within.

FIGURE 2: A damaged DNA molecule that can lead to cancer.

The Earth's atmosphere and its magnetic field (H)

The Earth is surrounded by its own **magnetic field**. The magnetosphere is the region round the Earth occupied by this magnetic field.

FIGURE 3: The Earth's magnetic field protects us from the solar wind.

The Sun is constantly emitting a swarm of particles (electrons, protons and neutrinos) known as the **solar wind**. The Earth's magnetic field acts as a 'shield' and deflects most of the solar wind away from the Earth. Some of the solar wind reaches as far as the Earth's atmosphere where it ionises the gas molecules. Hence the Earth's magnetic field and its atmosphere protect us from excessive exposure to dangerous ionising radiation from outer space. The **atmosphere** also stops a significant amount of harmful **ultraviolet** radiation from the Sun reaching the surface.

The magnetosphere around the Earth is not perfect at stopping the solar wind. The weak spots are at the magnetic poles where the Earth's magnetic field is the strongest. Here, the charged particles spiral down towards the Earth's surface. As they do so, the particles ionise the gas molecules in the atmosphere and produce spectacular aurora borealis (dancing lights) in the night sky.

FIGURE 4: Aurora borealis is caused by the solar wind and the Earth's magnetic field.

...*mutation* ...*safety* ...*solar wind* ...*ultraviolet*

Glowing in the dark

SELF-CHECK ACTIVITY

CONTEXT

In the Second World War pilots were trained to fly at night, using their instruments to show their height, speed and position. That meant, of course, that they had to be able to read the instruments in the dark. Having a light in the cockpit would make the plane visible to others and affected the pilot's ability to see outside the plane. Instead the instrument dials were painted with radium.

Radium is radioactive and emits alpha and beta particles and gamma rays. It has a half life of around 1600 years. The paint was made by mixing radium with zinc sulphide and glue. When the radioactive particles hit the zinc sulphide it glowed.

At the end of the war many aircraft were broken up. Others had crashed or been shot down. Sometimes the instruments were kept as souvenirs by people who found them.

Radium is potentially dangerous. The dials were painted by hand, usually by girls. This fine work was only possible if the tip of the brush was at a very fine point and the easiest way to do this was to lick the end of the brush. That usually meant a small amount of radium was transferred to the tongue and would work its way into the body. The radioactive poisoning caused cancers and weakening of the bones.

Aircrew appear to have been under no such risk. At a distance of about 70 cm from the instrument it is difficult to distinguish radiation from the instrument from normal background radiation. Modern aircraft don't have radium on the dials, but tritium, which is a beta source with a half life of 12.43 years.

CHALLENGE

STEP 1

What is meant by 'normal background radiation' and where does it come from?

STEP 2

The instruments had a glass front. What effect would this have had on the radiation being emitted from the instrument dial?

Why is it that the instruments become more dangerous if damaged or dismantled?

STEP 3

Draw a diagram showing the function of the molecules of zinc sulphide and the radioactive emissions from the radium in the luminous paint.

Use your understanding of radioactivity to explain why:
- tritium is safer than radium
- radium was much more dangerous to the instrument makers than to the aircrews.

For many years some types of alarm clock had radium instrument dials. Write a paragraph explaining why this was done, what the hazards are and whether you would be happy to have one.

Maximise your grade

These sentences show what you need to include in your work to achieve each grade. Use them to improve your work and be more successful.

Grade	Answer includes...
F	State different types of radioactive emission.
	State what background radiation is and how the emissions of various particles vary.
	Describe how radioactive emissions can be blocked.
C	Explain how the glass fronts affect radioactive emissions.
	Explain how the glass front on the instrument panel and the distance from the body meant that aircrews had little risk but the factory girls much more.
	Explain what makes zinc sulphide glow.
A	Assess and justify the acceptability of the risk from radioactivity from alarm clocks with radium-painted dials.
	Assess and justify the acceptability of the risk from radioactivity from alarm clocks with radium-painted dials, with particular clarity and command of evidence.

Dangers of electrostatics

You will find out:
- How insulators can be charged
- About the forces between charged objects
- How the dangers of sparks can be minimised

Thunderbolt and lightning!

When **insulators** rub against each other, electric charges can build up on their surfaces. This can lead to electric sparks. Lightning is a giant electric spark that can be quite dangerous!

Electrostatics

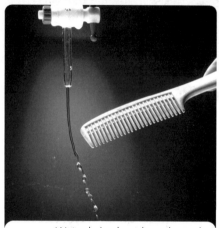

FIGURE 2: Water being bent by a charged comb.

Rub a plastic comb or a polythene rod with a dry woollen duster and hold it near a trickle of water from a burette or a tap. There is an attraction between the water and the plastic comb. **Friction** between the comb and the duster has made the comb charged. The charge on the comb is on its surface and does not move as in current electricity. These charges are referred to as **electrostatic charges**. In order to understand how insulators acquire a charge, we have to go back to the structure of the atom.

FIGURE 1: Lightning can look spectacular but it can be quite dangerous.

All objects are made up of atoms. The atom has a positive nucleus that is surrounded by orbiting negatively charged electrons. The nucleus is positive because it contains protons that are positively charged. There are also neutrons within the nucleus, but these carry no charge.

So what happens when you rub a polythene rod with a duster? All insulators acquire a charge because of **transfer of electrons**. The protons remain fixed. Rubbing causes some of the outer electrons of the atoms in the duster to be stripped off and get transferred onto the polythene rod. The duster has fewer electrons and therefore becomes positively charged. The polythene rod has gained extra electrons and therefore becomes negatively charged.

When a glass rod is rubbed against a dry woollen duster, the glass becomes positively charged and the duster becomes negatively charged.

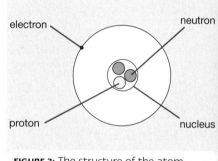

FIGURE 3: The structure of the atom.

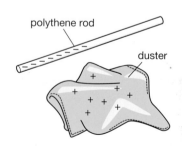

FIGURE 4: The polythene rod gains electrons and becomes negative. The duster loses the electrons and becomes positive.

QUESTIONS

1. What do you have to do in order to charge two insulators?
2. Name the charged particles that are transferred when two insulators rub against each other.
3. A glass rod rubbed with a duster becomes charged positive. Explain which object gains electrons and which one loses the electrons.

...attraction   ...earthing   ...electric field   ...electric sparks   ...electrons

Force between charged objects

Charged objects exert a force on each other because of their charge. There are two laws of force for charges:

- Opposite charges attract.
- Like charges repel.

The **attraction** and **repulsion** can be demonstrated easily by suspending a charged rod from a dry nylon thread and bringing other charged rods close by.

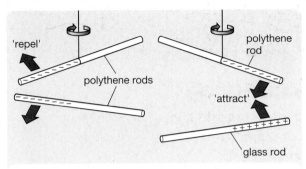

FIGURE 5: Like charges repel and opposite charges attract.

Electric sparks

Most of us are familiar with the crackling noise when removing clothes made from synthetic materials. The crackling is due to tiny **electric sparks**.

What causes a spark and what is it? When the amount of charge on an isolated insulator increases, the voltage between it and the earth increases. Air is normally a very good insulator but at high voltages, around 3 000 000 V it starts to conduct. The electrons and other charges moving through the air cause an electric spark.

Electric sparks can create high temperatures and this can make them dangerous. It is not sensible to have electric sparks on an oil tanker. This is why all the workers on oil tankers wear shoes with conducting soles. Electric sparks can be useful too. Car engines have spark plugs that help to ignite the fuel.

Most objects can be made safe by **earthing** the object. This involves having a metal conductor secured between the object and the ground. This helps to transfer the electrons from the object to the earth or vice versa, thus minimising the dangers of sparking.

Here are some examples:

- *Car*: moving cars gain a charge as the rubber tyres rub against the ground. To avoid an electric shock when getting out of the car, a metal earthing strap is fixed to the car.

- *Fuelling*: when fuelling aircraft, the friction between the fuel and the pipe makes each acquire opposite charges. The charges can build up and create a spark with devastating consequences. This is why aircrafts are earthed when refuelling.

Lightning conductors

What happens to the air surrounding a sharp pointed metal rod that is connected to a high-voltage supply? The sharp metal point creates a strong **electric field** that strips off the electrons from nearby air atoms and creates positive ions. The air around the sharp point becomes ionised. The positive point repels the positive ions and creates an 'electric wind'.

Tall buildings are protected from the dangers of lightning strikes by having a **lightning conductor** placed at their highest point. This conductor consists of thick copper strip secured to the outside of the building. It has a spike at the top and a metal plate embedded into the ground at the bottom.

FIGURE 6: This lightning conductor will protect the building.

When a negatively charged thundercloud passes overhead, it creates positive charges at the top of the lightning conductor. The spike repels the positive ions in the air towards the cloud to discharge the cloud so no lightning is produced. The electrons are attracted to the conductor and travel down to the earth. During a severe thunderstorm, the clouds suddenly discharge and produce huge sparks we call lightning.

QUESTIONS

4 Electrons are negative and protons are positive. What is the force between these particles?

5 Why are electric sparks dangerous near petrol vapours?

6 During a long car journey, the body of the car becomes negatively charged. The car has an earthing strap secured between it and the ground. How does this make it safe from electric sparks?

QUESTIONS

7 What happens to the air close to a sharp metal point held at a very high voltage?

8 Why may it be dangerous to be standing in an open field during a thunderstorm?

...*electrostatic charge*   ...*friction*   ...*insulator*   ...*lightning conductors*   ...*repulsion*

Uses of electrostatics

You will find out:
- How an electrostatic precipitator works
- How fingerprinting works
- How laser printing works

Life without photocopiers!

Johann Gutenberg printed the world's first book in 1456. His printing technique made it possible to make more copies in a few weeks than formerly could be produced in a lifetime by hand. This made mass circulation of literature possible. Copying documents has been made even easier now with photocopiers and computer scanners. It is hard to imagine life without such revolutionary devices.

FIGURE 1: Photocopiers can make life easier.

Making breezeblocks from soot

Electrostatic precipitators are used in coal-burning power stations to remove smoke particles (soot) before they can enter the environment.

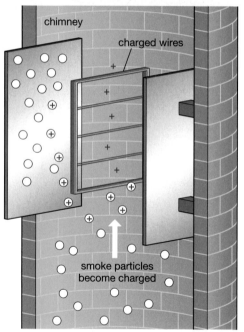

FIGURE 2: An electrostatic precipitator is used to remove smoke particles.

The precipitator is placed at the top of the chimney. It consists of positively charged wires held at a voltage of about 60 000 V. The air around these wires is ionised. As the smoke particles travel past the charged wires, they lose electrons and become positively charged. The positively charged smoke particles are repelled by the wires towards negative metal plates. The smoke particles stick to these plates. The soot is removed from the plates by repeatedly hitting them with a mechanical hammer. The soot is collected from the bottom of the chimney.

A coal-burning power station can produce up to 40 tonnes of soot every hour. This is not released into the atmosphere, but is used by the cosmetics industry and for making special house bricks known as breezeblocks.

FIGURE 3: A coal-burning power station produces tonnes of soot, which can be used to make breeze blocks.

QUESTIONS

1. Suggest why it is sensible to remove smoke particles from chimneys.
2. The smoke particles rising up the chimney carry no charge until they get close to the positively charged wires. How does this happen?
3. Why are the smoke particles attracted towards the negative metal plates?

...electrostatic ...electrostatic attraction

Fingerprinting

Taking photographs of **fingerprints** left by criminals on glass or tabletops has become a routine task at every crime scene in the world. The fingerprints can be used to identify known criminals.

What happens if the fingerprints are left on paper? A method similar to electrostatic precipitation can be used to show the fingerprint on paper. The paper is placed above electrically charged wires and fine black powder is sprinkled onto the paper. The powder sticks to the fingerprint but not the clean paper. This can be photographed and stored digitally in a computer.

FIGURE 4: This fingerprint could catch a criminal!

WOW FACTOR!

The chance of two people having the same fingerprints is almost zero.

In some companies, a computerised scanning technique is used to identify the workers.

FIGURE 5: A fingerprint scanner in use.

Paint spraying

The metal object to be painted, such as a car or bicycle, is charged negative. The paint is sprayed from a spray gun that is charged positive. The charged droplets of paint are attracted to the metal object and give it a uniform coat of paint. With this technique even the underside of the object receives a coat of paint and less paint is also used.

QUESTIONS

4   What technique is used to show the fingerprints on a piece of paper?

5   In paint spraying why does the spray gun have an opposite charge to that of the object being painted?

6   Name **one** benefit of using paint spraying compared with using a brush.

Laser printing

Chester Carlson, an American physicist, invented electrostatic photocopying in 1938. Unlike the earlier methods, which require liquid chemicals, his photocopier was completely 'dry'. His photocopying technique was known as Xerography. 'Xeros' in Greek means dry' and 'graphy' means writing.

In principle, modern photocopiers and laser printers are the same. Photocopiers can be used to produce high-quality copies of documents in a relatively short period of time.

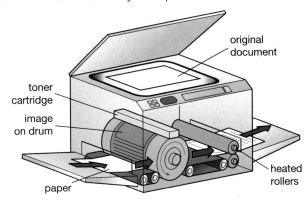

FIGURE 6: The inside of a photocopier.

The main component of a photocopier is a drum or plate that is sensitive to light. The drum is positively charged and its surface is coated with **selenium**, which becomes conducting when light shines on it. This is how a copy of the document is produced on paper:

- An image of the document to be copied is projected on the drum using lenses.
- The dark parts of the drum become positively charged and the regions exposed to light become uncharged.
- Very fine negatively charged '**toner**' particles stick to the dark parts of the drum because of **electrostatic attraction**.
- The powdered image of the document is transferred on to the paper by contact.
- The image is 'fixed' on to the paper by heating. This melts small plastic particles mixed in with the black toner powder, which makes the toner stick to the paper. (This is why the copies are warm when they come out of the photocopier and can smudge if handled too quickly.)

QUESTIONS

7   In a modern photocopier, what is the purpose of selenium?

8   Explain why the toner sticks to the regions on the drum that are dark.

9   Explain why the final stage of photocopying involves heating the paper.

Predictions and Einstein

You will find out:
- How scientists use theories and make predictions
- About Einstein's famous equation $E = mc^2$

Theories can be wrong

For almost one and a half thousand years, scientists believed that heavier objects fell faster on the Earth's surface. This idea or theory, proposed by the Greek philosopher Aristotle, did not take account of the effect of air resistance. It took a genius by the name of Galileo to conduct experiments that showed that all objects, irrespective of their mass, fell on the Earth with the same acceleration.

Theories and predictions

Most scientists carry out experiments. The results from the experiments can often be explained in terms of scientific ideas known as **theories**. Scientists use a theory to make **predictions**. If the predictions do not agree with the theory, then a revolution can occur, with the old ideas being replaced by a better theory.

FIGURE 1: Aristotle's ideas of motion were wrong.

FIGURE 2: Galileo showed that all objects fall at the same rate on the Earth.

For example, since the 1660s, Newton's law of gravitation was used to explain a range of things from the origin of tides to the orbits of planets and comets. The ideas of Newton were even used successfully to predict the existence of 'new' planets such as Neptune and Pluto. However, Newton's laws could not exactly explain the strange orbit of the innermost planet Mercury. Mercury's orbit showed a slight 'gyration', which could not be explained. It took a set of new ideas from the genius Albert Einstein to explain this phenomenon.

Here are some more theories and their successful or unsuccessful predictions:!

Individual	Theory	Prediction
Galileo Galilei 1569–1642	Falling objects	All objects, irrespective of their mass, roll down a slope with the same acceleration. This was a successful prediction.
Isaac Newton 1642–1727	Light	When light travels from air into water, it bends or refracts because the speed of light increases in water. In fact, light slows down in water, hence the prediction was wrong.
Albert Einstein 1879–1955	Gravitation and space	The gravity of a dense star distorts the space around it. This will make light travelling close to the star deviate slightly. This beautiful prediction was shown to be true.
George Gamov 1904–1968	Big Bang	The universe began from a hot explosion. The universe cooled as it expanded. The temperature of space at this moment in its history is about −270 °C. This prediction was spot on.

▪ QUESTIONS ▪

1 From the table above, which theory gave incorrect predictions?
2 What normally happens when a theory cannot explain something?
3 What did Gamov predict the temperature of the universe to be now?

...mass–energy   ...nuclear reactor   ...predictions   ...radioactive

ɛinstein's famous equation

ılbert Einstein, a German physicist, was a genius comparable to the likes of Isaac Iewton and Galileo. In 1905, while working as a clerk, he proposed an astonishing heory called the **special theory of relativity**. In it, he proposed many truly xtraordinary ideas. One of them was the theory that mass and energy were quivalent. He proposed an equation that most of us are familiar with, but what loes the equation really mean?

instein's **mass-energy** equation is written as:

$$E = mc^2$$

vhere m is the *change* in the mass in kilograms (kg), E s the *change* in energy in joules (J) and c is the speed of light (3.0×10^8 m/s) in vacuum.

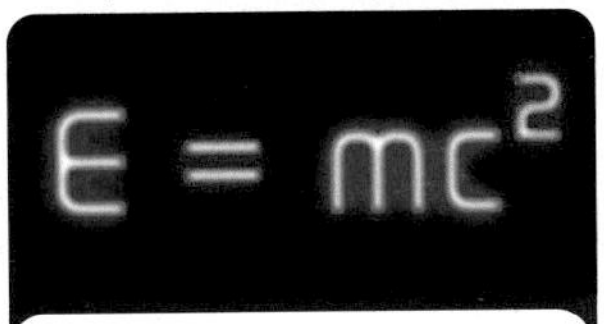

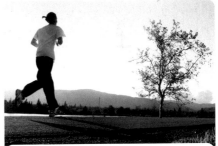

FIGURE 3: The famous mass–energy equation in neon lights.

According to this equation energy is *released* from a system whenever there is a *decrease* in the mass of the system.

- In the Sun, nuclear matter is being converted into energy at a phenomenal rate. The Sun shines because some of its mass is being converting directly into energy.
- In a **nuclear reactor**, small nuclear reactions produce kinetic energy because there is a tiny decrease in the mass of the nuclei in every reaction.
- A **radioactive** nucleus releases energy in the form of kinetic energy because there is a decrease in the mass of the nuclei.

Example: How much energy is produced when a mass of 1 gram (0.001 kg) is changed completely into energy?

The energy E released is given by:

$$E = mc^2$$

$$E = 0.001 \times (3.0 \times 10^8)^2 = 9.0 \times 10^{13} \text{ J}$$

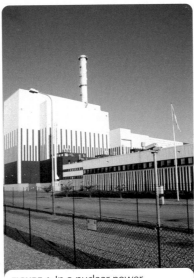

FIGURE 4: In a nuclear power station, mass is partly destroyed to produce energy.

WOW FACTOR!

In our Sun, about one billion tonnes of matter are converted into energy every second.

WOW FACTOR!

A mass of 1 gram produces the same nuclear energy as 3.6 million kilograms of petrol!

QUESTIONS

4 In the equation $E = mc^2$ what is c?

5 Calculate the energy released from completely destroying a mass of 0.5 kg (equivalent to a glass of water).

6 Calculate the energy released from completely destroying a mass of 0.000 01 kg (equivalent to a grain of sand).

7 Write an equation for m in terms of E and c.

More on $E = mc^2$

Einstein's mass–energy equation is much more profound than at first glance. The equation can be applied to everything, including us!

According to Einstein, when we *run* our total energy has increased because of the extra kinetic energy. Therefore according to $E = mc^2$, our mass must also increase. The reason we do not notice the change in mass is because it is so small. The following calculation makes this clear.

Example: A person running has kinetic energy of 500 J. What is the increase in the mass m of the runner?

FIGURE 5: A person running will have a greater mass than when at rest.

$$E = mc^2$$

$$m = \frac{500}{(3.0 \times 10^8)^2}$$

$$m = 5.6 \times 10^{-15} \text{ kg}$$

This increase in mass is quite insignificant and the runner would not notice it.

However, a tiny electron travelling very close to the speed of light can have a mass that could be a 20 times greater than its mass at rest. Just imagine how we would feel if we were the electron!

QUESTIONS

8 Why will the mass of a person running increase?

9 An object at the bottom of a mountain has a mass of 1 kg. It is lifted to the top of a mountain. The object gains potential energy. Explain whether its mass will be more than or less than 1 kg.

Nuclear fission

You will find out:
- About nuclear fission
- Why energy is released in a fission reaction
- About the fission of uranium-235
- About chain reaction

Splitting the nucleus?

Artificially splitting the **nucleus** is not an easy matter. Two German physicists, Otto Hahn and Fritz Strassmann, split the nuleus during some experiments in 1938. Amazingly, they did not realise what they had done! It had to be pointed out by two other physicists, Otto Frisch and Lise Meitner.

Nuclear fission

In natural radioactive decay, a nucleus disintegrates by emitting either an alpha particle or a beta particle. The decay is **spontaneous** and cannot be controlled by external factors such as pressure or temperature. The decay of the nucleus is a natural event that is not assisted by humans in any way.

In nuclear **fission**, a nucleus of uranium-235 is struck by a slow-moving neutron and splits up into two smaller nuclei (known as the **daughter nuclei**) and either two or three fast-moving neutrons.

The neutron has no charge. It can travel towards the nucleus without suffering any electrical forces because of the positive nucleus. When the neutron gets close to the nucleus it is quickly absorbed. However, this makes the new nucleus, with an extra neutron, highly unstable. As a result, the nucleus splits.

FIGURE 1: Hahn and Meitner were two pioneers of nuclear fission.

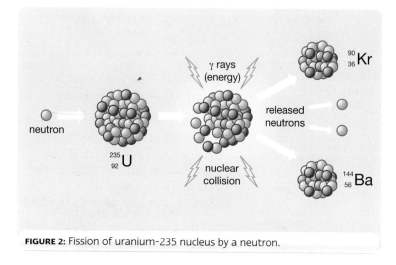

FIGURE 2: Fission of uranium-235 nucleus by a neutron.

Radioactivity is a natural event, but nuclear fission is artificial!

EXAM HINTS AND TIPS

Slow-moving neutrons are more easily absorbed by uranium nuclei than fast-moving neutrons.

QUESTIONS

1. What part of the atom does nuclear fission involve?
2. What happens to a uranium-235 nucleus that absorbs a neutron?
3. In what form is energy released from nuclear fission reaction?

...*chain reaction* ...*critical mass* ...*daughter nuclei* ...*decay series*

Fission produces energy

Energy is released in a fission reaction. This energy comes from a small amount of nuclear matter being changed into energy. Here is one of the many possible nuclear decay equations for the fission of uranium-235:

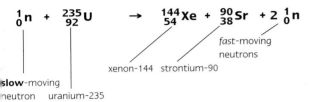

$${}^{1}_{0}n + {}^{235}_{92}U \rightarrow {}^{144}_{54}Xe + {}^{90}_{38}Sr + 2\,{}^{1}_{0}n$$

slow-moving neutron   uranium-235   xenon-144   strontium-90   fast-moving neutrons

FIGURE 3: Einstein's ideas about mass and energy help to explain why fission releases energy.

The total mass of xenon-144, strontium-90 and the fast-moving neutrons at the end is less than the total mass of the slow-moving neutron and uranium-235 at the start of the reaction. The difference in the mass is equivalent to the energy released. In this example, the difference in the mass m is about 4×10^{-28} kg. How much energy E is released in the fission reaction?

$$E = mc^2$$

energy released $= 4 \times 10^{-28} \times (3.0 \times 10^8)^2 \approx 3.6 \times 10^{-11}$ **joules**

If the fission neutrons split other uranium-235 nuclei, a **chain reaction** is set up. This is illustrated in Figure 4, where the daughter nuclei are different (krypton-91 and barium-142) and there are three fast-moving neutrons produced in every fission reaction.

- If the chain reaction continues to grow, then an enormous amount of energy can be produced in a very short time. This is the basis of a nuclear explosion.
- In a nuclear power station, the chain reaction is 'controlled', so that a single neutron is captured on average between one nuclear fission stage and the next.

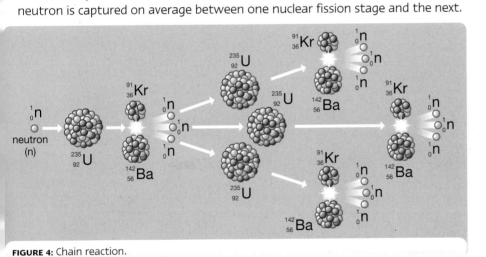

FIGURE 4: Chain reaction.

QUESTIONS

4   Is fission of uranium-235 produced by slow-moving or fast-moving neutrons?

5   Name the **two** daughter nuclei that can be produced when uranium-235 is involved in a fission reaction.

6   One kilogram of uranium has about 2.6×10^{24} uranium nuclei. Each fission reaction produces 3.6×10^{-11} joules. What is the total energy that can be released from 1 kg of uranium fuel?

This is all critical   (H)

If the mass of a lump of pure uranium exceeds a certain **critical mass**, then a single neutron can activate an uncontrolled chain reaction. The critical mass for uranium is about 15 kg. This is how colossal energy can be released in a short period of time in a nuclear explosion.

In all fission reactions, the daughter nuclei are themselves radioactive. Some of these by-products can have very long half-lives, which makes **disposal** a real environmental issue for future generations and us.

In the previous fission reaction, one of the daughter nuclei produced was that of strontium-90. The following diagram illustrates the **decay series** for strontium-90:

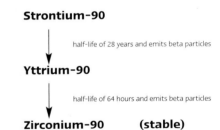

Strontium-90

half-life of 28 years and emits beta particles

Yttrium-90

half-life of 64 hours and emits beta particles

Zirconium-90   **(stable)**

Strontium-90 is very short lived compared with some daughter nuclei such as lanthanum-138, which has a half-life of 110 billion years!

QUESTIONS

7   What is the critical mass of uranium?

8   Explain why the by-products of fission reactions cannot be easily disposed of.

9   How could you make radioactive by-products from fission reactions safe by chemical changes?

...disposal ...fission ...nucleus ...spontaneous

Destructive and peaceful fission

You will find out:

- About the destructive use of fission
- How a chain reaction is controlled in a nuclear reactor

The first atomic bombs

German scientists at the start of the Second World War discovered nuclear **fission** in 1938. The race was on to produce the world's first atomic bomb. It took Europe's and America's best physicists and engineers only seven years to produce and detonate bombs on the Japanese cities of Hiroshima and Nagasaki with terrible consequences.

FIGURE 1: One of the few surviving structures in Hiroshima after the explosion of the first atomic bomb.

A timeline to destruction

- **1905**   Einstein proposed his famous equation: $E = mc^2$.

- **1934**   Enrico Fermi in Italy split heavy nuclei by bombarding them with neutrons.

- **1938**   Otto Hahn and Fritz Strassmann in Berlin announced that they had split the nucleus using neutrons.

- **1939**   Albert Einstein wrote a letter to the American President, Franklin D. Roosevelt, urging him to start a 'nuclear programme'.

- **1942**   Enrico Fermi (now in America) succeeded in producing the first nuclear **chain reaction**. His **nuclear reactor** was built secretly in an old squash court at the University of Chicago!

- **16 July 1945**   The world's first **atomic bomb** was tested successfully at Alamogordo, New Mexico.

- **6 August 1945**   The American aircraft *Enola Gay* dropped the first atomic bomb (named 'Little Boy') on Hiroshima in Japan. This killed about 140 000 people and seriously injured 100 000 people.

- **9 August 1945**   The United States dropped a second atomic bomb (named 'Fat Man') on the Japanese city of Nagasaki.

FIGURE 2: Enrico Fermi built the world's first nuclear reactor in a squash court!

QUESTIONS

1. What did Enrico Fermi, Otto Hahn and Fritz Strassmann have in common?
2. Where was the world's first nuclear reactor built?

The first atomic bomb was equivalent to 20 000 tonnes of TNT.

...*atomic bomb*   ...*chain reaction*   ...*critical mass*

Chain reaction and the atomic bomb

When a uranium-235 nucleus breaks up into a pair of daughter nuclei and a few extra neutrons, it releases energy. These extra neutrons can cause further fission reactions and produce a chain reaction. It is possible for a single neutron to trigger the release of enormous energy from uranium in a millionth of a second.

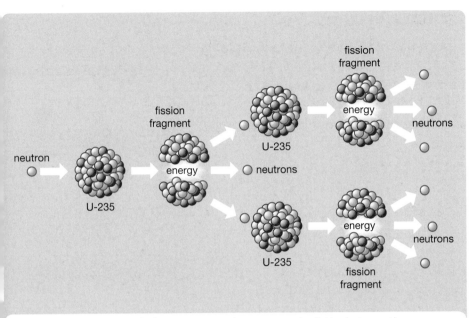

FIGURE 3: In an atomic bomb the neutrons produce an uncontrollable chain reaction.

A small amount of uranium-235 cannot maintain a chain reaction. Too many neutrons escape through the surface of the material and hence are not involved in further fission reactions. However, when the mass of uranium is about 15 kg, the number of neutrons escaping the surface of the material is compensated for by the additional neutrons produced from within the material from nuclear fission.

The minimum amount of fissile material (e.g. uranium or plutonium) required to maintain the chain reaction is known as the **critical mass**. Increasing the size and mass of the material leads to a large amount of energy being produced in a very short period of time. This is what happens in an atomic bomb.

Sadly, the nuclear weapon technology has advanced to a frightening end. Fission bombs have been taken over by **fusion** bombs and 'smart' neutron bombs that would kill the people but leave the buildings standing. Einstein never envisaged the destructive power behind his equation $E = mc^2$.

QUESTIONS

3 Why is it not possible to produce a chain reaction in a small amount of uranium?

4 Define the critical mass of a fissile material.

5 In an atomic bomb, the explosion is triggered by rapidly bringing two sections of a fissile material close together. For an atomic bomb using uranium, what is the minimum mass of the uranium in each section?

How to make a chain reaction safe in a nuclear reactor (H)

In an atomic bomb, an **uncontrolled fission** chain reaction can lead to a massive release of energy in a split second. However, by controlling the number of neutrons, it is possible to achieve a situation where on average, one neutron from the previous fission stage leads to fission in the next fission stage. This is how nuclear reactors produce a stable source of energy.

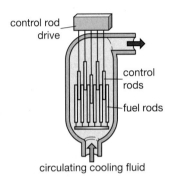

FIGURE 4: The control rods made from boron help to produce a controlled chain reaction.

In a **nuclear reactor**, the chain reaction occurs at a steady rate. This is achieved by reducing the number of neutrons produced from the fission reactions by using an absorbing material such as boron. Inserting or withdrawing the boron rods (also known as the control rods) among the uranium-rich fuel rods controls the amount of neutrons absorbed.

The nuclear reactor has a graphite core, known also as the moderator. The moderator slows down the fast-moving neutrons. Slow-moving neutrons have a greater chance of inducing fission than fast-moving neutrons.

QUESTIONS

6 What is the major difference between an atomic bomb and a nuclear reactor?

7 What is the purpose of the moderator?

8 What is the purpose of the boron rods?

9 Name **one** material used for the moderator.

...fission ...fusion ...nuclear reactor ...uncontrolled fission

Nuclear power stations

You will find out:

- How nuclear reactors produce thermal energy
- How thermal energy is transferred to electrical energy in a nuclear power station

Harnessing a chain reaction

There are many more power stations burning fossil fuel (coal, oil and natural gas) than nuclear power stations. Nuclear power stations have been producing energy since the 1950s. The number of nuclear power stations in the world has grown steadily. Some countries such as Sweden have over 50% of their energy needs produced by fission reactors. There are over 400 nuclear reactors operating around the world.

Producing electrical energy

In a conventional power station burning fossil fuel, the **chemical energy** from the fuel (coal, oil or natural gas) is used to generate **electrical energy**. Figure 2 shows how this is done.

FIGURE 1: A nuclear power station in Britain.

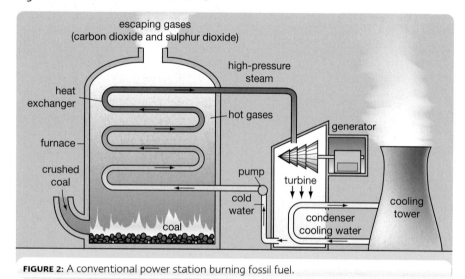

FIGURE 2: A conventional power station burning fossil fuel.

The fuel is burned and its chemical energy is used to produce high-pressure steam. The hot steam is used to turn a turbine, which then turns a generator to produce electrical energy. The National Grid transports this electrical energy to our homes and factories.

The major difference between a coal-burning power station and a nuclear power station is that the energy source is different. Instead of getting chemical energy from coal, the energy comes from the nuclei of uranium or plutonium atoms. The reactor of a nuclear power station does the same thing that a boiler does in a fossil fuel plant – it produces heat. In the nuclear reactor, the uranium fuel undergoes **controlled nuclear reactions.**

▌▌ QUESTIONS ▌▌

1 What energy changes take place in the boiler?
2 What energy changes take place in a generator?
3 What is the major difference between a coal-burning power station and a nuclear power station?

...chain reaction ...chemical energy ...controlled nuclear reactions ...control rods ...coolant

Nuclear power stations

The **thermal energy** (heat) in a nuclear reactor comes from the kinetic energy of the fission products (neutrons and the daughter nuclei). The diagram below shows a gas-cooled or water-cooled nuclear reactor.

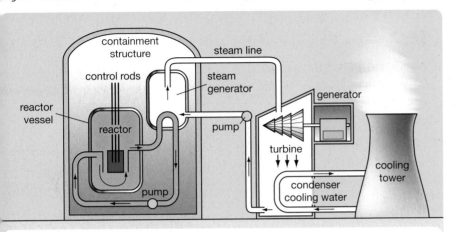

FIGURE 3: A diagram of a nuclear power station.

The basic components of a nuclear reactor are the **core**, **control rods**, **moderator**, **coolant** and **shielding**.

The *core* of a nuclear reactor contains the uranium **fuel rods** in the form of uranium oxide (UO_2). There may be 200 fuel rod assemblies in a typical reactor.

Movable *control rods* are inserted into the core of the reactor. When pushed in, they absorb neutrons and slow down the nuclear reaction and when pulled out they allow it to speed up again. In this way the **chain reaction** is controlled. The typical material for the control rods is either boron or cadmium.

A *moderator* is used to slow the fast-moving neutrons produced in the fission reactions. This is done deliberately because slow-moving neutrons have a greater chance of being absorbed by uranium nuclei, which will cause further fission with the fuel rods. The materials most commonly used as moderators are carbon in the form of graphite and water.

Fission of uranium nuclei occurring in the reactor generates an enormous amount of heat. A liquid or gas *coolant* removes this heat away from the reactor to a boiler where steam is made. Typical coolants used are carbon dioxide (CO_2) and water.

The entire reactor is enclosed in a *shielding*. The shielding is there to prevent ionising radiations from the reactor escaping into the environment. The shielding is typically made of steel and concrete.

WOW FACTOR!

The chance of being harmed by the nuclear industry is about 1 in 5 million. Compare this with the chance of heart disease, which is 1 in 200.

QUESTIONS

4   How is heat generated in a nuclear reactor?

5   Name the common type of fuel used in a nuclear reactor.

6   What is the purpose of the coolant?

The nuclear reactors around the world

All nuclear reactors operate on the same basic principles; however, there are many different designs used around the world. Natural uranium and plutonium oxide may be used as fuels, but uranium oxide is the most common type.

All the reactors in Britain are gas-cooled reactors. The coolant is carbon dioxide and the moderator is made from graphite.

The table shows the situation around the world in 2005.

Reactor type	Main countries
Pressurised water reactor (PWR)	USA, France, Japan, Russia
Boiling water reactor (BWR)	USA, Japan, Sweden
Gas-cooled reactor	UK
Pressurised heavy water reactor	Canada
Light water graphite reactor	Russia
Fast neutron reactor	Japan, France, Russia

The worst nuclear accident took place at Chernobyl power station in 1986. The nuclear reactor was a type known as 'pressurised water reactor' (PWR) and it had a graphite moderator. The accident was caused by the loss of cooling water, which caused the reactor to overheat. The escaping steam reacted with the graphite to produce the highly explosive gas hydrogen. The site remains radioactive even today.

QUESTIONS

7   Name a nuclear fuel other than uranium oxide.

8   In Britain, all 23 nuclear reactors are gas-cooled reactors. State the coolant and moderator used for these reactors.

Impact of nuclear power

You will find out:
- About the drawbacks and benefits of nuclear power
- About the storage and disposal of nuclear waste

What a waste!

Nuclear reactors produce radioactive nuclear waste that can remain active for millions of years.

Fossil fuels or nuclear power?

The nuclear disasters at Three Mile Island in the United States on 28 March 1979 and the Chernobyl nuclear power plant in Ukraine on 26 April 1986 have had a long lasting impact on the way we think about nuclear power. At the Three Mile Island power station, the uranium fuel rods started to 'melt-down' (become liquid), but they did not fall through the reactor floor and break through the concrete and steel shielding. It is understandable that nuclear power generates fear.

The world is facing a severe **energy crisis**. Fossil fuel resources are being used up very quickly. Even uranium, the fuel used in nuclear reactors, will eventually run out. The solution to the energy crisis may be in alternative resources such as solar, wind, biomass, wave, hydroelectric, tidal and geothermal. Perhaps the ultimate solution may lie in fusion reactors.

The table compares coal-burning and nuclear power stations.

FIGURE 1: An aerial view of Chernobyl soon after the accident.

Source	Advantages	Disadvantages
Coal	Very cheap fuel Easy to mine Accidents are less severe than nuclear disasters	Expensive air pollution controls Significant contributor to acid rain and global warming Extensive transportation system
Nuclear	No **greenhouse** or **acid rain** effects Waste is more compact than any other source Easy to transport as new fuel Little background radiation Low risks. The risk of a nuclear accident for an individual is 1 in 5 million	Larger capital cost The waste is radioactive for thousands of years May cause cancer/leukaemia **Storage** and **disposal** problems of waste

QUESTIONS

1. What type of power station contributes to acid rain?
2. Give **one** reason for opting for coal-powered stations.
3. Give **one** major disadvantage of nuclear power stations.

...*acid rain*   ...*disposal*   ...*energy crises*   ...*greenhouse effect*   ...*high-level waste*

Disposal and storage of nuclear waste

The waste from the nuclear industry is radioactive and therefore has to be disposed of with great care. Nuclear waste is divided into three categories: **low-level waste** (LLW), **intermediate-level waste** (ILW) **and high-level waste** (HLW).

Low-level waste consists of paper, rags, tools, clothing, filters, etc., which contain small amounts of mostly short-lived radioactivity. It does not require shielding during handling and transport and is suitable for shallow land burial.

This type of waste is stored in steel drums and buried in shallow trenches. The levels of radioactivity are so low that no shielding is required. The corrosion of the containers is minimised by choosing a site that has a dry climate.

FIGURE 2: Drums of nuclear waste being buried in a shallow trench.

Intermediate-level waste contains higher amounts of radioactivity and so it requires shielding. The shielding can be barriers of lead, concrete or water to give protection from penetrating radiation such as gamma rays. Generally the short-lived waste from nuclear reactors is buried under about 8 metres of clay.

High-level waste (HLW) contains the fission products generated in the nuclear reactor core, which are highly radioactive and hot. After some time, the fuel rods have to be replaced. The 'spent' fuel is generally removed from the reactor core under water and transferred to large water-filled pools where the fuel is held on racks underwater. The water both shields the radiation and cools the spent fuel that may be destined either for long-term storage or reprocessing. In reprocessing the uranium or plutonium is extracted from the old fuel rods. High-level waste can be stored deep under ground in either disused mines or special tunnels.

In the United States, a permanent storage site has been selected at Yucca Mountain, Nevada. Yucca Mountain is in an extremely dry area of Nevada. This storage site is projected to be ready by the year 2010.

FIGURE 3: The Yucca Mountain site in Nevada, United States.

High-level waste

High-level waste has to be buried deep under ground. The details of the Yucca Mountain storage site in Nevada in the United States are shown in Figure 4.

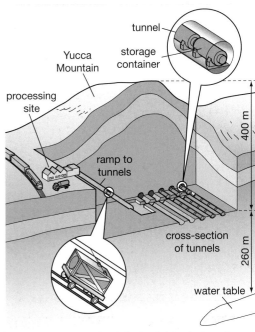

FIGURE 4: The details of the burial site below the Yucca Mountains.

The liquid waste from nuclear power stations can be **vitrified** (made into glass) before storage. Not many countries specialise in this type of technique. France leads in this technology. In the UK, British Nuclear Fuels Ltd (BNFL) is planning to recycle the waste from other countries and then bury the vitrified waste in steel canisters in deep tunnels under the sea.

QUESTIONS

4 Name the type of waste that does not require shielding.

5 Why is it sensible to bury nuclear waste in dry climate areas?

6 What type of waste would you store in a site where 'the waste containers are buried about 500 m underground and 100 km away from the nearest city'?

QUESTIONS

7 What type of nuclear waste can be vitrified?

8 Why is the vitrified waste still radioactive?

Fusion on the Earth

You will find out:

- About nuclear fusion
- About the difference between nuclear fission and nuclear fusion
- The scientific theory of 'cold fusion'

Fusion is everywhere

Use your naked eye or a telescope and have a look at the night sky. It is peppered with bright, multicoloured stars. The stars are giant balls of gas, producing energy from a process known as nuclear fusion. Can we produce energy from fusion on the Earth? Physicists and engineers have been trying to do this since the 1950s.

FIGURE 1: The stars produce energy because of fusion reactions.

Nuclear fusion

In a nuclear **fission** reaction, a neutron striking a nucleus of uranium splits it up into smaller nuclei and a few extra neutrons. The **splitting** of the uranium nucleus in this manner releases energy. We saw on page 270 that such reactions produce energy in nuclear power stations.

In a nuclear **fusion** reaction, two nuclei of hydrogen *join* (fuse) together and produce a nucleus of helium. The joining together of the hydrogen nuclei releases a colossal amount of energy. It is such fusion reactions at the centre of a star that keep it burning bright in the night sky. Our Sun generates its energy from fusion reactions.

In order to produce energy from fusion reactions, physicists have to create the conditions at the centres of stars. Figure 2 shows an experimental fusion reactor at Culham in Oxfordshire, England.

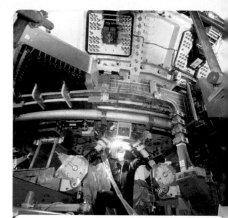

FIGURE 2: The world's biggest nuclear fusion machine.

QUESTIONS

1. What type of nuclear reactions produces energy in stars?
2. What element is produced when hydrogen nuclei fuse together in stars?

...cold fusion   ...energy   ...fission   ...fusion

The story of 'cold fusion'

On 23 March 1989, Stanley Pons of the University of Utah and Martin Fleischmann of Southampton University in England announced to the world that they had produced nuclear fusion at room temperature! This type of nuclear fusion reaction was referred to as **cold fusion**. This was astonishing news that was worthy of front-page coverage in all leading newspapers of the world. However, many scientists criticised Pons and Fleishman because they did not provide adequate technical details of their experiment. Scientists in laboratories around the world were unable to reproduce their experiment, which involved 'the electrolysis of heavy water in a cell with platinum anode and palladium cathode'. The experiment was alleged to cause nuclear fusion and release lots of **energy** and **neutrons** (uncharged particles within all nuclei).

The majority of scientists now believe that Pons and Fleishman failed to demonstrate the release of fusion energy.

FIGURE 3: Professors Stanley Pons (left) and Martin Fleischmann.

Fusion on the Earth (H)

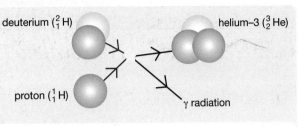

deuterium ($^2_1$H)

proton ($^1_1$H)

helium–3 ($^3_2$He)

γ radiation

FIGURE 4: A typical fusion reaction

Figure 4 shows one of the many nuclear fusion reactions between the isotopes of hydrogen. The reaction can occur only if the hydrogen nuclei are close enough to each other. This is not easy because the hydrogen nuclei have positive charges and therefore repel.

The **temperature** of the Sun at its centre is about 15 million °C. At this temperature, the hydrogen atoms are stripped of their electrons and they move very quickly. This state of matter is known as **plasma**. The hydrogen nuclei move fast enough to overcome the repulsive forces between the positive nuclei and fuse together.

In order to achieve fusion on the Earth in a reactor, scientists have to imitate the conditions at the centre of stars. The hydrogen gas has to be heated to an extremely high temperature of about 100 000 000 °C. The hydrogen nuclei have to be brought close together by squeezing them, using very strong **magnetic fields**. Physicists have managed to create fusion for a very short period of time. Large-scale production of energy from fusion reactions is still a long way away.

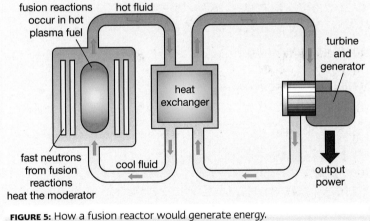

fusion reactions occur in hot plasma fuel

hot fluid

turbine and generator

heat exchanger

fast neutrons from fusion reactions heat the moderator

cool fluid

output power

FIGURE 5: How a fusion reactor would generate energy.

Figures 5 shows the International Thermonuclear Experimental Reactor (ITER) which will be the first ever full-scale fusion reactor producing energy. It is planned to come into operation in 2016 and could produce 500 million watts of power.

If fusion energy does become practical, it would offer cheap fuel because deuterium can be extracted from ocean water. The waste from fusion reactors would be low-level waste and the radioactivity would not last for long periods of time.

QUESTIONS

3 At what temperature was cold fusion assumed to occur?

4 Why do you think that scientists could not accept the physics of cold fusion?

QUESTIONS

5 Why are high temperatures necessary for fusion reactions?

6 Give **one** main advantage of a fusion reactor over a fission reactor using uranium.

...*magnetic fields*   ...*neutrons*   ...*plasma*   ...*splitting*   ...*temperature*

Unit summary

Concept map

All ionising radiations (including X-rays) are dangerous because they destroy cells and can alter DNA.

Some uses of radioactivity:
- Keeping fruit fresh for longer by irradiating them with intense gamma rays.
- Domestic smoke alarms use an alpha-source (strontium-90).
- Radioactivity is used to date relics and ancient rocks.
- Gamma rays from cobalt-60 are used to kill off cancerous cells.

Putting Radiation to Use

An atom consists of a tiny positive nucleus surrounded by negative electrons whizzing round it. An isotope is a nucleus of the same element with the same number of protons but a different number of neutrons.

The ionising radiations emitted by unstable nuclei in the order of decreasing ionising ability are:
- Alpha particles (helium nuclei)
- Beta particles (electrons)
- Gamma rays

We are all exposed to background radiation. Rocks such as granite emit radioactive radon gas that can be trapped in building if they are not properly ventilated.

The Earth's magnetic field protects us from dangerous charged particles from the Sun and space.

Radioactive nuclei decay randomly. The half-life of a nucleus is the average time taken for half of the nuclei to decay.

Uses of electrostatics:
- Removal of soot from the chimneys of coal-burning power stations.
- Laser printing (photocopiers).
- Fingerprinting.

Electrostatics

Insulators can be charged by rubbing them together.

- An insulator can be charged by the transfer of electrons.
- An electric spark is the results of charged particles being transferred through the air.
- Electric sparks can be dangerous when refuelling aircrafts.

Nuclear reactors produce radioactive waste that can remain active for thousands of years.

Power of the atom

The nucleus of an atom can release colossal amount of energy by turning a small fraction of its mass into energy. The amount of energy E released when the change in mass is m is given by Einstein's famous mass-energy equation:

$$E = mc^2.$$

- In nuclear fission, a neutron is absorbed by a nucleus of uranium-235. This splits the nucleus into two large fragments and two or more neutrons.
- Nuclear fission is used both in nuclear power stations and in atomic bombs.

- Our Sun produces its energy from fusion reactions. In a fusion reaction, hydrogen nuclei join together to form helium.
- Fusion reactors on the Earth are still in their experimental stages.

Unit quiz

1 How small is the nucleus of an atom compared with the size of the atom?

2 Name two particles emitted from radioactive nuclei.

3 An alpha particle consists of protons and neutrons. How many protons and neutrons are there in a single alpha particle?

4 A particular isotope of oxygen has 8 protons and 7 neutrons. What is the nucleon number for this isotope?

5 All radiations emitted by radioactive nuclei cause ionisation. Explain what is meant by ionisation.

7 State three natural sources of the background radiation.

8 Gamma rays are short-wavelength electromagnetic waves. Use the equation

$$c = f\lambda$$

to determine the frequency of gamma rays of wavelength 5.0×10^{-14} m.
(The speed of electromagnetic waves is 3.0×10^8 m/s)

9 Explain why excessive exposure to X-rays and gamma rays can be extremely dangerous to humans.

10 Describe how insulators can be charged.

11 A plastic sheet rubbed with a duster acquires a positive charge. Explain how the plastic sheet gains a positive charge.

12 What are the labels E, m and c in the famous equation $E = mc^2$?

13 Describe the process of nuclear fission of uranium-235.

14 Describe how the number of neutrons is controlled in a nuclear power station.

15 State one benefit of nuclear power station over conventional coal-burning power stations.

16 State whether the following nuclear reaction is a fission reaction or a fusion reaction:

    deuterium + proton → helium + gamma radiation

17 Explain why high temperatures are necessary for fusion reactions to occur.

18 Explain why most scientists do not believe in 'cold fusion'.

Numeracy activity

An experiment is carried out to determine the half-life of a particular isotope. The average background count-rate is found to be 9 counts per minute. The results from the experiment are shown in the table below.

time/minutes	0	1	2	3	4	5	6	7
Measured count-rate (counts per minute)	121	94	73	58	46	37	30	25
Corrected count-rate (counts per minute)								

QUESTIONS

1 Explain why the actual corrected count-rate at the start of the experiment is 112 counts per minute.

2 Copy the table above and complete the last row.

3 Plot a graph of corrected count-rate (y-axis) against time (x-axis).

4 Draw a smooth curve through the data points.

5 Use the graph to determine the half-life of the isotope. (Hint: The half-life is the time taken for the count-rate to be halved.)

Exam practice

 1 a Strontium-90 has a half-life of 28 years and decays by emitting a beta particle. Explain what is meant by:

    i half-life

    ii beta particle   [4]

b How long would it take for the activity of a sample of strontium-90 to fall to a quarter of its original value?   [2]

c Smoke detectors contain a radioactive source, americium-241. Americium-241 has a half-life of 460 years. Explain why it is desirable for this source to have a long half-life.   [2]

d The details of three radioactive sources are included in the table:

Source	Type of particle emitted	Half-life
Technetium-99	Gamma rays	6 hours
Californium-241	Alpha particles	4 minutes
Carbon –14	Beta particles	5600 years

Which source would be most suitable to use as a tracer in the human body? Explain your answer.   [3]

 2 a Explain why a plane may become positively charged as it flies through the air.   [2]

b The rubber on aeroplane tyres is specially made so it is an electrical conductor. Explain how this can reduce the chances of an explosion.   [2]

c A laser printer uses toner, which is powdered ink. Explain why the toner powder is given an electrostatic charge.   [2]

 3 Nuclear power uses fission reactions to generate thermal energy. The fission of one U-235 atom creates two daughter nuclei and two neutrons, which start a chain reaction in the fuel rod.

a Describe the energy changes that take place when thermal energy is transferred into electrical energy in a nuclear power station.

b Explain what is meant by:

    i fission reaction

    ii chain reaction.

c Describe how the chain reaction is slowed down in a nuclear reactor

d Many people say that we need new nuclear power stations to reduce global warming. State clearly one other advantage and one disadvantage of nuclear power.

e Explain why scientists were not aware of the many of the risks associated with radioactivity when it was first used for experiments.

(Total marks: 3

Radiation

a Explain what is meant by background radiation, giving one reason why it may vary throughout the British Isles. [3]

Radioactive sources may cause tissue damage.

b Explain why alpha radiation is less damaging outside the body, and more damaging when inhaled or swallowed. [4]

The pupil gets 2 marks. Background radiation is caused by our surroundings, including cosmic rays, rocks, buildings, food and drink, etc. It varies because some rocks give out a radioactive gas. A little more detail is needed for 3 marks.

a Background radiation is around us all the time. It is different around the UK because of the rocks.

b Alpha radiation cannot travel far in air. It is very ionising.

c Use tongues. Don't look at the source.

The student loses 3 marks. Alpha radiation cannot penetrate through the dead outer layer of skin cells to reach living cells, so it is not damaging outside the body. If inhaled, it can reach living lung cells and it is so ionising it can cause mutations and damage.

The pupil gets 1 out of 2 marks. They meant tongs, not tongues – try to remember correct spellings. Other precautions include limiting the time when sources are out of the box and keeping a safe distance from them.

Overall Grade: D

How to get an A

Make sure your answer is relevant to the question. Telling the examiner what you know does not tell them you can apply your answer to different situations.

Your guide to GCSE Additional Science

About GCSE Additional Science

During your GCSE Additional Science course, you will study the following units:

B2: pages 12–107	1. Inside Living Cells
	2. Divide and Develop
	3. Energy Flow
	4. Interdependence
C2: pages 108–193	5. Synthesis
	6. In Your Element
	7. Chemical Structures
	8. How Fast? How Furious?
P2: pages 194–277	9. As Fast as You Can!
	10. Roller coasters and Relativity
	11. Putting Radiation to Use
	12. The Power of the Atom

You will be examined on these units in two of three following ways:

- An internal assessment which your teacher will provide for you
- An externally-assessed test of multiple choice questions
- An externally-assessed exam of structured answer questions

These assessments and tests make up **60%** of your final grade, so it is very important to make sure you have studied everything thoroughly. Each test will take 20 minutes.

All of the external assessment for GCSE Additional Science is tiered. This means that if you are taking the Higher Tier you will be expecting to achieve grades A* to D, and if you are taking the Foundation Tier you will be expecting to achieve grades C to G. You might not necessarily be in the same tier for each subject though – for example, you might take Higher Tier Biology and Foundation Tier Chemistry and Physics. The final mark you achieve will be based on your overall performance in the assessments.

During your revision, the **Unit summaries** on pages 104, 190 and 274 will be a useful tool for checking that you can remember the key pieces of information in each topic.

Test your knowledge with the **Unit quiz** questions on pages 105, 191 and 275. Where you find gaps in your knowledge, go back and revise the section from this book.

When you feel confident you have done enough revision, practise answering the exam-style questions in **Exam practice** on pages 106, 192 and 276.

A further **40%** of your final mark will be gained by Internal Assessments that your teacher will give you a grade for. These will include:

- Assessment of your practical skills – including how well you follow instructions, how well you collect data, and how well you present the findings of your practical work. This section is worth **10%** of your marks.

- Assessment activities provided by Edexcel. These activities are designed to give you a good understand of how Science works. These are worth **30%** of your marks, included in which is a mark for Quality of Written Communication. You may produce more than one assessment activity and submit your best mark.

- Each of the Internal Assessments will take 45 minutes to carry out.

Each part of your written work – for your external tests and internal assessments – will also be assessed for Quality of Written Communication. To avoid losing marks, you should ensure that all your work:

- is presented in a clear format, for example, using tables and graphs, rather than a long list of data.

- uses accurate spelling, punctuation and grammar. Don't forget to proofread your work before you hand it in.

- has a good style and structure of writing. It should be easy for your teacher or an examiner to understand your work.

The periodic table

Key

| Atomic Number |
| Symbol |
| Name |
| Molar mass in g mol⁻¹ |

Group headings: Period | 1 | 2 | ... | 3 | 4 | 5 | 6 | 7 | 8

Period	1	2											3	4	5	6	7	8
1	1 H Hydrogen 1																	2 He Helium 4
2	3 Li Lithium 7	4 Be Berylium 9											5 B Boron 11	6 C Carbon 12	7 N Nitrogen 14	8 O Oxygen 16	9 F Fluorine 19	10 Ne Neon 20
3	11 Na Sodium 23	12 Mg Magnesium 24											13 Al Aluminium 27	14 Si Silicon 28	15 P Phosphorus 31	16 S Sulphur 32	17 Cl Chlorine 35.5	18 Ar Argon 40
4	19 K Potassium 39	20 Ca Calcium 40	21 Sc Scandium 45	22 Ti Titanium 48	23 V Vanadium 51	24 Cr Chromium 52	25 Mn Manganese 55	26 Fe Iron 56	27 Co Cobalt 59	28 Ni Nickel 59	29 Cu Copper 63.5	30 Zn Zinc 65.4	31 Ga Gallium 70	32 Ge Germanium 73	33 As Arsenic 75	34 Se Selenium 79	35 Br Bromine 80	36 Kr Krypton 84
5	37 Rb Rubidium 85	38 Sr Strontium 88	39 Y Yttrium 89	40 Zr Zirconium 91	41 Nb Niobium 93	42 Mo Molybdenum 96	43 Tc Technetium (99)	44 Ru Ruthenium 101	45 Rh Rhodium 103	46 Pd Palladium 106	47 Ag Silver 108	48 Cd Cadmium 112	49 In Indium 115	50 Sn Tin 119	51 Sb Antimony 122	52 Te Tellurium 128	53 I Iodine 127	54 Xe Xenon 131
6	55 Cs Caesium 133	56 Ba Barium 137	57 La Lanthanum 139	72 Hf Hafnium 178	73 Ta Tantalum 181	74 W Tungsten 184	75 Re Rhenium 186	76 Os Osmium 190	77 Ir Iridium 192	78 Pt Platinum 195	79 Au Gold 197	80 Hg Mercury 201	81 Tl Thallium 204	82 Pb Lead 207	83 Bi Bismuth 209	84 Po Polonium (210)	85 At Astatine (210)	86 Rn Radon (222)
7	87 Fr Francium (223)	88 Ra Radium (226)	89 Ac Actinium (227)	104 Unq Unnilquadium (261)	105 Unp Unnilpentium (262)	106 Uuh Unnilhexium (263)												

58 Ce Cerium 140	59 Pr Praseodymium 141	60 Nd Neodymium 144	61 Pm Promethium (147)	62 Sm Samarium 150	63 Eu Europium 152	64 Gd Gadolinium 157	65 Tb Terbium 159	66 Dy Dysprosium 163	67 Ho Holmium 165	68 Er Erbium 167	69 Tm Thulium 169	70 Yb Ytterbium 173	71 Lu Lutetium 175
90 Th Thorium 232	91 Pa Protactinium (231)	92 U Uranium 238	93 Np Neptunium (237)	94 Pu Plutonium (242)	95 Am Americium (243)	96 Cm Curium (247)	97 Bk Berkelium (245)	98 Cf Californium (251)	99 Es Einsteinium (254)	100 Fm Fermium (253)	101 Md Mendelevium (256)	102 No Nobelium (254)	103 Lr Lawrencium (257)

Some useful formulae

$$\text{acceleration} = \frac{\text{change in speed}}{\text{time taken}}$$

$$\text{force} = \text{mass} \times \text{acceleration}$$

$$\text{force} = \frac{\text{change in momentum}}{\text{time taken}}$$

$$\text{kinetic energy} = \times \text{mass} \times (\text{velocity})^2$$

$$\text{momentum} = \text{mass} \times \text{velocity}$$

$$\text{potential energy} = \text{mass} \times \text{gravitational field strength} \times \text{height}$$

$$\text{power} = \frac{\text{work done}}{\text{time taken}}$$

$$\text{speed} = \frac{\text{distance}}{\text{time}}$$

$$\text{work done} = \text{force} \times \text{distance moved in direction of force}$$

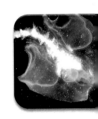

Glossary

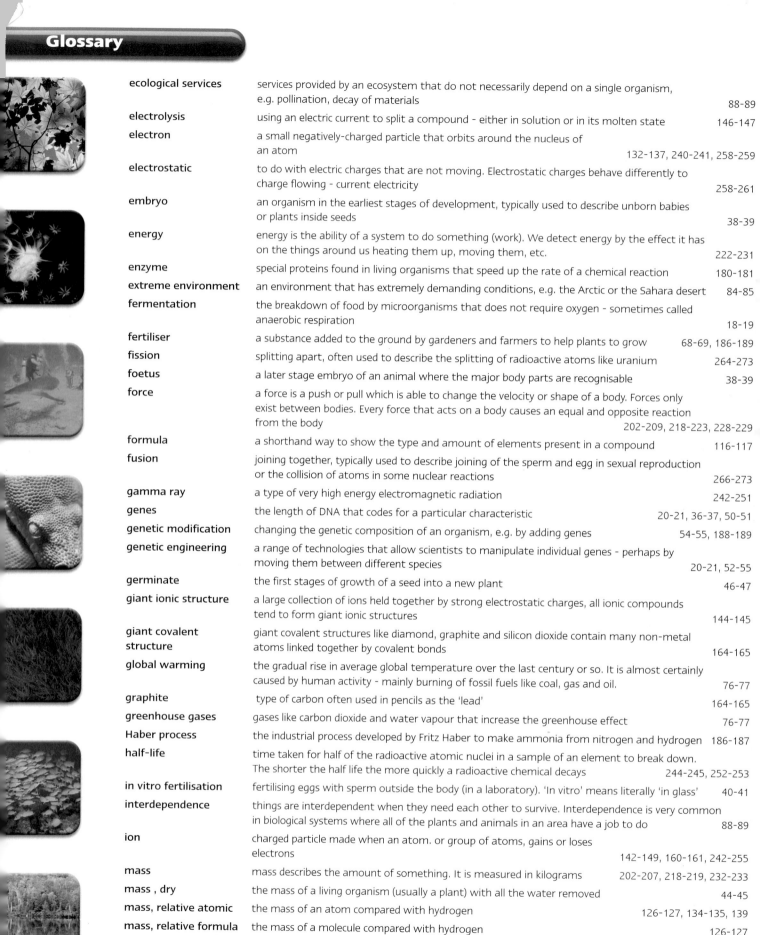

Term	Definition	Pages
ecological services	services provided by an ecosystem that do not necessarily depend on a single organism, e.g. pollination, decay of materials	88-89
electrolysis	using an electric current to split a compound - either in solution or in its molten state	146-147
electron	a small negatively-charged particle that orbits around the nucleus of an atom	132-137, 240-241, 258-259
electrostatic	to do with electric charges that are not moving. Electrostatic charges behave differently to charge flowing - current electricity	258-261
embryo	an organism in the earliest stages of development, typically used to describe unborn babies or plants inside seeds	38-39
energy	energy is the ability of a system to do something (work). We detect energy by the effect it has on the things around us heating them up, moving them, etc.	222-231
enzyme	special proteins found in living organisms that speed up the rate of a chemical reaction	180-181
extreme environment	an environment that has extremely demanding conditions, e.g. the Arctic or the Sahara desert	84-85
fermentation	the breakdown of food by microorganisms that does not require oxygen - sometimes called anaerobic respiration	18-19
fertiliser	a substance added to the ground by gardeners and farmers to help plants to grow	68-69, 186-189
fission	splitting apart, often used to describe the splitting of radioactive atoms like uranium	264-273
foetus	a later stage embryo of an animal where the major body parts are recognisable	38-39
force	a force is a push or pull which is able to change the velocity or shape of a body. Forces only exist between bodies. Every force that acts on a body causes an equal and opposite reaction from the body	202-209, 218-223, 228-229
formula	a shorthand way to show the type and amount of elements present in a compound	116-117
fusion	joining together, typically used to describe joining of the sperm and egg in sexual reproduction or the collision of atoms in some nuclear reactions	266-273
gamma ray	a type of very high energy electromagnetic radiation	242-251
genes	the length of DNA that codes for a particular characteristic	20-21, 36-37, 50-51
genetic modification	changing the genetic composition of an organism, e.g. by adding genes	54-55, 188-189
genetic engineering	a range of technologies that allow scientists to manipulate individual genes - perhaps by moving them between different species	20-21, 52-55
germinate	the first stages of growth of a seed into a new plant	46-47
giant ionic structure	a large collection of ions held together by strong electrostatic charges, all ionic compounds tend to form giant ionic structures	144-145
giant covalent structure	giant covalent structures like diamond, graphite and silicon dioxide contain many non-metal atoms linked together by covalent bonds	164-165
global warming	the gradual rise in average global temperature over the last century or so. It is almost certainly caused by human activity - mainly burning of fossil fuels like coal, gas and oil.	76-77
graphite	type of carbon often used in pencils as the 'lead'	164-165
greenhouse gases	gases like carbon dioxide and water vapour that increase the greenhouse effect	76-77
Haber process	the industrial process developed by Fritz Haber to make ammonia from nitrogen and hydrogen	186-187
half-life	time taken for half of the radioactive atomic nuclei in a sample of an element to break down. The shorter the half life the more quickly a radioactive chemical decays	244-245, 252-253
in vitro fertilisation	fertilising eggs with sperm outside the body (in a laboratory). 'In vitro' means literally 'in glass'	40-41
interdependence	things are interdependent when they need each other to survive. Interdependence is very common in biological systems where all of the plants and animals in an area have a job to do	88-89
ion	charged particle made when an atom. or group of atoms, gains or loses electrons	142-149, 160-161, 242-255
mass	mass describes the amount of something. It is measured in kilograms	202-207, 218-219, 232-233
mass , dry	the mass of a living organism (usually a plant) with all the water removed	44-45
mass, relative atomic	the mass of an atom compared with hydrogen	126-127, 134-135, 139
mass, relative formula	the mass of a molecule compared with hydrogen	126-127
mass, wet	the mass of a living organism including the water present in the body	44-45
Mendeleev, Dmitri	the scientist who first developed the periodic table	138-139

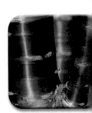

Glossary

regeneration	recreation of something, so some animals can regenerate a body part which has been removed	40-41
resistance	the amount that a conductor prevents the flow of electric current	208-209
respiration, aerobic	aerobic respiration breaks down glucose using oxygen to make energy available for chemical reactions in cells	18-19, 24-25
respiration, anaerobic	anaerobic respiration breaks down glucose without oxygen to make energy available for chemical reactions in cells. Anaerobic respiration in microorganisms is sometimes called fermentation	18-19, 24-25, 30-31

ribonucleic acid (RNA)	a type of nucleic acid found in cells but not used to build chromosomes. Some sorts of RNA are involved in protein synthesis	16-17
risk	a risk is something, usually bad, that might happen	213-214
selective breeding	two organisms are chosen because of desirable characteristics and mated together to produce offspring, hopefully with a combination of the desired characteristics	50-51
sewage	organic waste produced by human bodies. Sewage includes faeces and urine and the water used to flush them away	98-99
speed	how fast an object is moving	196-201, 228-229
speed of light	the speed of light is roughly 300,000 km per second in a vacuum. It slows down in a transparent medium like glass or air	230-233

sperm	special cells produced by the male. Sperm joins with an egg from a female to produce a baby	36-37
sustainable development	development that does not make it more difficult for the generations that come after us	128-129
theory of relativity	the theory put forward by Albert Einstein that suggested that time and space were linked together and were relative to the observer rather than absolute	230-233, 22-263
thorax	the scientific name for the chest region. It is applied to a range of organisms as well as humans	26-27
time	a measure of how quickly things happen	196-201
variation	the existence of a range of individuals of the same group with different characteristics	42-43

velocity	velocity is the speed an object is moving in a particular direction. A change in direction or speed will change the velocity. Velocity is usually measured in metres per second (m/s)	196-201, 228-229
weight	the force of gravity acting on a body on the Earth. Since weight is a force it is measured in newtons.	206-207
work	work is done when a force moves. The greater the force or the larger the distance the more work is done	218-227
x-rays	electromagnetic radiation used by doctors to look inside a patient's body or to destroy some types of cancer cells	248-255

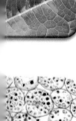

Acknowledgements

The authors and publisher are grateful to the following for permission to reproduce photographs. Whilst every effort has been made to trace the copyright holders, in cases where this has been unsuccessful or if any have been inadvertently overlooked, the Publishers will be pleased to make the necessary arrangements at the first opportunity.

Contents page: t – b ©Matthew Cole/istock.com, ©Stephen & Donna O'Meara/SPL, ©Marek Tihelka/istock.com, ©Professor Harold Edgerton/SPL, ©Charles D. Winters/SPL; p6 tl ©Phil Date/istock.com, bl ©Maartje van Caspel/istock.com, br ©Steve Cook/istock.com; p.7 all ©Gareth Price; p.8 tl ©Milan Radulovic/istock.com, tr ©Charles D Winters/SPL, bl ©Andrew Lambert Photography/SPL, br ©Roberto de Gugliemo/SPL; p.9 tl ©Laguna Design/SPL, tr ©David Mack/SPL; bl ©Charles D. Winters/SPL, br ©Charles D. Winters/SPL; p.10 tr ©Jason Lugo/istock.com, tl ©Oleg Prikhodko/istock.com, br ©Ashok Rodrigues/istock.com, bl ©Adam Booth/istock.com; p.11 tl ©Perttu Sironen/istock.com, tr ©David Parker/SPL, bl ©TEK Image/SPL, br ©Art-Y/istocck.com, p.12/13 ©Hybrid Medical Animation/SPL; p.14 ©Nancy Louie/istock.com; p.16 1 ©2006 Jupiterimages, 3 ©Dr Mark J. Winter/Science Photo Library; p.17 ©Hybrid Medical Animation/SPL; p.18 ©2006 Jupiterimages; p.19 ©2006 Jupiterimages; p.20 1 ©Rey Rojo/istock.com, 2 ©Julia Kamlish/SPL; p.21 ©Jim Orr/istock.com; p.22 1 ©Paul Cowan/istock.com, 2 ©Cordelia Molloy/SPL; p.24 1 ©David Parsons/istock.com, 2 ©Galina Barskaya/istock.com; p.26 ©Andy Lim/istock.com; p.27 3 ©Michele Bagdon/istock.com, 6 ©Francisco Orellana/istock.com; p.28 ©Susumu Nishinaga/SPL; p.30 1 ©ericsphotography/istock.com, 2 ©BSIP, Laurent/B. Hop AME/SPL; p.31 ©AFP/Getty Images; p.33 ©Getty Images; p.36 1 ©C C Studio/SPL, 2 ©Dr Bernard Lunaud/SPL; p.38 1 ©Elizabeth Shoemaker/istock.com, 2 ©Andy Walker, Midland Fertility Services/SPL, 3 ©Dopamine/SPL, 4 ©Dr Najeeb Layyous/SPL; p.39 ©Getty Images; p.40 1 ©Professor Miodrag Stojkovic/SPL, 2 ©Georgette Douwma/SPL; p.41 3 ©Getty Images, 4 ©Jan Bruder/istock.com; p.42 1 ©twka/istock.com, 2 ©Jason Stitt/istock.com; p.43 ©AFP/Getty Images; p.44 ©AtWaG/istock.com; p.46 1 ©Steve Cook/istock.com, 2 ©duckycards.com/istock.com; p.47 ©Steve McWilliam/istock.com; p.48 ©Matthew Cole/istock.com; p.49 5 ©Geoff Kidd/SPL; 6 ©Robert Lerich/istock.com; p.50 1 ©Richard Foote/istock.com, 2 ©Sue McDonald/istock.com, 3 ©Rhonda O'Donnell/istock.com, 4 ©arfo/istock.com; p.51 ©David Freund/istock.com; p.52 ©Holt Studios International Ltd/Alamy; p.54 1 ©Eric Herzog, Custom Medical Stock Photo/SPL, 2 ©AJ Photo/SPL; p.55 3 ©Jackie Lewin, Royal Free Hospital/SPL, 4 ©Klaus Guldbrandsen/SPL; p.56 t ©Galina Barskaya/istock.com, b ©Dr Bernard Lunaud/SPL; p.60/61 ©Kennan Ward/Corbis; p.62 both ©Gareth Price; p.63 ©Gareth Price; p.64 ©Gareth Price; p.66 ©Foodfolio/Alamy; p.67 ©Gareth Price; p.68 ©Ian Pritchard; p.69 ©Gareth Price; p.70 ©Greg Watts/Rex Featires; p.71 ©Michael P. Gadomski/SPL; p.72 1 ©Swim Ink 2, LLC/Corbis, 2 ©Gareth Price; p.73 ©Ian Beames/Ecoscene/Corbis; p.74 1 ©Richard Stouffer/istock.com, 2 ©Lidian Neeleman/istock.com; p.75 3 ©Peter Clark/istock.com; p.76 ©Cephas Picture Library/Alamy; p.78 ©Mehau Kulyk/SPL; p.79 NRSC Ltd/SPL; p.80 ©Danita Delimont/Alamy; p.82/83 ©nagelstock.com/Alamy; p.84 ©B. Murton/Southampton Oceanography Centre/SPL; p.85 2 ©Patrick Roherty/istock.com, 3 l ©Taxi/Getty Images; p.86 ©Matthew Noble/Alamy; p.87 ©Gareth Price; p.88 ©Gareth Price; p.89 2 & 3 ©Gareth Price; p.90 t ©Survival Anglia/Photolibrary .com, b ©Gareth Price; p.91 ©Popperfoto/Alamy; p.92 ©Gareth Price; p.93 ©Paul Inskip/istock.com; p.95 ©Vaughan Fleming/SPL; p.97 2 ©NASA, coloured by John Wells/SPL, 3 ©Sinclair Stammers/SPL; p.98 ©Gareth Price; p.100 ©Gareth Price p.103 ©Kyle Maass/istock.com; p.108/109 ©P. J. Stewart/SPL; p.110 1 ©Richard Folwell/SPL, 2 ©Steve Allen/SPL, 3 ©Comstock Images/Alamy; p.111 ©Andrew Lambert Photography/SPL; p.112 ©2006 JupiterImages; p.113 © Andrew Lambert Photography/SPL; p.114 1 ©Mike Tingle, 2 ©Jostein Hauge/istock.com; p.115 3 ©Mike Tingle, 4 ©istock.com, 5 ©Mike Tingle; p.117 ©SPL; p.118 1 ©Astrid & Hans Frieder Michler/SPL, 2 ©Mike Tingle; p.119 ©Martyn F. Chillmaid/SPL; p.120 1 ©BMW AG, used with kind permission, 2 ©Lawrence lawry/SPL, 3 ©Michael Maretn/SPL; p.121 4 ©Dr Jeremy Burgess/SPL, 5 ©Eye of Science/SPL; p.122 1 ©Jerry Mason/SPL; 2 ©George Haling/SPL; p.123 3 ©David Parker/SPL, 4 ©Francoise Sauze/SPL; p.124 ©David Nunuk/SPL; p.125 2 ©Will & Deni McIntyre/SPL, 3 ©Geoff Tompkinson/SPL p.126 1 ©IBM/SPL, 2 ©Victor de Schwanberg/SPL; p.127 ©Charles D. Winters/SPL; p.128 1 ©Steve Chenn/Corbis, 2 ©Yann Arthus-Bertrand/Corbis; p.129 3 ©Mike Tingle, 4 ©BMW AG used with kind permission, 5 ©Lori Martin/istock.com; p.131 ©Andrew Holt/Alamy; p.132 ©Text 100 Agents for IBM; p.135 ©Michal Wozniak/istock.com; p.136 ©Andrew Lambert Photography/SPL; p.138 1 ©Eye of Science/SPL, 2 ©SPL; p.139 3 ©SPL; p.140 1 ©Charles D. Winter/SPL, 2 ©John Heseltine/SPL; p.141 3 ©Charles D. Winters/SPL, 5 ©Andrew Lambert Photography/SPL; p.142 ©Tony & Daphne Hallas/SPL; p.143 ©Andrew Lambert Photography/SPL; p.144 1 ©Stephen & Donna O'Meara/SPL, 2 ©Charles D. Winters/SPL; p.145 ©Andrew Lambert Photography/SPL; p.146 1 ©Comstock Images/Alamy, 2 ©SPL, 3 ©Charles D. Winters/SPL; p.148 1 ©Tony Craddock/SPL, 2 ©Jason Stitt/istock.com; p.149 4 ©Pasieka/SPL, 5 ©Steve Allen Travel Photography/Alamy; p.154/155 ©Digital Archive Japan/Alamy, p.156 1 Image ©Murray Robertson 1999-2005, Royal Society of Chemistry, 2 l ©Timothy Babasade/istock.com, 2 r ©Marek Tihelka/istock.com; p.157 4 ©Jonathan Blair/Corbis, 5 ©Philip Wallick/Corbis; p.158 1 ©Elzbieta Lewandowska/istock.com, 2 ©2006 JupiterImages.com; p.159 3 ©Amanda Rohde/istock.com, 4 ©Lise Gagne/istock.com; p.160 1 ©Lance Bellars/istock.com, 2 ©Klaus Guldbrandsen/SPL; p.162 1 ©J-L Charmet/SPL, 2 ©Laguna Design/SPL; p.163 3 ©Digital Art/Corbis, 4 ©Laguna Design/SPL, 5 ©Peter Steiner/Alamy; p.164 1 ©Lawrence Lawry, 2 ©Andrew Lambert Photography/SPL; p.165 4 ©Sciencephotos/Alamy, 5 ©Mike Tingle; p.166 ©Osca Burriel/SPL; p.167 2 ©Ross Nicholas, 3 ©Chris Knapton/SPL; p.168 1 ©Francoise Sauze, 2 ©Scott Camazine/SPL; p.169 4 & 5 ©Andrew Lambert Photography/SPL; p.172 1 ©Peter Bowater/SPL, 2 ©Charles D. Winter/SPL; p.173 3 ©Andrew Lambert Photography/SPL; p.174 1 ©Tex Image/SPL, 2 ©Adam Hart-Davis/SPL; p.175 3 ©Kenneth Eward/Biografx/SPL; p.176 1 ©NREL/US Department of Energy/SPL, 2 ©Robert Brook/SPL; p.178 ©Charles D. Winters/SPL; p.179 ©Martyn F.Chillmaid/SPL; p.180 1 ©Cordelia Molloy/SPL, 2 both ©Martyn F. Chillmaid/SPL; p.181 1 ©Scott Camazine/SPL, 2 ©Reuters/Corbis; p.182 1 ©Charles D. Winters/SPL, 2 ©David Hughes/istock.com; p.184 both ©Rob King; p.185 ©IFM-GEOMAR, used with kind permission; p.186 1 ©Guy Erwood/istock.com, 3 ©Andrew Lambert Photography/SPL; p.188 1 ©Mauro Fermariiello/SPL, 2 ©Sheila Terry/SPL; p.189 3 ©Andrew Sacks/AGStock/SPL, 4 ©Victor Habbick Visions/SPL; p.194/195 ©Keith Kent/SPL; p.196 1 ©Caitriona Dwyer/istock.com, 2 ©Hasan Shaheed/istock.com; p.198 ©Jason Lugo/istock.com; p.199 1 ©Michael Napoleon/istock.com, 2 ©Sascha Reiterer/istock.com; p.200 ©Steve Lovegrove/istock.com; p.202 1 ©Archivberlin Fotoagentur GmbH/Alamy, 2 Travis Lynton, Ontario's Strongest Man 2004, photo appears courtesy of OntarioStrongman(www.ontariostrongman.ca); p.203 1 ©Firehorse/istock.com, 2 ©Kerstin Klaassen/istock.com; p.204 ©Sue Colvil/istock.com; p.205 4 ©SPL, 5 ©Carsten Madsen/istock.com; p.206 1 ©Christine Balderas/itock.com, 2 ©Andrew Lambert Photography/SPL; p.210 ©NASA/SPL; p.212 2 ©Action Press/Rex Features; p.214 1 ©Jim Parkin/istock.com, 2 ©Andrea Gingerich/istock.com; p.218 1 ©Frances Twitty/istock.com, 2 ©Lee Pettet/istock.com; p.219 ©Dennis MacDonald/Alamy; p.220 1 t ©Doug Mauck/istock.com, 1 b ©Alan Collins/istock.com; p.221 ©Nick Jay/istock.com; p.222 1 ©Robert Deal/istock.com, 2 ©Professor Harold Edgerton/SPL; p.223 3 ©Arlene Gee/istock.com, 4 ©SPL; p.224 1 ©2006 Jupiterimages, 2 ©Jean Schweitzer/istock.com; p.226 1 ©Science Museum/ Science & Society Picture Library, 2 ©Konrad Steynberg/istock.com; p.229 ©Vasile Tiplea/istock.com;